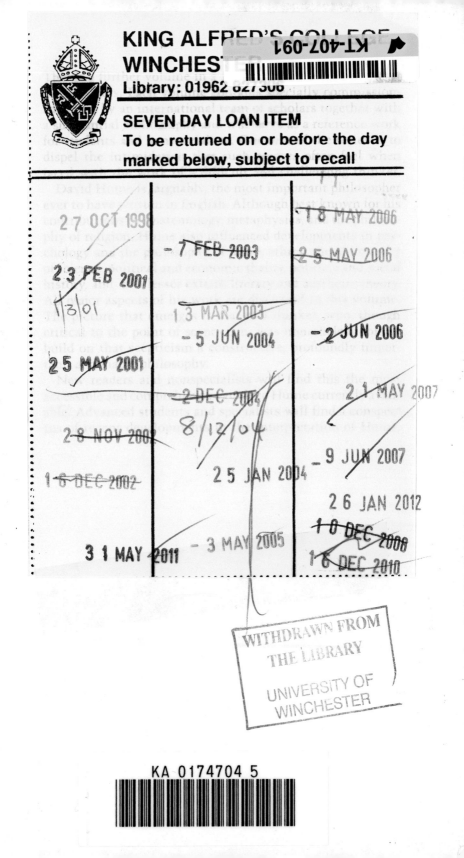

THE CAMBRIDGE COMPANION TO

HUME

OTHER VOLUMES IN THIS SERIES OF CAMBRIDGE
COMPANIONS:

AQUINAS Edited by NORMAN KRETZMANN and
ELEONORE STUMP
ARISTOTLE Edited by JONATHAN BARNES
BACON Edited by MARKKU PELTONEN
BERKELEY Edited by KENNETH WINKLER
EARLY GREEK PHILOSOPHY Edited by
A. A. LONG
FOUCAULT Edited by GARY GUTTING
FREUD Edited by JEROME NEU
HABERMAS Edited by STEPHEN P. WHITE
HEGEL Edited by FREDERICK BEISER
HEIDEGGER Edited by CHARLES GUIGNON
HOBBES Edited by TOM SORRELL
HUSSERL Edited by BARRY SMITH and
DAVID WOODRUFF SMITH
KANT Edited by PAUL GUYER
LEIBNIZ Edited by NICHOLAS JOLLEY
LOCKE Edited by VERE CHAPPELL
MARX Edited by TERRELL CARVER
MILL Edited by JOHN SKORUPSKI
NIETZSCHE Edited by BERND MAGNUS
PLATO Edited by RICHARD KRAUT
SARTRE Edited by CHRISTINA HOWELLS
SPINOZA Edited by DON GARRETT
WITTGENSTEIN Edited by HANS SLUGA and
DAVID STERN

The Cambridge Companion to
HUME

Edited by David Fate Norton

McGill University

 **CAMBRIDGE**
UNIVERSITY PRESS

Published by the Press Syndicate of the University of Cambridge
The Pitt Building, Trumpington Street, Cambridge CB2 IRP
40 West 20th Street, New York, NY 10011-4211, USA
10 Stamford Road, Oakleigh, Victoria 3166, Australia

First published 1993

Printed in the United States of America

Library of Congress Cataloging-in-Publication Data
The Cambridge companion to Hume / edited by David Fate Norton.
  p.   cm. – (Cambridge companions to philosophy)
  Includes bibliographical references and index.
ISBN 0-521-38273-4. – ISBN 0-521-38710-8 (pbk.)
  1. Hume, David, 1711–1776. I. Norton, David Fate. II. Series.
B1498.C26   1993
  192–dc20   92-47406
                                                            CIP

A catalog record for this book is available from the British Library.

ISBN 0-521-38273-4 hardback
ISBN 0-521-38710-8 paperback

CONTENTS

List of contributors   *page* vii

Method of citation   x

1 An introduction to Hume's thought   1
DAVID FATE NORTON

2 Hume's new science of the mind   33
JOHN BIRO

3 Hume and the philosophy of science   64
ALEXANDER ROSENBERG

4 Hume's scepticism   90
ROBERT J. FOGELIN

5 Hume's moral psychology   117
TERENCE PENELHUM

6 Hume, human nature, and the foundations of morality   148
DAVID FATE NORTON

7 The structure of Hume's political theory   182
KNUD HAAKONSSEN

8 David Hume: Principles of political economy   222
ANDREW S. SKINNER

9 Hume's literary and aesthetic theory   255
PETER JONES

10 David Hume, "the historian"   281
DAVID WOOTTON

v

vi   Contents

11 Hume on religion   313
    J. C. A. GASKIN

    Appendix: Hume's autobiographies   345
        I. A Kind of History of My Life [1734]   345
        II. My Own Life [1776]   351

    Bibliography   357

    Index of names and subjects   377

    Index of citations and references   392

CONTRIBUTORS

JOHN BIRO is Professor of Philosophy at the University of Florida. He has published numerous papers on eighteenth-century philosophy, as well as on topics of current interest in the philosophy of mind and the philosophy of language. He is co-editor of two volumes, *Spinoza* (University of Oklahoma Press, 1978) and *Mind, Brain, and Function* (University of Oklahoma Press, 1982).

ROBERT J. FOGELIN is Professor of Philosophy at Dartmouth College. He is author of *Hume's Skepticism in the* Treatise of Human Nature (Routledge, 1985), *Evidence and Meaning* (Routledge, 1967), *Wittgenstein* (Routledge, 1976), and *Understanding Arguments* (Harcourt Brace Jovanovich, 1978), and of many articles on a wide range of philosophical topics.

J. C. A. GASKIN is a Fellow of Trinity College Dublin, where he has lectured since 1963. His publications include *Hume's Philosophy of Religion* (Macmillan; second edition, 1988), *The Quest for Eternity: An Outline of the Philosophy of Religion* (Penguin, 1984), and, as editor, *Varieties of Unbelief* (Macmillan, 1989). He is the author of numerous articles on Hume and on the philosophy of religion, and the editor of the World's Classics edition of Hume's works on religion.

KNUD HAAKONSSEN, Senior Research Fellow, Research School of the Social Sciences, the Australian National University, has published widely on topics in the history of natural law theory. He is author of *The Science of a Legislator, The Natural Jurisprudence of David Hume and Adam Smith* (Cambridge University Press, 1981) and editor of Thomas Reid's *Practical Ethics* (Princeton University Press, 1990), David Hume's *Political Essays* (Cambridge University

Press, forthcoming), and of *The Cambridge History of Eighteenth-Century Philosophy* (Cambridge University Press, forthcoming).

PETER JONES is Professor of Philosophy and Director of the Institute for Advanced Studies in the Humanities at the University of Edinburgh. He has published extensively on the history of philosophy, particularly eighteenth-century Scottish philosophers, and in aesthetics; his books include *Philosophy and the Novel* (Oxford University Press, 1975) and *Hume's Sentiments* (Edinburgh University Press, 1982).

DAVID FATE NORTON is Macdonald Professor of Moral Philosophy, McGill University. He is co-editor of *David Hume: Philosophical Historian* (Bobbs-Merrill, 1965) and *McGill Hume Studies* (Austin Hill Press, 1978) and the author of *David Hume: Common-Sense Moralist, Sceptical Metaphysician* (Princeton University Press, 1982), as well as numerous articles on Hume and eighteenth-century Scottish philosophy. He is at present preparing the first critical edition of Hume's *A Treatise of Human Nature* for Oxford University Press.

TERENCE PENELHUM is Professor Emeritus of Religious Studies at the University of Calgary, where he was formerly professor of philosophy and director of the Calgary Institute for the Humanities. His books include *Religion and Rationality* (Random House, 1971), *Hume* (Macmillan, 1975), *God and Skepticism* (Reidel, 1983), *Butler* (Routledge, 1985), and most recently, *David Hume: An Introduction to his Philosophical System* (Purdue University Press, 1992).

ALEXANDER ROSENBERG is Professor of Philosophy at the University of California, Riverside. He is the author (with Tom L. Beauchamp) of *Hume and the Problem of Causation* (Oxford University Press, 1981). He has published five books in the philosophy of the social and biological sciences, as well as many articles. His most recent book is *Economics – Mathematical Politics or Science of Diminishing Returns?* (University of Chicago Press, 1992).

ANDREW S. SKINNER is Daniel Jack Professor of Political Economy at the University of Glasgow. In addition to many papers on the history of economic thought, he is the author of *A System of Social Science: Papers Relating to Adam Smith* (Clarendon Press, 1979) and co-editor of *Essays on Adam Smith* (Clarendon Press, 1975) and of Smith's *An Inquiry into the Nature and Causes of the Wealth of Nations* (Clarendon Press, 1976).

DAVID WOOTTON is Lansdowne Professor in the Humanities at the University of Victoria (Canada). He is the author of *Paolo Sarpi: Between Renaissance and Enlightenment* (Cambridge University Press, 1983) and the editor of *Divine Right and Democracy* (Penguin, 1986) and *Locke on Politics* (Penguin, forthcoming). He is co-editor of *Atheism from the Reformation to the Enlightenment* (Clarendon Press, 1992).

METHOD OF CITATION

Citations to Hume's texts are given parenthetically, although on a few occasions such references may be combined with an endnote. Parenthetical references invariably follow this form: an abbreviation followed without punctuation by book, part, section, or chapter number if these are standardly used, then, following a comma, the page number of the particular edition of the text being cited. Thus (T 1.3.2, 75) refers to *A Treatise of Human Nature*, book 1, part 3, section 2, p. 75, in the edition described at T in the list of abbreviations, while (HE 11, 1: 445) refers to *The History of England*, chapter 11, volume 1, p. 445, of the edition described at HE. In order that the reader may always know precisely which of Hume's many essays is being referred to, references to the *Essays* include, following a hyphen, an abbreviation of the title of the particular essay cited. Thus (E-ST, 230) refers to *Essays Moral, Political, and Literary*, "Of the Standard of Taste," p. 230, in the edition described at E, where all additional abbreviations of essay titles are listed.

LIST OF ABBREVIATIONS

A   *An Abstract of a Book lately Published; Entituled* A Treatise of Human Nature, &c. *Wherein the Chief Argument of that Book is farther Illustrated and Explained* (first published 1740), cited from the edition of P. H. Nidditch included in *A Treatise of Human Nature*, ed. L. A. Selby-Bigge and P. H. Nidditch, 2d ed. (Oxford: Clarendon Press, 1978).

D   *A Dialogue* (first published 1751), cited from *Enquiries concerning Human Understanding and concerning the Principles of Morals*, ed. L. A. Selby-Bigge and P. H. Nidditch, 3d ed. (Oxford: Clarendon Press, 1975).

DNR *Dialogues concerning Natural Religion* (first published 1778), ed. N. K. Smith (Oxford: Clarendon Press, 1935; 2d ed. London: Thomas

x

Nelson & Sons, 1947; New York: Library of Liberal Arts [1962]). All with same pagination.

DP   *Dissertation on the Passions* (first published 1757), cited from vol. 4 of *David Hume: The Philosophical Works*, ed. T. H. Green and T. H. Grose (London: Longman, 1882–6; reprinted Darmstadt: Scientia Verlag Aalen, 1964).

E   *Essays Moral, Political, and Literary*, ed. E. F. Miller (Indianapolis: Liberty*Classics*, rev. ed., 1987). Abbreviations of the individual essays cited in this volume, with date of first publication:

E-BG   Whether the British Government inclines more to Absolute Monarchy, or to a Republic (1741)
E-BT   Of the Balance of Trade (1752)
E-CL   Of Civil Liberty (1741)
E-Co   Of Commerce (1752)
E-CP   Of the Coalition of Parties (1760)
E-CR   A Character of Sir Robert Walpole (1742; withdrawn after 1768)
E-DM   Of the Dignity or Meanness of Human Nature (1741)
E-DT   Of the Delicacy of Taste and Passion (1741)
E-Ep   The Epicurean (1742)
E-FP   Of the First Principles of Government (1741)
E-IM   Of Impudence and Modesty (1741; withdrawn after 1760)
E-In   Of Interest (1752)
E-IP   Of the Independency of Parliament (1741)
E-IPC   Idea of A Perfect Commonwealth (1752)
E-IS   Of the Immortality of the Soul (1777, after having been withdrawn in 1757)
E-JT   Of the Jealousy of Trade (1760)
E-LP   Of the Liberty of the Press (1741)
E-Mo   Of Money (1752)
E-NC   Of National Characters (1748)
E-OC   Of the Original Contract (1748)
E-OG   Of the Origin of Government (1777)
E-PA   Of the Populousness of Ancient Nations (1752)
E-PC   Of Public Credit (1752)
E-PG   Of Parties in General (1741)
E-PGB   Of the Parties of Great Britain (1741)
E-PR   That Politics may be reduced to a Science (1741)
E-PS   Of the Protestant Succession (1752)
E-RA   Of Refinement in the Arts (1752)
E-RP   Of the Rise and Progress of the Arts and Sciences (1742)

E-Sc   The Sceptic (1742)
E-SE   Of Superstition and Enthusiasm (1741)
E-SH   Of the Study of History (1741; withdrawn after 1760)
E-SR   Of Simplicity and Refinement in Writing (1742)
E-ST   Of the Standard of Taste (1757)
E-Su   Of Suicide (1778, after having been withdrawn in 1757)
E-Ta   Of Taxes (1752)
E-Tr   Of Tragedy (1757)

EHU   *An Enquiry concerning Human Understanding* (first published 1748 as *Philosophical Essays concerning Human Understanding*), cited from *Enquiries concerning Human Understanding and concerning the Principles of Morals*, ed. L. A. Selby-Bigge and P. H. Nidditch, 3d ed. (Oxford: Clarendon Press, 1975).

EPM   *An Enquiry concerning the Principles of Morals* (first published 1751), cited from *Enquiries concerning Human Understanding and concerning the Principles of Morals*, ed. L. A. Selby-Bigge and P. H. Nidditch, 3d ed. (Oxford: Clarendon Press, 1975).

HE   *The History of England* (first published 1754–62), 6 vols. (Indianapolis: LibertyClassics, 1983).

HL   *The Letters of David Hume*, ed. J. Y. T. Greig, 2 vols. (Oxford: Clarendon Press, 1932).

KHL   *A Kind of History of My Life*, cited from the appendix of this volume.

L   *A Letter from a Gentleman to His Friend in Edinburgh: containing Observations on . . . the Principles . . . said to be maintain'd in . . . A Treatise of Human Nature* (first published 1745), ed. E. C. Mossner and J. V. Price (Edinburgh: Edinburgh University Press, 1967).

MOL   *My Own Life* (first published 1777), cited from the appendix of this volume.

NHL   *New Letters of David Hume*, ed. R. Klibansky and E. C. Mossner (Oxford: Clarendon Press, 1954).

NHR   *The Natural History of Religion* (first published 1757), cited from vol. 4 of *David Hume: The Philosophical Works*, ed. T. H. Green and T. H. Grose (London: Longman, 1882–6; reprinted Darmstadt: Scientia Verlag Aalen, 1964).

T   *A Treatise of Human Nature* (first published 1739–40), ed. L. A. Selby-Bigge and P. H. Nidditch, 2d ed. (Oxford: Clarendon Press, 1978).

W   *David Hume: The Philosophical Works*, ed. T. H. Green and T. H. Grose (London: Longman, 1882–6; reprinted Darmstadt: Scientia Verlag Aalen, 1964).

Note: The several editions of Hume's works inconsistently use large and small capitals for certain kinds of emphasis. Except for titles, this volume uses small capitals on all such occasions. For words in small capitals in titles, we use an initial capital and then lower case. Unless otherwise indicated, italics in quoted passages are in the original texts. The idiosyncratic spelling in these texts has also been retained.

1 An introduction to Hume's thought

David Hume (1711–76) may be best understood as the first post-sceptical philosopher of the early modern period. Many of Hume's immediate predecessors, particularly the Cartesians, had attempted to refute philosophical scepticism. In contrast to these predecessors, Hume was a self-proclaimed sceptic who consciously developed a philosophical position that is at one and the same time fundamentally sceptical and fundamentally constructive. His position is sceptical in so far as he shows that knowledge has nothing like the firm, reliable foundation the Cartesians or other rationalists had claimed to give it; his position is constructive in so far as he undertook to articulate a new science of human nature that would provide for all the sciences, including morals and politics, a unique and defensible foundation. For nearly two centuries the positive side of Hume's thought was routinely overlooked – in part as a reaction to his thoroughgoing religious scepticism – but in recent decades commentators, even those who emphasize the sceptical aspects of his thought, have recognized and begun to reconstruct Hume's positive philosophical positions.

I. INTELLECTUAL BEGINNINGS

Hume was born in Edinburgh and divided his youth between that city and Ninewells, his family's small landholding a few miles from the Scottish Borders town of Berwick-upon-Tweed. Little is known of Hume's early childhood. His father died when Hume was two years old, and his early education was in the charge of his mother,

I wish to thank David Raynor for his helpful comments on an earlier version of this essay.

who reported that young Davie was "uncommonly wake-minded" –
that is, uncommonly *acute*, in the local dialect of the period – and
this report is confirmed by all else we know of the young Hume. He
was himself concerned about his vanity in thinking himself cleverer
than his schoolmates,[1] while his earliest surviving letter (HL 1: 9),
written soon after he turned sixteen, indicates that he was even then
engaged in the writing that was to result in the publication, at age
twenty-seven, of the first two volumes of *A Treatise of Human
Nature*.

   A detailed account of Hume's early reading and education is only
now beginning to emerge, but it is clear that by the time he left college
(c. 1726) he would have had a thorough grounding in classical authors
(especially Cicero and the major Latin poets); in natural philosophy
(particularly that of Robert Boyle, whose use of the experimental
method obviously impressed Hume) and elementary mathematics;[2]
and in logic (including theory of knowledge), metaphysics (including
natural religion), and moral philosophy (including moral psychology
or the theory of the passions). There is also evidence that he attended
lectures on world history, and that soon after leaving college he undertook study of the theory of fluxions (calculus). His early reading also
included many of the English poets and essayists of the period –
Milton, Dryden, Rochester, Prior, Pope, Swift, Addison, Steele, for
example. He reports that in the three years ending about March 1734
he had read "most of the celebrated Books in Latin, French & English," and also learned Italian (KHL). Thus, although Hume's
thought has been routinely represented as the outcome of his intellectual engagement with only a few philosophers – with Locke and
Berkeley, or Hutcheson or Newton – the fact is that Hume read
widely, and that the list of those who had a significant, but not necessarily positive, impact on his early thought must be expanded to
include not only the writers already mentioned, but also a great many
others, among them such relatively well-known figures as Plutarch,
Seneca, Machiavelli, Montaigne, Francis Bacon, Grotius, Descartes,
Gassendi, Pascal, Boileau, Pufendorf, Hooke, Malebranche, Bayle,
Collins, Shaftesbury, Samuel Clarke, Mandeville, Joseph Butler, Montesquieu, and Bolingbroke, as well as many other figures now obscure.
This breadth of study and reading does not necessarily distinguish
Hume from other philosophers of his time, but it does suggest that,
despite his obvious preference for what he called the "experimental

Method of Reasoning," no single writer or philosophical tradition can be relied upon to provide a comprehensive key to his thought. Readers of Hume should be wary of those commentators who engage in the kind of historical reductivism that claims to unlock the secrets of Hume's thought by reference to one or two authors or one intellectual tradition.

II. PHILOSOPHICAL BEGINNINGS

1. Hume's most often cited works include *A Treatise of Human Nature* (3 volumes, 1739–40); the *Abstract* (1740) of volumes 1 and 2 of the *Treatise*; *Essays, Moral, Political, and Literary*, a collection of approximately forty essays (first published, for the most part, between 1741 and 1752); *An Enquiry concerning Human Understanding* (1748); *An Enquiry concerning the Principles of Morals* (1751);[3] *The Natural History of Religion* (1757); a six-volume *History of England* from Roman times to 1688 (1754–62); a brief autobiography, *My Own Life* (1777); and *Dialogues concerning Natural Religion* (1778). These works span a wide range of topics, which make them in the end significantly heterogeneous, but they are unified in at least one fundamental characteristic: their author's commitment to the experimental method, or to a form of empiricism that sees both the advantages and the necessity of relying on experience and observation to provide the answer to intellectual questions of all kinds.

In the Introduction to the earliest of his works, *A Treatise of Human Nature*, Hume traces the beginning of the use of the experimental method in the natural sciences to Francis Bacon (d. 1626). The moral sciences, he argues, particularly the foundational science of human nature that he proposes to develop, must also make use of this method: "And as the science of man is the only solid foundation for the other sciences, so the only solid foundation we can give to this science itself must be laid on experience and observation" (T Intro, xvi).[4] A page later he insists that, while we must try

to render all our principles as universal as possible, by tracing up our experiments to the utmost, and explaining all effects from the simplest and fewest causes, 'tis still certain we cannot go beyond experience; and any hypothesis, that pretends to discover the ultimate original qualities of human nature, ought at first to be rejected as presumptuous and chimerical.

(T Intro, xvii)

Recognizing that moral philosophy cannot make its experiments "purposely, with premeditation, and after such a manner as to satisfy itself concerning every particular difficulty which may arise," he tells us that

> we must therefore glean up our experiments in this science from a cautious observation of human life, and take them as they appear in the common course of the world, by men's behaviour in company, in affairs, and in their pleasures. Where experiments of this kind are judiciously collected and compared, we may hope to establish on them a science, which will not be inferior in certainty, and will be much superior in utility to any other of human comprehension. (T Intro, xix)

In the *Abstract* Hume "promises to draw no conclusions but where he is authorized by experience" (A, 646). He concludes *An Enquiry concerning Human Understanding* with the now notorious injunction to commit to the flames any book that contains neither *"any abstract reasoning concerning quantity or number"* nor *"any experimental reasoning concerning matter of fact and existence"* (EHU 12.3, 165), but not before he has subjected experimental reasoning itself to a severe, experimental scrutiny (EHU 4.2, 32–9).[5] *An Enquiry concerning the Principles of Morals* undertakes to discover "the foundation of ethics." As this, Hume says, "is a question of fact, not of abstract science, we can only expect success, by following the experimental method, and deducing general maxims from a comparison of particular instances" (EPM 1, 174). In "Of the Original Contract," an essay first published in 1748, Hume tells us that "A small degree of experience and observation suffices to teach us, that society cannot possibly be maintained without the authority of magistrates," and that, moreover, the "observation of these general and obvious interests is the source of all allegiance, and of that moral obligation, which we attribute to it" (E-OC, 480). "Of the Standard of Taste," first published in 1756, tells us that the "rules of composition" are obviously nothing more than "general observations, concerning what has been universally found to please in all countries and in all ages," and that in this regard their "foundation is the same with that of all the practical sciences, [namely] experience" (E-ST, 231).[6]

Hume presumably felt less need to be explicit about his commitment to experience and observation in his primarily historical works, the *Natural History of Religion* and *History of England*. The first of these works attempts to discover "the origin of religion in human nature" by extrapolating from present facts (religion and human nature as they are at present found to be) and the historical record of the beginnings and development of religion. This exercise is a *natural* history because the explanation is carried out within the limits of observable, natural phenomena; no supernatural beings or principles are appealed to or presupposed.[7] In short, *The Natural History of Religion* is a manifestation of Hume's commitment to observational empiricism.[8]

Much the same can be said of *The History of England*. Motivated to a considerable degree by the exaggerated claims of Whig and Tory alike – of those who insisted that the political institutions of eighteenth-century Britain should be made to reflect a perfect model found either in the mists of their Anglo-Saxon beginnings (a Whig tendency) or in a timeless, sacred beginning (a Tory tendency) – Hume attempted an impartial history of England, a history free of the essentially metaphysical commitments of both parties. He undertook to produce a history that recorded the *development* of political institutions over time, that treated these institutions not as derivations from pre-existing principles, but as the hard-won and still developing products of centuries of experience and observation.[9]

2. For most of the 250 years since the publication of his *Treatise*, Hume has standardly been interpreted as the philosopher who advanced empiricism to its logical and sceptical conclusion. Hume is better understood as a post-sceptical philosopher. By this I mean to suggest that Hume supposed (a) that the Cartesians (especially Malebranche) and Locke and Berkeley had in fact already taken traditional metaphysics and epistemology to its sceptical conclusions; (b) that these sceptical conclusions had been soundly and validly established; and (c) that the most important remaining task of philosophy, given these well-established and obvious conclusions, was to show how we are to get on with our lives, particularly our intellectual lives. Prior to Hume, one or another philosopher had, often unintentionally, thoroughly discredited the claim of humans to have certain knowledge of the true nature of space, causal relations, external objects, and mind. As Hume put it, even the "rabble," the crowd outside the philosophical hall, can tell, from the noise within, that

the philosophical enterprise is not going well. "The most trivial question escapes not our controversy, and in the most momentous we are not able to give any certain decision" (T Intro, xiv). Time, surely, to start afresh, to provide a new foundation, the science of human nature, on which all other sciences will rest.

But notice where Hume begins: the "elements of this philosophy" are, in the most literal sense, the immediate objects of thought and the relations between or among these objects of the "mental world." The elements themselves are called *perceptions* and are divided into two kinds, *impressions* and *ideas*. Of these, impressions are the more forceful or lively and also causally prior; ideas are complementary in that they are said to be "the faint images" of impressions, and causally dependent on them. In addition, Hume classifies as impressions "all our sensations, passions and emotions, as they make their first appearance in the soul" or mind and then divides this class into two sub-classes, *impressions of sensation* and *impressions of reflection*. The latter sort, impressions of reflection, are "derived in a great measure from our ideas." Impressions of sensation, he says, arise "*in the soul originally, from unknown causes*" (italics added). He then adds that "the examination of our sensations belongs more to anatomists and natural philosophers than to moral; and therefore shall not at present be enter'd upon" (T 1.1.1–4, 1–13). The phrase "not at present" we in time discover means "not in this work," for at no time does Hume take up the task which he has assigned to anatomists and natural philosophers.[10] Indeed, he begins Book 2 of the *Treatise* with much the same disclaimer:

'Tis certain, that the mind, in its perceptions, must begin somewhere; and that since the impressions precede their correspondent ideas, there must be some impressions, which without any introduction make their appearance in the soul. As these depend upon natural and physical causes, the examination of them wou'd lead me too far from my present subject, into the sciences of anatomy and natural philosophy.   (T 2.1.1, 275–6)

Between these two remarks Hume tells us clearly why he has left to others the task of explaining the origins of impressions of sensation. Such an explanation is irrelevant to the philosophical enterprise in which he is engaged. As he puts it:

As to those *impressions*, which arise from the *senses*, their ultimate cause is, in my opinion, perfectly inexplicable by human reason, and 'twill

always be impossible to decide with certainty, whether they arise immediately from the object, or are produc'd by the creative power of the mind, or
are deriv'd from the author of our being. Nor is such a question any way
material to our present purpose. We may draw inferences from the coherence of our perceptions, whether they be true or false; whether they represent nature justly, or be mere illusions of the senses.   (T 1.3.5, 84)[11]

But notice, I repeat, where Hume begins: the "elements of this
philosophy" are, in the most literal sense, the immediate objects of
thought and the relations between or among these objects in the
"mental world." And his concern is not to advance from this base in
order to deny that there are causes, objects, or minds – his concern is
not to make the case for scepticism about objects, causes, or minds.
The case for scepticism about these momentous questions was well-
known to Hume. He knew those sections of Bayle and Locke that
reveal the inadequacy of Descartes's attempts to prove that there is
an external world. He appreciated the sceptical force of the objections brought by Bayle, then significantly amplified by Berkeley,
against the primary-secondary quality distinction championed by
Locke.[12] He saw that philosophers of all kinds were, in the matter of
explaining the interaction of mind and body, sceptics in spite of
themselves. He saw that the leading Cartesian of the day, Malebranche, had concluded that there are no natural causes of any kind,
and that there is no human or natural knowledge of the existence of
causes or objects; what we do know of these things is the result of,
essentially, an act of divine grace.[13] In short, Hume was satisfied that
the battle to establish reliable links between thought and reality had
been fought *and lost* and hence made his contributions to philosophy from a post-sceptical perspective that incorporates and builds on
the sceptical results of his predecessors.[14]

3. The once-standard reading of Hume credited him with seeing the
sceptical implications of the representative theory of perception,[15]
and with seizing on these implications in the cause of a destructive
scepticism. It seems likely that Hume was fully aware of the
sceptical implications of this theory, but, given his expressed disin-
terest in the connections between impressions of sensation and their
possible causes, we must conclude either that he did not adopt the
theory, or that he adopted only one part of it. Hume agrees that the
immediate objects of mind are always perceptions, but he does not

take these to be, in one cardinal sense, representative of objects – neither impressions nor ideas *resemble* objects.[16]

In fact, Hume gave the "way of ideas" a kind of phenomenological turn. That is, his primary concern in Book 1 of the *Treatise* is with our perceptions, qua perceptions, with perceptions as, simply, the *elements or objects of the mind* and not as *representations* of external existences. Having focused on perceptions as the only objects of the mind, Hume goes on in Book 1 to show how some of these perceptions are interrelated or associated to produce still further perceptions, which are then projected onto a world putatively outside the mind.[17] *Somehow* the mind is furnished with impressions of sensation. On examination, we find that not one of these *impressions* can of itself be taken as an accurate representation of space or time, causal connection, an external object, or even our own mind. We simply do not have sensory *impressions* of space, causal connection, external existence, and so on. But, notwithstanding this fact – and the further fact that all our ideas are derived from impressions – we nonetheless do have *ideas* of space, causal connection, external existence, and so on and are nonetheless irredeemably committed to believing that there are real entities that correspond to each of these *ideas*.[18] The mystery to be explained, given the success of scepticism, is how we come to have these important ideas and, moreover, to believe that they represent, not impressions, but external existences or realities. To put this differently, Hume's greater goal is to show how, despite the success of scepticism, we are rescued from scepticism.

The first book of the *Treatise* is an effort to show how our perceptions "cohere" to form ideas of those fundamental items (space, causal connection, external existence) in which, sceptical doubts notwithstanding, we repose belief and on which "life and action entirely depend." In Book 1, Part 2, Hume argues that we have no direct impressions of space and time, and yet we do have the ideas of space and time.[19] He accounts for our idea of space by appealing to a "manner of appearance" in the following way. By means of two senses, sight and touch, we have impressions that array themselves as so many points related to one another. These particular impressions are by the *imagination* transformed into a "compound impression, which represents extension" or the abstract idea of space itself. Our idea of time is, *mutatis mutandis*, accounted for in the same way. "As 'tis from the disposition of visible and tangible objects we receive the idea of space, so from the succession of ideas and impressions we form the idea of time." The abstract idea of time, like all other abstract ideas, is represented in the imagination by a "particular individual idea of a determinate quantity and quality" joined to a term, "time," that has general reference (A, 647; T 1.2.3, 34, 38, 35). In short, the imagination, a faculty not typically assigned so significant a role, achieves what neither the senses nor reason can achieve.

Hume's account of our derivation and belief in the idea of causal connection (of "necessary connection," in his terms) follows this same pattern. He is often said to have denied that there is physical necessity and that we have any idea of necessary connection. This interpretation is significantly mistaken. Hume had been convinced by the Cartesians, especially by Malebranche, that neither the senses nor reason can establish that one object (a cause) is connected together with another object (an effect) in such a way that the presence of the one necessarily entails the existence of the other. Hume's own analysis of what we suppose to be experiences of cause and effect reveals only that objects taken to be causally related are contiguous in time and space, that the cause is prior to the effect, and that similar objects have been constantly associated in this way. These are the only perceptible features of such putative causal connections. And yet there seems to be more to the matter. "There is," he says, "a NECESSARY CONNECTION to be taken into consideration," and our belief in that relation must be explained (T 1.3.2, 77). Despite our demonstrated inability to see or prove that there are necessary causal connections, we continue to think and act as if we had knowledge of such connections. We act, for example, as though the future will necessarily resemble the past, and "wou'd appear ridiculous" if we were to say "that 'tis only probable the sun will rise tomorrow, or that all men must dye" (T 1.3.11, 124). To explain this phenomenon, Hume asks us to imagine what life would have been like for Adam, suddenly brought to life in the midst of the world and in "the full vigour of understanding." Adam would have been unable to make even the simplest predictions about the future behaviour of objects. He would not have been able to predict that one moving billiard ball, striking a second, would cause the second to move (A, 650–1). And yet we, endowed with the same faculties, can not only make, but are unable to resist making, this and countless other such predictions. What is the difference between ourselves and this puta-

tive Adam? Experience. We have experienced the constant conjunction (the invariant succession of paired objects or events) of particular causes and effects, and, although our experience never includes
even a glimpse of a causal connection, it does arouse in us an expectation that a particular event (a "cause") will be followed by another
event (an "effect") previously and constantly associated with it.
Regularities of experience give rise to these feelings and thus determine the mind to transfer its attention from a present impression to
the idea of an absent but associated object. *The idea of necessary
connection is copied from these feelings* (T 1.3.14, 162–6). The idea
has its foundation in the mind and is projected onto the world, but
there is nonetheless such an idea. That there is an objective physical
necessity to which this idea corresponds is an untestable hypothesis,
nor would demonstrating that such necessary connections had held
in the past guarantee that they will hold in the future. From these
considerations we see that Hume does not explicitly and dogmati-
cally deny that there are real causal connections. We have no experience of such necessary connections and hence can be, at best,
sceptical or agnostic about their existence. There is, however, an
idea of necessary connection, but, although we ordinarily and naturally believe that reality corresponds to this idea, the correct philosophical analysis reveals that the idea is derived from a feeling, or an
impression of reflection, and hence this analysis leaves us able to
suppose that our belief, however natural, may be mistaken.

Hume's account of our *belief* in future effects or absent causes – of
the process of mind that enables us to *plan effectively* – is a part of
this same explanation. Such belief involves an idea or conception of
the entity believed in but is clearly different from mere conception
without belief. This difference cannot be explained by supposing
that some further idea, an idea of belief itself, is present when we
believe but absent when we merely conceive. There is no such idea.
Moreover, given the mind's ability freely to join together any two
consistent ideas, if such an idea were available we by an act of will
could, contrary to experience, combine the idea of belief with any
other idea, and by so doing cause ourselves to believe anything.
Consequently, Hume concludes that belief can only be a "different
MANNER of conceiving an object"; it is a livelier, firmer, more vivid
and intense conception. Belief in certain "matters of fact" – the belief that because some event or object is now being experienced,

some other event or object not yet available to experience *will in the future* be experienced – is brought about by previous experience of the constant conjunction of two impressions. These two impressions have been associated together in such a way that the experience of one of them automatically gives rise to an idea of the other and has the effect of transferring the force or liveliness of the impression to the associated idea, thereby causing this idea to be believed or to take on the lively character of an impression (T 1.3.7, 94–8; A, 653–4).

Our beliefs in continuing and independently existing objects and in our own continuing selves are, on Hume's account, beliefs in "fictions," or in entities entirely beyond all experience. We have impressions that we naturally but mistakenly suppose to be themselves continuing, external objects, but analysis quickly reveals that these impressions are by their very nature fleeting and observer-dependent. Moreover, none of our impressions provides us with a distinctive mark or evidence of an external origin (T 1.4.2, 187–93). Similarly, when we focus on our own minds, we experience only a sequence of impressions and ideas and never encounter the mind or self in which these perceptions are supposed to inhere. To ourselves we appear to be merely "a bundle or collection of different perceptions, which succeed each other with an inconceivable rapidity, and are in a perpetual flux and movement" (T 1.4.6, 252). How, then, do we come to believe in external objects or our own selves and self-identity? Neither reason nor the senses, working with impressions and ideas, provide anything like compelling proof of the existence of continuing, external objects, or of a continuing, unified self. Indeed, these two faculties cannot account for our *belief* in objects or selves. If we had only reason and the senses, the faculties championed by previous philosophers, we would be mired in a debilitating and destructive uncertainty. So unfortunate an outcome is avoided only by the operation of that apparently unreliable third faculty, the *imagination*. It, by means of what appear to be a series of outright mistakes and trivial suggestions, leads us to believe in our own selves and in independently existing objects. The scepticism of the philosophers is in this way both confirmed (we can provide no arguments, for example, proving the existence of the external world) and shown to be of little practical import. As Hume summed up his point:

Almost all reasoning is there [the *Treatise*] reduced to experience; and the belief, which attends experience, is explained to be nothing but a peculiar sentiment, or lively conception produced by habit. Nor is this all, when we believe any thing of *external* existence, or suppose an object to exist a moment after it is no longer perceived, this belief is nothing but a sentiment of the same kind. Our author insists upon several other sceptical topics; and upon the whole concludes, that we assent to our faculties, and employ our reason only because we cannot help it. Philosophy wou'd render us entirely *Pyrrhonian*, were not nature too strong for it.   (A, 657)

4. Books 2 and 3 of the *Treatise* focus on the remaining element in Hume's mental world, the *impression of reflection*, or "those other impressions . . . call'd secondary and reflective, as arising either from the original impressions, or from their ideas" (T 2.1.1, 276). There are in these two books no questions about the existence of causes, objects, or minds. Having once explained how we form ideas of and come to believe in these entities, Hume simply takes them for granted and pushes on to discuss our principal impressions of reflection: the passions and the will in Book 2, and the moral sentiments, a particular species of passion, in Book 3.[20]

In general terms, Hume can be said to have attempted to rescue the passions from the ad hoc explanations and negative assessments of his predecessors. From the time of Plato and the Stoics, the passions had been routinely characterized as irrational, inexplicable, and unnatural elements which, given their head, will undermine and enslave reason, the essential and defining characteristic of humans. In contrast to this long-standing orthodoxy, Hume assumes that the passions constitute an integral and legitimate part of human nature, and a part that can be explained observationally (although introspectively) without recourse to physical or metaphysical speculation. On Hume's view, the passions can be treated as of a piece with other perceptions: they are secondary impressions that derive from prior impressions and ideas.

When we look at the passions in this way, we find differences between them. They may be divided into two classes, the *direct* and the *indirect*. The *direct* passions – desire, aversion, hope, and fear, for example – are feelings *caused* immediately or directly by pleasure or pain, or the prospect thereof, and take entities or events as their intentional objects, as when I desire food or fear political change. The *indirect* passions – pride and humility, love and hatred – are more complex. They arise as the result of a double relation of impressions and ideas and take persons as their objects. Their *causes* are, typically, the qualities of persons or of things belonging to persons, while their *objects* are the persons possessing these qualities or things. As Hume explains the matter, the object of pride or humility is always oneself, while the object of love or hatred is always some other person. The important point in the present context has not to do with the details of Hume's account, but with the fact that in giving it he demonstrates his commitment to treating the passions as nothing more or less than an integral part of the natural, mental world. The passions, like the ideas discussed in Book 1 of the *Treatise*, are further products of the observable natural processes Hume undertook to analyze and explain.

At first glance, the third and final book of the *Treatise* may appear to launch Hume on a course entirely different from that followed in the preceding volumes. This book is subtitled *Of Morals* and begins with a discussion of the question, "*Whether 'tis by means of our ideas or impressions we distinguish betwixt vice and virtue, and pronounce an action blameable or praise-worthy?*" (T 3.1.1, 456). The ensuing discussion seems never to deal explicitly with the apparently more fundamental genetic question, *How do the original elements of the mental world, those original* impressions of sensation, *give rise to the* impressions of reflection *and* ideas *associated with morality?* Hume simply takes it as given that we make moral distinctions, and that our moral discourse is carried out competently. We use a wide-ranging moral vocabulary that includes such terms as *virtue, vice, motive, duty, laudable, blameable, benevolence,* and *justice,* to mention only a few, and we understand one another's meaning – not perfectly, of course – but well enough to be able to spot inappropriate or incorrect uses of these terms (T 3.2.2, 500; 3.3.1, 579). This latter fact means that Hume also supposes that there are relatively clear moral *ideas,* ideas that are referred to by, or (to use his idiom) that are *annexed to,* these moral terms. Pursuing the genetic question about these ideas may give us the clearest and most fundamental answer to the question Hume *does* ask.

Hume appears never to think of renouncing the principle that "all ideas are deriv'd from, and represent impressions" (T 1.3.14, 161; see also 1.3.7, 96).[21] Given that he explicitly tells us that we have no sensory impressions of virtue and vice (T 3.1.1, 468–9), it follows that the idea of virtue is no more a copy of an *impression of sensation* than the idea of necessary connection is the copy of that type of impression. Hume also tells us that the ideas of virtue and vice are not the products of unaided reason; *reason alone* can no more give us the idea of vice than it can give us the idea of necessary connection (T 3.1.1, 456–68; 1.3.14, 157). And yet he assumes that we can talk as intelligently about virtue and vice as we do about extension and necessary connection (T 1.2.2, 32; 1.3.14, 162). Consequently, we must conclude that our moral terms are not meaningless – which is to say that they are "annexed" to ideas, and that these ideas refer to specifiable impressions. Just as there is an alternative account of the "nature and origin" of the idea referred to by the term *necessary connection* (T 1.3.14, 162), so is there an alternative account of the nature and origin of our moral ideas. Earlier we saw that impressions of sensation give rise, albeit indirectly, to the idea of necessary connection. Now we need to discover which impressions give rise, again indirectly, to the ideas of virtue and vice, and just how this is done. We also need to ask the same questions about our ideas of such particular virtues and vices as justice, injustice, and benevolence, and of such other moral concepts as duty and blame.

When we have answered these questions, we will understand why it is that Hume insists that it is by means of certain *impressions* that we distinguish betwixt vice and virtue. For Hume, to make a moral distinction – to do so competently, so that, for example, Nero is judged to have been vicious – is to apply rightly a moral term (*vicious*) and its annexed idea (the idea of *vice*) to an individual with distinctive characteristics, the observation of which characteristics has given rise to a distinctive and unpleasant feeling (an *impression of reflection*), or a "moral sentiment." If we think of this *kind* of experience as happening only once, it seems likely that there would be little more to it than the felt disapprobation. There would be an observation, and there would be a feeling of disapprobation, but there would be no *idea* of vice. But, because this kind of experience is encountered repeatedly, it gives rise to an idea that serves to "represent" it, or that represents at least its most notable aspect, the feeling of disapprobation. Thus we see not only how it is that moral ideas arise, but why it is that moral distinctions depend on particular impressions, the moral sentiments. Moral distinctions cannot depend ultimately on ideas, not even on moral ideas, because all ideas derive from, and represent, impressions. If our experience were not such that it gave rise to some distinctive and relevant differences among our impressions of reflection, we would have no distinctive and intelligible *moral* ideas. Just as only a portion of the conjunctions we experience lead us to make causal judgements, so, too, do only a portion of our approvals and disapprovals – and we can specify the features of those that do so – lead us to make moral judgements. In other words, only a relatively small part of our impressions of reflection give rise to, and are represented by, moral ideas.

This account of the origin of moral distinctions serves as an important reminder of another of Hume's points of departure, namely, the assumption that morality is an entirely human affair founded on human nature and the circumstances of human life. Since morality, he wrote as he was revising Book 3 of the *Treatise*, "is determin'd merely by Sentiment, it regards only human Nature & human Life" (HL 1:40). Morality exists only because human beings as a species possess several notable dispositions which, over time, have given rise to it. The tendency just discussed – to feel approbation and disapprobation in response to the motives and actions of others, and to form moral ideas as a consequence – is such a disposition. In addition, we have a disposition to form bonded family groups, another disposition (called *sympathy*) to communicate and thus share sentiments, and also a disposition to form general rules. Our disposition to form family groups results in small social units in which a natural generosity operates. The fact that such generosity is possible provides a foundation for the distinction between virtue and vice. The fact that we respond very differently to distinctive motivations – we feel approbation in response to well-intended actions, and disapprobation in response to ill-intended ones – provides a necessary starting place for the entire moral enterprise. To claim that "Nero was vicious" is to make a judgement about Nero's motives or character in consequence of an observation of him that has caused an impartial observer to feel a unique sentiment of disapprobation. That our moral judgements have this affective foundation accounts for the practical and motivational character of morality. Reason itself is "perfectly inert," and hence there is another ground for concluding that moral distinctions, which are practical or action-guiding, must derive from impressions, and, more particularly, from the sentiments or feelings provided by our moral sense.

Hume distinguishes, however, between the "natural virtues" (generosity, benevolence, for example) and the "artificial virtues" (justice, allegiance, for example). These differ in that the former not only produce good on each occasion of their practice, but are also on every occasion approved. In contrast, any particular instantiation of justice may be "contrary to the public good" and be approved only in so far as it is entailed by "a general scheme or system of action, which is advantageous" in so far as it conforms to one of the general rules we have been disposed to form (T 3.3.1, 579). The artificial virtues differ also in being the result of ad hoc decisions and contrivances arising from "the circumstances and necessities of mankind" (T 3.2.1, 477). In our original condition, we did not need the artificial virtues because our natural dispositions and responses were adequate to maintain the order of small, kinship-based units. But as human numbers increased, so, too, did the scarcity of some material goods lead to an increase in the possibility of conflict – particularly over property – between these units. As a consequence, and out of self-interest, our ancestors were gradually led to establish conventions governing property and its exchange. In the early stages of this necessary development our disposition to form general rules was an indispensable component; at later stages, sympathy enables many individuals to pursue the artificial virtues from a combination of self-interest and a concern for others, thus giving the fully developed artificial virtues a foundation in two different kinds of motivation. Just how these important and complex philosophical claims are to be understood is a matter of considerable debate, but it is clear that for Hume morality is an artifact – the product of an entirely human activity that has enabled the species to organize itself, in response to different and changing circumstances, for an ordered and sometimes propitious survival.[22]

III. RECASTINGS AND CONTINUATIONS

1. Within a few years, Hume came to regret the publication of the *Treatise*. The work was never a commercial success: Hume alleged that it fell *"dead-born from the press"* (MOL), by which he may have meant that the work failed to reach a second edition; indeed, about 1760 nearly 300 copies of volumes 1 and 2, and 200 of volume 3, were sold at auction in two lots, and at cut-rate prices. But

Hume's greater regret was over his own performance in the work, that he had bungled his attempt to introduce a new system of philosophy. Even before volume 3 was published (November 1740), he wrote, "I wait with some Impatience for a second Edition principally on Account of Alterations I intend to make in my Performance" (HL 1:38–9). In March of that year he had published the *Abstract* of the *Treatise*, a short work that attempts *"to render a larger work more intelligible to ordinary capacities, by abridging it,"* or, more accurately, to further illustrate and explain the "CHIEF ARGUMENT" of that work (A, [641, title]).[23] Still not satisfied, he was to include in the third volume of the *Treatise* an appendix in which some passages of Book 1 "are illustrated and explain'd" (T 3, title). Despite these attempts at clarification, Hume was later to say of the *Treatise*: "I was carry'd away by the Heat of Youth & Invention to publish too precipitately. So vast an Undertaking, plan'd before I was one and twenty, & compos'd before twenty five, must necessarily be very defective. I have repented my Haste a hundred, & a hundred times" (HL 1:158).

In 1748 Hume published *Philosophical Essays concerning Human Understanding* (later to be titled *An Enquiry concerning Human Understanding*), a recasting of materials from, for the most part, Book 1 of the *Treatise*. Of this work he said that he thought it contained "every thing of Consequence relating to the Understanding, which you woud meet with in the Treatise; & I give you my Advice against reading the latter. By shortening & simplifying the Questions, I really render them much more complete. *Addo dum minuo*. The philosophical Principles are the same in both" (HL 1:158).[24]

The recast version of Book 3 of the *Treatise, An Enquiry concerning the Principles of Morals*, the work which Hume took to be, "of all my writings, historical, philosophical, or literary, incomparably the best" (MOL), was published in 1751. *A Dissertation on the Passions*, a recasting of Book 2 into what Hume described as one of several "small pieces," was published in 1757. Late in his life Hume grew impatient with his critics for focusing their attention on the *Treatise* rather than his recastings of it, and so in 1775 he composed a short notice which he asked to be affixed to all existing and future copies of his *Essays and Treatises on Several Subjects*.[25] This "Advertisement" asks that the *Treatise* be ignored.

Most of the principles, and reasonings, contained in this volume, were published in a work in three volumes, called A Treatise of Human Nature: *A work which the Author had projected before he left College, and which he wrote and published not long after. But not finding it successful, he was sensible of his error in going to the press too early, and he cast the whole anew in the following pieces, where some negligences in his former reasoning and more in the expression, are, he hopes, corrected. Yet several writers, who have honoured the Author's Philosophy with answers, have taken care to direct all their batteries against that juvenile work, which the Author never acknowledged, and have affected to triumph in any advantages, which, they imagined, they had obtained over it: A practice very contrary to all rules of candour and fair-dealing, and a strong instance of those polemical artifices, which a bigotted zeal thinks itself authorized to employ. Henceforth, the Author desires, that the following Pieces may alone be regarded as containing his philosophical sentiments and principles.*

(EHU, [3])

Reasonable though Hume's desire may have seemed to him, few if any serious readers have been able to concur with it. For Hume's critics, the *Treatise* is an irresistible target; for those who believe him to have been a profound and constructive student of human nature, the work is too rich to ignore.

2. About the works that are said to represent the *Treatise* "cast . . . anew," two things are obvious. First, as noted in section II.1, Hume's commitment to the experimental method continued unabated in these later works. Second, Hume does not merely, as he suggests, add or improve by subtraction. His recastings include some lengthy and important additions, most notably some attention-getting discussions of matters relating to religion. In an effort to make his views religiously innocuous so that they might be considered calmly and on their philosophical merits, he had carefully excised from the *Treatise* anything that could be taken as anti-religious. This effort failed. The views of the *Treatise* and *Essays, Moral and Political* were too thoroughly secular to pass unremarked in a religious age, and by 1745 Hume had been branded a religious sceptic with atheistic tendencies. He seems in consequence to have decided to challenge openly the rationality of religious belief. In any event, *An Enquiry concerning Human Understanding* included two of Hume's most provocative forays into the philosophy of religion, "Of Miracles" and "Of a particular Providence and of a future State," while

The Natural History of Religion was denounced as atheistic even before it was published.[26]

These works established beyond all doubt Hume's character as a religious sceptic. Taken together, they challenge the value of religious belief and attempt to curb its excesses by undertaking to show that this form of belief has its beginnings in sources or causes about which we must be deeply suspicious. In "Of Miracles," for example, Hume argues that belief in miracles, a kind of putative fact used to justify a commitment to certain creeds, can never provide the secure foundation such creeds require. He sees that these commitments are typically maintained with a mind-numbing tenacity and a disruptive intolerance toward contrary views. To counter these objectionable commitments, he argues that the widely held view that miracles are violations of a law of nature is incoherent; that the evidence for even the most likely miracle will always be counter-balanced by the evidence establishing the law of nature which the miracle allegedly violates; and that the evidence supporting any given miracle is necessarily suspect. His argument leaves open the possibility that violations of the laws of nature may have occurred, but shows that the logical and evidential grounds for a *belief* in any given miracle or set of miracles are much weaker than the religious suppose. There are and will be those who believe that miracles have occurred, but Hume's analysis shows that such beliefs will always lack the force of evidence needed to justify the arrogance and intolerance that characterize so many of the religious.

"Of a particular Providence and of a future State" (posthumously supplemented by the *Dialogues concerning Natural Religion*) has a similar effect. Philosophers and theologians of the eighteenth century commonly argued (the *argument from design*, as it is known) that the well-ordered universe in which we find ourselves can only be the effect of a supremely intelligent cause, that each aspect of this divine creation is well-designed to fulfil some beneficial end, and that these effects show us that the Deity is caring and benevolent. Hume argues that these conclusions go well beyond the available evidence. The pleasant and well-designed features of the world are balanced by a good measure of the unpleasant and the plainly botched. Our knowledge of causal connections depends on the experience of constant conjunctions; these cause the vivacity of a present impression to be transferred to the idea associated with it and leave us believing in that idea. But in this case the effect to be explained, the universe, is unique, and its cause unknown. Consequently, we cannot possibly have experiential grounds for any kind of inference about this cause. On experiential grounds the most we can say is that there is a massive, mixed effect, and, as we have through experience come to believe that effects have causes commensurate to them, this effect probably does have a commensurately large and mixed cause. Furthermore, as the effect is remotely like the products of human manufacture, we can say "*that the cause or causes of order in the universe probably bear some remote analogy to human intelligence*" (DNR 12, 227). There is indeed an inference to be drawn from the unique effect in question (the universe) to the cause of that effect, but it is not the "argument" of the theologians, and it provides no foundation for any form of sectarian pretension or even the mildest forms of intolerance.

The *Natural History of Religion* focuses on the question of "the origin of religion in human nature." Hume asks, that is, what features of human nature account for the widespread, but not universal, belief in invisible and intelligent power(s). He delivers a thoroughly deflationary and naturalistic answer: religious belief "springs not from an original instinct or primary impression of nature," not from any universal and fundamental principle of our natures, but from features of human nature that are derivative and whose operation "may easily be perverted by various accidents and causes ... [or] altogether prevented" (NHR Intro, 4:309–10). Moreover, it is the darker, less salubrious features of our nature that take the principal parts in this story. Primitive peoples did not find nature orderly and reassuring as though produced by a beneficent designer, but arbitrary and fearsome. Motivated by their own ignorance and fear, they came to think of the activities of nature as the effect of a multitude of petty powers – gods – that could, through propitiating worship, be influenced to ameliorate the lives of those who engaged in this worship. Subsequently, the same fears and perceptions transformed polytheism into monotheism, the view that a single, omnipotent being created and still controls the world and all that transpires in it. From this conclusion Hume goes on to argue that monotheism, seemingly the more sophisticated position, is in fact *morally* retrograde, for, once having established itself, monotheism tends naturally toward zeal and intolerance, encourages debasing, "monkish virtues," and proves itself a danger to society because it proves to be a cause of violent and immoral acts directed against those found to be hetero-dox. In contrast, polytheism is tolerant of diversity and encourages genuine virtues that improve humankind, and hence from a moral point of view is superior to monotheism. The important point here, however, is that all religious belief appears to derive from fear and ignorance, and, moreover, to foster the continued development of these undesirable characteristics.

3. In a number of respects, Hume's *Essays* and his *History of England* constitute *continuations* of his earliest work. They are, of course, further manifestations of his attempt to extend the experimental method into moral subjects. They are also further manifestations of his attempt to gain understanding by means of an examination of origins or beginnings. Their titles alone indicate, often enough, this interest: "That Politics may be reduced to a Science," "Of the First Principles of Government," "Of the Origin of Government," "Of the Rise and Progress of the Arts and Sciences." Others, with less tell-tale titles, are nonetheless a part of the same project. "Of the Liberty of the Press" traces the unparalleled liberty of the press British subjects enjoy to the "mixed form of government" found in Britain and thus serves as an argument in support of that form. In "Of the Independency of Parliament" Hume draws attention to the fact that the House of Commons could easily wrest all power from the king and lords, but does not do so. He resolves this "paradox" by looking for an explanation that is "consistent with our experience of human nature" and concluding that a fundamental feature of that nature, the self-interest of the individual members of the Commons, acts as a brake on the expansion of the power of Parliament (E-IP, 44–5). "Of Parties in General" looks for the sources, again in human nature, of parties, or those detestable factions that "subvert government, render laws impotent, and beget the fiercest animosities among men of the same nation, who ought to give mutual assistance and protection to each other." (E-PG, 55) "Of Superstition and Enthusiasm" outlines the pernicious effects on government and society of the two types of false religion named in the title of the essay.[27] And so on.

There is at least one additional sense in which the *Essays* and *The History of England* represent a continuation of the project that began with *A Treatise of Human Nature*: the work for which Hume is remembered is all fundamentally historical. That is, all this work attempts to explain something that we at present believe, feel, say, think or do, to explain some present state of affairs, whether that state be in the mental, moral, or political world, by tracing perceptions, actions, or states – various *effects* – to discernible *causes*. Our experiments in the science of human nature, he said in the often-quoted line, must be gleaned "from a cautious observation of human life," from the "common course of the world, by men's behaviour in company, in affairs, and in their pleasures." Observation of what humans have done, how their minds work, how their institutions have formed: these are *historical* observations of several different kinds.

Hume reveals something more of his view of explanation in one of the essays just mentioned, "Of the Rise and Progress of the Arts and Sciences." Enquiries into human affairs, he says there, require us to distinguish between "what is owing to *chance*, and what proceeds from *causes*." If we say that an event is owing to chance, we are in effect confessing our ignorance, and putting an end to attempts at explanation. But if we suppose some event or state of affairs is the result of causes, we leave ourselves the opportunity of "assigning these causes" and displaying our "profound knowledge." As a general rule, he says, "*What depends upon a few persons is, in a great measure, to be ascribed to chance, or secret and unknown causes: What arises from a great number, may often be accounted for by determinate and known causes*" (E-RP, 111–12). Consequently, explanations of, say, the course of domestic politics or the rise of commerce will be easier to come by than explanations of cultural or artistic development. And yet a cautious enquirer may perhaps show that there is something to learn about this latter subject, may perhaps as a result of careful observation detect regularities between prior conditions and the flourishing of the arts and sciences. In this particular essay, Hume turns his hand to giving just such an explanation. But, more important, the *Essays* taken together, and *The History of England*, are the result of many attempts to push back the frontiers of ignorance or misunderstanding by assigning *causes* to phenomena previously attributed to the workings of *chance*, or what to Hume amounted to the same thing, the workings of providence. The *Treatise* and its several recastings are the result of other such attempts.

IV. REFORM

In August 1776, a few days before his death, Hume was visited by Adam Smith, one of his closest friends. On observing that Hume, who had been seriously ill for some months, was cheerful and apparently full of the spirit of life, Smith "could not help entertaining some faint hopes" of his friend's recovery. "Your hopes are groundless," Hume replied, and eventually turned the conversation onto Lucian's *Dialogues of the Dead*, and the excuses offered to Charon the boatman for not entering his boat to be ferried to Hades. None of the classical excuses fitted him, Hume noted. He had no house to finish, no children to provide for, no enemies to destroy. "He then diverted himself," Smith continues,

with inventing several jocular excuses, which he supposed he might make to Charon, and with imagining the very surly answers which it might suit the character of Charon to return to them. "Upon further consideration," said [Hume], "I thought I might say to him, 'Good Charon, I have been correcting my works for a new edition. Allow me a little time, that I may see how the Public receives the alterations.' But Charon would answer, 'When you have seen the effect of these, you will be for making other alterations. There will be no end of such excuses; so, honest friend, please step into the boat.' But I might still urge, 'Have a little patience, good Charon, I have been endeavouring to open the eyes of the Public. If I live a few years longer, I may have the satisfaction of seeing the downfal[l] of some of the prevailing systems of superstition.' But Charon would then lose all temper and decency. 'You loitering rogue, that will not happen these many hundred years. Do you fancy I will grant you a lease for so long a term? Get into the boat this instant, you lazy, loitering rogue.' "[28]

Of the many anecdotes about Hume that have survived, none, I think, better reveals his character. There is, first, the fact that a man, correctly convinced of his imminent death, and equally satisfied that death is simply annihilation, would treat the matter lightly.[29] Serious topics treated at times with nonchalance: this has been enough to lead some of his critics mistakenly to suppose that Hume lacked seriousness of purpose, to suppose that *effect* was to him more important than *truth*. Of course, Hume did treat serious topics lightly, and he did have reservations about claims to have found the truth, but these facts are entirely consistent with his most fundamental and unmistakably serious aim.[30]

In the conversation with Smith, for example, Hume's humour is focused on two topics of genuine concern to him. He was, surely, as he candidly tells us in "My Own Life," concerned with his literary reputation, and seems very likely to have taken pleasure in being recognized as one of Europe's leading literary figures. But it was not merely *fame* that Hume sought; it was also *reputation*. Before he had published anything he said that he "wou'd rather live & dye in Obscurity" than publish his views in a "maim'd & imperfect" form (KHL). With the *Treatise* finally published, he discouraged a friend from pursuing a scheme to increase sales; his first concern was not with commercial success, but with earning the approbation of those capable of judging his writings (NHL, 4). And, as his first excuse to Charon indicates, he constantly revised and altered his *Essays and Treatises*, and *History of England* – indeed, he did so, apparently, on his death-bed – when he had no other reason for doing so than his own inner compulsion to improve them. We can agree that Hume wrote for effect, but we need not conclude from his occasional or even typical lightness of tone that he lacked serious purpose.[31]

Hume's second excuse to Charon reveals much about that purpose. He has, he says, "been endeavouring to open the eyes of the Public" and would like to remain alive long enough to have "the satisfaction of seeing the downfal[l] of some of the prevailing systems of superstition." Hume the *reformer* is only seldom noticed.[32] And yet from early days *reform* was the effect at which he aimed. In the beginning, it was "reformation" of the science of man at which he aimed, a reformation which would, if successful, have the effect of reforming all the other sciences, for these are all – even *"Mathematics, Natural Philosophy, and Natural Religion"* – dependent on the science of human nature (T Intro, xv). Habit, he says elsewhere, is a "powerful means of reforming the mind, and implanting in it good dispositions and inclinations"; the great value of philosophy derives from the fact that, properly undertaken, "it insensibly refines the temper, and it points out to us those dispositions which we should endeavour to attain, by a constant *bent* of mind, and by repeated *habit*" (E-Sc, 170–1). "Moral Philosophy," he says at the very beginning of *An Enquiry concerning Human Understanding*, "may contribute to the entertainment, instruction, and reformation of mankind" (EHU 1, 5).

Hume had no thought of reforming human nature itself. Human

nature he took to be fixed,[33] and utopian schemes dependent on a changed constitution of humanity he dismissed without qualification. "All plans of government, which suppose great reformation in the manners of mankind, are plainly imaginary" (E-IPC, 514). Reformation, if it is to take place, will affect individuals, and will be in the form of that refinement of temper which results from new habits of *mind*, and, most particularly, from new habits of *belief*. It will be the effect of individuals melding, as Hume melded, the "experimental Method of Reasoning" into an updated version of the "Academic or Sceptical philosophy." This latter species of philosophy has, he says, a clear advantage over all other kinds: by its very nature it protects those who adopt it from the excesses characteristic of other forms of philosophy. The academic sceptic, noting the dangers of hasty and dogmatic judgement, emphasizes continually the advantages of "doubt and suspense of judgment . . . of confining to very narrow bounds the enquiries of the understanding, and of renouncing all speculations which lie not within the limits of common life and practice" (EHU 5.1, 41). Hume's post-sceptical philosophy does not counsel us to suspend all judgement or belief and affirmation. Instead, accepting the basic lessons of scepticism, it attempts to show us how to moderate our beliefs and attitudes. Those who practised his principles would, Hume thought, learn how to avoid that combination of arrogance, pretension, and credulity that he found so distasteful and stifling, so *dangerous* in its typical manifestations, namely, religious dogmatism and the spirit of faction. Hume did not suppose that he would effect changes in human nature, but he did hope that he could moderate individual belief and opinion, and, in consequence, actions and even institutions.[34] A simple but profound goal: "to open the eyes of the Public," and thereby undercut "prevailing systems of superstition."

V. TEN ESSAYS ON HUME'S THOUGHT

Although best known now for his contributions to epistemology, metaphysics, and the philosophy of religion, Hume also made substantial and influential contributions to morals and moral psychology, political and economic theory, political and social history, and, to a lesser extent, literary and aesthetic theory. The essays in this volume approach Hume in this topical way. They introduce readers to his wide-ranging thought by focusing on ten overlapping areas of interest. The essays themselves are arranged in a pattern that reflects, first, the structural order of *A Treatise of Human Nature*, Hume's earliest and most systematic philosophical publication, and then the pattern of his later publications. Some essays show how Hume's thought may be linked to that of his predecessors and contemporaries. Others are more concerned with links to the twentieth century. Each provides an accessible account of some central aspect of Hume's thought.

The first essay outlines Hume's plans for a new science of human nature, a science that is to serve as the foundation of all the other sciences, moral as well as natural. This science, John Biro argues, has significant affinities to what is at present thought of as cognitive science and offers insights that will be of use to those engaged in this contemporary enterprise. Alexander Rosenberg looks at Hume's views on a set of issues – empirical meaning, causation, induction, and explanation, for example – and argues that it is because he raised these issues, and made significant contributions to our understanding of them, that Hume in the middle of the present century "came to be regarded as the most important philosopher to have written in the English language." Noting that Hume describes the philosophy of the *Treatise* as "very Sceptical," Robert Fogelin attempts to see what this scepticism amounts to, and how it is related to other aspects of his philosophical program. He concludes that while Hume clearly did not recommend a wholesale suspension of belief (he thought this impossible), he is, in so far as he presents us with a thoroughgoing critique of our intellectual faculties, a radical, unreserved, unmitigated sceptic, and that to think otherwise is to miss much of Hume's genius.

Of the three essays that take Hume's moral theory as a point of departure, that by Terence Penelhum considers those elements – the self, the passions, the will, for example – of Hume's view of human nature that are most intimately related to his objectives as a moral philosopher, but not before he has considered Hume's character and the important questions some have raised about his psychological qualifications for doing philosophy. In the second of these essays I situate Hume's moral theory within a centrally important debate about the foundations of morality. According to Hume, it is because our unchanging human nature is as it is that we are able to mark genuine differences between virtue and vice, justice and injustice, and other moral relations: morality has human nature as its foundation. Knud Haakonssen argues that Hume undertook to show that most early modern views of society and politics, founded as they were on two forms of false religion,–superstition or enthusiasm, were philosophically misconceived, empirically untenable, and, often enough, politically dangerous. In contrast, Hume offered a humanistic account of political morality – an account that sees our political institutions as human constructs that depend on human nature and human experience.

With the publication of his *Political Discourses* in 1752, Hume established himself as an important political economist. Andrew Skinner sketches the background of economic theory in which Hume's work appeared, outlines Hume's insightful alternative views, and concludes by noting Hume's influence on the economic writings of, among others, his good friend, Adam Smith. In 1757, with the publication of "Of the Standard of Taste" and "Of Tragedy," Hume provided his readers with the surviving pieces of what he had intended to be a systematic work on "criticism" – a combination of literary theory, aesthetics, and moral psychology. Peter Jones's essay brings together Hume's somewhat scattered remarks on these topics, thus enabling us to see and understand his general perspective on the arts and how it relates to his other views about humanity and society.

Because of the popularity of his six-volume *History of England*, Hume was, and still is, referred to as "the historian." David Wootton examines the motivations – personal, moral, and political – that led to this monumental narrative of social and political circumstance and suggests that it is, to a large extent, Hume's story of the development of the uncommon liberty enjoyed by the English. The last of Hume's major publications, his *Dialogues concerning Natural Religion*, was published only in 1778, two years after his death. In the final essay in the volume, John Gaskin reviews the whole of Hume's critique of religion – a critique that is at least implicit in all of his works, and that, we are shown, is "subtle, profound and damaging to religion in ways which have no philosophical antecedents and few successors."

The Appendix supplies the reader with two brief autobiographies. Hume wrote the first of these in 1734, some years after he had begun work on, but still five years before he published, the *Treatise*. The second he wrote forty-two years later, only a few months before his death in 1776. A bibliography provides the reader with information about Hume's works, the titles of the principal early reactions to them, and a selection of monographs and articles that discuss his writings.

NOTES

1 Reported by Hume to James Boswell. See "An Account of My Last Interview with David Hume, Esq." (DNR, 76).

2 On Hume's knowledge of the science of his time, and of Boyle in particular, see Michael Barfoot, "Hume and the Culture of Science in the Early Eighteenth Century," in *Oxford Studies in the History of Philosophy*, ed. M. A. Stewart (Oxford, 1990), pp. 151–90.

3 From 1758, Hume's essays and *An Enquiry concerning Human Understanding*, *A Dissertation on the Passions*, *An Enquiry concerning the Principles of Morals*, and *The Natural History of Religion* were published together as *Essays and Treatises on Several Subjects*.

4 For more on this topic, see John Biro, "Hume's New Science of the Mind," Part I, this volume.

5 On Hume's sceptical challenge to experimental reasoning, see Robert Fogelin, "Hume's Scepticism," Part II, this volume.

6 Here again Hume shows that he is aware of the limitations of his chosen principle, for he goes on to add: "But though all the general rules of art are founded only on experience and on the observation of the common sentiments of human nature, we must not imagine, that, on every occasion, the feelings of men will be conformable to these rules. Those finer emotions of the mind are of a very tender and delicate nature, and require the concurrence of many favourable circumstances to make them play with facility and exactness, according to their general and established principles. . . . [I]f any of these circumstances be wanting, our experiment will be fallacious, and we shall be unable to judge of the catholic and universal beauty. The relation, which nature has placed between the form and the sentiment, will at least be more obscure; and it will require greater accuracy to trace and discern it" (E-ST, 232–3). For a discussion of Hume's views on aesthetic and literary matters, see the essay by Peter Jones, this volume.

7 This attitude is made explicit in *The History of England*. In the midst of his discussion of Joan of Arc, Hume writes: "It is the business of history to distinguish between the *miraculous* and the *marvellous*; to reject the first in all narrations merely profane and human; to doubt the second;

and when obliged by unquestionable testimony, as in the present case, to admit of something extraordinary, to receive as little of it as is consistent with the known facts and circumstances" (HE 20, 2:398).

8 For a discussion of Hume's use of a historical, observational method, see Andrew Skinner's essay, "David Hume: Principles of Political Economy," Part III, this volume.

9 On Hume's *History of England*, see David Wootton's essay in this volume. In the process of producing historical work Hume made use of an implicit critical method to decide what the facts of experience had been. For a brief discussion of this method and, more generally, the relationship of Hume's philosophical and historical writings, see my "History and Philosophy in Hume's Thought," in *David Hume: Philosophical Historian*, ed. David Fate Norton and Richard H. Popkin (Indianapolis, 1965), pp. xxxii–l.

10 Although Hume wanted nothing to do with a physical anatomy attempting to explain sensation, he does repeatedly describe himself as engaged in *an anatomy of human nature* (T 1.4.6, 263; 3.3.6, 620–1; HL 1:32–3; A, 646).

11 This comment is made in the midst of Hume's attempt to explain how we come to have the idea of, and to believe in, necessary connection. But the suggestion that the explanations of Book 1 are confined to an examination of the "coherence" of "elements" within the "mental world" is repeated in other forms in other places. See, for example, 1.4.2 ("Of scepticism with regard to the senses"), where the discussion is focused on the way in which impressions and ideas cohere to give us, not *knowledge* of, but only *belief* in, external objects; and the Appendix (633), where Hume contrasts theories of the material world with his "theory of the intellectual world."

12 Locke argued that certain ideas (those of extension and shape, for example) caused by what he called the "primary qualities" of objects resemble these qualities in such a way that they provide us with accurate, reliable information about the qualities that cause them. Other ideas (those of colour and taste, for example) caused by what he called the "secondary qualities" of objects fail to resemble the qualities causing them and in fact lead us to attribute to objects characteristics (colour, taste) which they do not actually possess. Bayle suggested, and Berkeley argued – successfully, it is generally believed – that this distinction is epistemologically untenable. See Pierre Bayle, *Historical and Critical Dictionary*, ed. and trans. Richard H. Popkin (Indianapolis, 1965), Article "Pyrrho," Note B; George Berkeley, *A Treatise concerning the Principles of Human Knowledge*, I.9–15. For a helpful account of Berkeley's impact on Hume, see David Raynor, "Hume and Berkeley's *Three Dia-*

logues, Studies in the Philosophy of the Scottish Enlightenment" (Oxford, 1990), pp. 231–50.

13 Hume says, for example: "But so little does any *power* discover itself to the senses in the operations of matter, that the *Cartesians* have made no scruple to assert, that matter is utterly deprived of energy, and that all its operations are perform'd merely by the energy of the supreme Being" (A, 656).

14 It does not follow that Hume made no contributions to the arsenal of scepticism. His critique of induction, mentioned in note 5, is one such contribution. For others, see John Gaskin, "Hume on Religion," this volume.

15 This theory maintains that the immediate objects of the mind are *ideas* (in Hume's vocabulary, *perceptions*, or *impressions* and *ideas*), some of which are supposed accurately to represent various kinds of entities outside the mind. The problem was to determine which ideas do represent, and, given that ideas and only ideas are immediate objects of the mind, to find independent evidence that any given idea represents accurately or at all – that it *resembles*. The theory is sometimes referred to as the "way of ideas."

16 Hume repeatedly insists that *ideas* are derived from and represent impressions. Impressions themselves are of two types: impressions of sensation and of reflection. Our senses, he says, cannot represent their impressions as distinct from us and hence fail to represent a crucial feature of external objects. Nor, he says, can any of our sense impressions, not even our impressions of touch, "represent solidity, nor any real object," because there is not the "least resemblance" between these impressions and solidity (T 1.4.2, 190; 1.4.4, 230–1; see also 1.2.3, 34). A passion, Hume says, "contains not any representative quality, which renders it a copy of any other existence or modification" (T 2.3.3, 415). We see, then, that neither type of impression can in this sense *represent* external reality.

Hume's reasons for agreeing that the immediate objects of mind are always perceptions are discussed in Alexander Rosenberg, "Hume and the Philosophy of Science," Part I, this volume. It should also be noted that Hume is not, as another strain of interpretation suggests, a *phenomenalist*, or one who supposes our perceptions constitute objects.

17 Husserl, the founder of phenomenology, himself recognized this feature of Hume's thought. See R. A. Mall, *Experience and Reason: The Phenomenology of Husserl and its Relation to Hume's Philosophy* (The Hague, 1973), esp. pp. 19–28.

18 We remain irredeemably committed to these beliefs in the sense that, while philosophical analysis may on occasion bring us to doubt them,

this doubt cannot be sustained. Even a sceptic must, with rare exception, believe in causes and objects. The sceptic may very well, however, modify the manner or intensity of these unavoidable beliefs. On this latter point, see my "How a Sceptic May Live Scepticism," in *Faith, Scepticism and Rationality: Essays in Honour of Terence Penelhum*, ed. J. J. MacIntosh and Hugo Meynell (University of Calgary Press, forthcoming).

19 It should be understood that Hume is concerned with the source of our most abstract or general ideas of space and time – of space, for example, as something like continuous, unbounded, or unlimited extension in every direction, regarded as void of matter, or without reference to matter (*Oxford English Dictionary*). Of such a space we neither have, nor could have, a direct sensory impression, but from the fact that we can intelligibly discuss the subject, it follows, on Hume's view, that we have an idea of space to which the word "space" refers: "Now 'tis certain we have an idea of extension; for otherwise why do we talk and reason concerning it?" (T 1.2.2, 32).

20 On Hume and the will, see Terence Penelhum, "Hume's Moral Psychology," Part IV, this volume. This same essay also includes a substantial discussion of Hume's theory of the passions.

21 Hume's views on the relationship of ideas to meaning are scattered throughout his writings, but see, for a start, T 1.2.2, 32 and T 1.3.14, 162. See also Alexander Rosenberg, "Hume and the Philosophy of Science," Part I, this volume.

22 For a more detailed discussion of Hume's moral theory, see my "Hume, Human Nature, and the Foundations of Morality," this volume.

23 As it is now clear that Hume is the author of the *Abstract*, this short work can be enthusiastically recommended to those who wish to consider Hume's own account of the chief argument of the *Treatise*. For recent discussions of the question of who wrote the *Abstract*, see David Raynor, "The Authorship of the *Abstract* Revisited," and my "More Evidence that Hume Wrote the *Abstract*," both in *Hume Studies* 19 (1993).

24 In "My Own Life" (reprinted in the Appendix to this volume), Hume was to say: "I had always entertained a notion, that my want of success in publishing the Treatise of Human Nature, had proceeded more from the manner than the matter, and that I had been guilty of a very usual indiscretion, in going to the press too early. I, therefore, cast the first part of that work anew in the Enquiry concerning Human Understanding."

25 See note 3.

26 Hume at one point included "Of Miracles" in the manuscript of the *Treatise* but excised it as part of his program to eliminate religiously

offensive material from that work. Hume's reputation as a religious sceptic, and even an atheist, was instrumental in his failure, in 1745, to be appointed to the chair of moral philosophy at the University of Edinburgh. See *A Letter from a Gentleman to His Friend in Edinburgh* (Edinburgh, 1745; facsimile reprint, Edinburgh, 1967). On the controversy surrounding the publication of *The Natural History of Religion*, see Ernest Campbell Mossner, *The Life of David Hume* (Edinburgh, 1954), 319–35. Hume's views on religion are the subject of the essay by J. C. A. Gaskin in this volume.

27 For a discussion of these issues as they bear on Hume's political theory, see Knud Haakonssen, "The Structure of Hume's Political Theory," this volume.

28 Letter from Adam Smith, LL.D., to William Strahan, Esq. (DNR, 244–5).

29 A few weeks before his death Hume was able to satisfy Boswell that he sincerely believed it "a most unreasonable fancy" that there might be life after death (DNR, 76–7).

30 For an insightful discussion of this point, see Terence Penelhum, "Hume's Moral Psychology," Part I, this volume.

31 In the letter just cited, Smith went on to add: "And that gaiety of temper, so agreeable in society, but which is so often accompanied with frivolous and superficial qualities, was in him certainly attended with the most severe application, the most extensive learning, the greatest depth of thought, and a capacity in every respect the most comprehensive" (DNR, 247).

32 A recent and important exception is John B. Stewart, *Opinion and Reform in Hume's Political Philosophy* (Princeton, 1992); see esp. chaps. 5 and 6.

33 See "Hume, Human Nature, and the Foundations of Morality," Part III, this volume.

34 On the nature and import of Hume's scepticism, see the essay by Robert Fogelin in this volume and my "How a Sceptic May Live Scepticism," in *Faith, Scepticism and Rationality*.

2 Hume's new science of the mind

For Hume, understanding the workings of the mind is the key to understanding everything else. There is a sense, therefore, in which to write about Hume's philosophy of mind is to write about all of his philosophy. With that said, I shall nonetheless focus here on those specific doctrines that belong to what we today call the philosophy of mind, given our somewhat narrower conception of it. It should also be remembered that Hume describes his inquiry into the nature and workings of the mind as a *science*. This is an important clue to understanding both the goals and the results of that inquiry, as well as the methods Hume uses in pursuing it. As we will see, there is a thread running from Hume's project of founding a science of the mind to that of the so-called cognitive sciences of the late twentieth century. For both, the study of the mind is, in important respects, just like the study of any other natural phenomenon. While it would be an overstatement to say that Hume's entire interest lies in the construction of a science in this sense – he has other, more traditionally "philosophical" concerns, as well – a recognition of the centrality of this scientific conception of his subject is essential for understanding him.[1]

I. A NEW SCIENCE OF HUMAN NATURE

In one of the best-known passages in all of his writings, from the Introduction to *A Treatise of Human Nature*, Hume declares his aim

The work on which this chapter is based was begun during the tenure of a fellowship at the Institute for Advanced Studies in the Humanities at the University of Edinburgh. I am grateful to that institution, as well as to Martin Curd, William Morris, Wade Robison, and Corliss Swain for discussion, criticism, and advice.

of founding what he calls a new science of human nature. He argues that the development of such a science, based on "the experimental Method of Reasoning," must precede all other inquiry, since only it can serve to ground the rest of our knowledge:

> There is no question of importance, whose decision is not compriz'd in the science of man; and there is none, which can be decided with any certainty, before we become acquainted with that science. In pretending therefore to explain the principles of human nature, we in effect propose a compleat system of the sciences, built on a foundation almost entirely new, and the only one upon which they can stand with any security.   (T Intro, xvi)

For Hume, explaining the principles of human nature involves "examining the Mind . . . to discover its most secret Springs & Principles" (HL 1: 32). Although these principles may "lie very deep and abstruse," the new method, modelled after that used with such spectacular success by Newton in what might be called the new science of matter, holds out the hope of results no less far-reaching in this domain.[2] The method calls for "careful and exact experiments," in pursuing the aim of "render[ing] all our principles as universal as possible." This, in turn, requires "tracing up our experiments to the utmost, and explaining all effects from the simplest and fewest causes" (T Intro, xiv, xvii).

Hume's expectations for his project are at once great and modest. He sees his new science as the key to all others, indeed to all knowledge: "Human Nature is the only science of man." Yet his modest aim is only to bring it "a little more into fashion," as, in spite of its importance, it "has been hitherto the most neglected." Even more than the other sciences, it is still in its infancy: "Two thousand years with such long interruptions, and under such mighty discouragements are a small space of time to give any tolerable perfection to the sciences; and perhaps we are still in too early an age of the world to discover any principles, which will bear the examination of the latest posterity" (T 1.4.7, 273). Still, Hume's hope is that the new science may "discover, at least in some degree, the secret springs and principles, by which the human mind is actuated in its operations" (EHU 1, 14).

We should thus put the pursuit of this new science in the place of the "many chimerical systems" and "hypotheses embrac'd merely for being specious and agreeable," spawned by the "warm imagination" of philosophers. "Were these hypotheses once remov'd, we might hope to establish a system or set of opinions, which if not true (for that, perhaps, is too much to be hop'd for) might at least be satisfactory to the human mind, and might stand the test of the most critical examination" (T 1.4.7, 272–3). "The only solid foundation we can give to this science ... must be laid on experience and observation" (T Intro, xvi). This is, of course, true of all human knowledge; for Hume, there is no other source of knowledge besides experience, and no claim to knowledge based on anything else is legitimate. Where the application of the experimental method to "moral subjects" must differ from its more established use in "natural philosophy" is in the impossibility of making experiments "purposely, with premeditation." Here Hume is speaking of the controlled experiments typical of the laboratory sciences, as opposed to the kind of thought experiment, common in philosophy, that he himself often uses. In place of the former, however, we must "glean up our experiments in this science from a cautious observation of human life, and take them as they appear in the common course of the world, by men's behaviour in company, in affairs, and in their pleasures." In spite of this, the science of man need "not be inferior in certainty ... to any other of human comprehension" (T Intro, xix); indeed, it is in this science alone that we "can expect assurance and conviction" (T 1.4.7, 273).

Such assurance and conviction cannot extend to any claim concerning the ultimate reason for the principles governing human nature that our new method has revealed, that is, about *why* these are the way they are: "we can give no reason for our most general and most refined principles, beside our experience of their reality" (T Intro, xviii). Hume is adamant on this point. When he first introduces his famous principles of association – the three "universal principles" that "guide" the operations of the imagination in uniting our ideas – he claims that their reality requires no special proof beyond recognizing that their "effects are every where conspicuous." Yet he follows this claim immediately by reminding us that their causes "are mostly unknown, and must be resolv'd into *original* qualities of human nature, which I pretend not to explain" (T 1.1.4, 13). It would be a mistake, however, to complain about this "impossibility of explaining ultimate principles" in the science of man, as it is "a defect common to it with all the sciences, and all the arts, in which we can employ ourselves" (T Intro, xviii). Being sceptical about the possibility of answering certain questions posed by the metaphysician need not make one sceptical about the possibility of scientific knowledge.

Hume is, as we have seen, fully explicit about the nature and status of the project he wants to undertake. Yet his declarations have had remarkably little effect on the interpretation of that project by champions and critics alike, from his day to ours. It is only recently that some have begun to take him at his word and to see him as engaged in an inquiry at least continuous with what we think of as the scientific study of the mind. Philosophers of mind today often see themselves as being so engaged, as participating in an interdisciplinary inquiry they are happy to label "cognitive science." But it is an irony that would not escape Hume that they not infrequently explicitly contrast that inquiry with his science of man, rather than recognizing it as the latter's descendant.[3]

This is not to say, of course, that there are no differences between the two projects, separated as they are by two and a half centuries during which both science and philosophy have changed out of all recognition. The passages I have cited from Hume's announcement of his new science should alert us to some features of it that contrast sharply with those of its twentieth-century offspring. While Hume anticipated many of the difficulties and problems recently "discovered" by our contemporaries, he offers – or, at least, hints at – rather different solutions to them. As we will see, some of these solutions compare favourably with those prompted by later formulations of recognizably the same problems. One reason for this is that the method he so clearly outlines in the Introduction to the *Treatise* is more suited to the subject matter of the new science than is one modelled on that of the so-called hard sciences and favoured by many of his modern successors.

II. SCEPTIC OR SCIENTIST

For two centuries after its publication, Hume's philosophy was construed as essentially, perhaps entirely, negative.[4] His enquiries were seen as undertaken in a spirit of scepticism and as aiming to show how far that outlook can – and must – be carried if some seemingly compelling empiricist principles are followed out to their inevitable consequences. The barrage of arguments in the first book of the *Treatise*, apparently questioning the very possibility of knowing anything about the world and about ourselves, was seen as directed not against various philosophical doctrines on these subjects (as these arguments are construed, increasingly, today), but against the very possibility of such knowledge. That such scepticism is on the face of it incompatible with the project Hume announced in the Introduction to the work was either not noticed or dismissed as unproblematic by the simple expedient of not taking him at his word.[5]

There was, to be sure, some reason for such a response. Ever since Descartes, epistemological questions have occupied centre stage in philosophy, and epistemology has come to be seen as virtually consisting in coming to terms with, in one way or another, the kind of sceptical threat posed in the opening pages of Descartes's *Meditations*. It was natural for Hume's contemporaries to see him as struggling with the same problems that preoccupied them and as responding to his predecessors' treatment of them. His extensive and devastating criticisms of attempts to deal with the sceptical threat, either by an appeal to the power of reason to discover truths about the world or by relying on experience to convey those truths to us through perception, seemed then – and to many since – evidence that he shared their preoccupation with that threat. Yet Hume is quite explicit in disclaiming such an interest and tells us clearly, in a variety of contexts and ways, that the main aim of his enquiries is something very different. An example is his admonition in the opening paragraph of the section in the *Treatise* entitled "Of scepticism with regard to the senses" not to be concerned with the usual sceptical question about the existence of the external world: "We may well ask, *What causes induce us to believe in the existence of body?* but 'tis in vain to ask, *Whether there be body or not?* That is a point, which we must take for granted in all our reasonings." That such an injunction should appear in this very section, nominally concerned with scepticism, is surely not an accident and should clinch the case that whatever Hume is doing, he is neither pressing, nor looking for – and failing to find – an answer to the usual sceptical challenges. He tells us explicitly what he *is* doing: "The subject, then, of our present enquiry is concerning the *causes* which induce us to believe in the existence of body" (T 1.4.2, 187–8).

As noted earlier, Hume *is* sceptical about various philosophical attempts at justifying our beliefs, especially when it comes to the most basic of these, such as the belief in bodies, in the identity of our person, in causal connections, and the like, which even a sceptic cannot really reject or live without. He often insists that it is just as well that nature has made sure that, in spite of all philosophy, we take these for granted, as without them "human nature must immediately perish and go to ruin" (T 1.4.4, 225). But this recognition of our unreflective, instinctive, and unavoidable acceptance of certain basic beliefs must not be confused with claiming to have a justification of those beliefs. Philosophers' attempts at the latter are the targets of Hume's sceptical arguments, as are their pretensions to knowledge about the source of the principles a scientist of the mind can discover, and about the reasons why these principles are what they are.

In the crucial case of personal identity (to be discussed at greater length later in the chapter), Hume makes it equally clear that his interest lies in examining how one comes to form one's belief in one's identity and in what accounts for one's confidence in that belief, rather than in a philosophical justification of it. After dismissing the claim of philosophers that we are "every moment intimately conscious of what we call our SELF," he asks: "What then gives us so great a propension to ascribe an identity to these successive perceptions, and to suppose ourselves possest of an invariable and uninterrupted existence thro' the whole course of our lives?" (T 1.4.6, 251, 253). It should be clear that his powerful negative arguments are given not in the service of a purely sceptical conclusion, but as a necessary preliminary to refocusing our attention on giving an answer to these other questions in the spirit of descriptive – and explanatory – science.[6]

Thus, while there is a sense in which Hume can be said, as he so often is, to be a sceptic, his scepticism is better understood as one about pretended supra-scientific metaphysical knowledge, rather than about scientific knowledge itself. It is this kind of scepticism that separates him most sharply from other philosophers of his day, who conceived of philosophy as going beyond mere scientific knowledge to disclose a deeper and more certain knowledge of reality. An example of this more ambitious expectation is the common refusal of Leibniz and the Cartesians to admit that Newton had really *explained* anything. Hume, by contrast, thinks of explanation in a thoroughly scientific spirit. The "total alteration" and "revolution" he regards his new science as bringing to the intellectual scene consists in becoming what he calls an "anatomist" of human nature. As we saw earlier, Hume believes that the anatomist of human nature who proceeds in a systematic manner can discover the mind's "most secret Springs & Principles," even though these "must lie very deep and abstruse" (HL 1: 32; T Intro, xiv; see also A, 646). A *secret* principle need not be *occult*; it need not be inaccessible to the investigator using the right method. The true laws governing the mind can be discovered by science; in contrast, the claims of the metaphysician, based on his *a priori*, arm-chair, method are forever destined to remain mere speculation.

This shift of focus – from a vain attempt to give a philosophical justification of our fundamental beliefs to a scientific account of their origin in the operations of our minds – is what Hume, with a deliberate air of paradox, calls a "sceptical solution" to the sceptical challenge (EHU 5). The questions such a scientific account must answer are: How do we form our beliefs? How do we move from one belief to another? and What mechanisms and principles underlie and govern such processes? These are the questions for the new science of the mind, and these are the questions to which Hume constantly recurs as soon as he has discredited the arguments of those who think that they can answer the very different question of what entitles us (by some non-immanent, external standard) to hold the beliefs we in fact, and inevitably, do hold.

III. AN ANATOMY OF THE MIND

Hume's general answer to questions about how we come to have the various beliefs we have is that they are the product of a non-rational faculty. He labels this faculty variously as the "imagination," as an "instinct," or by what sometimes seems to be the name of its product, "habit" or "custom." The faculty in question is defined by a certain "propensity" to form ideas and beliefs. Some subtle differences behind this varying terminology notwithstanding, this faculty is contrasted with reason, the faculty whose standards and operations some philosophers think can serve to provide an answer to the sceptic's challenge.[7]

The raw materials on which this faculty works, and from which all mental life is constructed, are impressions and their "faint copies," ideas, both species of the genus, perception: "All the perceptions of the human mind resolve themselves into two distinct kinds, which I shall call IMPRESSIONS and IDEAS" (T 1.1.1, 1). Many of the most sceptical-sounding passages of the *Treatise* and the *Enquiry concerning Human Understanding* are devoted to showing that our stock of these materials is more limited than philosophers have supposed. Hume shows us again and again that the impressions from which some putative idea posited by the metaphysician would have to derive are just not to be found in experience.[8] But he does not deny the obvious, and remarkable, fact that from the rather limited stock of impressions that come my way, I am able to construct an edifice of beliefs that goes far beyond those impressions and the ideas traceable to them.

First, my complex ideas are not confined to the complex impressions I have actually had: I can combine simple impressions in novel ways, into new complex ideas. (These, often called by Hume "fictions," may give rise to belief, that is, be taken to represent real things, but often they do not, as with fictional ideas in the usual sense.) Second, the course of my experience, the various regularities among the perceptions that make it up, is exploited by the mind in forming the beliefs it does. In both these ways, the mind must be conceived as essentially active. It is what the mind does with what it gets that matters, and it is this that Hume's science is an attempt to describe.

According to that science, the mind is led from one idea to another by three "principles of association": resemblance, contiguity, and cause and effect. These principles involve the mind's "taking notice" of certain properties of, and regularities among, its perceptions. Such taking notice need not be, and typically is not, conscious. What matters is that these properties and regularities be detected by the mind in a way that makes a difference to its subsequent operations and contents. Were it not for this active contribution on the mind's part, the mere presence of such properties and regularities would not be sufficient to explain the combinations and transitions that actually occur among our ideas, nor the genesis of the beliefs we actually form.

The remarkable regularities in the transitions we make from idea to idea and from (some) ideas to beliefs are the result of certain characteristics of the imagination, the ever-active (and sometimes overactive) non-rational faculty, the story of whose workings in large part constitutes Hume's scientific account of human nature. "Custom" or "habit" are Hume's usual short labels for these characteristics, among them a certain inertia, a fundamental property of the imagination that plays a role in Hume's explanations of some of the most basic, often not even noticed, but remarkable, facts about the mind. These include the fact that in the absence of impressions from which the corresponding ideas could have been copied, we nonetheless come to believe that there are bodies and that we are the same person at one time as at another, even that we can "extend our identity beyond our memory" (T 1.4.6, 262).

In the pivotal section "Of scepticism with regard to the senses," where he undertakes his enquiry "concerning the *causes* which induce us to believe in the existence of body," the legitimately scientific enquiry he distinguishes from the vain attempt to answer the sceptic, Hume reminds us of his earlier explanation of our belief in the infinite divisibility of space and time through our natural tendency to extrapolate beyond what is given in experience: "I have already observ'd, in examining the foundation of mathematics, that the imagination, when set into any train of thinking, is apt to continue, even when its object fails it, and like a galley put in motion by the oars, carries on its course without any new impulse" (T 1.4.2, 187–8, 198). This tendency, automatic and non-reflective, is also ubiquitous: nothing, says Hume, is "more usual, than for the mind to proceed after this manner with any action, even after the reason has ceas'd, which first determin'd it to begin." In the sections on space and time, this tendency explained how we generate an "imaginary standard of equality," notions of "perfection beyond what [our] faculties can judge of," and of "correction[s] beyond what we have instruments and art to make." This, in turn, enabled Hume to account for the "fictions," "useless as well as incomprehensible," of the mathematicians who claim to give exact definitions and demonstrations (T 1.2.4, 48, 51).

Hume's purpose in that earlier discussion was to expose these fictions as "absurd" (T 1.2.4, 51–2). His recommendation there was to resist the mind's tendency and thus avoid the absurdity.[9] In the discussion of our belief in body, the same tendency to extrapolate is invoked in the interest of quite a different goal: that of explaining how naturally, even unavoidably, we form our "opinion of the continu'd existence of body." He writes: "Objects have a certain coherence even as they appear to our senses; but this coherence is much greater and more uniform, if we suppose the objects to have a continu'd existence; and as the mind is once in the train of observing an uniformity among objects, it naturally continues, till it renders the uniformity as compleat as possible" (T 1.4.2, 198).

Hume distinguishes between "principles which are permanent, irresistable, and universal" and those "which are changeable, weak, and irregular" (T 1.4.4, 225). This distinction is, of course, essential to the double use by Hume of the natural extrapolating tendency of the mind. When the tendency is guided by principles of the first sort, as it is in the formation of our fundamental common-sense beliefs, a recognition of this is what constitutes a "sceptical solution" to the sceptic's doubts, whether that doubt be about the external world or about personal identity. While Hume sometimes uses the term *fiction* to label a fundamental natural belief produced by this property of the mind, we must be careful not to be misled into thinking of such a belief as somehow fanciful and arbitrary. Fictions of this sort are not optional: they are forced on us by our nature. Distinguishing such fictions from those resulting from philosophical speculation floating free of common sense is a large, indeed, arguably the central, part of the overall aim of Hume's philosophy.

In cases of what we may call the natural fictions, the mind's extrapolating tendency operates "in such an insensible manner as never to be taken notice of," and the "imagination can draw inferences from past experience, without reflecting on it; much more without forming any principle concerning it, or reasoning upon that principle." Hume adds that this tendency "may even in some measure be unknown to us." It is important to see that by this he means only that we have no introspective access to the processes in question. In making causal inferences, for example, we obviously do not consciously recall the previous instances of constant conjunctions upon which the inference is based: "The custom operates before we have time for reflexion."[10] "I never am conscious of any such operation" and in deciding to "give the preference to one set of arguments above another, I do nothing but decide from my *feeling* concerning the superiority of their influence" (emphasis added). Thus it is that "all probable reasoning is nothing but a species of sensation" (T 1.3.8, 101–4).

This distinction between reason (a reflective faculty for making inferences on the basis of evidence) and the imagination (a non-reflective faculty that naturally moves from experience to belief) is fundamental to Hume's anatomy of the mind. To quote again from his discussion of our belief in external objects: "our reason neither does, nor is it possible it ever shou'd, upon any supposition, give us an assurance of the continu'd and distinct existence of body. That opinion must be entirely owing to the IMAGINATION: which must now be the subject of our enquiry" (T 1.4.2, 193). Nor is this particular kind of belief unique in this respect: quite generally, "*belief is more properly an act of the sensitive, than of the cogitative part of our natures*" (T 1.4.1, 183). When it comes to our most general and most fundamental beliefs (such as those in the existence of an external world, in our own identity, in causal relations), these are, therefore, quite impervious to the influence of reason, which can neither ground nor destroy them. "Cogitative part" here means our faculty of theoretical reasoning, at work when we construct demonstrations and philosophical arguments. There is, however, another sense of 'reasoning,' applicable to some of the natural and instinctive transitions we make from one perception to another, from perception to belief, and thus from one belief to another.[11] We are engaged, for example, in reasoning when we make a causal inference; indeed, that is what we primarily mean by 'reasoning' in ordinary, non-theoretical, contexts: "this inference is not only a true species of reasoning, but the strongest of all others" (T 1.3.7, 97n). Hume calls this kind of reasoning "experimental reasoning" and insists that we share it with infants, "nay even brute beasts" – who presumably do not "cogitate." It is this latter kind of reasoning "on which the whole conduct of life depends, [and it] is nothing but a species of instinct or mechanical power, that acts in us unknown to ourselves; and in its chief operations, is not directed by any such relations or comparisons of ideas, as are the proper objects of our intellectual faculties" (EHU 4.2, 39; 9, 108).

The great importance of causal reasoning is that it is the only kind by which we "can go beyond what is immediately present to the senses" or which "can be trac'd beyond our senses, and informs us of

existences and objects, which we do not see or feel" (T 1.2.3, 73–4).
The causal inferences that thus take us beyond our present impressions are, for Hume, indeed a form of reasoning, even though they
are, as we have seen, automatic and non-reflective. This sort of
reasoning is "stronger" than that which involves "the separating or
uniting of different ideas by the interposition of others, which show
the relation they bear to each other" (T 1.3.7, 96n). The latter, while
constituting demonstrations, as the former do not, do so only with
respect to "*philosophical* relations" – relations resulting from the
arbitrary comparison of ideas. We can, for example, ask of any two
objects, what is the distance or, more generally, the difference, between them. But if they are far, or wholly different, from each other,
the natural thing to say is that they are *not* related. Such "relations"
are contrasted by Hume with relations in the more usual sense,
which he calls "natural" (T 1.1.5, 13–14).

It is appeals to reasoning of the demonstrative sort to establish
facts about the world that Hume's sceptical arguments show to be
futile. Causal reasoning, by contrast, has the power to yield belief.[12]
The difference between merely having an idea and having a belief is
easy to know but difficult to explain. When Hume reflects in the
Appendix on his earlier attempt to distinguish them solely in terms
of their respective degrees of force and vivacity, he realizes that
"there are other differences among ideas, which cannot properly be
comprehended under these terms. Had I said, that two ideas of the
same object can only be different by their different *feeling*, I shou'd
have been nearer the truth" (T App, 636). Yet, as we have just seen,
the special feeling that marks out belief – "that certain *je-ne-scai-
quoi*, of which 'tis impossible to give any definition or description,
but which every one sufficiently understands" (T 1.3.9, 106) – is not
altogether involuntary and beyond rational control. The "great difference," Hume says, between "a poetical enthusiasm, and a serious
conviction . . . proceeds in some measure from reflexion and *general
rules*. . . . A like reflexion on *general rules* keeps us from augment-
ing our belief upon every encrease of the force and vivacity of our
ideas. . . . 'Tis thus the understanding corrects the appearances of
the senses" (T App, 631–2).

So Hume's recommendation is to replace endless and fruitless
"cogitating," in an attempt to give a philosophical justification of
our beliefs, with an attempt to find a scientific explanation of their

origin. Doing so is, as noted earlier, what the "sceptical solution" of the sceptical challenge consists in (EHU 5). It is to give up being a "metaphysician" and to become a scientist – an "anatomist" – of the mind, of human nature. This recommendation bears a striking resemblance to the so-called naturalizing programs common in recent philosophy of mind and epistemology. Here, too, the leading idea is to abandon an *a priori* method perceived as bankrupt in favour of an empirical one that holds out the promise of genuine progress. Many epistemologists have, in recent years, come to feel that the time-honoured philosopher's pastime of arm-chair conceptual analysis is unlikely to tell us much about the real nature of human knowledge.[13] Philosophers of mind, too, interested in understanding reasoning, perception, memory, language, and a host of other mental phenomena, increasingly look to the new discipline (or constellation of disciplines) called "cognitive science," rather than to traditional methods of philosophical analysis and argument.[14]

One of the most striking features of our cognitive capacities and performance, whether in perception, in linguistic processing, or in reasoning generally, is that the states, mechanisms, and operations our best theories of them posit must be thought of as *sub-doxastic*, *modular*, and *automatic*. First, since their subject – the entity to which they are attributed – is not the cognizer himself, but some component sub-system we regard as the locus or "agent" of the operation or process postulated to explain the cognitive function in question, we have to think of the states and processes involved as obtaining or taking place below the threshold of the cognizer's consciousness and, hence, as somehow "below" the level of belief. As a result, the subject is not necessarily a reliable source of information about them. Hence the preference in these studies for a third-person approach, rather than a first-person one, for laboratory experiments instead of arm-chair introspection. (Compare Hume's advocacy, noted earlier, of "careful and exact experiments," "judiciously collected and compared," requiring "a cautious observation of human life.") Second, the operations and processes involved are, in the overwhelming majority of cases, found to be task-specific, doing their work largely in isolation from each other and from the cognitive states we would attribute to the person taken as a whole. Thus the processes underlying one particular kind of cognitive capacity or performance often do not interact with those associated with others, and their respective outputs are similarly independent. (Think of the common case of the different senses delivering different verdicts on the properties of one and the same object or event, as with the half-immersed stick, seen to be bent yet felt to be straight.) The processes are also insensitive to the cognizer's beliefs – even if these are reflective and conscious, rather than merely tacit, and even if he makes an effort to bring them to bear on their workings. (Think of the robustness of perceptual illusions known to be such, as with parallel lines seeming to converge as they recede from the eye.)

I have already discussed Hume's recognition of our tendency to over-generalize. The same sort of inductive over-generalization, sometimes benign, sometimes not, has been found to be ubiquitous in recent empirical studies of our cognitive processes. We see it in language learning, and in various kinds of processing – phonological, morphological, even syntactic – as with so-called garden-path sentences, where we leap ahead to complete a sentence in the wrong way, as well as in prosody. We see it in perception, for example, in the detection of the edges and boundaries of objects and in the perception of the movement of rigid bodies. We see it in problem solving and reasoning generally, as in our lamentable tendency to make clearly fallacious probabilistic inferences. What all these instances of the tendency have in common is that the meanings we assign, the beliefs we form, and the inferences we draw, while often far outrunning the evidence available to us and, in many cases, recognized as doing so, are, nonetheless, all but irresistible. Hence the common characterization of many of the processes posited to explain our cognitive capacities and performance as "cognitively impenetrable" or "informationally encapsulated."[15]

This recognition, common to Hume and to modern cognitive scientists, of these features of our cognitive make-up raises some deep methodological issues. What these are, and how Hume's distinctive response to them differs from those of the latter, will help us see the full complexity of his approach to the task he has set himself, as well as the source of some of the tensions that are sometimes detected in it. But before turning to these matters, we must look in some detail at the topic on which discussion of Hume's philosophy of mind has traditionally centred, that of personal identity. Here, too, the conti-

nuity with some central concerns of modern cognitive science will
be striking.

IV. PERSONAL IDENTITY

The most general philosophical question about the mind had always
been an ontological one: What is it? But Hume's eschewal of speculative metaphysics leads him to substitute for this question two others to which there are clear answers: what kind of thing is my belief
about when I believe that I am a *self*, something that can be re-
identified as the same thing at different times; and, what is the
source of my belief that I am such a thing? It is important to see that
these questions are being asked from the first-person point of view,
thus rendering irrelevant the easy answer that to believe in one's
identity is to believe that one is, or is at least associated with, an
enduring body. Re-identification of a body depends only on general
criteria of identity applicable to physical objects. While Hume is
interested in those criteria, and indeed appeals to considerations
involving them in attempting to clarify the concept of identity in
general, when he comes to the topic of *personal* identity and tries to
explain "the identity, which we ascribe to the mind of man," he
knows that he cannot simply rely on those criteria, since they involve activities (remembering and associating, for example), and
hence the identity, of a mind, the very thing whose identity is at this
point in question (T 1.4.2, 200–204; 1.4.6, 253–9). For talk of a mind
doing something to make sense, there must be a temporally extended item of some sort denoted by the term *mind* (and by the
pronoun *I*), one to which the predicate "same at time$_2$ as at time$_1$"
can be applied.[16] Given this, before an account of my belief in the
identity of material objects in terms of various mental activities
attributed to me can be intelligible to me, I must believe that I *am* a
self: I must believe that I am a subject to whom such activities,
taking place over time, as activities must, can be attributed. Thus, as
Hume recognizes, the first belief standing in need of an analysis and
a genetic account is the belief one has in one's own identity.[17] He
therefore gives an account of what one believes when one has that
belief and of how one could come by a belief of that sort. That in his
analysis he must make use of the more general concepts which

themselves presuppose having such a belief can obscure this all-important point, as can, on occasion, Hume's language. But when he asks whether "in pronouncing concerning the identity of a person, we observe some real bond among his perceptions" (T 1.4.6, 259), he must be taken to be talking about a person pronouncing on his own identity on the basis of observing his own perceptions. There *is* no observing another's perceptions, as there is another's body. So, for an answer to the question that must be most basic – How do I come to think of myself as a self? – I must turn inward, I must look to see what there is in my experience to lead me to think of myself as the same person or mind over time. *That* I do so is a datum, one Hume is seeking to explain within the new scientific framework he has adopted.[18]

Thus Hume should be seen as having a theory about a certain fundamental belief that underlies and is presupposed by all other beliefs. The theory has two parts: an explication of what I think when I think of myself as a self (or a mind, a person); and an explanation of how I can come to think that I am such a thing on the basis of my experience. The answer philosophers, especially those in the Cartesian tradition, commonly give to the first question is that to think that one is a self is to think that one is a simple substance, one that endures essentially unchanged in spite of many accidental changes, in particular, changes in what perceptions one has. On this view, I am the owner of the many experiences I undergo, but I am distinct from those experiences, and what I am, in the metaphysically relevant sense, is independent of what they are.

But why should we believe such philosophers? Hume's negative arguments are intended to show that there is no good reason to do so. No demonstrative argument can prove the existence of such an entity (any more than of any other), and no evidence can be found in experience, the only source of non-demonstrative evidence for anything.[19]

Had Hume stopped here, we could say with some justice that his position was a sceptical one, though it would still be worth noting that his would have been a scepticism only about the particular philosophical doctrines he was examining. From his arguments against that doctrine, however, nothing follows concerning the prospects for constructing some other theory about the content and source of one's belief in one's identity. And, indeed, Hume does not stop with negative arguments against the substantial view of the self. He goes on to give an alternative account of how the belief in personal identity can be based on experience.

On Hume's alternative analysis – his famous "bundle" theory – a mind (self, person) is a collection of perceptions related to each other in certain ways so as to constitute a complex entity to which identity of one sort, though not of another, may be intelligibly and truly ascribed. The sort of identity that is appropriate to such an entity is what Hume calls "imperfect identity," thus distinguishing it from "perfect," (or "strict") identity, a property only simple and unchanging entities possess (T 1.4.6). Having argued that nothing in one's experience answers to a belief that one is such a simple and unchanging entity – "when I enter most intimately into what I call *myself*, I always stumble on some particular perception or other" (T 1.4.6, 252) – Hume goes on to show that the same experience can nevertheless serve to explain how one comes to believe in one's identity over time. This is a belief each of us has, and it is central to the commonsense picture of the world that we all accept when uncorrupted by bad philosophy. It is a belief implicated in all our other beliefs, a belief without which arguably even the sceptic's position could not be understood.

What, above all, unites the perceptions that collectively constitute a mind or self is *memory*, and the *natural relation of causation* with which memory is inextricably bound up. Memory is in one way the more fundamental here, since without it the natural relation would not arise: "Had we no memory, we never shou'd have any notion of causation, nor consequently of that chain of causes and effects, which constitute our self or person" (T 1.4.6, 261–2). One reason for this priority of memory is that Hume's account of causation requires that I remember the constant conjunctions between a pair of events if experience of such a conjunction is to lead me to think of them *as cause and effect* – that is, leads me to expect the second to always (where this means, necessarily) follow on the first. The mere occurrence of such a constant conjunction in my experience would not suffice. Suppose that my experience did include such repeated conjunctions of two events, A and B, but that it did not also include perceptions that are rememberings of previous co-occurrences of the pair. This *might* be sufficient for giving rise, upon a fresh experience of A, to an expectation of B. (There are reasons to doubt this: What would be the mechanism? What, in the absence of memory, would distinguish the umpteenth experience of A from the first?) Still, even that expectation would not be enough to give rise to the idea of necessary connection, whose genesis Hume is trying to explain. I may still lack the *felt* "determination of the mind," which, in that explanation, serves in lieu of an impression of necessary connection and gives rise to the idea of such a connection. Thus my expectation of B, while caused by its constant conjunction with A, would, in the absence of a memory of that constant conjunction, fail to be an expectation of an *effect*.

It is, then, the presence of memories among my perceptions that is the ultimate source of the idea that I am a temporally extended being. These memories need not be veridical: what matters is that they are what philosophers since Franz Brentano have meant by *intentional*, in the sense of referring to, being about, other things – here other perceptions – experienced at an earlier time. In the full story, forward-looking perceptions – anticipations – also play a role, as does the inertial tendency we have already seen at work elsewhere. "But having once acquir'd this notion of causation from the memory, we can extend the same chain of causes, and consequently the identity of our persons beyond our memory, and can comprehend times, and circumstances, and actions, which we have entirely forgot, but suppose in general to have existed" (T 1.4.6, 262).[20]

One of the chief insights emerging from this discussion of personal identity, with implications that go far beyond that topic, is that an entity of the sort Hume takes the mind to be (complex, dynamic, ever-changing) can be thought of as an active agent in the formation of our beliefs about everything (including even, as we have seen, the formation of the belief in its own identity). A generalization of this insight underlies virtually all of Hume's analyses of the concepts we employ in thinking about the world and our relation to it. Most important, it drives all Hume's hypotheses about how we come to believe what we believe, whatever the content and object of our belief. From the earliest parts of the *Treatise*, with its picture of complex ideas being generated from simple ones, through the account of the nature of belief (as well as of belief formation, of belief transition by way of the principles of association, of causal beliefs as expectations produced by experience and habit), to the practical philosophy (where almost every interesting principle of moral psychology, and of ethics, politics, and aesthetics involves it), the constant activity of this mind is what dominates the story and ties it together into a unified and coherent whole.

V. HUME'S SELF AND SOME RECENT THEORIES OF THE MIND

With this sketch of Hume's theory of the self in place, we are in a position to explore some parallels between Hume's concerns and some of those that have loomed large in recent theories of the mind. This exercise will illustrate the continuing relevance of the former, as well as help us to guard against some common misunderstandings of it. While the morals I shall draw apply to all aspects of these theories, I have singled out the topic of personal identity as my chief illustration, for three reasons. First, this is the topic that has received, historically, and continues to receive, today, by far the most attention from those interested in Hume's philosophy of mind. Second, while this emphasis on the so-called problem of personal identity has, I believe, stood in the way of achieving a satisfactory overall interpretation of Hume's theory of the mind, it is, nonetheless, true that any theory on the subject must offer, or presuppose, an answer to it. For Hume, given his particular account of the workings of the mind, and his self-imposed empiricist constraints, finding a satisfactory answer is especially pressing. Third, appreciating the nature of the answer Hume offers is a good way of understanding the rest of his account, particularly those aspects of it that centre on the ubiquitous activity of the mind, the aspects I have been highlighting as fundamental.

A much favoured strategy in recent philosophy of mind has been to look for decompositions, along functional lines, of the various kinds of behaviour we think of as distinctive of creatures with minds. When we try to understand a piece of behaviour we regard as intelligent (not in the honorific and comparative sense, but in the deeper and more general one of involving mental, as opposed to merely physical, processes), we are urged to seek to identify simpler – and, importantly, *dumber* – processes, which, in combination, would explain, perhaps literally constitute, the behaviour in question. The way we decide what simpler processes to postulate is to ask what the function of the bit of behaviour in question is in the overall mental economy of the creature we are studying – for example, what role a particular belief we are inclined to attribute to it plays, in combination with other beliefs and desires we can attribute to it, in making it act the way it does. As with mental states such as beliefs and desires, so with mental processes and operations: we hypothesize that our creature goes through various transitions from mental states to other mental states by way of specifiable steps falling into specifiable patterns. Within this framework, it is the business of normal empirical science – of the burgeoning field of "cognitive science," which includes cognitive psychology, linguistics, neuro-physiology, and more – to generate the best hypotheses about what states and processes would best explain the creature's observable behaviour.

I said that the simple steps and processes we seek to identify as underlying, indeed, in some sense constituting, complex intelligent behaviour are supposed to be themselves "dumb," merely mechanical. This requirement springs from a metaphysical concern: it is felt that only thus will intelligent behaviour, and thus the mind, be explainable in respectably physicalistic terms, that is, as subject to the same laws as the rest of the natural world. In our day, this physicalistic assumption is not considered to be in need of defence: the alternative of accepting, with Descartes, a radical division of nature into separate material and mental realms, and the concomitant bifurcation of our knowledge, is deemed a non-starter, incompatible with the scientific outlook.

Whether one shares this physicalistic assumption or not – and one may well feel that it poses a false dilemma – one can see its pull and the considerations that make it seem inevitable. A more interesting question in the present context is, What was Hume's attitude to the ontological question? Was he, ultimately. a materialist, as some have suggested?[21] Or does his declared distaste for metaphysical speculation make the very question misplaced? Whatever the answer, what we can, and must, note is that a functional approach to the mind is separable from an attempt to reduce it to the physical, and that the former can prove scientifically and philosophically fruitful even if the latter, metaphysical, ambition is eschewed or frustrated.

This so-called top-down picture, of seeing intelligent behaviour as the tip of an iceberg of unintelligent, mechanical, processes subserving it, has indeed proven to be most fruitful in the cognitive sciences, though it is certainly not unchallenged.[22] As Daniel Dennett, one of the pioneers of this approach has emphasized, however, it can be illuminating only if we can avoid positing an intelligent subpersonal agent – a "homunculus" – as the subject of the processes and activities alleged to underlie and constitute the personal-level behaviour that we are trying to explain. Otherwise, it is thought, we are engaged in a futile enterprise: to explain the intelligence of people by positing intelligent homunculi is to embark on a hopeless and philosophically pointless regress. Functional decomposition can be illuminating and useful even when couched in thoroughly mentalistic language, as it often is in empirical science. But there must come a point at which such *pro tem* mentalism must be redeemed in the physicalistic coin of the realm, or else no philosophical progress will have been made.

As we have just observed, this obligation is to some extent the result of a metaphysical assumption we – and Hume – may not want to make. Nonetheless, we can ask how various theories, Hume's included, fare in meeting the physicalist's demand, assuming it to be legitimate and pressing.

It has been a commonplace since Brentano to think of the mental as essentially *intentional* (in the sense explained in the previous section) or, what is much the same thing, *representational*. Simply put, this just means that mental states are *about* things (not necessarily physical things) other than themselves.[23] Now when in our top-down, decompositionalist, strategy we posit processes that involve mental states of a creature that are said to represent things (most likely, things in the creature's environment, either as it is, or as it seems – perhaps mistakenly – to be to the creature), we must remember that in doing so we incur a philosophical debt. If our explanation of the intelligent behaviour is not to be on a par with "explaining" the action of a sedative by an appeal to its *virtus dormitiva* (its sedating power), that debt must be redeemed in a physicalistically acceptable way. Since a representation represents only to or for someone, each state that is said to represent – each intentional state, that is – must be thought of as having an interpreter. If we make that interpreter the creature as a whole, we are not explaining what *that* is in the way the decompositional strategy is meant to do. The alternative seems to be to posit a sub-personal interpreter, a homunculus, as the subject of the representation. Unless, however, we are ultimately able to get rid of such a homunculus by explaining how its functions, including the interpretive one, can be carried out by dumb physical components of the system, we are left with an "exempt agent" whose intelligence is unexplained. But then we will not have repaid the "loan" we took out in our decomposition of the original intelligent behaviour, and from a philosophical point of view (though not, perhaps, from a scientific one), we may as well not have started. Dennett explicitly dubs this conundrum "Hume's problem," and others have also seen Hume's theory as incapable of dealing with it. According to Dennett, "Hume wisely shunned the notion of an inner self that would intelligently manipulate the ideas and impressions." This left him only one alternative, if he wished to avoid a mysterious duplication of personal-level properties. He was left, Dennett suggests, "with the necessity of getting the ideas to 'think for themselves.' " Even though "this associationistic coupling of ideas and impressions, [the] pseudo-chemical bonding of each idea to its predecessor and successor, is a notorious non-solution to the problem," Dennett thinks that Hume had no alternative but to take it seriously.[24]

But is Hume really forced into the position Dennett attributes to him? Only if the alternatives of a homunculus-self, of just the sort he claims is not to be found in experience, or no self at all – the sceptical position – are exhaustive. To think that these are the only choices is, however, a mistake, a surprising one in the light of the fact that Hume's bundle theory may be plausibly seen as designed precisely to find a middle way between these two equally unacceptable extremes.

Hume's purpose is not to deny that there is a self. Nor is it to deny that the self is the thing that thinks – has beliefs, desires, and other cognitive states and dispositions. However, telling us what such a self is does require him to spend considerable time telling us what it is not. Thus he can easily appear to be saying that it is not anything. But this impression is mistaken, as is the one behind Dennett's suggestion that Hume's "solution" is to make perceptions themselves the possessors of purposive or intentional properties. On the contrary, Hume's real argument is that only a self constituted in the way he describes can be intelligibly said to do the things people (and, perhaps, other intelligent creatures) are said to do. Only such a self can be made the subject of the predications – in particular, of the intentional ones – peculiarly appropriate to intelligent creatures, and to persons in particular.

Part of what complicates matters is that Hume does indeed make perceptions, as opposed to bundles of them, the subjects of certain intentional verbs: perceptions are said to do things such as "producing" and "attracting" each other. (Such verbs are intentional in the sense that, taken literally, they presuppose intelligence and, hence, the possession of representational states, states with content. While we do say that clouds produce rain and magnets attract nails, such uses of these verbs are clearly not intentional in the sense an account of intelligence requires.) That Hume frequently talks this way can encourage us to ascribe to him the so-called Newtonian picture, so-called because of its obvious reliance, to describe the bonds among perceptions, on metaphors drawn from Newton's picture of gravitational attraction among bodies.[25] If these metaphors are taken seriously, it does seem that these sub-personal components of a person are the real, and ultimately, the only, subjects of intentional attributions, with personal-level attributions being derived from them. But then we have to be able to make sense of perceptions doing other, much more puzzling-sounding, things, such as understanding each other and themselves. As Dennett points out, this parallels exactly the modern cognitivist's problem of either making sense of representation without an exempt agent or ending up with an uninformative theory.

What is the evidence that Hume is more successful than some modern cognitivists in avoiding this trap? Briefly, it is that he almost never makes anything other than a person the subject of a seriously intentional – as opposed to what we may call a quasi-intentional – predication. While he talks of perceptions "attracting," "producing," "destroying," and "influencing" each other, he never talks of them as thinking, understanding, willing, or desiring. Expressions of the former sort should be taken for the metaphors they are, as indeed they must be in descriptions of the physical world itself. One may even suggest that, if anything, these descriptions themselves must get their content from their analogues at the personal level: our understanding of what is meant when a body is said to attract or influence another is based ultimately on our understanding of what it is for people to do these things.[26]

There may, indeed, be a mystery about how a mind constituted of perceptions, in the way that Hume's account has it, can do the things we say it does in our ordinary, non-philosophical, discourse. But there is no analogous mystery about how the *perceptions* that constitute a mind can do these same things, for the simple reason that they are not said by Hume to do them in the first place, and, *contra* Dennett, nothing in Hume's theory commits him to say that they do. That theory is addressed to the first – real – mystery, and it is about as promising a solution to it as any in the history of philosophy.

VI. SCIENTIST OR PHILOSOPHER?

As I remarked earlier, the kind of picture both Hume and modern cognitive science present of the cognitive agent has as one of its more surprising consequences that such an agent is not always the best source of information and insight about his own cognitive life. If we want to find out about the nature of someone's cognitive (perceptual, linguistic, deliberative) processes, asking him is sometimes not only not very helpful but can be positively misleading. One of the most robust general findings in recent cognitive science has been that we can often get more interesting, more detailed, and more reliable information from experiments and tests that measure response times, error patterns, comprehension, and the like.

The modern cognitive scientist can accept this lesson with equanimity, even with relish. But can Hume, in spite of his scientific ambitions? I have suggested that his own general picture of the science of the mind, and even his specific insights about how the mind works, anticipate some of these results. And he certainly emphasizes the need for experiments, although, as we have noted, he has something in mind rather different from the kind of laboratory experiment on which modern science thrives. But, of course, Hume still has a deep commitment, inherited from the "way of ideas" tradition of both the Cartesians and his empiricist predecessors, to introspection as a way of finding epistemological bedrock. So, for him, the need to find the right balance between the subjective, phenomenological, approach so central to that tradition, and the objective, third-person, experimental methods needed in scientific theory, is more pressing than for anyone before or since.

Nor could Hume's commitment to the introspective method be

eliminated on the grounds that it is merely the result of his inability to free himself of a pervasive pattern of thought, one that contributes nothing to the substance of his account. Hume's aims are, as we saw earlier, ambitious, and require him to look for a certain kind of grounding of the very concepts a non-philosophical scientist can take for granted. *He* cannot be a naive realist about external objects, causation, or the self in the way a working scientist can, indeed must, be. His account of our mental lives must include explanations, in some sense philosophically legitimizing, of beliefs that are, from a purely scientific point of view, unproblematic. It is not that cognitive science has nothing to say about such fundamental concepts and about their role in our mental life. It is, rather, that they are used, uncritically, in the very theories that purport to explain, for example, their acquisition. They are not seen as themselves standing in need of a certain legitimation, as they are for Hume.

We have seen that the so-called naturalization programs in recent epistemology and philosophy of mind bear a striking resemblance to Hume's project in at least some respects. The most important of these involves a somewhat similar shift from the justification of beliefs in the traditional sense to an explanation of their provenance through an examination of our cognitive endowments. The shift also includes, as it did for Hume, a scepticism about the usefulness, indeed, the coherence, of the traditional notion of justification and, as a result, a re-assessment of the value of traditional epistemological projects.

Yet the similarity should not be over-emphasized. There are significant differences, as well – in particular, as just noted, Hume's continued adherence to the time-honoured introspective method. Equally, and perhaps ultimately, more important is Hume's refusal to abandon those elements of the traditional framework that derive from common sense and our everyday practices, rather than from the rarefied and esoteric activities of philosophers *or* scientists. That is why, to return once again to the clear and explicit explanation of his method set out at the very start of his project, the experiments in his science must consist of a *"cautious* observation of human life" and must be taken "as they appear *in the common course of the world"* (my emphases).

Hume therefore has a much more complex task than the modern cognitive scientist, or even the modern naturalizing philosopher. He must try to fit together into a coherent whole a number of elements that do not easily go together: innocent scientific theorizing; self-conscious and self-reflective, even self-referring, philosophical analysis; and an ultimate allegiance to common sense as the touchstone for both. Hume does not, one must say, fully succeed in weaving together the different strands in his thought that are responsive to these different demands. It is no wonder that the debates that have dogged the interpretation of his work since his own day, debates about whether he is a philosopher or "just" a psychologist, a naturalist or a sceptic, continue unabated.

Take, for example, the thesis that our natural beliefs are irresistible. We have seen that a recognition of, indeed, insistence on, this is a cornerstone of Hume's account of the mind. Yet even if no amount of philosophical reflection can halt the operations that produce these beliefs or can influence their outcome, such reflection can still lead us to question the epistemological status of our natural beliefs. When unchecked by common sense, this reflection can lead to the "deepest darkness" of total scepticism. Fortunately, when common sense reasserts itself, as it inevitably does, the sceptic's speculations are seen as "cold, and strain'd, and ridiculous" (T 1.4.6, 269). Yet they, too, are in a sense natural and, at least for some minds, irresistible, and perhaps the ultimate and deepest challenge for a philosopher is to find a way of living with these irreconcilable demands of his own nature.

The tensions in Hume's method reveal something else about him that is not frequently recognized. More than any other thinker of the modern period, he feels the pressure to find an accommodation between the scientific spirit of his era and the perennial ambitions of philosophy. This explains the complexity of his thought, as well as the puzzles and perplexities that have plagued interpretations of it. An appreciation of what leads to this complexity should teach us something about our own intellectual situation and, in particular, about methodological problems we face no less than he did. And reading Hume in this light can be more help than many realize in grappling with these problems on our own behalf.

NOTES

1 For a discussion of how this aspect of Hume's philosophy relates to other, non-scientific, concerns of his, see my "Memory, Mind,

and Society." Paper presented at *the São Paulo Hume Conference*, 1987.

2 There is considerable controversy about the extent and nature of Newton's influence on Hume. For some of the relevant literature on this topic, see Alexander Rosenberg, "Hume and the Philosophy of Science," note 3, this volume.

3 An example is Jerry Fodor, "Mental Representation: An Introduction," in *Scientific Inquiry in Philosophical Perspective*, ed. N. Rescher (Washington, 1987).

4 This reading was in part due to the emphasis placed on the early parts of the *Treatise*. Even when attention was paid to the rest of Hume's works, these were typically read in the same way, with emphasis on sceptical or destructive passages, often taken out of context. A striking example is the singling out of the notorious passage about the impossibility of deducing *ought* from *is* (T 3.1.1, 469–70) as representative of his practical philosophy.

5 There is, of course, also the possibility that Hume is simply contradicting himself. But attributing to Hume inconsistency on a such a massive scale strikes me as far less plausible than re-interpreting his scepticism in the way recommended here. One way of not taking Hume at his word is to stress the role of irony in his writings; see, for example J. V. Price, *The Ironical Hume* (Austin, 1965). While I agree that this can be illuminating – Hume is surely as subtle, complex, and, at times, esoteric, a writer as any in the history of philosophy – it is also important to know when to take what he says literally. I believe, though I cannot defend the claim here, that the definitions, principles, and doctrines he flags in various ways as canonical (for example, by their placement in introductory or annunciatory passages, by techniques such as CAPITALIZATION, by a certain hard-to-define but recognizable tone of voice) are best read in this way.

6 On the relation between description and explanation, see J.-P. Monteiro, "Hume's Conception of Science," *Journal of the History of Philosophy* 19 (1981): 327–42; and my "Description and Explanation in Hume's Science of Man," *Transactions of the Fifth International Congress on the Enlightenment*, Voltaire Foundation (1979): 449–57.

7 Care has to be exercised with Hume's terminology here. While he sometimes distinguishes reason from the imagination, he himself recognized that his terminology could be confusing (T 1.3.9, 117–18). When he distinguishes *reason* from the *imagination*, he speaks of the latter's "general and more establish'd properties." However, the imagination in this form can also be distinguished from "the trivial suggestions of the fancy" (T 1.4.7, 267). This makes sense only if we recognize that Hume

uses the terms *reason* and *reasoning* in two very different ways. In one sense, these terms refer to the kind of abstract reflective operation involved in the arbitrary comparison of ideas that constitutes what he calls "philosophical relations." But they can also denote the kind of automatic, non-reflective, transitions that count as "natural relations," most important among them, causation. For a discussion of the several senses in which Hume uses *reason*, see David Fate Norton, *David Hume: Common-Sense Moralist, Sceptical Metaphysician* (Princeton, 1982), pp. 96–8.

8 What Hume calls his "first principle" – sometimes labelled by commentators "the copy principle" – states that *"all our simple ideas in their first appearance are deriv'd from simple impressions, which are correspondent to them, and which they exactly represent"* (T 1.1.1, 4).

9 Some find *Treatise* Book 1, Part 2, one of the most perplexing of the whole work, and its purposes are much disputed; see, for example, Robert Fendel Anderson, *Hume's First Principles* (Lincoln, Neb., 1966), and Robert J. Fogelin, *Hume's Scepticism in the* Treatise of Human Nature (London, 1985). It is worth noting that at least at times Hume seems to be interested there in making an *anti*-sceptical argument. Having argued that the idea of extension as infinitely divisible is incoherent, he says: "Now 'tis certain we have an idea of extension; for otherwise why do we talk and reason concerning it? ... Here then is an idea of extension, which consists of parts or inferior ideas, that are perfectly indivisible: consequently this idea implies no contradiction: consequently 'tis possible for extension really to exist conformable to it: and consequently all the arguments employ'd against the possibility of mathematical points are mere scholastick quibbles, and unworthy of our attention" (T 1.2.2, 32).

10 As indicated before, we do take notice of them in a non-reflective, non-conscious way, and the mind does retain them, so as to make use of them in making the inference.

11 It is Hume's frequently expressed view that a belief is nothing but a lively perception. See, for example, T 1.3.5, 86.

12 Not all transitions between ideas grounded in natural relations, however, deserve the title "reasoning" in the more honorific sense. We must remember the distinction between beliefs resulting from principles of the imagination "permanent, irresistable, and universal" and those due to principles "changeable, weak, and irregular" (T 1.4.4, 225). Only the former, and these only when tempered by the reflective use of "general rules" (T 1.3.13, 146ff.; 1.3.15, 173–6), are to be relied upon. This "second influence of general rules" (T 1.3.13, 150) is the work of our judgement and understanding, and it must be sharply distinguished from the first, which involves their "rash" use in unqualified generalization from

small samples by the uncontrolled imagination or fancy. This first "influence" of general rules is what is at work in the kind of inertial extrapolation to "imaginary standards" in mathematical reasoning which we saw Hume criticize. It is also what makes us declare that "an *Irishman* cannot have wit, and a *Frenchman* cannot have solidity" on the basis of a few examples we have encountered; and in this use they are "the source of what we properly call PREJUDICE" (T 1.3.13, 146). For helpful discussions of general rules, see Thomas K. Hearn, "'General Rules' in Hume's *Treatise,*" *Journal of the History of Philosophy* 8 (1970): 405–22, and "General Rules and the Moral Sentiments in Hume's *Treatise,*" *Review of Metaphysics* 30 (1976): 57–72. I have also benefited from reading S. Monder's unpublished "Hume on Regular and Irregular General Rules."

13   The uninspiring history of the so-called Gettier problem, involving increasingly arcane and artificial counter-examples to ever more byzantine definitions of knowledge is often taken to be proof of this. For details of this history, see R. K. Shope, *The Analysis of Knowing: a Decade of Research* (Princeton, 1983).

14   The fountainhead of modern naturalizing programs in epistemology and the philosophy of mind is W. V. O. Quine. For recent examples, see Alvin Goldman, *Epistemology on Cognition* (Cambridge, Mass., 1987); Stephen Stich, *The Fragmentation of Reason: Preface to a Pragmatic Theory of Cognitive Evaluation* (Cambridge, Mass., 1990). For a useful volume of papers on the subject, see H. Kornblith, *Naturalized Epistemology* (Cambridge, Mass., 1985).

15   Details about these matters may be found in Shimon Ullman, *The Interpretation of Visual Motion* (Cambridge, Mass., 1979); Daniel Kahneman, Paul Slovic, and Amos Tversky, eds., *Judgements under Uncertainty: Heuristics and Biases* (Cambridge, 1982); Zenon Pylyshyn, *Computation and Cognition: Toward a Foundation for Cognitive Science* (Cambridge, Mass., 1984); Goldman, *Epistemology on Cognition;* and Stich, *Fragmentation of Reason.*

16   Hume's general account of identity involves thinking of the mind as surveying objects and "trac[ing] the succession of time" (T 1.4.2, 201) – something that seems to presuppose *its* identity over time. So, it may seem, does talking of *one's* believing and re-identifying, as I just have. It may seem to beg the question against the very sceptic Hume is often taken to be, namely, one who doubts that there *is* a self. Does such talk not already imply, by virtue of its grammar alone, that there is one?

One may be tempted to say that if the sceptic were right, "he" could not state "his" view. However this may be, Hume's discussion is better seen, as I have suggested here, as one about what kind of thing the self is, rather than one about whether there is one. (The similarity with his treatment of belief in body, discussed earlier, should not be overlooked.) Once we understand his answer – essentially, that the self believed in is a complex object united by certain crucial relations – we can also see that there is no puzzle about how it can be the subject of so-called intentional verbs such as those used to attribute actions. For additional discussion of these issues, see my "Hume on Self-Identity and Memory," *The Review of Metaphysics* 30 (1976): 19–38, and "Hume's Difficulties with the Self," *Hume Studies* 5 (1979): 45–54.

17 This is why Hume insists on the need to account for one's belief in one's self first: that belief is required for one's belief in external objects. See T 1.4.2, 189.

18 The relation between the first-person and the second-person elements in Hume's method is discussed below, Part VI, and in my "Hume's Methods," a paper presented to the 1992 Hume Conference.

19 In the second book of the *Treatise*, concerned with the passions (with what we would today call moral psychology), Hume insists that "the idea of ourselves is always intimately present to us" (T 2.2.4, 354). The appearance of inconsistency here evaporates once we remind ourselves that the kind of self-awareness Hume requires in his account of the passions does not entail anything about the nature of the object we are aware of. We should distinguish the question of what the self is from the question of what role it plays in our emotional life. The two questions are independent; having answered the first, Hume can quite consistently expect the reader to be aware of this answer in giving his answer to the second. For more on the passions, see Terence Penelhum, "Hume's Moral Psychology," this volume.

20 For further details, see my "Hume and Cognitive Science," *History of Philosophy Quarterly* 2 (1985): 257–74, reprinted in *Historical Foundations of Cognitive Science*, ed. J-C. Smith (Boston, 1990).

21 See, for example, Anderson, *Hume's First Principles*.

22 The chief recent challenge to its classical computational version has come from connectionism; for a useful introduction, see W. Bechtel and A. Abrahamsen, *Connectionism and the Mind: An Introduction to Parallel Processing in Networks* (Cambridge, Mass., 1991).

23 This is not, perhaps, true of all mental states: sensations, such as pains, moods, emotions, and the like are perhaps not – at least not straightforwardly – about anything. But the kind of states most centrally involved in understanding intelligent behaviour – beliefs and desires – do seem to be essentially intentional in this sense.

24 See Daniel Dennett, *Brainstorms* (Cambridge, Mass., 1978), pp. 101–2.

25 For discussion of the "Newtonian" picture of the self, see Jane L. Mc-

Intyre, "Is Hume Self Consistent?" in *McGill Hume Studies*, ed. David Fate Norton, Nicholas Capaldi, and Wade L. Robison (San Diego, 1979), and my "Hume's Difficulties with the Self."

26 This is actually somewhat overstated. Especially in modern physics, the content of the informal descriptions of the behaviour of bodies offered by a theory ultimately depends largely on the mathematically statable laws of the theory. But, first, this should make us in any case suspicious of taking what the informal descriptions suggest at face value and, second, in so far as we do so, we must recognize them as stemming from their ordinary, non-metaphorical, use. Either way, the point stands: there is no independent meaning to be assigned to informal scientific descriptions beyond what comes from either the (strictly and non-metaphorically expressed) laws of a theory or from non-theoretical, common-sense uses of the terms in the descriptions. On the interplay and interdependence of models noted in different areas of discourse, see my "Persons as corporate entities and corporations as persons," *Nature and System* 3 (1981): 173–80.

3   Hume and the philosophy of science

Among all the philosophers who wrote before the twentieth century none is more important for the philosophy of science than David Hume. This is because Hume is widely recognized to have been the chief philosophical inspiration of the most important twentieth-century school in the philosophy of science – the so-called logical positivists. These philosophers began to work in Vienna in the late twenties, but by the end of the Second World War most of them had come to the United States. Many of them preferred the name logical empiricists, in part to emphasize their greater debt to Hume than to Comte.[1] They recognized that Hume raised a variety of issues that set the agenda for their program in the philosophy of science. It is jointly because of his impact on this agenda and because of the influence the philosophy of science acquired over this period that, after the First World War, Hume came to be regarded as the most important philosopher to have written in the English language.

Hume's knowledge of the science of his time is a matter of some controversy. Although in the *Treatise* he announced that he intended to bring "the experimental method of reasoning" to moral subjects, substantive science plays only a small role in Hume's writings, and there is little discussion of issues raised by Newtonian mechanics, the focus of much work in the philosophy of science in the twentieth century. As Noxon says, the *Treatise* "is as unmathematical as Ovid's Metamorphoses."[2] Yet there seems ample evidence to suppose that Hume's philosophy was animated by his inter-

I wish to thank Brian Copenhaver for extensive comments on a previous draft of this essay, comments that led to many material improvements, and David Owen for permitting me to read some as yet unpublished material on Hume's understanding of the laws of nature.

64

pretation of Newton's substantive and methodological views, as well as those of Hooke and Boyle.[3]

In Hume's philosophy, epistemology is the dominant force. His commitment to empiricism – to the thesis that the scope, limits, and justification of our knowledge is given by experience – drives almost all of his other views. It would force Hume to take sides on almost all of the questions that preoccupied the philosophy of science two hundred years later: the nature of empirical significance and the problem of demarcating scientific from non-scientific discourse, the foundations of inductive inference, the character of scientific laws, the structure of scientific theories and the nature of scientific explanation, the character of space and time, and the cognitive status of mathematics.

In one respect, Hume's approach to many of these issues differs sharply from that of his twentieth-century positivist successors. Unlike them, but like many of their successors, Hume organized much of his epistemology and his discussion of issues in the philosophy of science around his analysis of causation.[4] As he said in the *Enquiry concerning Human Understanding*, "All reasonings concerning matter of fact seem to be founded on the relation of *Cause and Effect*" (EHU 4.1, 26). Following Bertrand Russell,[5] the positivists viewed the concept of causation as an obscure one, without a role to play in science, and therefore of doubtful relevance to the philosophy of science. However, its role for Hume, and any serious empiricist philosophy of science, is so central that the absence of an analysis of causation from the positivist accounts of science makes them read like Hamlet without the melancholy prince. And twentieth-century physics and philosophy of mind have returned the notion of causality to the central place in epistemology and the philosophy of science that Hume accorded it.

I. COGNITIVE SIGNIFICANCE, DEMARCATION, AND THE EMPIRICAL MEANING OF SCIENTIFIC TERMS

The role Hume's theory of meaning plays in his account of the nature of causation cannot be overstated. Like empiricists after him, Hume takes on Locke's theory of meaning and of meaningfulness.[6] He does so largely without argument.[7] What he does argue is that every idea is caused by an impression. Hume defines impressions as

"sensations, passions and emotions, as they make their first appearance in the soul," and "ideas" as the "faint images of these in thinking and reasoning" (T 1.1.1, 1). We may understand "ideas" as the
mental tokens with which we reason, and "impressions" as the
immediate and unavoidable sensations or feelings that, according to
Hume, cause ideas. In the *Treatise* the argument that every idea or
concept is a copy of impressions that cause it is based on an inductive inference from past constant conjunctions and the temporal
priority of impressions (the argument relies on a prior analysis of
causation, of course) (T 1.1.1, 4–5). To this inductive argument
Hume adds an observation about sensory deprivation: "A blind man
can form no notion of colours; a deaf man of sounds" (EHU 2,20; T
1.1.1, 5).[8]

But Hume shifts without argument from the causal claim that
ideas are the effects of impressions to the semantic claim that ideas
refer to impressions. Though rejected by post-positivist philosophy
of language,[9] some views in late twentieth-century philosophy of
language vindicate this shift.[10] According to Hume's theory, since a
term names an idea, the meaning of a term is ultimately given by a
set of impressions that cause the idea it names, and terms without
such a pedigree are meaningless noises. In effect this theory of meaning constitutes a criterion of cognitive significance indistinguishable from one of the positivists' earliest attempts to frame a principle of verifiability. According to this early version of this principle,
every meaningful term required a set of observationally necessary
and sufficient conditions of application.[11] Unlike Hume, positivists
realized that this criterion was too stringent, for many theoretical
terms could not be provided anything approaching such observational conditions. For that matter, neither could the common sense
vocabulary of everyday objects. Hume did not recognize these limitations of his verifiability criterion of meaning. But he used it mainly
to condemn a wide variety of concepts of traditional philosophical
thought (*substance, substantial form, mode, essence,* for example)
as without cognitive significance. In doing so, Hume followed a
tradition, one dating from Descartes or before, that rejected the central concepts of Aristotelian metaphysics.

Hume sought a sensory pedigree for some of these concepts – an
account that would explain why common sense, science, and philosophy persisted in employing them despite their meaninglessness.

This empirical meaning is of course wholly different from what previous philosophy or common sense supposed. Thus, for instance, "causal necessity" is not stigmatized as meaningless, but is assigned reference to a sensation – an impression of reflection – caused in us, but mistaken by the mind for a property of causal sequences independent of us (see Part II). Hume provided these alternative meanings for concepts strictly meaningless by his standards, because as a psychologist he was interested in explaining how we come by certain beliefs and certain notions. But his purely epistemological interests should lead him to condemn as unintelligible the definitions usually accorded many of the terms of "school" philosophy, of common sense, and even of scientific theory. (See the discussion of gravity and of "fictions" which follows.)

One of Hume's most famous dictums expresses the consequences of his theory of meaningfulness for traditional philosophy and theology:

When we run over libraries, persuaded of these principles, what havoc must we make? If we take in our hand any volume; of divinity or school metaphysics, for instance; let us ask, *Does it contain any abstract reasoning concerning quantity or number?* No. *Does it contain any experimental reasoning concerning matter of fact and existence?* No. Commit it then to the flames: for it can contain nothing but sophistry and illusion.   (EHU, 12.3, 165)

Unlike his positivist successors, Hume apparently treated his claims about ideas and impressions, and his theory of the meaning of terms, as part of a contingent empirical theory. For, on the one hand, he invites counter-examples and, on the other hand, produces one of his own, the famous missing shade of blue: in the *Treatise*, and the *Enquiry*, Hume grants that if someone is acquainted with all colors except one particular shade of blue, he could still generate the idea of this shade without ever having had the relevant impression. But, writes Hume, "this instance is so singular, that it is scarcely worth our observing, and does not merit that for it alone we should alter our general maxim" (EHU 2, 20–1; see also T 1.1.1, 5–6).

Twentieth-century empiricism has had great difficulty reconciling its claims about empirical meaningfulness with the apparent commitment of scientific theory to the existence of entities beyond our observational access. Empiricists since Hume have either sought to translate claims about theoretical entities into statements about what we can observe or sought to treat such claims as convenient instruments or heuristic devices with only apparent semantic content. Hume had a similar problem as the result of his attack (inspired by Berkeley) on Lockean "representative realism," the thesis that substances existing independently of us cause us to have impressions, some of which represent the real properties of these objects – the so-called primary qualities, extension, mass, and other properties that figure in the scientific theory of the time. In addition, these substances cause us to have impressions that do not represent their real properties – color, taste, heat, the so-called secondary qualities. Hume took over Berkeley's arguments to reject the primary/secondary quality distinction. More important, he held that claims about the existence of unperceived objects and the suggestion that they cause our perceptions are both unintelligible, on the grounds of his theory of meaning. But of course because of his psychologistic interest in explaining how we come by the words we employ to express these meaningless claims, Hume also provides an alternative account of how we come to have these terms and make these claims. This account gives our statements about objects, perceived and unperceived, an empirical meaning altogether foreign to our intentions in the use of these expressions. Thus, in the section of the *Treatise* titled "Of scepticism with regard to the senses," Hume begins by saying that we cannot doubt the existence of bodies, but ends up saying that terms that seem to name physical objects really refer to (sets of) sense impressions (a position now called "linguistic phenomenalism"). *Mutatis mutandis*, Hume is committed to treating the theoretical claims of science similarly.

Hume is also explicit in his rejection of the intelligibility of powers or dispositions independent of their manifestation in our observations. Hume's treatment of gravity illustrates this attitude towards dispositions and at the same time the difficulties empiricists have accounting for theoretical entities. He writes: "when we talk of gravity, we mean certain effects, without comprehending that active power. It was never the meaning of Sir ISAAC NEWTON to rob second causes of all force or energy. . . . On the contrary, that great philosopher had recourse to an etherial active fluid to explain his universal attraction" (EHU 7.1, 73n). Leaving aside the accuracy of Hume's exegesis of Newton, note first the reduction of gravity as a dispositional force to its effects, and the reference to Newton's view that an underlying mechanism (an etherial active fluid to transmit causal forces the way that water transmits waves) eliminates the need to posit any secret powers, occult forces, or the appearance of action at a distance. But this etherial active force is just the sort of concept that on Hume's own analysis lacks a pedigree in impressions. Elsewhere, faced with terms for which no such impressions can be produced, Hume does not shrink from reading them out of the language of science. But he could hardly repudiate the theoretical terms of Newtonian mechanics. For, after all, his stated objective in the *Treatise* was to introduce methods he took to have been experimental (if not explicitly Newton's) to the moral sciences. He could scarcely endorse Newton's methods, while repudiating Newton's most significant "experimental" results.

Locke's representative realism is widely held to have been motivated by seventeenth-century physical theory. Although he did not attack the physical theory, Hume did reject the theory of "double existence," as he called it – the theory that while we experience only impressions and ideas, there is also another set of existences, namely, objects. Hume's strictures against the "double existence" of objects and perceptions caused by them, are epistemically akin to twentieth-century arguments against taking seriously the theoretical entities of modern physics. Hume noted that we could have no experience of the putative causes of our impressions, and that this makes unintelligible the claim that a Lockean "something I know not what" is their cause. That this "something" should have properties, some of which are represented in our impressions and some not, is equally unintelligible on Hume's theory of meaning, since we could have no notion of the objects independent of impressions.

Hume described as "fictions" certain of the terms he stigmatized as meaningless. By fiction he meant "the pure offspring of the fancy" (T 1.3.10, 122). Thus, of the notion of "substance" he says, "In order to reconcile . . . contradictions the imagination is apt to feign something unknown and invisible, which it supposes to continue the same under all these variations; and this unintelligible something it calls a *substance, or original and first matter*" (T 1.4.3, 220). Yet as noted earlier, Hume elsewhere sought an explanation for our employment of many of these fictions. He did so by way of an account of how experience gives them a role and a meaning different from the meaning we suppose these terms to have.

Much earlier in the *Treatise*, for example, Hume had offered a very different view of "substance":

The idea of substance must therefore be deriv'd from an impression of reflexion, if it really exist. But the impressions of reflexion resolve themselves into our passions and emotions; none of which can possibly represent a substance. We have therefore no idea of substance, distinct from that of a collection of particular qualities, nor have we any other meaning when we either talk or reason concerning it.

The idea of a substance . . . is nothing but a collection of simple ideas, that are united by the imagination, and have a particular name assigned them.   (T 1.1.7, 16)

Hume's strategy of finding a provenance in impressions for terms whose strict philosophical definitions would render them meaningless has led to suggestions that these concepts serve as heuristic devices – although they are meaningless, they serve a useful function in our cognitive economy.[12] But it is difficult to establish that by "fiction" Hume means something more than a meaningless term used illegitimately. For, as we have seen, he so stigmatizes many of the terms of Aristotelian metaphysics,[13] terms that few empiricists would identify as practically or scientifically useful. Indeed, Hume occasionally identifies as a fiction a notion of evident importance in science. The relation of perfect equality, for example, involving as it does "any correction beyond what we have instruments and art to make," is not to be met with in experience. It "is a mere fiction of the mind, and useless as well as incomprehensible" (T 1.2.4, 48).

Applied to modern science, Hume's strictures would favor an interpretation of the meaning of theoretical claims that treats these claims as mere manners of speaking about actual and possible sensations. For, on the one hand, he claimed that "we must take for granted" that there is body, and on the other, in describing material objects, he refers to "a hat, or shoe, or stone, or any other impression" (T 1.4.2, 187, 202). That there are sensations we cannot doubt; that there are bodies we cannot doubt; that there are substances existing independent of our sensations is unintelligible. *Ergo*, bodies, macroscopic, microscopic, or cosmic, must be sensations. In the twentieth century, this view came to be called phenomenalism. Latter-day phenomenalists found in Hume's discussion of the constancy and coherence of our impressions of objects (T 1.4.2, 194–7) a precursor to their own account of how statements about material objects turn into statements about sense data.[14]

II. CAUSATION AND INDUCTION

Causation is the center stage for Hume's application of the empiricist theory of meaning to problems in philosophy and scientific method. Hume defined causation at least twice in the *Treatise* and provided definitions in the *Abstract* and the *Enquiry* (T 1.3.14, 170; A, 649–51, 656–7; EHU 7.2, 76–7). Rendering a single interpretation that does justice to all these explicit definitions has kept many philosophers occupied for a fair portion of the twentieth century.[15] Without attempting explicitly to reconcile apparently conflicting definitions or their interpretations, what follows is one consistent interpretation of the relevant texts.

A strictly empiricist examination of the notion of cause led Hume to conclude that causation was fundamentally a relation between concrete *events*, although he did use other expressions, especially "objects," to refer to the relata of the causal relation. On his view, causation consists in three conditions: (a) spatio-temporal contiguity – there is no "action at a distance";[16] (b) temporal priority of the cause – there is no future or retrocausation, and, for that matter, no simultaneous causation among distinct events;[17] and (c) the instantiation of general regularities by particular causal sequences. Most crucially for Hume, the difference between causal sequences and merely accidental ones does not consist in some real metaphysical connection between individual events present in particular causal sequences and absent in particular accidental sequences. Rather, causation in one sequence of events requires constant conjunction of other events of the same types.[18] Hume notes that " 'tis commonly suppos'd, that there is a necessary connexion betwixt the cause and effect, and that the cause possesses something, which we call a *power*, or *force*, or *energy*." But, he goes on, "so little does any *power* discover itself to the senses in the operations of matter, that the *Cartesians*" concluded that matter is devoid of all power, and that the (apparent) operations of matter are all effected by God himself. Moreover, "our own minds afford us no more notion of energy than matter does." We must conclude, then, that "either we have no idea at all of force and energy, and these words are altogether insignificant, or they can mean nothing but that determination of the thought, acquir'd by habit, to pass from the cause to its usual effect" (A, 656–7; see also EHU 7.1, 63). Thus, there is, according to Hume, nothing "in the objects" taken in pairs that distinguishes causal and non-causal sequences. The distinction between these two types of sequence consists in every causal sequence instantiating some law(s) or other while no accidental sequences do so. This claim is the nub of Hume's theory of causation, and in one way or another has been the subject of the sharpest controversy in twentieth-century debates about causation. By grounding the causal relation in constant conjunctions, Hume made the problem of the nature of scientific laws, and their differences from merely accidentally true regularities, the central issue in the philosophy of science.

Previous philosophers, including, of course, Locke,[19] and subsequent opponents of Hume's theory have held that the causal relation obtains directly between individual events and does not require that they instantiate a general law. Moreover, on these views causal sequences are directly observable in individual sequences. Among twentieth-century proponents of the primacy of singular causal sequences in our causal knowledge are C. J. Ducasse and G. E. M. Anscombe.[20] Both argue vigorously against Hume. Like Locke, both claim that the efficacy of causes is also directly perceivable in individual sequences. And some philosophers persist in holding that there is a real tie between individual causes and effects, one that reflects the operation of distinct causal powers. These dispositions to bring about effects are held to be distinct from the manifest properties of objects, or the actual bringing about of effects. They are supposed to be absent in accidental sequences, while their presence in causal sequences underwrites the existence of general laws that subsume such sequences.[21]

Hume's arguments against these views employ principles that fix much of the rest of his philosophy of science. As noted, for Hume the meaning of a term is the idea it represents, and all ideas have their origin in sensory impressions. Since there is no impression of a causal power in objects, but only impressions of their succession in space and time, the term "causal power" is, strictly speaking, meaningless. Hume writes:

In reality, there is no part of matter, that does ever, by its sensible qualities, discover any power or energy, or give us ground to imagine, that it could produce any thing, or be followed by any other object. . . . It is impossible, therefore, that the idea of power can be derived from the contemplation of bodies, in single instances of their operation. (EHU 7.1, 63–4)

Imagine that our sensory apparatus were far more powerful than it is, so powerful that we could observe the transactions among the most minute particles of matter. What would we see? Nothing but displacement in space and time. We cannot even conceive of properties of objects or relations between them, observable or not, that would effect a necessary connection among things or the events they participate in.

Thus, notions of efficacy or causal power or causal necessity in the objects are without the requisite pedigree in experience to be meaningful. Indeed, the whole notion that causation rests on or reflects the intelligibility or rationality of sequences among events is a mistake. Accordingly, for Hume, the aim of science cannot be to reveal the intelligible character of the universe, but simply to catalogue the regularities that causal sequences reflect. (See the discussion of explanation in Part III.)

Hume relegated the necessity widely attributed to the causal connection to the mind, as an impression of reflection that we mistakenly attribute to the relation among the objects of causation. This impression is produced in us, according to Hume, by our experience of constant conjunctions – that is, by the perception of regularities in our experience. Thus Hume explains our common-sense distinction between accidental sequences and causal sequences by an appeal to a subjective sort of necessary connection, a feeling produced in the mind:

For after we have observ'd the resemblance in a sufficient number of instances, we immediately feel a determination of the mind to pass from one object to its usual attendant. . . . The several instances of resembling conjunctions lead us into the notion of power and necessity. . . . Necessity, then, is the effect of this observation, and is nothing but an internal impression of the mind, or a determination to carry our thoughts from one object to another. (T 1.3.14, 165)

All events in themselves, Hume tells us, "seem entirely loose and separate" (EHU 7.2, 74). There is no necessity in the objects of causation.

But cannot accidental sequences pile up to a large enough number to generate the same feeling of necessity, and furthermore, will this doctrine relegate causation to an at least partly mental contingency? The latter issue especially troubled Hume. Indeed, he forcefully posed it himself:

What! the efficacy of causes lie in the determination of the mind! As if causes did not operate entirely independent of the mind, and wou'd not continue their operation, even tho' there was no mind existent to contemplate them, or reason concerning them. Thought may well depend on causes for its operation, but not causes on thought. This is to reverse the order of nature, and make that secondary, which is really primary.   (T 1.3.14, 167)

In response to this charge, Hume insists that there is in fact no necessary connection among the objects; there is only contiguity and succession. But this means that the only basis for distinguishing real law-like – nomological – generalizations from generalizations based on purely accidental regularities is in the evidence that the mind can adduce for the former but not for the latter. Twentieth-century empiricists followed Hume's claim that "the mind has a great propensity to spread itself on external objects" and sought the difference between laws and those generalizations drawn from accidental regularities in our beliefs about them (T 1.3.14, 167–8). Thus, A. J. Ayer, for example, argued that the difference "lies not so much on the side of the facts which make [law-like generalizations] true or false as in the attitude of those who put them forward."[22] He held that the conviction that a generalization is really law-like is the result of the much greater amount and variety of evidence we can secure for laws as compared to merely accidental regularities.

This empiricist approach has, however, not withstood the test of time. Most philosophers continue to search for some causally relevant difference in the objects themselves, and not just in our beliefs about them, a difference that provides an objective foundation for the distinction between law-governed and accidental sequences. Mostly, the search for such differences has focused on what makes certain counterfactual conditional statements true, and others false. For it is the difference between true and false counterfactual conditionals that reflects our strong commitment to the existence of some sort of causal necessity, not merely in our beliefs, but in the world.

For present purposes, we need to consider counterfactual statements of the form, "if it hadn't been the case that . . . then it would not have been the case that. . . ." Causal sequences, for example, the striking of a match causing it to catch fire, make *true* counterfactual statements such as "if the match had not been struck, it would not have caught fire." By contrast, accidental sequences, for instance, the marking of a match with an X and its catching fire, do not make true counterfactuals: "if the match had not been marked with an X, it would not have caught fire" is a false counterfactual. Philosophers have sought the difference between causal and accidental sequences in the different conditions in the objects that make the first counterfactual true and the second false.[23] In large measure, those attempting to explain this difference have found themselves pressed to employ the very notion of causal necessity that Hume repudiated. Yet few have embraced "heroic Humeanism" – the doctrine that there is no difference between a law-like or nomological generalization and a universal truth drawn from exceptionless accidental regularities.[24] Nevertheless, this is the doctrine I believe most consistent with the rest of Hume's philosophy and the theory of language on which it is based.

Hume is almost universally credited with discovering the problem of induction. The problem arose for Hume in his search for the nature of causal necessity. Failing to find an impression of necessity in the objects, Hume turned to an examination of inference from past experience to future predictions, in the hope that beliefs about causal necessity could either be shown to emerge rationally from such reasoning, or perhaps be shown to be presupposed by it. However, Hume succeeded only in undermining inductive reasoning in general (although whether he intended to do the latter is by no means clear).

Hume recognized that inductive conclusions could only be derived deductively from premises (such as the uniformity of nature) that themselves required inductive warrant, or from arguments that were inductive in the first place. The deductive arguments are no more convincing than their most controversial premises and so generate a regress, while the inductive ones beg the question.[25] Accordingly, claims that transcend available data, in particular predictions and general laws, remain unwarranted. In the most succinct expression of this view, Hume asks for the basis of inferences from the past to the future:

But you must confess that the inference is not intuitive; neither is it demonstrative: Of what nature is it, then? To say it is experimental, is begging the question. For all inferences from experience suppose, as their foundation, that the future will resemble the past. . . . If there be any suspicion that the course of nature may change, and that the past may be no rule for the future, all experience becomes useless, and can give rise to no inference or conclusion.   (EHU, 4.2, 37–8)

It is difficult to square with Hume's own further writing about causal inference the allegation, almost universally attributed to him, that induction is groundless. To begin with, in the very same part of the *Treatise* in which he discusses the problem of justifying induction, Hume offers a series of methodological "Rules by which to judge of causes and effects" (T, 1.3.15, 173).[26] Moreover, Hume advocated and employed inductive methods in his histories, essays, and works on the nature of religion. Indeed, many of the crucial claims of the *Treatise* and *Enquiry* rest on inductive arguments. For example, Hume's claim that every idea is caused by impressions is justified by induction from observations. Just what the nature of Hume's scepticism about induction really is has thus become one of the enduring controversies of Hume scholarship.

Much of the controversy surrounding historical interpretations of Hume begins with problems raised by his apparent scepticism about induction. These interpretations of the whole corpus of Hume's works and his intentions have not bulked large in the philosophy of science. Nevertheless, any account of Hume's views about induction must at least take note of some of these interpretative projects. Among the most influential attempts to reconcile Hume's apparent scepticism with his practices are those of a tradition of "naturalists," from Norman Kemp Smith in the early 1940s to Barry Stroud in the late 1970s. Their aim is broadly to treat Hume as a psychologist who emphasizes the role of custom and habit, feeling, and sentiment as the ruling forces of cognition, and who accepts the authority of custom and habit as fitting and proper. On this view, Hume's aim is not to propound a philosophical conundrum, but to reveal the subordination of reason and evidence to instinct: "Hume's philosophy is not fundamentally skeptical; it is . . . naturalistic . . . in tendency."[27] Thus, the sceptical challenge about induction is "directed against the claims of a certain traditional conception of reason or rationality," and not against our ordinary claims to knowledge.[28] Other interpretations argue that Hume was not a naturalist in this sense, that his aims were not purely descriptive or psychological, and that, still less, did he suppose that normative epistemology could be inferred from an understanding of the "natural" processes of feeling and imagination. On these views, the target of Hume's apparent attack on induction was not empirical knowledge, but rather the pretense of the rationalists that the results of induction could be certified as necessarily true.[29]

Much twentieth-century thought about induction has focused on the notion of probability and on the nature of probabilistic inference. And some have argued that such inference entirely escapes Hume's objections against inductive methods. Most sustained of these arguments is that of David Stove.[30] Stove adopts the conventional view that Hume's argument aims to show that all inductive inferences are unreasonable because deductively invalid. He then argues that probabilistic inferences escape Hume's arguments because they are reasonable and non-deductive. Positive evidence increases the probability of a hypothesis, even though it does not entail the hypothesis. For instance, the observation of five black ravens increases the probability that all ravens are black, and the observation of a hundred does so even more strongly, without the inference from the evidence to the conclusion being deductive (since the evidence is still consistent with there being non-black ravens). And as the probability of a hypothesis increases, it becomes more reasonable to believe it. Induction increases probability. Accordingly, it makes the hypothesis more reasonable. Thus, Stove solves Hume's problem of induction. This view turns, of course, on an account of probability that avoids some standard Hume-inspired empiricist objections to the standard interpretations.[31]

Despite the interpretative controversies, what can be said with some confidence is that Hume held inductive reasoning to be inevitable for creatures like us, and that scientific claims rest on it. It is also indisputable that the preoccupation of twentieth-century philosophy of science with providing foundations for inductive inference was inspired by its reading of Hume.

III. EXPLANATION, LAWS, AND THEORIES

Hume gave no explicit account of the nature of general laws. But much of what contemporary philosophers have to say about such laws begins by outlining a view of them drawn directly from Hume's analysis of causation as constant conjunction: laws are the instantiation of contingent regularities whose evidential strength enables them to support counterfactuals – and thus sustains an attribution of some sort of necessity to the connections they report. He also held laws to be the essential ingredients in explanation. Hume's own practice, throughout the *Treatise* and the *Enquiry concerning Human Understanding*, is to explain psychological phenomena by subsuming them under general laws. Moreover, given his view of the centrality of the causal relation to all understanding, it is beyond question that for Hume the explanation of natural phenomena must proceed causally, and therefore must involve derivation from general laws.[32]

But what makes derivation from laws explanatory? Nothing in Hume's epistemology will allow such derivations to provide intelligibility or any sort of illumination, still less any sort of necessity rationalists might have held out for in a real explanation. Why does the derivation of phenomena from general laws explain? There is a revealing passage in which Hume announces his commitment to the explanatory role of general laws, both in the explanation of individual events and in the explanation of derivative generalizations. But in doing so he adopts the view that laws explain only because they unify and systematize, and that the ultimate explainers of science are such more particular laws as those of Newtonian mechanics. Hume raises the question, How, assuming that we have explained particular events by subsumption under a general law, do we explain the laws – the general causes, as he calls them – under which we have subsumed particular events?

> But as to the causes of these general causes, we should in vain attempt their discovery; nor shall we ever be able to satisfy ourselves, by any particular explication of them. These ultimate springs and principles are totally shut up from human curiosity and enquiry. Elasticity, gravity, cohesion of parts, communication of motion by impulse; these are probably the ultimate causes and principles which we shall ever discover in nature; and we may esteem ourselves sufficiently happy, if, by accurate enquiry and reasoning, we can trace up the particular phenomena to, or near to, these general principles. The most perfect philosophy of the natural kind only staves off our ignorance a little longer.   (EHU 4.1, 30)

"Tracing up the particular phenomena" means subsuming them under more and more general laws. Of course, quantum mechanics has staved off our ignorance further than Newtonian mechanics. But in a wider sense Hume's point about explanation remains unaffected. In the search for explanations we secure acquaintance with generalizations of ever greater range and precision, but they remain for all that statements of constant conjunction, not revelations of recognizable ultimate springs, still less claims of metaphysical necessity. And what makes them explanatory is the degree to which they unify diverse phenomena by providing a small number of general causes from which a large number of special ones follow.

Hume said remarkably little about the nature of scientific theories. But his approach to explanation, together with his commitment to a regularity theory of causation, and his phenomenalism about theoretical terms, narrow the range of accounts of scientific theory he could have given. The importance he attached to the "laws of matter and motion," found in Newtonian mechanics (E-Su, 580–6), as a means of unifying phenomena under a small number of general principles, makes an axiomatic account of scientific theories obviously attractive for Hume. For axiomatic systems are just those systems of propositions in which a small number of underived assumptions (axioms) work together to entail a large number of derived statements (theorems). The only axiomatic system discussed explicitly in the Humean corpus is geometry, which Hume distinguished from the rest of mathematics as a theory of the nature of space. Though axiomatic, geometry was for Hume (in the *Treatise,* but not in the *Enquiry*) a contingent theory. Unlike pure mathematics, geometry, he says, "can scarce be esteem'd a perfect and infallible science," for it "never attains a perfect precision and exactness. Its first principles are still drawn from the general appearance of the objects; and that appearance can never afford us any security, when we examine the prodigious minuteness of which nature is susceptible" (T, 1.3.1, 71; see also the discussion of mathematical knowledge in Part IV).

As with geometry, then, theories are composed of hypotheses that must be subjected to test by experience. Empirical regularities are much more strongly supported by experience than are explanatory theories. "The phaenomenon may be real, tho' my explication be chimerical," says Hume: "having establish'd any doctrine upon a sufficient number of experiments, [the natural philosopher should] rest contented with that, when he sees a farther examination would lead him into obscure and uncertain speculations. In that case his enquiry wou'd be much better employ'd in examining the effects than the causes of his principle" (T 1.2.5, 60; 1.1.4, 12–13). Hume thus seems to have anticipated a version of "hypothetico-deductivism," the twentieth-century thesis that theories are developed to explain empirical regularities by subsuming them under more general hypotheses, which gain their credence through their relation to these lower level generalizations.

In a way, this view sits uncomfortably with Hume's phenomenalism and his theory of meaning. And it generates for Hume the puzzle of accounting for the empirical scientist's need of theoretical laws couched in unobservable notions that transcend experience.[33] Meaningful terms for Hume must be definable in terms of sense impressions. A hypothesis composed of such terms can therefore not transcend experience – except inductively. But an explanatory theory must transcend the phenomena it seeks to explain; otherwise it merely redescribes them. If it transcends observations, however, it becomes meaningless. Therefore, all explanatory theories must consist in what Hume called "obscure and uncertain speculations" – hypotheses in the pejorative sense that Hume sometimes shared with Newton, and which they both stigmatized as superfluous to the aims of science. In the end Hume's epistemology is too narrow to permit post-Humean philosophers of science to borrow from him a cogent explanation for the theoretical character of science.

IV. MATHEMATICS AND THE NATURE OF SPACE AND TIME

Empiricist philosophers have always been embarrassed by the need to account for mathematical knowledge. For mathematical truths have a sort of certainty that experience can never convey. Generally, empiricists have dealt with this problem in one of two ways. Either they have concluded, with Mill, that mathematical truths are extremely well confirmed but nevertheless contingent propositions that experience could conceivably overturn, or they have held, with Hume, that such statements are certain because they express claims we know to be true by definition and therefore have no empirical content, and make no contingent claims about the way the world works.

Hume draws an epistemological distinction between two kinds of statements:

> All the objects of human reason or enquiry may naturally be divided into two kinds, to wit, *Relations of Ideas*, and *Matters of Fact*. Of the first kind are the sciences of Geometry, Algebra, and Arithmetic. . . . *That the square of the hypothenuse is equal to the square of the two sides*, is a proposition which expresses a relation between these figures. *That three times five is equal to the half of thirty*, expresses a relation between these numbers. Propositions of this kind are discoverable by the mere operation of thought, without dependence on what is anywhere existent in the universe. Though there never were a circle or triangle in nature, the truths demonstrated by Euclid would for ever retain their certainty and evidence.   (EHU 4.1, 25)

Mathematical statements can be established by considering the relation of ideas that the terms of these statements name. If these ideas give the meanings of the terms, then Hume's claim is that mathematical statements are true in virtue of the relations between the meanings of their terms. In the terminology Kant introduced, they are analytic truths – statements true in virtue of the meanings of their terms. As definitions and their consequences, it will be no surprise that mathematical propositions are certain, that they can be established by the mere operation of thought, and that they do not depend for their truth on the existence of anything anywhere existent in the universe. Analytic truths are to be contrasted with synthetic truths – statements that as Hume said, report contingent matters of fact.

It is because ideas can be measured against precise standards of equality and proportion only in algebra and arithmetic that "we can carry on a chain of reasoning to any degree of intricacy, and yet preserve a perfect exactness and certainty" (T 1.3.1, 71). Thus, the certainty of mathematical knowledge is no reason to question the fallibility of empirical science, for the certain claims of mathematics are without empirical content.

This account of the nature of mathematical truths was eclipsed by Kant's arguments that mathematics constituted synthetic truths known *a priori*. Both Hume's and Kant's views of the nature of mathematical truths have been overturned by subsequent discoveries in mathematics. Non-Euclidean geometries undercut Kant's claim that Euclidean geometry was necessarily true, and Gödel's incompleteness theorem showed that mathematical claims cannot be merely analytical propositions reporting the relations of ideas. For this reason, Hume's view of mathematics as a body of definitions and their consequences, which was embraced by most empiricists in the early twentieth century, has now fallen out of philosophical favor.

Perhaps the one area of the philosophy of science in which Hume's views have never been influential is the discussion of the nature of space and time. As noted, the *Treatise* excludes geometry from the realm of mathematical certainty and exactness because "its first principles are still drawn from the general appearance of the objects." In particular, Hume challenged certainty about the postulate of the parallels, Euclidian geometry's claim that one and only one line parallel to a given line can be drawn through a point outside that line. Hume insisted that we have no standard of straight lines "so precise as to assure us of the truth of this proposition" (T 1.3.1, 71). Here Hume prefigured subsequent doubts about the postulate of the parallels, doubts that led to the development of non-Euclidean geometries. But Hume's doubts, like most others before the nineteenth century, simply reflect the greater complexity of this fifth axiom of Euclid's system compared with the other four axioms. It betokens no intimation of non-Euclidean geometry.

Other reasons for treating geometry as a potentially fallible theory of space derive from Hume's strictures on infinite divisibility in relation to the nature of space and time. Both geometry and physics seem to require that space be infinitely divisible, and the infinite divisibility of time is required by physical theory. But infinite divisibility has posed a problem for philosophy since Zeno's proofs that motion is impossible. In brief, these "proofs" purport to show that motion is impossible because displacement even across the shortest distance requires passage through an infinity of points, and no infinite series can be completed. Hume makes no mention of this argument, but he does attempt to undercut it.[34]

Experience can never provide an impression of a mathematical point, and we have no notion of infinite divisibility. It follows, then, that these notions are meaningless, and that the claims that space and time are composed of mathematical points or are infinitely divisible are equally meaningless. Yet Hume simply holds the claims that space and time are both infinitely divisible to be false, not unintelligible. And after noting that we can have no impression of infinite divisibility, he provides arguments against the theses that space and time are so divisible. Both arguments trade on misunderstandings of limits and of the possibility of infinite series summing to finite magnitudes (T 1.2.2, 30–1).[35]

Hume went further and made a positive psychological claim: experience does provide impressions that cannot be divided further – perceptual minima (T 1.2.1, 27). This is a claim subsequent philosophy leaves to empirical science, psychophysics in particular, but Hume employs it to provide an alternative to infinite divisibility. Perceptual minima are not further divisible, because dividing them simply annihilates them. In experience, the apparent size of an ink-spot becomes smaller and smaller as its distance from the observer increases until some point when abruptly it disappears. Space is apparently like this: "But my senses convey to me only the impressions of colour'd points, dispos'd in a certain manner. . . . [W]e may conclude with certainty, that the idea of extension is nothing but a copy of these colour'd points, and of the manner of their appearance" (T 1.2.3, 34). The expression "the manner of their appearance" is critical. Hume uses a similar expression when he comes to account for our idea of time. Both expressions reveal the defects of Hume's theory of meaning and reflect deep circularities in his analyses of space and time.

The idea of time, Hume tells us, is derived from an impression of succession: "time cannot make its appearance to the mind, either alone, or attended with a steady unchangeable object, but is always discover'd by some *perceivable* succession of changeable objects" (T 1.2.3, 35). It seems to have escaped Hume's notice that the notion of succession is a temporal one itself. If our concept of time derives from a succession of impressions, we need to ask: A succession in what? If the answer is "in time," Hume's analysis has proved circular. Similarly, consider the "manner of appearance" that relates the sensible minima: the manner of appearance of these coloured points has them either to the left or, to the right of, above, or below one another. But where do these ideas come from? They presuppose space. If so, just as succession is already a temporal term, the "manner of appearance" of extended minima must be spatial itself, and of no help in an empiricist account of the nature of time.

Because of its confusions about the infinite, its admixture of psychological issues with physical and mathematical ones, and its fundamentally circular character, Hume's treatment of space and time has been of little influence in subsequent discussions of these concepts in the philosophy of science.

V. CONCLUSION

Much of the Humean corpus beyond what is treated here is also of significance for Hume's view of science and scientific method, especially as it relates to subsequent social science. Psychology, economics, sociology, political science – all are areas in which Hume's accounts of human affairs has bulked large. His studies of the nature and origin of religious belief, his history of England, his essays on economics and political theory – all are pursued in accordance with methodological maxims drawn from the *Treatise* and the *Enquiry concerning Human Understanding*. In particular, Hume's other works all reflect a principle he enunciated in Book 2 of the *Treatise*: "in judging of the actions of men we must proceed upon the same maxims, as when we reason concerning external objects" (T 2.3.1, 403). Like the empiricists who followed him, Hume held that the methods of the social sciences must be fundamentally the same as those of natural science.

There is among philosophers of science little agreement with any of Hume's particular arguments. But it is a remarkable fact that many of the conclusions he reached about topics of interest in the philosophy of science have withstood the test of scientific change and philosophical fashion. As other essays in this volume show, the same can be said for almost all of the philosophy of David Hume.

NOTES

1 Positivism's heyday extended from the late thirties to the early sixties. Over the period of its flourishing, its leading figures were Rudolph Carnap, Hans Reichenbach, Herbert Feigl, and Carl Hempel. For a logical positivist's account of the history of philosophy and Hume's place in it, see Hans Reichenbach, *The Rise of Scientific Philosophy* (Berkeley, 1951), esp. chap. 5. A. J. Ayer, *Language, Truth and Logic* (London, 1936) is the *locus classicus* for logical positivism in the English-speaking philosophy world. Ayer writes, "The views which are put forward in this

treatise derive from . . . the logical outcome of the empiricism of Berkeley and Hume" (p. 31).

2 James Noxon, *Hume's Philosophical Development* (Oxford, 1972), p.
112.

3 In addition to Noxon, see, for example, Mary Shaw Kuypers, *Studies in
the Eighteenth Century Background of Hume's Empiricism* (Minneapolis, 1930; reprinted New York, 1983); Nicholas Capaldi, *David Hume
the Newtonian Philosopher* (Boston, 1975); Peter Jones, *Hume's Sentiments* (Edinburgh, 1982); James Force, "Hume's Interest in Newton and
Science," *Hume Studies* 13 (1987): 166–216; David Fate Norton, "Hume
and the Experimental Method," unpublished typescript, 1989. The extent of Hume's probable exposure to science is discussed in Michael
Barfoot, "Hume and the Culture of Science in the Early Eighteenth Century," *Oxford Studies in the History of Philosophy*, ed. M. A. Stewart
(1990), pp. 151–90. Barfoot and Norton draw attention to the influence
of Boyle on Hume.

4 See, for example, Wesley Salmon, *Scientific Explanation and the Causal
Structure of the World* (Princeton, 1984), pp. 135–238.

5 "On the Notion of Cause," *Mysticism and Logic* (London, 1917). It was
in this essay that Russell claimed that the notion of cause has survived
on the mistaken assumption that, like the monarchy, it can do no harm.
In fact, he actually adopted Hume's account of causation as lawful regularity, while affecting to repudiate the entire notion.

6 Locke writes, "But so far as Words are of Use and Signification, so far is
there a constant connexion between the Sound and the *Idea*; and a
Designation, that the one stand for the other: without which Application of them, they are nothing but so much insignificant Noise." *An
Essay Concerning Human Understanding*, ed. P. H. Nidditch (Oxford,
1975), 3.2.7, 408.

7 For a discussion of Hume's implicit argument for Locke's theory of
meaning, see Jonathan Bennett, *Locke, Berkeley, Hume: Central
Themes* (Oxford, 1971), sec. 47.

8 In a letter only recently discovered, Hume defends his view of the relationship of impressions and ideas from the criticism of Thomas Reid.
Reid affirmed, wrote Hume, that "I had been hasty, & not supported by
any Colour of Argumen[t] when I affirm, that all our Ideas are copy'd
from Impressions. I have endeavourd to build that Principle on two
Arguments. The first is desiring any one to make a particular Detail of
all his Ideas, where he woud always find that every Idea had a correspondent & preceding Impression. If no Exception can ever be found, the
Principle must remain incontestible. The second is, that if you exclude
any particular Impression, as Colours to the blind, Sound to the Deaf,

you also exclude the Ideas." Quoted from Paul B. Wood, "David Hume . . . A New Letter to Hugh Blair from July 1762," *Mind* (1986): 411–16.

9 Especially under the influence of Wittgenstein, whose "private language" argument in the *Philosophical Investigations* (Oxford, 1956) was long held to be a direct attack on the Humean theory of meaning.

10 See, for example, Jerry Fodor, *Theory of Content* (Cambridge, Mass., 1990), pp. 231–51.

11 For a full account of positivist principles of verification, see Carl Hempel, *Aspects of Scientific Explanation* (New York, 1965), chap. 4.

12 See, for example, Saul Traiger, "Impressions, Ideas, and Fictions," *Hume Studies* 13 (1987): 381–99.

13 See the extended discussion in *"Of the antient philosophy"* (T 1.4.3, 219–25).

14 See, for example, A. J. Ayer, *Foundations of Empirical Knowledge* (London, 1949), pp. 166–84.

15 For an introduction to this controversy, see J. A. Robinson, "Hume's Two Definitions of 'Cause'," in *Hume*, ed. V. C. Chappell (New York, 1966).

16 Interestingly, the *Enquiry* does not stipulate spatial contiguity as a requirement for causal connection. Hume's motives for requiring contiguity probably reflect strictures of seventeenth-century science. See Kuypers, *Studies*, chaps. 1–4. The *Treatise* makes it clear that Hume requires a chain of contiguous causes and effects to link distant events said to be causally related: "Tho' distant objects may sometimes seem productive of each other, they are commonly found upon examination to be link'd by a chain of causes, which are contiguous among themselves, and to the distant objects; and when in any particular instance we cannot discover this connexion, we still presume it to exist. We may therefore consider the relation of CONTIGUITY as essential to that of causation" (T 1.3.2, 75). Note Hume's usual form of argument here, which relies on ordinary presumptions as an argument for this necessary condition for causation. See also the discussion of gravity later in this chapter.

17 Although Hume offers no specific argument against future causation, he provides an intricate one against simultaneous causation: " 'Tis an establish'd maxim both in natural and moral philosophy, that an object, which exists for any [not *some*] time in its full perfection without producing another, is not its sole cause . . . . Now if any cause may be perfectly co-temporary with its effect, 'tis certain, according to this maxim, that they must all of them be so [that is, all "sole" or "com-

plete" causes must be simultaneous]; since any one of them, which retards its operation for a single moment, exerts not itself at that very individual time, in which it might have operated; and therefore is no proper cause. The consequence of this wou'd be no less than the destruction of that succession of causes, which we observe in the world" (T 1.3.2, 76). The exegesis of this reductio argument remains a matter of controversy. See Tom Beauchamp and Alexander Rosenberg, *Hume and the Problem of Causation* (New York, 1981), pp. 192–200. It is worth noting that the special theory of relativity vindicates Hume's conclusion, if not his argument. There is a further twentieth-century controversy surrounding the question of whether Hume's account of causal directionality in terms of the temporary priority of causes can be accepted. For an introduction, see Beauchamp and Rosenberg, chap. 6.

18 An alternative, necessitarian reading of Hume's account is to be found in John P. Wright, *The Sceptical Realism of David Hume* (Manchester, 1983), and Galen Strawson, *The Secret Connection* (Oxford, 1989). Strawson's work is inspired by passages like the following: "An object may be contiguous and prior to another, without being consider'd as its cause. There is a NECESSARY CONNECTION to be taken into consideration; and that relation is of much greater importance, than any of the other two above-mention'd" (T 1.3.2, 77). In my view, this passage does not constitute an endorsement of Strawson's interpretation. The passage in question is a part of Hume's introduction to the problem of accounting for the common belief that necessary connections obtain between causes and effects. For a critical assessment of Strawson's interpretation, see Simon Blackburn, "Hume and Thick Connections," *Philosophy and Phenomenological Research* 50 (1991): 237–50.

19 *An Essay concerning Human Understanding*, 2.21, 233–87, and 2.26, 324–8.

20 See C. J. Ducasse, "On the Nature and the Observability of the Causal Relation"; and G. E. M. Anscombe, "Causation and Determination," in *Causes and Conditionals*, ed. Ernest Sosa (Oxford, 1975), pp. 63–81, 114–25.

21 As Edward Madden and Rom Harre argue in *Causal Powers* (Oxford, 1975).

22 "What Is a Law of Nature," in *The Concept of a Person* (London, 1963), p. 230. See also Ayer's *Probability and Evidence* (New York, 1972), chap. 1; and Frank Ramsey, *Collected Papers* (Cambridge, 1990), pp. 140–4.

23 See, for instance David Lewis, *Counterfactuals* (Cambridge, Mass., 1972), chap. 2; and "Causation" in *Causes and Conditions*, pp. 180–92.

24 For a discussion and qualified defence of heroic Humeanism, see Beau-

champ and Rosenberg, chaps. 1 and 4. For further discussion, see J. L. Mackie, *The Cement of the Universe* (Oxford, 1974), chap. 8.

25 For example, consider a deductive argument like the following:

   1. If the sun has risen in the past, it will rise in the future.
   2. The sun has risen in the past.
      therefore
   3. The sun will rise in the future.

This deductively valid argument remains unconvincing until its first premise is established. How can it be established? By another deductive argument from an equally controversial premise? This begins the regress. To infer that the sun will rise tomorrow or every day hereafter since it has done so indefinitely many times in the past, from the fact that this statement has been true in the past, is a form of circular reasoning: justifying inductive reasoning by an inductive argument.

26 Note, especially, rules 4 through 7, which prefigure Mill's methods of induction.

27 Norman Kemp Smith, *The Philosophy of David Hume* (London, 1941), p. 155.

28 Barry Stroud, *Hume* (London, 1977), p. 60.

29 See Beauchamp and Rosenberg, especially chap. 2.

30 David C. Stove, *Probability and Hume's Inductive Skepticism* (Oxford, 1973). See also Mackie, *The Cement of the Universe*, chap. 1.

31 For an excellent introduction to contemporary versions of the problem of induction, with due recognition of its Humean origins, see Wesley Salmon, *Foundations of Scientific Inference* (Pittsburgh, 1966).

32 Hume certainly inspired the "covering law" model of explanation, according to which particular events are explained by deduction from a statement of general laws and initial or boundary conditions, and laws are explained by their derivation from more general laws. For the classic discussion of "covering law" explanations, see Carl Hempel, *Aspects of Scientific Explanation* (New York, 1965), pp. 331–496. It is important to remember that Hume's account of explanation cannot be identified with the covering law model. Not the least of the reasons for distinguishing Hume's account is the fact that he would insist that scientific explanations be causal, a view that covering law theorists reject. Hume's insistence on this point preserves him from several objections to the covering law model.

33 For a discussion of this problem, see Hempel, "The Theoretician's Dilemma," in *Aspects of Scientific Explanation*.

34 Kemp Smith has argued convincingly that Hume's discussion of the nature of space and time follows and at the same time criticizes those of

the seventeenth-century sceptic Pierre Bayle, whose *Historical and Critical Dictionary* Hume knew well. See *The Philosophy of David Hume*, pp. 284–90. See also Robert J. Fogelin, *Hume's Skepticism in the Treatise of Human Nature* (London, 1985), pp. 25–7. The relevant texts of Bayle may be found in his *Historical and Critical Dictionary*, ed. and trans. Richard H. Popkin (Indianapolis, 1965).

35 For a discussion of some of these problems, see A. Flew, "Infinite Divisibility in Hume's *Treatise*," in *Hume: A Re-evaluation*, ed. Donald W. Livingston and James T. King (New York, 1976), pp. 257–69.

4 Hume's scepticism

By all that has been said the reader will easily perceive, that the philosophy contain'd in this book is very sceptical, and tends to give us a notion of the imperfections and narrow limits of human understanding. Almost all reasoning is there reduced to experience; and the belief, which attends experience, is explained to be nothing but a peculiar sentiment, or lively conception produced by habit. Nor is this all, when we believe any thing of *external* existence, or suppose an object to exist a moment after it is no longer perceived, this belief is nothing but a sentiment of the same kind. Our author insists upon several other sceptical topics; and upon the whole concludes, that we assent to our faculties, and employ our reason only because we cannot help it. Philosophy wou'd render us entirely *Pyrrhonian*, were not nature too strong for it.   (A, 657)

The above passage comes from a pamphlet written by David Hume to secure a readership for his largely unappreciated *Treatise of Human Nature*. Though not successful in this regard, the *Abstract* remains a valuable guide to Hume's *Treatise*, for it offers his own assessment of the significance of that work. Here, at least, Hume is unequivocal in describing his philosophy as "very sceptical." But even if Hume describes his philosophy in this way, and even if, at the time, his philosophy was almost universally taken in this light, it remains unclear, first, what this scepticism amounts to and, second, how this scepticism is related to other aspects of his philosophical program. The goal of this essay is to answer both of these questions. I begin by giving a broad sketch of the role of scepticism in Hume's philosophy and then, in succeeding sections, offer a detailed analysis of the central sceptical arguments.

I. SCEPTICISM AND BELIEF

One clue to the nature of Hume's scepticism is given in the sentence that immediately follows his claim that the philosophy found in the *Treatise* "is very sceptical, and tends to give us a notion of the imperfections and narrow limits of human understanding." "Almost all reasoning is there reduced to experience; and the belief, which attends experience, is explained to be nothing but a peculiar sentiment, or lively conception produced by habit." Now the reduction of all reasoning to experience (*empiricism*) does not, by itself, yield sceptical consequences, at least of the strong (Pyrrhonian) kind referred to at the end of the passage. Empiricism can lead to a mild version of scepticism if we insist (perhaps incorrectly) that knowledge must involve certainty and then further insist (perhaps incorrectly) that empirical claims that go beyond reports of immediate experience always fall short of certainty. Scepticism of this kind might better be called *fallibilism*, not scepticism. In fact, a thoroughgoing empiricist typically abandons claims to certainty over a wide range of cases where most people think they possess certainty, but traditional empiricists did not think that their position forced a wholesale suspension of belief. With an important exception to be noted later,[1] it is not Hume's empiricism but primarily his theory of belief that pushes his philosophy in the direction of extreme (or Pyrrhonian) scepticism.

The story, broadly sketched, is this: a central part of Hume's project of introducing the experimental method of reasoning into moral subjects involved giving a naturalistic account of how human beings come to believe certain things about the world that (they suppose) surrounds them. A single example will serve our purposes. As human beings, we naturally suppose that we are directly aware of a world that is independent of us and continues to exist when we are not aware of it. What is the source of this belief? It cannot be the result of sound argument, for, first, the great bulk of mankind is wholly unacquainted with any arguments on these matters. They believe, but do so in a total absence of justifying arguments.[2] Furthermore, those arguments intended to prove the existence of an enduring external world are easily shown to be irreparably no good. Thus, for Hume, the common belief in an external world is not based on any sort of reasoning to begin with and cannot be supported by sound reasoning after the fact. This is one side of Hume's scepticism.

A second side of Hume's scepticism emerges when he lays bare what he takes to be the mechanisms that do, in fact, govern the formation of beliefs on these matters. The wording in the passage from the *Abstract* is revelatory:

the belief, which attends experience, is explained to be nothing but a peculiar sentiment, or lively conception produced by habit. Nor is this all, when we believe any thing of *external* existence, or suppose an object to exist a moment after it is no longer perceived, this belief is nothing but a sentiment of the same kind.

Now, in describing a belief as *nothing but* a peculiar sentiment produced by habit, Hume is obviously contrasting his position with that of others who hold that there must be more to belief formation than this. That view, crudely put, is that belief is the result of reasoning, and sound beliefs are the result of sound reasoning. Over against this rationalist or Cartesian conception of belief formation, Hume holds that reasoning, by itself, is generally incapable of fixing belief and, in this particular case, incapable of establishing a belief in the existence of an external world.

These sceptical motifs are further developed by the details of Hume's explanation of how this fundamental belief is formed. Presented with Hume's causal account of the actual mechanisms that lead us to believe that we are aware of an independent external world, we are simply appalled that our beliefs should be formed on such an arbitrary basis. Furthermore, when this arbitrary basis for our fundamental beliefs is revealed to us, then, for a time at least, belief itself evaporates. In the *Enquiry concerning Human Understanding*, Hume describes scepticism generated in this way as follows:

There is another species of scepticism, *consequent* to science and enquiry, when men are supposed to have discovered, either the absolute fallaciousness of their mental faculties, or their unfitness to reach any fixed determination in all those curious subjects of speculation, about which they are commonly employed. Even our very senses are brought into dispute, by a certain species of philosophers; and the maxims of common life are subjected to the same doubt as the most profound principles or conclusions of metaphysics and theology.   (EHU 12.1, 150)[3]

From all this it appears that Hume's writings contain two sceptical strategies. The first we might call the *argumentative* strategy; the second the *genetic* strategy. When using the argumentative strategy, Hume adopts the common sceptical ploy of presenting arguments intended to show that some class of beliefs is not capable of rational justification. In this class, we find many of the enduring features of Hume's philosophy, the most important being his scepticism concerning induction,[4] his scepticism concerning the external world (T 1.4.2; EHU 12.2), and, more exotically, his scepticism with regard to reason (T 1.4.2). His criticism of the argument from design found in the *Dialogues concerning Natural Religion* and his examination of arguments involving miracles found in Section 10 of the *Enquiry* can also be placed in this category of argumentative scepticism.

What I have called Hume's *genetic* strategy reflects his idea of a scepticism that is consequent upon science and enquiry. A system of beliefs can be discredited by revealing its disreputable provenance. Thus, in his discussion of *"scepticism with regard to the senses,"* Hume offers a detailed account of the manner in which fictions are piled upon fictions in a way that leads us to adopt what he calls the "extraordinary opinion" that the objects of our awareness (which, for Hume, are perceptions) can enjoy a continued and distinct existence (T 1.4.2, 195). Here, then, is a double movement in the development of Hume's sceptical position. First, *reasoning* shows us that our belief in an external world is not based on sound argument, for no such sound argument on this matter exists, and, second, when *empirical investigation* lays bear the actual mechanisms that lead us to embrace this belief, we are immediately struck by their inadequacy.

This contrast between argument-based and genetic-based scepticism has another side. If, as is not true, our most general beliefs about the world rested on arguments, then sound sceptical arguments, once encountered, would deprive us of these beliefs. But this does not happen. Sceptical arguments may confound us for the moment, but lack lasting effects. Hume makes this point nicely in commenting on the nature and force of some of Berkeley's arguments: "But that all his arguments, though otherwise intended, are, in reality, merely sceptical, appears from this, *that they admit of no answer and produce no conviction.* Their only effect is to cause that momentary amazement and irresolution and confusion, which is the result of scepticism" (EHU 12.1, 155n).

I think that we can now understand why, on Hume's terms, sceptical arguments "produce no conviction." An examination of the actual mechanisms of belief formation shows that beliefs are rarely based on ratiocination. For this reason, a sceptical argument, even if correct, removes nothing that previously supported beliefs. It is more deeply disturbing to come face to face with the actual mechanisms that do generate beliefs, for then we cannot help being struck by their inadequacy. With these mechanisms explicitly displayed before us, we do, in fact, *find* ourselves in a state of radical doubt. But as our thoughts return to the common concerns of life, the authority of these normal mechanisms is restored, and we *find* ourselves believing largely as we had before we began our inquiries. This is our sole defence against radical scepticism, for philosophy, as Hume tells us in the *Abstract*, "wou'd render us entirely *Pyrrhonian*, were not nature too strong for it." The irony is that the ways of nature, when revealed, hardly fill us with confidence or with a sense of human dignity.

II. HUME'S INDUCTIVE SCEPTICISM

1. From his lifetime down to the present, no aspect of Hume's philosophy has attracted more attention than the things that he says about the related notions of causality, necessity, and induction. The limitations of the present essay preclude a close examination of his important ideas on necessity and causality,[5] but, broadly, for Hume, causality and inductive reasoning are related in the following way. In both the *Treatise* and the *Enquiry*, Hume argues that causal connections cannot be established by any form of *a priori* reasoning. Nor can a causal relationship be ascertained through immediate experience, for inspection of the cause reveals no connecting link between it and its effect. Simplifying, it is only our experience of a constant conjunction between two sorts of events that leads us to suppose that one is the cause of the other. We reach the problem of induction by raising the following question: How does the experience of events being consistently conjoined in the past license an inference to the claim that they will continue to be so conjoined in the future? This, as it turns out, raises a question that proves very difficult to answer.

In Hume's words: "But if we still carry on our sifting humour, and ask, *What is the foundation of all conclusions from experience?* this implies a new question, which may be of more difficult solution and explication" (EHU 4.2, 32).

Hume poses his difficult question three times – first in the *Treatise*, then in the *Abstract*, and finally in the *Enquiry* – and though there are important differences in detail, the basic move is the same in each. Our reliance on past experience rests, he tells us, on the principle "*that instances, of which we have had no experience, must resemble those, of which we have had experience,*" and, with respect to the future, this amounts to the assumption there will not be "a change in the course of nature." On what basis, Hume asks, can we justify this assumption? His claim – and this is his core thesis – is that no argument can justify this assumption. There can be no demonstrative argument to prove it, for it is at least conceivable that the course of nature might change: what is conceivable is possible; what is possible cannot be demonstrated to be false; therefore, it cannot be demonstrated that the course of nature will not change. (T 1.3.6, 89)

For Hume, the only alternative to demonstrative reasoning is reasoning involving probability. In the *Treatise*, Hume dismisses this alternative quickly, and somewhat obscurely:

probability is founded on the presumption of a resemblance betwixt those objects, of which we have had experience, and those, of which we have had none; and therefore 'tis impossible this presumption can arise from probability. The same principle cannot be both the cause and effect of another; and this is, perhaps, the only proposition concerning that relation, which is either intuitively or demonstratively certain.   (T 1.3.6, 90)

By *probability* (as opposed to *demonstration*), Hume seems to mean any form of inductive reasoning based upon past experience. His basic point, which he puts rather quaintly, is that such reasoning itself presupposes that the course of nature will not change, and thus cannot be used, without circularity, to prove it. Hume makes this point more clearly in the *Abstract*, where he tells us that it is not possible to "prove by any *probable* arguments, that the future must be conformable to the past. All probable arguments are built on the supposition, that there is this conformity betwixt the future and the past, and therefore can never prove it" (A, 651). Given that neither demonstra-

tive nor probable arguments can prove that the future must be conformable to the past, it seems that nothing could prove this.[6]

Hume's basic argument for inductive scepticism gets its most
elaborate statement in the *Enquiry*. In the *Abstract*, he brought the
core argument into sharp focus; in the *Enquiry* he made it a center-
piece of his philosophy. The argument in the *Enquiry* has the same
underlying structure as those in the *Treatise* and the *Abstract*, but it
employs an essentially new argumentative device: the distinction
between *relations of ideas* and *matters of fact* for argumentative
purposes.[7] Presented with any claim on any subject, we can always
ask: Can this claim be established as a relation of ideas? If not, can it
be established as a matter of fact? If its truth can be established in
neither way, then its truth cannot be established at all. Antony Flew
calls this argumentative device *Hume's Fork*.[8]

Unfortunately, Hume's distinction between relations of ideas and
matters of fact raises problems of its own. First, the distinction is
hastily, and perhaps incoherently, drawn. Second, by resting his argument on this distinction, Hume opens himself to serious objections
concerning the distinction itself, objections that do not bear directly
upon the problem of induction. I will take up these points one at a
time.

Hume introduces his distinction between relations of ideas and
matters of fact as follows:

All the objects of human reason or enquiry may naturally be divided into
two kinds, to wit, *Relations of Ideas*, and *Matters of Fact*. Of the first kind
are the sciences of Geometry, Algebra, and Arithmetic; and in short, every
affirmation, which is either intuitively or demonstratively certain. . . .
Propositions of this kind are discoverable by the mere operation of thought,
without dependence on what is anywhere existent in the universe. . . .

Matters of fact, which are the second objects of human reason, are not
ascertained in the same manner; nor is our evidence of their truth, however
great, of a like nature with the foregoing. The contrary of every matter of
fact is still possible; because it can never imply a contradiction, and is
conceived by the mind with the same facility and distinctness, as if ever so
conformable to reality.   (EHU 4.1, 25)

Though it is not spelled out fully, in this passage Hume divides
relations of ideas and matters of fact along *two* lines: one logical, the
other epistemological. His criterion for a relation of ideas is epistemological. That is, the criterion is drawn in terms of how we come

to know such relations: "Propositions of this kind are discoverable by the mere operation of thought." Thus, statements expressing relations of ideas can be known to be true *a priori*.[9] In contrast, Hume's criterion for a matter of fact is both epistemological and logical. First, matters of fact differ epistemically from relations of ideas in that they "are not ascertained in the same manner"; that is, they are not ascertained by the mere operations of thought. Second, they differ logically from relations of ideas, in that "the contrary of every matter of fact is still possible; because it can never imply a contradiction."

Now, given Hume's initial claim that "all the objects of human reason or enquiry may naturally be divided into two kinds," his use of dual criteria for distinguishing relations of ideas from matters of fact has the following consequence: no proposition that is not a relation of ideas can be known to be true *a priori*. Thus, in the guise of merely classifying the "objects of human reason or enquiry," Hume has embraced a strong thesis without offering any argument in its behalf.

Furthermore, by basing his argument on the distinction between relations of ideas and matters of fact, Hume has opened himself to criticisms that have nothing to do with the issue at hand, namely, the problem of induction. In particular, propositions exist that seem not to fit into either of Hume's categories, for example, that the west wall of a building cannot be simultaneously both entirely white and entirely green. Of course, if propositions exist which cannot be accommodated within Hume's classification, then that classification is no longer exhaustive and the argumentative strategy known as Hume's Fork fails. It seems, then, that before we can evaluate the argument in the *Enquiry* in behalf of inductive scepticism, we will have to enter into a more general investigation of the kinds of propositions that exist and the methods of justification appropriate to them. This is an excursion from which we might never return.

Perhaps there is a shorter route back to Hume's original concern with inductive scepticism. The drawing of a distinction between relations of ideas and matters of fact can be viewed as the argumentative counterpart of a tactic used in both the *Treatise* and in the *Abstract*, namely, that of holding (or just assuming) that all arguments fall into two distinct categories: demonstrative and probable. Hume, of course, can be challenged on just this point. But we can get back to the center of Hume's argument if we recall that he was interested in the possibility of an argument establishing the truth of quite a specific claim, namely, that *the future must be conformable to the past*. On its face, this seems to be a substantive claim about how the future will unfold and thus not something susceptible to any form of *a priori* justification.[10] Furthermore, the second part of Hume's argument seems persuasive as well: any attempted inductive justification of this claim will be question begging.

Elsewhere, I have claimed that Hume put forward what I called a *no-argument argument* concerning induction, namely, an argument intended to show that no argument could possibly justify the claim that the future will be conformable to the past.[11] The text, I believe, clearly shows that this was his intention. It now also seems clear to me that Hume's no-argument argument fails. In both the *Treatise/Abstract* version and in the *Enquiry* version, an important step is missing. In the early version, we need a proof showing that all arguments may be divided into demonstrative arguments and probable arguments in the sense in which Hume describes them. In the later version, we need a proof showing that "all the objects of human reason or enquiry may naturally be divided into two kinds, to wit, *Relations of Ideas*, and *Matters of Fact*." In fact, Hume seems to face a more difficult problem with the *Enquiry* version of his argument than with the earlier versions, for there seem to be a number of clear examples of propositions that fall into neither of his two categories. But perhaps a related complaint might be made against the *Treatise/Abstract* version of the argument, namely, that there are legitimate modes of argumentation that Hume has not considered. Again, because Hume has not eliminated this possibility, his argument fails as a no-argument argument.

2. In the first part of this essay I indicated that Hume's scepticism had two chief sources, one based on arguments, the other based on accounts of how human beings actually form beliefs. The second theme will play a central role in the discussion of Hume's scepticism with regard to reason and his scepticism with regard to the senses, but his account of how we actually come to project past regularities into the future has sceptical consequences as well. As we shall see, however, these are not as dramatic as those found in his discussion of reason and the senses.

In the *Treatise*, Hume's sceptical argument concerning induction is embedded in a psychological account of the component parts of our reasoning concerning causes and effects.[12] In the *Enquiry*, the two discussions are neatly partitioned into two successive sections. Section 4 of the *Enquiry* is entitled "Sceptical Doubts concerning the Operations of the Understanding." Its intended results are essentially negative: no argument can justify inference from past to future experience. Section 5 has the curious title "Sceptical Solution of these Doubts." The following passage gives some idea of what Hume has in mind in speaking of a "sceptical" solution:

> If the mind be not engaged by argument to make this step, it must be induced by some other principle of equal weight and authority; and that principle will preserve its influence as long as human nature remains the same. What that principle is may well be worth the pains of enquiry.
>
> (EHU 5.1, 41–2)

Presumably, a non-sceptical solution to the doubts raised in Section 4 would be some sort of argument that would justify the step in question. In that sense of *solution*, a *sceptical solution* is no solution at all; instead, it is a mere description of the mechanisms that lead the mind to operate as it does. The description of these mechanisms will not resolve sceptical doubts, and, to the extent that their operations strike us as arbitrary, our sceptical doubt may be heightened by their discovery.

What principle leads us to make this transition to a belief in a matter of fact beyond the present testimony of the senses given that no argument can vindicate it?

> This principle is Custom or Habit. For wherever the repetition of any particular act or operation produces a propensity to renew the same act or operation, without being impelled by any reasoning or process of the understanding, we always say, that this propensity is the effect of *Custom*.

More specifically, after experiencing "the constant conjunction of two objects – heat and flame, for instance, weight and solidity – we are determined by custom alone to expect the one from the appearance of the other (EHU 5.1, 43).[13]

A recognition that all our inferences beyond present or past experience derive from this source may or may not make us more sceptical concerning them, but this discovery, at the very least, deflates our intellectual pretensions by revealing that some of our most important modes of inference are made in the complete absence of rational insight.

> As nature has taught us the use of our limbs, without giving us the knowledge of the muscles and nerves, by which they are actuated; so has she implanted in us an instinct, which carries forward the thought in a correspondent course to that which she has established among external objects; though we are ignorant of those powers and forces, on which this regular course and succession of objects totally depends.   (EHU 5.2, 55)

We are so constructed that under certain circumstances our minds irresistibly make transitions from one idea to another. In this regard we do not differ in any essential way from animals, who also learn from experience and who also do so without any comprehension of the underlying mechanisms that bring this about – a point that Hume dwells upon in both the *Treatise* and the *Enquiry* (T 1.3.14; EHU 9).

Hume gives the argument a nice turn by commenting upon the wonder we feel concerning the complex instinctual endowment possessed by animals:

> But our wonder will, perhaps, cease or diminish, when we consider, that the experimental reasoning itself, which we possess in common with beasts, and on which the whole conduct of life depends, is nothing but a species of instinct or mechanical power, that acts in us unknown to ourselves; and in its chief operations, is not directed by any such relations or comparisons of ideas, as are the proper objects of our intellectual faculties.
> (EHU 9, 108)

We can think of scepticism as a set of arguments intended to undercut claims for knowledge or even rational belief. Section 4, with its sceptical doubts concerning the human understanding, illustrates this first strategy. We can also think of the central aim of scepticism as an attempt to destroy the pretensions of reason. Section 5, with its sceptical – as opposed to rational – solution to these doubts, illustrates this second strategy.

III. HUME'S SCEPTICISM WITH REGARD TO REASON

1. The target of Hume's scepticism is not simply the writings of philosophers, but the faculties of the mind that generate these

writings. Hume does, of course, discuss the philosophical positions of others, and allusions to other philosophical standpoints occur throughout his writings, but, more often than not, such references are made in the service of developing his science of man. Bad, even nonsensical, philosophical arguments are revelatory of the underlying faculties that generate them.[14]

Although Hume is not careful in his use of terminology, the first book of the *Treatise* is largely concerned with four faculties: understanding, reason, the senses, and the imagination. By the understanding, Hume usually has in mind reasoning from experience, notably, causal reasoning. By reason, Hume usually has in mind demonstrative and intuitive reasoning.[15] By the senses, Hume has in mind that faculty which (seemingly) gives us information about a surrounding world. By the imagination, Hume has in mind a faculty that generates new ideas from old by means of principles of association. Hume's general strategy is to argue that the operations of the first three faculties are ultimately grounded in the operations of the fourth: the imagination or, as he sometimes calls it, the fancy. Hume's standard strategy in furthering this project is to produce sceptical arguments intended to show that beliefs generated by the first three faculties cannot be grounded in any form of ratiocination. He then attempts to show how they are generated by the instinctive mechanisms of the imagination.[16] We have already seen this double strategy at work in Hume's treatment of our reasoning from past experience, but it is most striking in the section of the *Treatise* entitled "*Of scepticism with regard to reason*" (T 1.4.1).

Hume's scepticism with regard to reason has not fared well. Most writers on Hume say little or nothing about it. Hume did not repeat it in his later writings. This almost universal neglect probably springs from one of two sources: (a) a belief that the basic sceptical argument is no good, or (b) a revulsion against the total scepticism that it would entail if it were correct. However this may be, it is clear in the *Treatise* that Hume accepted the sceptical argument he put forward and explicitly embraced the radical sceptical consequences it entailed.

Hume's overall argument depends upon two sub-arguments that I call the *regression argument* and the *diminution argument*. That argument, presented largely in Hume's own words, has the following form:

The regression argument

a. In every judgment, which we can form concerning probability, as well as concerning knowledge, we ought always to correct the first judgment, deriv'd from the nature of the object, by another judgment, deriv'd from the nature of the understanding.

b. As demonstration is subject to the controul of probability, so is probability liable to a new correction by a reflex act of the mind, wherein the nature of our understanding, and our reasoning from the first probability become our objects.   (T 1.4.1, 181–2)

The diminution argument

a. Having thus found in every probability, beside the original uncertainty inherent in the subject, a new uncertainty deriv'd from the weakness of that faculty, which judges, and having adjusted these two together, we are oblig'd by our reason to add a new doubt deriv'd from the possibility of error in the estimation we make of the truth and fidelity of our faculties.

b. No finite object can subsist under a decrease repeated *in infinitum;* and even the vastest quantity, which can enter into human imagination, must in this manner be reduc'd to nothing.

c. [Thus,] all the rules of logic require a continual diminution, and at last a total extinction of belief and evidence.   (T 1.4.1, 182–3)

I have called the first step the *regression argument* because it tells us that in our judgements we must not only attend to the object under consideration, but we must also *step back* and ask the prior question whether – or to what extent – those procedures we use in dealing with the object are reliable. For example, that someone has been very careful in casting a horoscope should not lead us to trust his predictions until we satisfy ourselves on the prior question whether horoscopes can be trusted. Similarly, Hume tells us that we should rely on our faculties only to the extent that they have shown themselves to be trustworthy.

We must, therefore, in every reasoning form a new judgment, as a check or controul on our first judgment or belief; and must enlarge our view to comprehend a kind of history of all the instances, wherein our understanding has deceiv'd us, compar'd with those, wherein its testimony was just and true.   (T 1.4.1, 180)

For Hume, all faculties are subject to this restraint, including reason – the source of demonstrative and intuitive knowledge. Even with reason, before trusting it, we must step back and ask how reliable it has proven to be. The upshot of this, Hume tells us, is that "all knowledge degenerates into probability; and this probability is greater or less, according to our experience of the veracity or deceitfulness of our understanding, and according to the simplicity or intricacy of the question" (T 1.4.1, 180). Hume is here probably wrong in saying that "knowledge *degenerates* into probability," for the fact that there may be some chance that a demonstrative argument is invalid does not change it into a different kind of argument.[17] But for Hume's purposes, it might be sufficient to hold that every claim for knowledge inevitably *leads us* to a prior claim concerning probability that must be answered before we assess the knowledge claim.

Part (b) of the *regression argument* tells us that just as every knowledge claim must be checked by regressing to a probability claim, so, too, must every probability claim be checked against a further probability claim. This leads to an infinite regress of probability judgements concerning probability judgements, forming a stack of the following kind.

> . . . .
>
> . . . .
>
> (4) (3) has a probability of n_4.
> (3) (2) has a probability of n_3.
> (2) (1) has a probability of n_2.
> (1) $17 + 39 = 56$ has a probability of 1.

Here probability claims are being nested *inside* one another. What (4) says is

> that that that $17 + 39 = 56$ has the probability 1 has the probability n_2 has the probability n_3 has the probability n_4.

The human mind buckles under the complexity of such a proposition: a fact that Hume will exploit in offering what might be called his sceptical solution to the problem he here raises.

At this point, Hume could have moved directly to a traditional sceptical conclusion by pointing out that, as rational creatures, we are committed to an unstoppable regress of higher-order probability assessments. That, it would seem, would be sufficient for his purposes. Instead, he gives this traditional sceptical argument a turn of his own by arguing that with each ascent to a higher probability assessment, the base proposition $(17 + 39 = 56)$ loses some measure of its probability. Finally, since we must perform infinitely many such assessments – each diminishing the initial probability at least to some extent – Hume concludes that "all the rules of logic require a continual diminution, and at last a total extinction of belief and evidence" (T 1.4.1, 183).

This is not the place to examine the technical details of Hume's probabilistic arguments, but it is important to note both the breadth and the depth of Hume's sceptical conclusion.[18] With respect to breadth, Hume's scepticism seems nearly all-encompassing. His original target was demonstrative reasoning, but, having reduced demonstrative reasoning, as he thought, to probabilistic reasoning, he then applies the same argument to probabilistic reasoning, finally depriving us of all those things we believe on that basis as well. The only thing we may be left with as objects of belief are immediate reports of experience, and, perhaps, certain simple intuitive truths. This is not a mere fallibilism – a cautionary reminder that we lack certainty in areas where people commonly suppose we possess it. If Hume's argument is correct, we find ourselves in the deep scepticism traditionally associated with Pyrrhonism.[19]

When I reflect on the natural fallibility of my judgment, I have less confidence in my opinions, than when I only consider the objects concerning which I reason; and when I proceed still farther, to turn the scrutiny against every successive estimation I make of my faculties, all the rules of logic require a continual diminution, and at last a total extinction of belief and evidence.   (T 1.4.1, 183)

2. Yet for all of Hume's sceptical arguments, experience shows that this total extinction of belief does not take place. Of course, most people – indeed, most philosophers – have never heard of Hume's scepticism with regard to reason. Others, who have heard of it, hold that it is incorrect and are thus immune to its force. But Hume, who propounded the argument, thinks that it is irrefutable, yet continues to believe many things on many topics. How, on his own terms, is this possible? In response to this question, Hume offers what again amounts to a "sceptical solution" to his doubts: since rational mechanisms cannot sustain our beliefs, and, indeed, lead to their extinction, there must be non-rational mechanisms that do this for us.

I answer, that after the first and second decision; as the action of the mind becomes forc'd and unnatural, and the ideas faint and obscure; tho' the principles of judgment, and the ballancing of opposite causes be the same as at the very beginning; yet their influence on the imagination, and the vigour they add to, or diminish from the thought, is by no means equal. . . . The attention is on the stretch: The posture of the mind is uneasy; and the spirits being diverted from their natural course, are not govern'd in their movements by the same laws, at least not to the same degree, as when they flow in their usual channel.   (T 1.4.1, 185)

The sole reason that we are not total sceptics is that we lack the mental capacity to pursue our reflections to this, their predetermined, end. Toward the end of the concluding section of Book I, Hume puts the matter this way:

We save ourselves from this total scepticism only by means of that singular and seemingly trivial property of the fancy, by which we enter with difficulty into remote views of things, and are not able to accompany them with so sensible an impression, as we do those, which are more easy and natural.
                                                            (T 1.4.7, 268)

Thus, it is the weakness of the mind, not its strength, that saves reason from the sceptical destiny implicit in it.

IV. HUME'S SCEPTICISM WITH REGARD TO THE SENSES

1. Hume's examination of the senses begins with a comparison between the sceptical problem concerning reason and the sceptical problems concerning the senses:

Thus the sceptic still continues to reason and believe, even tho' he asserts, that he cannot defend his reason by reason; and by the same rule he must assent to the principle concerning the existence of body, tho' he cannot pretend by any arguments of philosophy to maintain its veracity.
                                                            (T 1.4.2, 187)

Hume holds that there are unanswerable sceptical arguments against the pretensions of both of these faculties, but his mode of exposition is different in the two cases. As we have just seen, in his discussion of scepticism with regard to reason, Hume begins by stating his sceptical argument and then, briefly, describes those non-rational mechanisms that preserve belief despite the existence of a contrary sceptical argument.[20] In his discussion of the senses, Hume reverses this order. He begins by merely alluding to a sceptical argument concerning the senses and then announces that his main task will be to examine "the *causes* which induce us to believe in the existence of body" (T 1.4.2, 187–8). What follows is a long, complex, and rather perplexing examination of those causal mechanisms that lead human beings to adopt the false belief that our inner perceptions can enjoy an existence distinct from our minds and can continue to exist even when unperceived. The standard sceptical argument concerning the external world appears only after this causal account of the common belief is completed.

The sceptical argument, when it does appear in the *Treatise*, has two parts. The first is intended to show that "our perceptions [those things, that is, of which we are aware] are not possest of any independent existence." Here Hume uses standard arguments from perceptual variability.

When we press one eye with a finger, we immediately perceive all the objects to become double, and one half of them to be remov'd from their common and natural position. But as we do not attribute a continu'd existence to both these perceptions, and as they are both of the same nature, we clearly perceive, that all our perceptions are dependent on our organs, and the disposition of our nerves and animal spirits.   (T 1.4.2, 210–11)

Convinced, perhaps wrongly, that we are only aware of our own private perceptions, the philosopher steps in and suggests that some of these perceptions are images or representations of external objects. This theory, sometimes called representational realism, holds that we are not directly aware of external objects, but we are aware of perceptions that serve as their representations. Here Hume speaks of "the opinion of a double existence and representation," a view he obviously associates with the philosophy of John Locke (T 1.4.2, 202).

The second step in Hume's sceptical argument is aimed at such double existence theories and is intended to show that no argument can establish the existence of external objects resembling our perceptions. In the *Treatise*, Hume states the basic argument in only a few sentences:

The only conclusion we can draw from the existence of one thing to that of another, is by means of the relation of cause and effect. . . . The idea of this relation is deriv'd from past experience, by which we find, that two beings are constantly conjoin'd together, and are always present at once to the mind. But as no beings are ever present to the mind but perceptions; it follows that we may observe a conjunction or a relation of cause and effect between different perceptions, but can never observe it between perceptions and objects. 'Tis impossible, therefore, that from the existence or any of the qualities of the former, we can ever form any conclusion concerning the existence of the latter, or ever satisfy our reason in this particular.

(T 1.4.2, 212)

The counterpart argument in the *Enquiry* is equally succinct.

It is a question of fact, whether the perceptions of the senses be produced by external objects, resembling them: how shall this question be determined? By experience surely; as all other questions of a like nature. But here experience is, and must be entirely silent. The mind has never anything present to it but the perceptions, and cannot possibly reach any experience of their connexion with objects. The supposition of such a connexion is, therefore, without any foundation in reasoning.   (EHU 12.1, 153)

Hume thought that this sceptical argument was completely unanswerable, telling us that "this is a topic, therefore, in which the profounder and more philosophical sceptics will always triumph, when they endeavour to introduce an universal doubt into all subjects of human knowledge and enquiry" (EHU 12.1, 153). It seems that sound reasoning leads us to abandon our naive belief in a direct awareness of an external world, and then further sound reasoning leads us to a scepticism that casts doubt on the very existence of such a world. For Hume, things get worse the more we reason.

There is another important side of the story that cannot be pursued in detail here. We have seen before that Hume's scepticism is strengthened by his account of the actual mechanisms that fix belief. In the *Treatise*, though not as much in the *Enquiry*, Hume emphasizes the sheer arbitrariness of the mental mechanisms that lead us to believe, quite falsely, that we are directly aware of an external world. The upshot of this move, combined with the sceptical argument that forecloses any help from the philosopher, is one of Hume's deepest expressions of scepticism:

Having thus given an account of all the systems both popular and philosophical, with regard to external existences, I cannot forbear giving vent to a certain sentiment, which arises upon reviewing those systems. I begun this subject with premising, that we ought to have an implicit faith in our senses, and that this wou'd be the conclusion, I shou'd draw from the whole of my reasoning. But to be ingenuous, I feel myself *at present* of a quite contrary sentiment, and am more inclin'd to repose no faith at all in my senses, or rather imagination, than to place in it such an implicit confidence. I cannot conceive how such trivial qualities of the fancy, conducted by such false suppositions, can ever lead to any solid and rational system.

(T 1.4.2, 217)

2. The literature on the so-called problem of the external world – on the questions, whether the external world exists and how one would prove that it does – is too large to summarize in any detail. Here there is only room to note that the form of Hume's argument suggests two possible strategies for responding to these questions. First, we can attempt to block the argument intended to show that we are only directly aware of our own perceptions and not directly aware of external objects; second, we can grant this much of the argument and then attempt to find some form of inference that will take us from beliefs concerning our private perceptions to well-founded beliefs concerning objects external to them. The first strategy was championed in Hume's day by Thomas Reid and in this century most notably by J. L. Austin; the second is the more traditional way of responding to scepticism concerning the external world.[21] Though tremendous effort has been expended on these matters, no consensus has emerged that either of these approaches is successful in meeting Hume's challenge.

V. THE WORDS OF PHILOSOPHERS

In the previous section we saw that Hume presented a sceptical challenge to those who held what he called a "double existence" theory of perception.[22] Hume cannot be credited with a great deal of originality in presenting this challenge, for here he is largely casting into his own vocabulary arguments found in the writing of George Berkeley.[23] But in this same context, Hume makes a move that seems to be entirely original and of great importance for understanding his attitude toward philosophical reflection.

According to Hume – and surely he was right in this – the theory of double existence (or representational realism) was introduced by philosophers as a replacement for the naively realistic view of perception held by the plain man. We have already seen that Hume rejected this replacement since it was subject – or so he thought – to a decisive sceptical refutation. Here Hume follows Berkeley. But Hume goes beyond Berkeley in making the following further criticism of double existence theories: "There are no principles either of the understanding or fancy, which lead us directly to embrace this opinion of the double existence of perceptions and objects, *nor can we arrive at it but by passing thro' the common hypothesis of the identity and continuance of our interrupted perceptions*" (T 1.4.2, 211, italics added). Hume's remarkable suggestion is that the theory of double existence is not simply the result of rational reflection, but is the *causal* product of competing forces operating in the mind.

> The imagination tells us, that our resembling perceptions have a continu'd and uninterrupted existence, and are not annihilated by their absence. Reflection tells us, that even our resembling perceptions are interrupted in their existence, and different from each other. The contradiction betwixt these opinions we elude by a new fiction, which is conformable to the hypotheses both of reflection and fancy, by ascribing these contrary qualities to different existences; the *interruption* to perceptions, and the *continuance* to objects.   (T 1.4.2, 215)

Thus, the double existence theory is not simply a rational replacement for the naive view; instead, it is a position that naturally presses itself on philosophers because the naive view still exerts a force upon them. The doctrine of double existence is not simply a hypothesis that philosophers conjure up; it is something they find themselves constrained to believe. Paradoxically, the source of this belief is the naive position they claim to have overcome.

> Nature is obstinate, and will not quit the field, however strongly attack'd by reason; and at the same time reason is so clear in the point, that there is no possibility of disguising her. Not being able to reconcile these two enemies, we endeavour to set ourselves at ease as much as possible, by successively granting to each whatever it demands, and by feigning a double existence, where each may find something, that has all the conditions it desires.
>
>   (T 1.4.2, 215)

Hume tells a similar story concerning the traditional idea of *substance*. Briefly, provided that the changes in an object are gradual, the easy transition from one perception of it to the next will lead us to believe that an object has remained the self-same thing even though it has undergone considerable alteration. "The smooth and uninterrupted progress of the thought . . . readily deceives the mind, and makes us ascribe an identity to the changeable succession of connected qualities." Yet a shift in perspective can lead us to the reverse opinion:

> But when we alter our method of considering the succession, and instead of traceing it gradually thro' the successive points of time, survey at once any two distinct periods of its duration, and compare the different conditions of the successive qualities; in that case the variations, which were insensible when they arose gradually, do now appear of consequence, and seem entirely to destroy the identity.   (T 1.4.3, 220)

So whether a changing object will seem to preserve its identity or lose it depends upon the perspective we take on it. Furthermore, since both perspectives are readily available and seem entirely natural, the mind, following its own principles, seems to be driven toward what Hume calls a contradiction. From one perspective, we are naturally inclined to ascribe identity to an object gradually changing over time; from another perspective, we are inclined to withdraw this ascription.[24]

Again, the mind seems to be at odds with itself, and again, it tries to extricate itself from this difficulty through the introduction of a fiction. "In order to reconcile [these] contradictions the imagination is apt to feign something unknown and invisible, which it supposes to continue the same under all these variations; and this unintelligible something it calls a *substance, or original and first matter*" (T 1.4.3, 220).

I do not think that Hume supposes that this fiction of substance, or original and first matter, is part of the ordinary person's conceptual apparatus. For Hume, ordinary human beings (the *vulgar*, in his eighteenth-century vocabulary) live blissfully innocent of the fact that the greater part of their beliefs is either false or unfounded. It is the philosophers who, having lost their innocence, stand in need of the notion of substance, or original and first matter. They need this notion precisely because they cannot fully stifle their natural inclination to suppose that changing objects preserve their identity over time, while yet holding that we are only aware of fleeting internal perceptions. The notion of substance is a surrogate for those lost beliefs of the vulgar.

This philosophical fiction of substance has a feature that ordinary fictions lack: strictly speaking, it is unintelligible. Examination reveals that the term *substance*, at least as employed by the philosopher, has no idea, either simple or complex, associated with it. All the same, if we press our enquiries far enough, at a certain stage we are naturally led to embrace this doctrine. "The whole system, therefore, is entirely incomprehensible, and yet is deriv'd from principles as natural as any of these above-explain'd" (T 1.4.3, 222).

But how can a system that is "entirely incomprehensible" become an object of belief? What would the object of such a belief be? Hume answers these questions in a passage that anticipates developments in twentieth-century linguistic philosophy. Since it has been neglected, it is worth citing in its entirety:

> But as nature seems to have observ'd a kind of justice and compensation in every thing, she has not neglected philosophers more than the rest of the creation; but has reserv'd them a consolation amid all their disappointments and afflictions. This consolation principally consists in their invention of the words *faculty* and *occult quality*. For it being usual, after the frequent use of terms, which are really significant and intelligible, to omit the idea, which we wou'd express by them, and to preserve only the custom, by which we recal the idea at pleasure; so it naturally happens, that after the frequent use of terms, which are wholly insignificant and unintelligible, we fancy them to be on the same footing with the precedent, and to have a secret meaning, which we might discover by reflection.   (T 1.4.3, 224)

Broadly speaking, this is Hume's assessment of man's intellectual condition: for the most part, the fundamental beliefs of ordinary persons are either false or unfounded. The philosophers' attempts to put something better in their place is "wholly insignificant or unintelligible."

VI. HUME'S SCEPTICISM

To what extent was Hume a sceptic? This question does not admit of a direct answer, for two reasons. First, describing a philosopher as a sceptic can mean a variety of things, and, depending upon what is meant, our assessment of Hume's scepticism can vary. Second, and more deeply, Hume's own philosophical position precludes any simple attribution of doctrines to him.

Concerning the first point, various things can be meant by describing a philosopher as a sceptic. Scepticism is often associated with doubt or with the suspension of belief. The Pyrrhonists, at least as Hume understood them, recommended something close to a total suspension of belief.[25] Clearly, Hume did not recommend a wholesale suspension of belief, for he held, first, that it would be disastrous to human life, and, second, that it is not something we are capable of achieving. We are naturally determined – hardwired, as it were – to form certain beliefs in certain circumstances. If scepticism is equated with Pyrrhonism (as Hume understood it), then Hume was not a sceptic – but he at several places says that he is a sceptic.[26]

Scepticism can also be understood as a critique of the capacities of our intellectual faculties. Taken this way, Hume is a radical, unreserved, unmitigated sceptic. The doctrine of the *Treatise* is that our rational faculties, left to themselves, are wholly destructive of belief: "sceptical doubt arises naturally from a profound and intense reflection on those subjects, it always encreases, the farther we carry our reflections, whether in opposition or conformity to it" (T 1.4.2, 218). As we have seen, Hume supports this claim in two ways: by producing what he takes to be irrefutable sceptical arguments and through displaying the arbitrariness of our actual, non-rational modes of belief formation. His fundamental idea is that we are saved from total scepticism only because the non-rational aspects of our nature overwhelm the doubts that reason attempts to force upon us, but we must not lose sight of the fact, as some have, that this is a sceptical conclusion.

The second, deeper, reason it is difficult to decide whether, or to what extent, Hume was a sceptic is that his own account of belief formation precludes simple ascriptions of beliefs. On his own theory, a person's beliefs, including a philosopher's beliefs, will be a function of the level of inquiry at which they are formed. This applies to Hume's expression of his own beliefs, even in his theoretical writing. In these writings he often expresses himself in a manner that suggests that he accepts a completely naive notion of perception. There are passages that suggest a commitment to a causal theory of perception – what Hume called a "double existence" theory. There are also passages intended to show the inadequacies of both these positions. Finally, there are passages that reflect a near-Pyrrhonian despair of basing any belief upon the senses. Which is the real Hume? The most appropriate answer on Hume's own terms is that his writings simply exhibit "that propensity, which inclines us to be positive and certain in *particular points*, according to the light, in which we survey them in any *particular instant*" (T 1.4.7, 273). This radical perspectivalism had historical precedents – perhaps in Protagoras, certainly in Sextus Empiricus – but Hume was one of a few philosophers to understand it and trace out its implications.

In the closing section of the *Enquiry*, Hume recommends a moderate or mitigated scepticism as a middle way between naive acceptance and Pyrrhonism. This may suggest that he was a sensible fellow after all. His scepticism might be nothing more than a version of fallibilism, the appropriately cautious attitude of a hard-working social scientist attempting to "introduce the experimental method of reasoning into moral subjects." This reading diminishes Hume's genius. His own account of how one arrives at a moderate or mitigated scepticism is of a piece with his account of how other philosophical positions emerge: they come into existence because of a clash between brute irresistible common beliefs and philosophical reflection that shows these beliefs to be groundless.

[A] species of *mitigated* scepticism which may be of advantage to mankind, and which may be the natural result of the Pyrrhonian doubts and scruples, is the limitation of our enquiries to such subjects as are best adapted to the narrow capacity of human understanding. The *imagination* of man is naturally sublime, delighted with whatever is remote and extraordinary.... A correct *Judgement* observes a contrary method, and avoiding all distant and high enquiries, confines itself to common life, and to such subjects as fall under daily practice and experience.... To bring us to so salutary a determination, nothing can be more serviceable, than to be once thoroughly convinced of the force of the Pyrrhonian doubt, and of the impossibility, that anything, but the strong power of natural instinct, could free us from it.

(EHU 12.3, 162)

Like other philosophical positions, mitigated scepticism is the product of a conflict between philosophical doubts and instinctual beliefs. Here, as in other cases where philosophy and instinct clash, it is instinct, not philosophical reflection, that maintains belief.

NOTES

1 This occurs in his scepticism concerning the senses, discussed in Part IV of this essay.

2 Hume makes this point explicitly: "And indeed, whatever convincing arguments philosophers may fancy they can produce to establish the belief of objects independent of the mind, 'tis obvious these arguments are known but to very few, and that 'tis not by them, that children, peasants, and the greatest part of mankind are induc'd to attribute objects to some impressions, and deny them to others" (T 1.4.2, 193).

3 Hume's *Enquiry concerning the Principles of Morals* is not discussed in this essay, although its opening two sections do discuss sceptical motifs. I discuss Hume's ethical scepticism in *Hume's Skepticism in the* Treatise of Human Nature (London, 1985). There are excellent discussions of Hume's ethical scepticism in J. L. Mackie, *Ethics: Inventing Right and Wrong* (Harmondsworth, 1977) and *Hume's Moral Theory* (London, 1980); and David Fate Norton, *David Hume: Common-Sense Moralist, Sceptical Metaphysician* (Princeton, 1982). Useful commentary may be found in Jonathan Harrison, *Hume's Moral Epistemology* (Oxford, 1976).

4 This is at least foreshadowed in *Treatise* 1.3, then stated explicitly in the *Abstract*, and in Section 4 of the *Enquiry*.

5 My *Hume's Skepticism*, chap. 4, provides a detailed discussion of Hume's treatment of the interrelated notions of causality, necessity, and induction. Detailed examinations of Hume's definition of causality can be found in Tom L. Beauchamp and Alexander Rosenberg, *Hume and the Problem of Causation* (New York, 1981); and in J. L. Mackie, "Causes and Conditions," *American Philosophical Quarterly* 2 (1965): 245–64, and *The Cement of the Universe* (Oxford, 1974).

6 Janet Broughton has argued that the *Treatise* does not contain a sceptical argument concerning induction, but that Hume is simply arguing that it is past experience plus the imagination, rather than past experience plus reason, that cause us to project past regularities into the future. ("Hume's Skepticism about Causal Inferences," *Pacific Philosophical Quarterly* 64 [1983]: 3–18). I think that Broughton is right in identifying this contest between the faculties of imagination and reason as the major theme of *Treatise* 1.3. I think she is also right to say that the examination of the causes of our causal reasoning is the central theme of *Treatise* 1.3.6. All the same, it seems to me that part of Hume's attack against the claims of reason is that reason cannot account for our tendency to project past regularities into the future simply because no argument derived from reason can justify such projections. Hume's scepticism concerning induction is present in the *Treatise*, but deeply embedded in a larger program. In contrast, in both the *Abstract* and the *Enquiry concerning Human Understanding*, this argument is given prominence as a free-standing philosophical move.

7 The distinction between relations of ideas and matters of fact appears in

the *Treatise* as well, but its use as a dialectical weapon emerges clearly only in the *Enquiry*.

8 Antony Flew, *Hume's Philosophy of Belief* (London, 1961), p. 53.

9 In passing, we can note that Hume seems to forget that the *falsehood* of certain propositions can also be discoverable by the mere operation of thought. As a result, if we take Hume's statement literally, it seems that he would have to classify a proposition like 2 + 2 = 5 as a matter of fact. A similar confusion occurs in Kant's classification of judgements in the Introduction to his *Critique of Pure Reason*.

10 Barry Stroud emphasizes this point, for, among other things, it helps to clear Hume of the charge of being a deductive chauvinist, that is, of holding or assuming that the only form of proof is a sound deductive argument. See his *Hume* (London, 1977), pp. 56ff.

11 See my *Hume's Scepticism*, chap. 4 and Appendix A.

12 This discussion stretches over 1.3.4–14. The sceptical argument appears (or at least is adumbrated) in 1.3.6.

13 Hume seems to have forgotten liquid mercury.

14 This is the central theme of Part V of this essay.

15 In a number of places Hume does not honour this contrast between reason and understanding, but this, at least, is his general tendency.

16 For more details on this, see my *Hume's Scepticism*, chap. 5, "Scepticism and the Triumph of the Imagination." This same theme is developed by Annette Baier, *A Progress of the Sentiments: Reflections on Hume's Treatise* (Cambridge, Mass., 1991).

17 The expression "invalid demonstrative argument" is not a solecism.

18 For more on this, including references to others who have discussed this topic, see my *Hume's Scepticism*, chap. 2; and Ian Hacking, "Hume's Species of Probability," *Philosophical Studies* 33 (1978): 21–37.

19 A good introduction to the effects of Pyrrhonism on early modern philosophy is Richard H. Popkin, *The History of Scepticism from Erasmus to Spinoza* (Berkeley, 1979) and *The High Road to Pyrrhonism* (San Diego, 1980). For a helpful introduction to the character of ancient Pyrrhonism, see Myles Burnyeat, "Can the Sceptic Live His Scepticism," in *Doubt and Dogmatism*, ed. M. Schofield, M. Burnyeat, and J. Barnes (Oxford, 1980).

20 Later, in the *Enquiry*, Hume adopted this same order of exposition in discussing inductive inference.

21 See "Essay I" in Thomas Reid, *Essays on the Intellectual Powers of Man* (Edinburgh, 1785); and J. L. Austin, *Sense and Sensibilia* (Oxford, 1963). Among Hume's predecessors, Locke and Descartes attempted the second strategy. In this century it has been adopted by many philosophers, including Bertrand Russell in *Problems of Philosophy* (Oxford, 1912).

22 Much of what is said in this section is stated in more detail in my
   Hume's Scepticism, chap. 7, "Hume's Natural History of Philosophy."
23 See, for example, Berkeley's *Principles of Human Knowledge*, secs. 9–
   15, and the first dialogue of *Three Dialogues between Hylas and
   Philonous. Treatise* 1.4.4, "*Of the modern philosophy*," in which Hume
   derives sceptical consequences from the distinction between primary
   and secondary qualities, also follows Berkeley, although Hume does not
   say so. On Berkeley and Hume, see David Raynor, "Hume and Berkeley's
   Three Dialogues, in *Studies in the Philosophy of the Scottish Enlightenment*, ed. M. A. Stewart (Oxford, 1990), pp. 231–50.
24 Hume follows this discussion of the identity of an object over time with
   a parallel discussion of the simplicity or unity of an object at a given
   time (T 1.4.3, 221).
25 Hume's understanding of Pyrrhonism was probably historically inaccurate, but this is rather a complex topic, since scholars today disagree on
   the proper interpretation of Pyrrhonism. Discussions revealing the competing views on the nature of Pyrrhonism are to be found in Jonathan
   Barnes, "The Beliefs of a Pyrrhonist," in *Proceedings of the Cambridge
   Philosophical Society*, ed. E. J. Kenny and M. M. MacIntyre (Cambridge,
   1982); Myles Burnyeat, "Can the Sceptic Live His Scepticism"; and
   Michael Frede, "The Skeptic's Beliefs," in *Essays in Ancient Philosophy*
   (Minneapolis, 1987).
26 In addition to the several passages already cited, see, for example, the
   closing paragraph of *Treatise*, Book 1.

5 Hume's moral psychology

Within Hume's philosophical system and his account of human nature one finds a number of elements that are intimately related to his moral objectives. I refer, widely, to his moral objectives, rather than more restrictedly to his ethical theory, because his whole system has a moral thrust that can be discerned in many places where the immediate subject-matter is not ethical at all.

I. HUME AND HIS PHILOSOPHICAL SYSTEM

In 1927, A. E. Taylor concluded his Leslie Stephen Lecture *David Hume and the Miraculous* with a judgement of Hume's attitude to his philosophical work that has been held by many others:

What kind of response one makes to life will, no doubt, for better or worse, depend on the sort of man one is for good or bad. . . . But we can all make it our purpose that our philosophy, if we have one, shall be no mere affair of surface opinions, but the genuine expression of a whole personality. Because I can never feel that Hume's own philosophy was that, I have to own to a haunting uncertainty whether Hume was really a great philosopher, or only a "very clever man."[1]

Taylor is here expressing an attitude toward Hume that many of us have felt: that his philosophy does not deserve to be taken too much to heart, because for all his intellectual vitality and the disturbing character of much that he says, there is a streak of frivolity in him that leads him to follow arguments to outrageous conclusions without serious consideration of the effect such conclusions may have on those who are driven to them; and that the love of literary reputation that he openly expressed, was of far greater personal importance to him than philosophical truth.

This estimate of Hume is a deeply mistaken one, and it involves a misconstruction of elements in his writings and his personality that have a very different explanation.

There is no doubt that Hume writes with a lightness of touch, an ironic humor, and a degree of self-depreciation that are rare among great philosophers. He is not hard enough to read for a judgement of greatness to come readily to our minds, in fact. He is also able to deal with the issue immediately before him without labouring its connections with those other parts of his system not presently being considered; and this, too, to readers in an era when system-building is unfashionable, makes it harder to suppose he is trying to construct one in the way great philosophers do. And no thinker who is so frequently successful in the art of philosophical criticism can escape the charge of caring first and foremost about scoring points. Such features are most easily explained as the result of a temperamental immunity to philosophical anxieties.

But the evidence is clearly against this explanation, and another is called for. The lightness is deliberately assumed for philosophical reasons by someone who is not immune to philosophical anxieties but knows very well, and says, what it is like to be their victim. There are two well-known places where he tells us about this. One, not originally destined for our eyes, is the letter he wrote to an unnamed physician in 1734, did not (it seems) send, but preserved (KHL). In this letter he outlines, with remarkable acuity, the symptoms of breakdown that he had suffered as a result of his philosophical exertions in the period prior to the composition of the *Treatise* – symptoms such as "scurvy spots" on the fingers, "wateriness in the mouth," and a compulsive appetite, which he interpreted as signs of the "disease of the learned." The other is the famous concluding section of Book 1 of the *Treatise* itself, where he tells us of the effects that his researches have had upon him (T 1.4.7, 263–74). He fancies himself to be "some strange uncouth monster," to be "in the most deplorable condition imaginable, inviron'd with the deepest darkness, and utterly depriv'd of the use of every member and faculty." On both occasions, he seeks release from these anxieties, which are the dark underside of the intellectual exhilaration that so frequently bursts through in the text of the *Treatise*; and this release is something he thinks to be available to him only if he makes himself balance the excesses of his philosophical reflections with deliberate absorption in business or social activities. These allow the resources of his nature to overcome the debilitating effects of over-indulgence in philosophical reasoning.

This clear evidence shows us that Hume was not someone for whom philosophy was an activity of minor consequence, but someone who saw himself as likely to be thrown off balance by his predilection for it. So the affable and corpulent gentlemanly loiterer (to use a phrase from Taylor)[2] whom some see as the historical Hume is, at most, a deliberately assumed *persona* beneath which a much more complex and serious reality is at work. The *persona* is not the duplicate of the reality, but a product of experience and theory: experience of what philosophy leads to when practised in a way that does violence to our nature, and a theory that puts philosophy in its proper place.

What sort of theory is it? Any theory that suggests limits be placed on philosophy itself has an appearance of inconsistency if it is itself a philosophical theory; and the fact that Hume belongs somewhere in the sceptical tradition might seem to accentuate this risk. To a large extent, Hume's theory of human nature is not, in our terms, philosophical, but psychological, even though one of its key purposes is to determine the proper limits of philosophical thought. He certainly thinks that philosophical activity, properly pursued, sustains personal equilibrium and can keep threats to it in check – as when it protects us from the far more dangerous risks that arise from superstition (T 1.4.7, 271–2). But to know when to pursue philosophy and when not, one has to understand human needs and weaknesses, and make philosophy take account of them. Hume does not *confuse* philosophy and psychology, as some suppose; but he does mix them, in a special blend of his own.

Hume, then, is a Socratic thinker. He believes that in order to avoid being plagued by anxiety we must achieve self-knowledge. The philosopher stands in need of it as much as his fellows do. Socrates would have agreed; but he did appear to think that self-knowledge was to come through the pursuit of the dialectical questioning in which the philosopher is expert, whereas Hume does not think this. Hume thinks that he has available a scientific mode of understanding that illuminates our nature for us, and that the philosopher must turn to this to save himself. Our nature is intelligible; and once we have learned its key features, we can avoid those influences in philosophy (and in religion) that would lead us to do violence to it. The understanding of human nature that Hume urges upon us is very different, indeed, from that deriving from Socrates, at least as Plato presents him to us.

II. HUMAN NATURE, THE SELF, AND THE PASSIONS

Hume confidently proclaims the importance of his theory of human nature in the introduction to the *Treatise*:

Here then is the only expedient, from which we can hope for success in our philosophical researches, to leave the tedious lingring method, which we have hitherto followed, and instead of taking now and then a castle or village on the frontier, to march up directly to the capital or center of these sciences, to human nature itself. . . . There is no question of importance, whose decision is not compriz'd in the science of man; and there is none, which can be decided with any certainty, before we become acquainted with that science. In pretending therefore to explain the principles of human nature, we in effect propose a compleat system of the sciences, built on a foundation almost entirely new, and the only one upon which they can stand with any security.   (T Intro, xvi)

This is ambitious language, fully comparable to Descartes's claim, a century earlier, to be rebuilding all knowledge afresh. But the bases the two thinkers offer for this rebuilding are very different. The differences help us to understand why Hume has always had the reputation of being a spoiler rather than a builder, in spite of the positive thrust of this programmatic proclamation.

In Descartes's reconstruction of human knowledge, the metaphysical separation of the mental and the physical dictates limits to science: science gets the autonomy that it deserves (and which the church had denied it in condemning Galileo) because it is confined in its subject-matter to the physical world; the mind is exempted from scientific scrutiny because of its simplicity, its freedom, and its self-consciousness. The essence of Hume's reconstruction is to be found in the insistence that there can, indeed, be a science of mind, and that it is "experimental," or observational. The scientific ideal Hume has is often described as Newtonian, and the evidence for this claim is his proclamation of the theory of the association of ideas.

This theory seems to duplicate Newtonian explanation in the physical realm. It does so by identifying, first, the ultimate corpuscular units that our observation of mental life reveals to us; Hume calls these *perceptions* and divides them into *impressions* and *ideas*. He then provides a principle roughly corresponding to that of gravitation to account for the constant inner movement and change that characterize the mental life we are able to introspect. This analogue to gravitation is *association*, which determines one perception to call up, or lead on to, another. In spite of a wise and cautionary statement that "we are only to regard it as a gentle force, which commonly prevails" (T 1.1.4, 10), the gravitational analogy is offered with pride, along with a similarly Newtonian reticence about what may lie beneath that gentle force:

Here is a kind of ATTRACTION, which in the mental world will be found to have as extraordinary effects as in the natural, and to shew itself in as many and as various forms. Its effects are every where conspicuous; but as to its causes, they are mostly unknown, and must be resolv'd into *original* qualities of human nature, which I pretend not to explain. (T 1.1.4, 12–13)

In the *Abstract,* his own anonymous puff of the *Treatise,* Hume says that if anything justifies calling "the author" an inventor, it is the use he makes of the principle of association.

Peter Jones has argued, persuasively, that the influence of Newton on Hume has been overrated, and that Hume's direct acquaintance with Newton's writings was probably limited.[3] This may be true. It may also be that the doctrine of association is less prominent in his later writings than it is in the *Treatise,* and that the *Treatise* itself, as we shall see, leans heavily on psychological theories that do not combine with it without difficulty. Nonetheless, I think that the impact of something like a Newtonian picture of the science of mind lingered in Hume's system long after the details of associationism ceased to interest him. There are two places where this can be seen most clearly. One is in his view of the self. The other is in his famous claim that reason is the slave of the passions. In both these places we find ourselves at the heart of his moral psychology.

To say there can be a science of the mental, as Hume sees the matter, is to say that what we think, feel, or will can be explained as the effect of a cause and the instance of a natural law. Human minds are not strangers in nature, but inextricably parts of it. Hume tries to demonstrate this in detail in the *Treatise* by showing how our beliefs and our emotive and conative commitments arise. The accounts are intended to treat thoughts and feelings and volitions (all *perceptions*, in his vocabulary) as the units of explanation, and to show how they give rise to one another. This form of explanation, at least nominally, gives the mind *itself* no role to play. If the never-ending changes in the physical world are all to be explained in terms of the attraction of material particles to one another, there is no room for the suggestion that the world itself, which merely *contains* them, exerts a force of its own. It is just the place where the events being described occur. Similarly, if the course of my mental history is determined by the associative attraction of my perceptions, so that they cause one another to arise, there seems no place, perhaps even no clear sense, to the suggestion that *I*, the mind or soul that *has* them, can exert any influence over their course. All the mind does is *include* them. The self, or ego, as he says, is just "a kind of theatre, where several perceptions successively make their appearance." The denial of an independent real self is not an awkward consequence of Hume's theory of knowledge, which requires us to say that it is not there because we cannot find it when we look for it (although this is true); it is a cornerstone of his system, required by the supposed fact of a science of man conceived in quasi-Newtonian terms. This science is deterministic, since mental events occur as a result of laws that supposedly govern the sequences of such events alone; and if they mention minds or agents themselves, these are construed to be mere bundles, collections, or sequences of such events. "They are the successive perceptions only, that constitute the mind; nor have we the most distant notion of the place, where these scenes are represented, or of the materials, of which it is compos'd" (T 1.4.6, 253).

This understanding of human nature stands in sharp contrast to another, which for convenience I shall call the rationalist model. This derives, historically, from Plato's *Phaedo*, in which Socrates is presented as teaching that the human soul is not part of nature but is alien to it. It can choose how far it allies itself with the alien forces of its present environment, and how far it asserts its independence from them. These alien forces make inroads upon it through the passions and desires, to which the soul can say yes or no. The implication of this understanding is that some of the elements of our inner life, namely, the passions and desires, are not truly parts of ourselves at all; what is to be identified with the true self is the reason that says yes or no to them.

This Platonic view of the soul has taken deep root in our culture in many popular, and sophisticated, doctrines that are not overtly ascribed to Plato. There is the common contrast between reason and the passions, a contrast that yields the assumption that when one acts from passion one acts *in passivity*, so that what one does is not fully an act at all, or that one is not fully oneself in doing it. There is the correlative assumption, philosophically expressed in modern times in the Cartesian tradition, that the self is to be equated with the rational faculty and that one is fully oneself only when this faculty dictates what one believes and what one chooses. Descartes indeed carried this to the extent of holding that one has full freedom whether to say yes or no, not only to the passions, but to the presentations of sense, so that we can always suspend judgement when grounds are inconclusive.[4] This theory is the epistemological aspect of the general view that the unique dignity of the human soul consists in its possession of a special kind of freedom to assent to, or to reject, the promptings of the senses, the emotions, and the instincts. We can readily wonder whether all the elements in this view of ourselves are necessarily connected, and even whether they are consistent, but they are all powerfully present in popular culture and rationalist philosophical theory.

Hume's understanding of human nature is at odds with this rationalist picture of it at every important point, and he sees all its main contentions as inconsistent with the very possibility of a science of man. So he assaults it in every possible way, and in assaulting it ensures that he acquires a destructive reputation among philosophers who feel the dignity of human nature and the dignity of their own profession are both linked to the truth of the rationalist picture. One way Hume assaults that picture is by making statements of high shock-value for those whose thinking is formed by it. The most famous of these is his dictum that "reason is, and ought only to be the slave of the passions, and can never pretend to any other office than to serve and obey them" (T 2.3.3, 415). This dictum is fundamentally an insistence that there can be a science of human nature in a way the rationalist picture would (in Hume's opinion) make impossible. It is, of course, more than this: it is also a claim that when we look and see, we shall find that human beings are creatures of instinct and feeling whose rational powers cannot, or at least should not, be used in any way at odds with these instincts and feelings.

Norman Kemp Smith and others have made it clear that Hume's theory of knowledge is itself an application of this claim about human nature.[5] Hume sees our most fundamental beliefs as products of instinct; and he thinks we are lucky that they are. The rational queries of the philosophical sceptic would have the effect, if the rationalist view of the mind were true, of reducing us to a condition of chronic anxiety and indecision through our inability to justify the claims of our senses or the expectation of regularity in nature or the identity of the self. The sceptic is quite right about what we cannot rationally justify, but he is also, fortunately, quite wrong about what we are able to disbelieve. His doubts are intellectually correct but are *vain* or impotent doubts. Hume is himself a sceptic in his estimate of the soundness of sceptical arguments but sides with the most truculent of the common-sense philosophers in denying that these arguments can disturb us for more than brief periods.[6] These brief periods, however, are anxious ones, to be avoided by distraction, social or intellectual. Hume rejects the contention of the sceptics of antiquity that the recognition of reason's inability to support the commitments of common sense leads of itself to inner peace. On the contrary, as he makes clear in the concluding section of Book 1 of the *Treatise*, such recognition would lead to despair if not overcome by the resources of instinct.

Hume does see our nature as creative: in generating our fundamental beliefs, it invests our perceptions with meaning. But it is instinct and not reason that does this.

Why is it that our instincts manage to invest our perceptions with meanings that are so useful and adaptive? Hume does not profess to know and contents himself with an ironical suggestion that there must be a pre-established harmony at work (EHU 5.2, 54). He never says the lifeworld our instincts create for us is one we know to be the true one.[7] His view of our beliefs is essentially a Darwinian view.

I turn now to a more detailed account of the way Hume's view of human nature underlies his account of our conduct and our morality, leaving aside his epistemology with the comment that, as Kemp Smith made clear to us, Hume's views on the interrelation between reason and passion run parallel in the two areas.

III. HUMAN CHOICE AND THE PASSIONS

Epistemology has never had much of a place in popular culture. But the rationalist understanding of human nature has a strong hold on the common understanding of our choices. We pride ourselves on the supposed fact that we are able sometimes to choose courses of action that override our passions and desires in the light of a greater good. We pride ourselves on the supposed fact that when we do this, we exercise the power to be free from the influences and temptations that would otherwise condemn us to what Kant called heteronomy. And we particularly pride ourselves on the supposed fact that we are able to pursue the austere demands of duty and so, by putting inclination aside, function as pillars of society.

Hume denies none of the experiences on which these popular self-estimates depend. We can, and do, choose the good over the attractive and resist many of the passions that agitate us. We are, indeed, entitled to talk of ourselves as acting freely on many such occasions – and also on those when we yield to passions, and choose the attractive rather than the good. And we do, indeed, choose many actions because they are our duty, even though they do not appeal to us, and our society depends for its health on the fact that we do this. But none of these familiar experiences is to be interpreted in the way rationalists interpret them. I shall take each of these three popular views in order, and try to show how Hume offers an alternative account of the relevant phenomena. I begin with those occasions when we pursue our good in the face of inclination.

The rationalist holds that when I do this, reason triumphs over passion. Hume's alternative account of this familiar experience depends upon his analysis of the passions, which he develops at length in the largely neglected second book of the *Treatise*.[8]

The two technical classifications that are essential for understanding Hume's analysis of conflict and choice are his distinctions between direct and indirect passions, and between calm and violent passions. Both distinctions are introduced in the first section of Book 2 (T 2.1.1, 276–7). Every passion is a unique, simple secondary impression. What makes it the passion it is, rather than some other, is therefore the felt quality it has. Questions about how it arises and how it leads to other experiences or to actions are construed by Hume as causal questions to be dealt with within his Newtonian mental science. In calling them secondary impressions, Hume seeks to distinguish them from the sensory impressions, which he calls "original" – a term indicating (here at least) that they do not occur in us in consequence of prior perceptions, as the secondary ones do. Passions, then, always arise in us from mental causes: sensory impressions, ideas, or other passions. When they arise from other passions, they do so by association. There is, therefore, an association of impressions (based on resemblance), as well as an association of ideas.

The distinction between direct and indirect passions is a distinction between two ways in which passions may arise. Direct passions "arise immediately from good or evil, from pain or pleasure," which seems to mean that they arise when something has given us pleasure or pain, or is believed to offer us the prospect of them (T 2.1.1, 276). This at least is what Hume says at the outset of Book 2; but when he discusses the direct passions in more detail later in the same book, he adds that some of them "frequently arise from a natural impulse or instinct, which is perfectly unaccountable," a remark that comes close to making them original after all (T 2.3.9, 439).[9] The indirect passions "proceed from the same principles, but by the conjunction of other qualities" (T 2.1.1, 276). This "conjunction" is described in much detail in parts 1 and 2 of Book 2; but the key element in it is the fact that the indirect passions require a distinction between their *causes* and their *objects*: between roughly the qualities that occasion them and the persons (that is, oneself or another or others) who have them.[10] The fundamental indirect passions are those of pride and humility (that is, shame), where the object is oneself, and love and hatred, where the object is another person or persons. In each case, the passion only arises when we are conscious not only of the quality that causes it, but of the fact that it is possessed by, or due to, the self or another – the "object, to which it is directed" (T 2.1.3, 280).

The direct passions are a very mixed group, indeed; but the critical fact about them for present purposes is that they not only include such reactive emotions as joy or grief or despair, but some of the most fundamental determinants of human conduct, namely, the *desires*. Hume not only includes desires for perceived objects like clothes, or for bodily satisfactions like food or sex, but mentions "the desire of punishment to our enemies, and of happiness to our friends" (T 2.3.9, 439), and even "the general appetite to good, and aversion to evil, consider'd merely as such" (T 2.3.3, 417). It does not seem particularly natural to write of desires as passions, unless they are agitating and overwhelming ones, but Hume's psychology depends on his being able to counter our resistance to his doing this. This he does by means of his important distinction between calm and violent passions. When introducing this distinction, Hume says that it is common for us to distinguish between gentle and intense emotions, and to use the word "passion" only of the latter, but he calls this a "vulgar and specious division" (T 2.1.1, 276). One and the same passion can be both mild and intense, though a given passion will usually be one or the other. It is critically important that when a passion has become "the predominant inclination of the soul, it commonly produces no longer any sensible agitation" (T 2.3.4, 419). We must therefore distinguish between the violence of a passion, which is a matter of its felt intensity, and its strength, which is a matter of its degree of influence on our choices and conduct. A passion can be strong but calm; and such a passion may overcome a more violent or agitating one. This is presumably what happens when we choose the good over the alluring – so that the aching longing for the dessert loses out to the wish to stay slim, which agitates not at all. So those occasions when we think our reason has won out over passion are actually cases in which a calm passion has shown more strength than a violent one.[11]

The doctrine of calm passions is Hume's main card in the game against rationalist psychology. Its main internal difficulty is the fact that it requires him to say that passions can be "in a manner, imperceptible," while classing them as impressions (T 2.1.1, 276), despite the fact that he has earlier distinguished impressions from ideas on the basis of their force and vivacity and has even used the very word "violence" in doing so (T 1.1.1, 1).

He supports his positive analysis of choice by some famous negative arguments against rationalism. They are to be found in *Treatise* 2.3.3, entitled "Of the influencing motives of the will." They are intended to show that "reason alone can never be a motive to any action of the will" and that "it can never oppose passion in the direction of the will" (T 2.3.3, 413). Hume argues for the first contention in two ways: he says that reason has two functions only, namely, the discovery of relations of ideas, as in mathematics, and the description of matters of fact, as in the empirical sciences and common life.[12] Reason in the former function has practical import only when calculation plays a role in empirical investigation; and in its empirical function reason can affect practice only by showing us the causes or effects of objects that we already desire or shun. In other words, it is our desires that prompt us to pursue or flee from the objects of our choice. Reason merely shows us what leads to, or away from, that in which our desires make us take interest. It is never itself the source of such interest.

If reason is thus shown to be incapable of originating our choices and inclinations, then on those occasions when we make choices in opposition to a passion, it cannot be reason that moves us: reason cannot provide the necessary contrary "impulse" itself. At most, reason can serve the several desires or aversions that are in conflict.

Hume tries to clinch these arguments by drawing on a fundamental feature of his theory of the passions: that they are secondary impressions, and not ideas. Only ideas, because they are copies, have "reference to any other object," whereas passions, as impressions, do not have any such "representative quality." They cannot, therefore, be "contradictory to truth and reason," since such contradiction entails a defect in that very representative quality. This self-containedness, or lack of reference, that supposedly characterizes all passions is a feature of them even when they are desires. Hume gives the example of anger, which on his view is a desire for harm to another (what we would call hostility). "When I am angry," he says, "I am actually possest with the passion, and in that emotion have no more a reference to any other object, than when I am thirsty, or sick, or more than five foot high" (T 2.3.3, 415).

As a consequence of this wildly implausible denial of the intentionality of passions and desires, Hume maintains that they cannot properly be called unreasonable. This term, though often applied to them, should, he says, be applied only to the judgements that *accompany* them. "In short, a passion must be accompany'd with some false judgment, in order to its being unreasonable; and even then 'tis not the passion, properly speaking, which is unreasonable, but the judgment." Hence, there is no unreasonableness in preferring "the destruction of the whole world to the scratching of my finger" or in choosing "my total ruin, to prevent the least uneasiness of an *Indian* or person wholly unknown to me," or to prefer my lesser good to my greater (T 2.3.3, 416). None of these preferences requires any false judgements and could only be unreasonable if they did.

If we put aside the attention-drawing rhetoric, we can see that Hume does not deny reason an essential role in human conduct. Reason shows us how to satisfy our desires, and in enabling us to recognize that which we then come to want, it can even prompt them, although he does not concede this explicitly. What reason cannot do is to motivate us of itself. It is the *slave* of the passions. But there are many things that we can do with the help of a slave that we could not do if we did not have one, and for all the air of paradox with which Hume pronounces his theories, he does not deny this.[13]

IV. FREEDOM

Hume believes that if there is to be a science of human nature, our actions and choices must show the same sorts of regularity that we find in the physical world. In tracing our choices to the workings of the passions, which arise in us through the mechanisms of association, he has tried to show that these regularities do indeed govern those choices. Such a program seems to imply a denial of the freedom that we think distinguishes us from other beings, and that is associated in rationalist theory with the assertion of the supposed authority of reason. Hume seeks to show that his human science can accommodate our freedom without exempting human choice from the regularity and predictability that he finds in our natures. Hence, his philosophical system contains the best-known classical statement of what is now known as *compatibilism*.[14]

Compatibilism is the thesis that there is no inconsistency in holding that human actions are caused and yet are free. This is a logical thesis, normally combined with the substantive claim that our actions always *are* caused, and that they are sometimes free as well. I shall use the title to comprise the combination of all three propositions. I shall use the common term *libertarianism* to name the view that it is indeed inconsistent to hold human actions can be free yet always caused; that some of them are indeed free; and that some are therefore, in some manner, exempt from causation.

Hume's position is presented most clearly in section 8 of the first *Enquiry* (*An Enquiry concerning Human Understanding*), though most of what he says there is anticipated in *Treatise* 2.3.1–2. The *Treatise* version is more aggressive, and in the *Enquiry* he describes his argument as a "reconciling project." This phrase might suggest that he thinks his position is fully in accord with common sense, but it clearly is not, and Hume does not seriously pretend it is. What he thinks he is reconciling are the needs of a human science and the needs of our ordinary moral discourse, and he argues that common opinion is in error about those needs. Popular opinion holds that we need one sort of freedom that we do not have, instead of another that we do have.

In the *Treatise*, Hume uses scholastic terminology to name these two kinds of freedom: he distinguishes between "liberty of spontaneity" and "liberty of indifference" (T 2.3.2, 407). Liberty of spontaneity consists in the absence of hindrances to the execution of one's decisions. He describes it in the *Enquiry* thus: "*a power of acting or not acting, according to the determinations of the will*; that is, if we choose to remain at rest, we may; if we choose to move, we also may." He immediately adds that it is possessed by "every one who is not a prisoner and in chains" (EHU 8.1, 95). He thinks, correctly, that this last claim is not controversial. He is also correct in thinking that liberty of spontaneity, so defined, is compatible with universal causation; for it is merely the absence of interference with the exercise of one's choices, not the absence of causal determination in the making of those choices.

Hume's view becomes controversial when he turns to the other sort of freedom, the freedom that we think we have, but that in his view we do not have. We think that sometimes, when we choose one way, we could equally have chosen another way. In Hume's language, we believe that sometimes, when we choose to remain at rest, we might (even though we do not) choose instead to move; and that if we choose to move, we might (even though we do not) choose instead to remain at rest. We believe in the reality of unexercised powers of choice and see this reality as essential to our freedom as agents. Hume calls this sort of freedom "liberty of indifference," interprets it as a denial of the universality of causation in human affairs, and insists we neither have it nor need it. Indeed, he believes the requirements of our moral thinking and decision making are inconsistent with its existence.

Hume attacks liberty of indifference in three ways. First, he asserts the universality of causation, and the unreality of chance, and emphasizes that human affairs do not differ in these respects from the natural world. For example: "It is universally allowed that nothing exists without a cause of its existence, and that chance, when strictly examined, is a mere negative word, and means not any real power which has anywhere a being in nature" (EHU 8.1, 95). To this dogmatic metaphysical argument, he adds that we can infer and predict human actions from the motives and characters of human agents in a way that is fully comparable to our ability to explain and predict natural phenomena; and when people seem to act in bizarre or unpredictable ways, we can postulate, and discover, hidden causes that account for this – again, as we are able to do for surprising physical events. So we must acknowledge "necessity" in human affairs, as well as in physical nature – this term being understood, as he stresses, in the same way as he has interpreted it in his earlier analysis of causal inferences. (It is important to recall that when Hume outlines what he calls some "corollaries" of that analysis in the *Treatise*, he remarks, with astonishing casualness, that "the distinction, which we often make betwixt *power* and the *exercise* of it, is . . . without foundation" [T 1.3.14, 171]. One of the ways in which we "often make" this distinction is, of course, in the commonplace ascription of an unexercised power of choice to agents.)

Hume's second line of attack on liberty of indifference is the more practical one that we need predictability in human affairs in order to make our decisions. He gives the melancholy example of the prisoner condemned to the scaffold, who recognizes he will get no help in escaping from his jailer or his guards by observing their characters, and decides that, rather than in trying to change their resolution, he would be better employed in trying to weaken the bars of his cell (T 2.3.1, 406). The multitude of examples that human experience offers us of regular connections between character and action would not be open to us if liberty of indifference were a reality.

Hume's third argument against liberty of indifference consists in refutations of the natural, but in his view misguided, suggestion that we can introspect its reality (T 2.3.1, 408). What he says here parallels the many important things he says in opposition to the claim that we can detect within ourselves the experience of the power that we ascribe to natural causes (see, for example, EHU 7.1, 64–9). Hume does not deny there are volitions, as some have;[15] he sees them as a readily detectable component in the mechanism of human choice.[16] But he denies that we can ever detect that volitions are themselves "subject to nothing." Liberty of indifference, then, is a myth; but we have never had any need of it and, in fact, presuppose its absence in practical reflection. Its reality would be inconsistent with both morality and the possibility of a science of man, as Hume conceives that.

It is impossible here to explore the question of the relationship between human science and determinism, which is raised by Hume's stance. Instead, I mention an important implication of his view for his moral psychology.

If Hume is right, we are often in a position to enact the choices we make, and also to enact the alternative choices that we do not make. But we are never in a position to choose in a way other than the way we do choose. He believes in the reality of unexploited opportunities; but not in the reality of unexercised powers of choice. This entails, however, that moral praise or blame can never be applied on the ground that someone has chosen a course of action that he or she *need not have chosen*. Common opinion follows rationalism in thinking that this is the basis of much praise or blame; and Hume must deny it.

He does indeed deny it, and offers an account of moral virtue that connects it with the very predictability that he insists we can find in human affairs, not with the liberty of indifference that he says does not exist.

V. OBLIGATION AND VIRTUE

We have seen that Hume traces all choice to the passions and rejects the rationalist understanding of human freedom. But we are now led to what he seems to see as the major problem of his moral philosophy. Rationalists might concede the main features of his account of prudential choice but still say that when I choose what I think is good for me, instead of what I am now inclined to, I remain the servant of my desires. I do not cease to serve them when I merely postpone their satisfaction to the future. We do, however, sometimes manage to act in the face of all our desires, short-term or long-term. We do this when we act from duty. When we do this, reason does indeed triumph over passion.

The best-known version of this view from Hume's time is that of Joseph Butler, who insists on the supremacy of conscience in human nature.[17] He accords it supremacy over all other springs of action, including self-love, benevolence, and particular desires. Hume's account of our regard for duty is one that concedes the reality of duty but still derives this regard from our emotional natures as his science of man depicts them.

His account depends on a principle he enunciates as an "undoubted maxim," namely, *"that no action can be virtuous, or morally good, unless there be in human nature some motive to produce it, distinct from the sense of its morality"* (T 3.2.1, 479). He recognizes that this claim has to contend with the fact that we do sometimes act from a sense of duty alone; and his attempt to accommodate this fact is at the heart of his account of justice and is the most extensive and important of his three forms of attack on the rationalist view of human nature.

We must begin with his account of the role of the passions, or sentiments, of approval and disapproval, since he views the sense of duty as a derivative of these. Hume holds that moral judgements, in which we describe behavior as virtuous or vicious, express these sentiments. Like all other passions, they are unique secondary impressions and cannot therefore be analyzed; but we can say how they arise and what their effects are. The story is complex; but we can see at the outset that if, indeed, the sense of duty is a product of the sentiments of approval and disapproval, it is a product of sentiments that arise when we pass judgement on human behavior that must already be produced by something other than the approval and disapproval to which it gives rise. I draw in what follows on *Treatise* 3.3.1–3, and from the *Enquiry concerning the Principles of Morals* (the second *Enquiry*), sections 5–8.

Hume maintains that moral approval and disapproval have human characters, rather than individual actions, as their objects. It is significant that he takes the terms "virtuous" and "vicious" as the paradigms of moral language, thus making it easier to persuade us that evaluations are directed toward persons rather than their deeds. "If any *action* be either virtuous or vicious, 'tis only as a sign of some quality or character." He says that actions that do not reflect settled states of character in their agents "are never consider'd in morality" (T 3.3.1, 575). Reason assists in the generation of approval and disapproval by showing us the effects that certain states of character have. If by a disinterested examination (an examination conducted "without reference to our particular interest") we find that a particular character trait is agreeable or useful, or disagreeable or harmful, to the agent who has it, or to others, then the mechanism that generates approval or disapproval can commence (T 3.1.2, 472).

The mechanism is complex and involves the workings of the principle of *sympathy*. This principle is not to be confused with the sentiment of compassion, which is merely one of its products. The principle is the one that enables us to participate in the emotional life, and the pleasures and pains, of others. Hume first discusses sympathy in *Treatise* 2.1.11.[18] According to his account of it there, I become aware of the passion of another by observing its manifestations in his or her behavior; I have, therefore, an idea of it. So far, however, I am not moved by the other's passion. For this to happen, my idea has to be enlivened: then it will turn into an impression, and I shall have the very passion I have inferred in the other person. Hume says, to the regular surprise of the readers who encounter this so early in Book 2, with memories of *Treatise* 1.4.6 still in their minds, that what enlivens the idea I have of the other's passion is the "idea, or rather impression" of myself (2.1.11, 317). He cannot here refer to the impression of the pure ego that he so emphatically stated in Book 1 that he did not have, but must refer to "that succession of related ideas and impressions, of which we have an intimate memory and consciousness" (T 2.1.2, 277). This is so lively and vivid that its liveliness is communicated to the idea of the other's passion, which I then come to have myself. It can then lead on to other emotions, through the principle of association.

The sympathetic mechanism enables me to share in the pleasures and pains that are the effects, in the agent or others, of those character traits I am disinterestedly surveying. The association of impressions causes me then to experience approval (when these effects are pleasant) or disapproval (when they are painful). I *express* these sentiments in my moral judgements, and I call the character traits I have assessed in this way the virtues or vices, respectively, of individuals. (Their virtuousness or viciousness consists in their capacity to arouse these sentiments in observers; but these sentiments have not, of course, caused these character traits to be present in the observed agents in the first place.)

Hume describes approval and disapproval as calm forms of the indirect passions of love and hatred (T 3.3.5, 614). Love and hatred are caused by the qualities or actions of persons but have the persons themselves as their objects. Approval and disapproval are aroused by the qualities agents display but are directed towards the agents themselves as the bearers of the characters they manifest.

We have yet to account for the sense of duty, however. The account comes in two parts. The first is Hume's explanation of how it is that we sometimes perform acts from a sense of duty that others perform from (say) benevolence. He says that someone may be conscious of the fact that he lacks a character trait (such as kindness to children) that causes us to approve of those who have it. He may then come to "hate himself upon that account" and may perform the action "from a certain sense of duty, in order to acquire by practice, that virtuous principle" (T 3.2.1, 479). On this view, the sense of duty is a conscious substitute for more natural motives and is a product of self-hatred. To feel it is to feel the disapproval of your own lack of a virtuous inclination.

These phenomena occur, though we may well doubt whether they are the key to the *origin* of the sense of duty. But even if they are, they do not include a much larger range of cases: those occasions when we seem willing to act from duty even when there is no prior natural motive. These are the cases when we act from *justice*. There is no natural inclination (such as benevolence) to explain our willingness to pay our taxes or return money borrowed from bankers. Yet justice is esteemed as a virtue, and its denial is judged vicious.

The latter is the more important for the psychology of duty. The wider story of the nature and origins of justice cannot be told here.[19] But in Hume's system justice is not a natural virtue but an artificial one: that is, it is not a settled state of character that is due to innate causes within us but is a condition we acquire because of the influence on us of social institutions. We do have some socially unifying motives in our natural benevolence and love of family; but these motives are too restrictive to sustain large social groupings. We are able, however, to see the value of conventions that would safeguard such things as property rights, and we adopt them through an implicit recognition of common interests. Both in the *Treatise* and in the second *Enquiry*, Hume uses the analogy of oarsmen who row together without any explicit mutual undertaking to do so. Such conventions often entail inconvenience for us, but we sustain them through self-interest.

Once these conventions are established, it is easy to understand how they acquire the extra status given them through the operation of approval and disapproval. Each of us is able, through sympathy, to be conscious of the unpleasant results of unjust actions for those who suffer from them. We may suffer from them ourselves. We express our displeasure at these effects by saying that just actions are our duty and avoid inner discomfort by doing our duty ourselves. Hence, justice becomes virtuous without being attractive. Hume's most succinct summary of his account of the genesis of the sense of duty is perhaps this:

All morality depends upon our sentiments; and when any action, or quality of the mind, pleases us *after a certain manner*, we say it is virtuous; and when the neglect, or non-performance of it, displeases us *after a like manner*, we say that we lie under an obligation to perform it.   (T 3.2.5, 517)

VI. HUME AND COMMON OPINION

For all his willingness to express himself paradoxically, Hume's moral psychology is designed to accommodate the phenomena of our daily moral experience, and to reject only a rationalist interpretation of them. He does not seek to overturn the moral conventions of common sense but, on the contrary, seeks to support them anew on foundations of experiment and observation, free of misleading and disruptive theory.[20] It is therefore important, in assessing his successes and failures, to determine how far his opinions conform to common opinion, and how far not.

I begin with a comment on his theory of obligation. For many readers, its very ingenuity presents an immediate difficulty. Is it so obvious that the sense of duty is derivative? Hume is free of the worldly-wise cynicism of psychological egoism. In the second appendix of the second *Enquiry* he argues against it, much in the manner of Joseph Butler, and maintains that those who hold it (like Hobbes) are forcing a theory on the observable facts of conduct.[21] But why not follow Butler further and say that the observable facts also show we have a natural tendency to feel and act on a sense of obligation? The reason is probably to be found not only in the determination to undermine ethical rationalism, but also in Hume's equally strong determination to avoid any theory that might seem to require, or invite, theological underpinnings, and to offer instead a purely secular account of all the phenomena he explains. But in seeking to offer an explanation of conscience at all, instead of taking the fact of it as a datum as he takes benevolence to be, Hume is forced to interpret it as a product of the institutions of social justice, when the latter are probably regarded by most as deriving some of their hold on us from the power of our sense of obligation, not the other way about. The fact that many other philosophers try to explain them as deriving from self-interest, much as Hume does, puts them at odds with common opinion also.

There is another place where Hume's account of moral virtue puts him at odds with common opinion, and where he himself shows signs of greater discomfort at the fact. In his story of the ways we come to feel moral approval, he tells us that it is directed toward established character traits in our natures and arises when we disinterestedly recognize that these character traits are useful or agreeable to ourselves or others – that they have utility, in the language of the second *Enquiry*. This account prompts a question: there are many human characteristics that have utility in this way that we delight in, but are not objects of moral approval. Similarly, many human traits that are harmful or disagreeable do not elicit moral disapproval. We praise charm, wit, or eloquence, but not *in the manner* of benevolence, industry, or temperance. Why not? Hume addresses this potentially vexing question in *Treatise* 3.3.4, and in the fourth appendix to the second *Enquiry*. He tries to dismiss it as not "very material," and in entitling the *Enquiry* appendix "Of some verbal Disputes" evinces a lamentable and atypical inclination to dismiss a serious conceptual issue as what misguided theorists today sometimes call a "mere" question of semantics (T 3.3.4, 608).

But it *is* a problem; and Hume shows a degree of recognition of the sort of problem that it is by trying to fend off one possible explanation of the distinction we do indeed make between virtues, on the one hand, and talents, on the other. This is the suggestion that virtues are voluntarily acquired and talents are not. He says, perhaps correctly, that there is no ground for maintaining this and suggests instead that the relevant consideration is that virtues (and vices) can be changed by laws and by education, whereas talents cannot. This is interesting, but seems wrong: one thinks of the work of remedial

language instructors, long-suffering piano teachers, or physiothera-
pists, who all seem to be in the thankless but not-wholly-ineffectual
business of modifying our talents by training.

What, then, is the ground of our distinction? We can approach it
by noticing that in order to assimilate talents to virtues, Hume has
to assume that the talents are used well or wisely. A virtue cannot
(necessarily cannot) be used badly by its possessor, but a talent can.[22]
A virtue is, in part, the predictable tendency to use some talent well,
rather than badly. But using a talent well involves using it at the
right times and not using it at the wrong times. We praise those who
can be predicted to do this (by calling them virtuous), because they
choose to use the talent when it is good to do so, and not to use it
when it would be bad to do so. They are praiseworthy because they
use the talent in good ways when they *could* use it in bad ways
instead. We praise the predictability of virtuous action precisely because we think it could be done otherwise. On Hume's view of
freedom, this is what we can never say about anyone's choices.

Hume's science of human nature, then, seems to have the unat-
tractive consequence that we accord moral approval and disapproval
to patterns of choice that could not be other than what they are. A
good character is just a piece of good fortune. While popular ethical
thinking is frequently forced to give ear to this view, it is still seen as
paradoxical. Good character is, for the most part, still regarded as the
regular tendency to make free choices that are good, not merely to
perform pleasing acts habitually.

This brings us to the bedrock of Hume's understanding of what a
science of human nature has to be like. I have suggested that the
common distinction between virtues and talents, which he finds a
source of difficulty, exists because the popular ascription of virtue to
someone involves ascribing some degree of what Hume calls liberty
of indifference to that person. But Hume would respond that this
ascription entails the denial of the very predictability of human
conduct that our ethical thinking requires, and is inconsistent with
the scientific status of the study of mankind. Critics of a libertarian
turn of mind would say that Hume's difficulties merely show we
must jettison the Newtonian model of the human sciences. We
must, they would say, accept that the social sciences are able to
predict human behaviour (such as voting patterns) as well as they do
because, in fact, most people do choose in roughly the same ways in

similar situations, even though they could, *if* they chose, not do so. But some people do, now and then, surprise us (when they could have chosen not to!) and we have to be content with statistical predictions in consequence.

So far, we have found aspects of Hume's moral psychology that are at odds with common opinion in ways that seem inevitable consequences of his understanding of the science of human nature. There is another well-known claim that he makes that is indeed at odds with common opinion, but in a way he could have avoided. This is his claim that erroneous or bizarre emotions are not contrary to reason. Hume recognizes that the understanding can give rise to passion by producing opinions that give rise to such states as grief or joy or resentment, or by prompting desires or volitions when we see that some course of action will lead to what we already want or think good. But he insists that this does not ever entitle us to call the passions or desires unreasonable, or to hold that "reason and passion can ever oppose each other, or dispute for the government of the will and actions" (T 2.3.3, 416). What Hume has done here is emphasize the importance of passion or desire in the genesis of choice and conduct, while continuing to accept, indeed to stress, the rationalist insistence on the sharp separation of reason and emotion. Hume teaches the *a-rationality* of passion where the rationalist teaches the *ir-rationality* of passion. Both, in fact, misinterpret common moral opinion, which is committed to neither view, but accepts that emotion, as well as opinion, can be both reasonable and unreasonable.

Hume seems to think that the only cases where the moral evaluations of common sense require the ascription of irrationality to the passions are cases where these are deemed to be the result of false judgements. But this is not so. On the contrary: if I pursue an objective that is harmful to me, because I mistakenly think it will be good for me, then my desire for it may be judged to be erroneous, since my judgement is; but it is not thereby judged to be unreasonable. If common sense agrees that the course I am following will lead to the objective I am pursuing, but holds me to be mistaken in thinking it will be good for me; or if common sense holds me to be right in thinking the objective I am pursuing would be good for me but wrong in thinking the course I am following will help me attain it, common sense is still likely to call my choice a *reasonable* one. The error of my judgement is the very thing that makes my action reasonable in cases of this sort. If I grieve at the supposed loss of a loved one who is in fact alive and well, my grief is mistaken, but not unreasonable. We apply the term "unreasonable" to an emotion or to a desire where that emotion or desire is thought to be in some way *inappropriate* to the situation in which the agent finds himself, or herself – when it is the wrong way to respond, emotionally or conatively, to a situation of that sort. If the situation is not of that sort, the response is mistaken as well. But it can be quite free of error and still be either reasonable or unreasonable: by being moderate or excessive, helpful or unhelpful, sane or silly. These are all dimensions of rationality that can be manifested *by the passions themselves*. Hume has perceived the importance of the passions for all our choice and conduct but has mistakenly felt obliged to deny their rationality in order to accommodate this fact. In this respect, he shares with the rationalists whose theories he contests a mistaken estimate of the passions. This mistake is one from which common sense is already free.

VII. MORAL PSYCHOLOGY AND THE SELF

We have seen that Hume's conception of a science of human nature reduces mental life to the interplay of impressions and ideas, and treats the mind itself as the theatre wherein this interplay occurs, not as a participant in it. The scholarly literature contains many criticisms and reappraisals of what Hume says about the self, almost all directed to his treatment of it in Book 1 of the *Treatise*. Two of the criticisms prominent in this literature are of particular importance.

The first criticism is that in spite of the quasi-Newtonian account of perceptions that Hume proclaims at the outset of the *Treatise*, and again in the first *Enquiry*, his accounts of the origins of our beliefs lean heavily on the ascription to us of propensities, tendencies, or habits. This leads some to suggest that he is committed to a crypto-Kantian psychology in which the subject of explanations is the mind and its dispositions, rather than the perceptions it contains.[23] The second criticism is that the ascription of a propensity (in this case the propensity to confuse one sort of succession with another) is essential to Hume's account of the genesis of the belief in the unity of the mind itself – thus opening him to the objection that he cannot explain how we come to have the belief he criticizes without first assuming its truth.[24]

It is possible to respond on Hume's behalf to the first criticism by suggesting that talk of the mind's propensities should be construed as popular shorthand for a genuinely Newtonian account that speaks instead of how impressions and ideas give rise to one another *in* the mind. It is possible to respond similarly to the second by saying that the perceptions the mind has can well include perceptions *of* the series that constitute it, without there having also to be any supervenient subject beyond the series' successive members. Such responses seem to save him from charges of formal inconsistency.

But the transition to the passages about the self in Book 2 is still a surprising one for the reader of Book 1. Hume has tried to prepare us for it by telling us to distinguish "betwixt personal identity, as it regards our thought or imagination, and as it regards our passions or the concern we take in ourselves" (T 1.4.6, 253). He also tries to ease the transition by clarifying his use of the term "self" in its first introduction in Book 2 as the name of the object of the indirect passion of pride: "This object is self, or that succession of related ideas and impressions, of which we have an intimate memory and consciousness" (T 2.1.2, 277). This makes it clear that he is not reverting to the pure owner-self whose existence he rejects so brusquely in Book 1. But this does not prepare us for the claim that "the idea, or rather impression of ourselves is always intimately present with us, and that our consciousness gives us so lively a conception of our own person, that 'tis not possible to imagine, that any thing can in this particular go beyond it" (T 2.1.11, 317). More serious perhaps, is the fact that the aetiology of the indirect passions requires the use of the idea of the self as *distinct from others*; and the account of the origins of our belief in self-identity in Book 1 is confined to our belief in the self's own inner unity over time and tells us nothing of how we come to be aware of the existence of other minds. This is a serious gap in his system, but perhaps not a manifest inconsistency. Let us turn instead to the role he ascribes to this lively notion of our self in our emotional life.

Whatever this role is, Hume does not think it undermines his Newtonian mental science. There is no place in his system for the suggestion that choices are the product of anything other than the series of passions and cognitions that lead to them. His denial of liberty of indifference permits no consideration of what has been called agent-causation: the theory that in free action it is the agent, rather than the agent's desires or volitions, that is the *locus* of causality.[25] This denial is coupled with great stress on the claim that our understanding and evaluation of human agency depends on our recognition of settled states of character. This raises, in the sphere of action, a perplexity parallel to that raised by Hume's critics in the sphere of epistemology: that his view seems to require a continuing self that has the character traits he feels necessary for prediction and evaluation. We can perhaps offer a similar answer: that talk of an agent's character is shorthand for talk of that agent's emotions and desires.

However we respond to these difficulties of interpretation, there is a vital dimension to Hume's theory of the self in Book 2 that is only lately beginning to be recognized as central to his moral psychology.[26] It permeates his whole vision of the human condition. We find its clearest expression in the introduction of the principle of sympathy, in *Treatise* 2.1.11. Scholars have interpreted sympathy as a mechanism to explain my concern for others, which emerges through my having myself the very feelings I discern in them. This is correct, but incomplete. The principle is introduced by Hume as a "secondary" source of the self-regarding indirect passions of pride and humility. Pride does not merely come about through my taking pleasure in qualities that I recognize to belong to me; it also comes about through my sympathetically sharing the admiration (that is, in Hume's terms, the love) that others have toward me when they, too, discern these pleasing qualities. So my own pride is in part the product of the mentality of others, not only of my own. And since I am loved, or admired, for qualities I have or objects I possess, my emotional life is such that I shall pride myself on those qualities or objects for which others admire me and be ashamed of those qualities or objects for which they hate (or despise) me. They are the co-creators of my self-image, and to understand the character of my self-concern it is necessary to take the measure of the society of which I am a member.

As Annette Baier points out, many of the features others thus make part of my self-image will be physical ones, so the self of the passions is a physicalized construct, and not the quasi-solipsist monster of Book 1.[27] Once this is recognized, it is also evident that I sometimes come to have pride or humility in some characteristic I ascribe to myself only after others admire or despise it: their evaluation of it and of me may not only augment my own, but actually engender it. And I may, of course, come to simulate, or actually develop, some character trait they would praise in order to prevent their blaming me (and hence my blaming myself) for its absence. This, as we have already seen, is part of Hume's account of the origin of the sense of duty, an account that seeks to turn the rationalist's key ethical endowment into an internalized social product (see again T 3.2.1, 479).

The sort of story this tells us about the self as social construction is one we have heard since from Freud, Marx, and the existentialists, always with ideological accretions wholly foreign to Hume's naturalism. His own summary statement is as follows: "In general we may remark, that the minds of men are mirrors to one another, not only because they reflect each others emotions, but also because those rays of passions, sentiments and opinions may be often reverberated, and may decay away by insensible degrees" (T 2.2.5, 365).

It is easy to see from this insistence that the self is not discernible within but largely ascribed by transference from without, why Hume has such deep hostility to all systems that view persons as alien to the social world they inhabit. His negativity toward rationalism and its craving for autonomy is the result of its being a theoretical force that can only encourage self-distancing from the sources of emotional nourishment that make us what we are. And his intemperate rejection of the religious austerities of the "monkish virtues" can be seen as having the same theoretical source (EPM 9.1, 270). Each is life-denying, and in a quite literal sense self-destructive. Human nature does not need to be mastered, nor does it need to be redeemed. It needs social nurture. Both reason and "true" religion are the *slaves* of the passions.

VIII. CONCLUSION

I have argued that Hume is a neo-Hellenistic thinker, one who follows the Stoics and Epicureans and Sceptics in maintaining that we should avoid anxiety by following nature. This prescription is notorious among philosophers for combining descriptive and normative elements. Hume is not, in any general way, confused between descriptive and normative claims: there is nothing in principle confused about seeing an understanding of our nature as a guide to one's way of life, or even to the proper practice of philosophy. There is more than one way of getting and using such guidance. Hume thinks a philosopher must, first and foremost, learn to accept his or her nature for what it is. This means recognizing that it is so programmed that our instincts furnish us with beliefs that we cannot survive without, or supply independently, or seriously question. Faced with this fact, the philosophical enterprises of sceptical doubt and rationalist reconstruction are doomed to failure on psychological grounds alone, and the attempts to pursue them can only generate and exacerbate anxiety.

When we turn to Hume's moral thought, we find the parallel insistence that we must recognize the dominance of the passions in our nature, and not risk misery by attempting to follow eccentric programs of choice that frustrate them in the supposed interests of reason or the mortifications of religion. Once again, we have to accept our nature, not violate it. Here Hume risks confusion in a fundamental respect: while there is nothing incoherent in describing our nature and then saying we must accept it and not violate it, it *is* incoherent to say this if we are *unable* to violate this nature. To combine the descriptive with the normative without incoherence, it is necessary to permit freedom of choice in a form for which Hume's own account of liberty allows no space. The price of using the study of human nature as a guide to choice is the price of recognizing that it is part of our nature to be *able* to choose. But if this is admitted, we can then follow him in saying that if we make certain kinds of choice, we may ruin ourselves and end up anxious, or incapacitated, or otherwise miserable, by frustrating our basic needs. Read this way, his system tells us that the polite society human beings had by his day developed in property-owning Western Europe, with all its protective artifices, meets the needs of human nature better than its alternatives. While this may be judged by some to be complacent or enervating, the experience of more radical programs that are based on ideologies that attend less to the details of human nature should make us hesitate to dismiss his advice too readily.

NOTES

1 A. E. Taylor, *David Hume and the Miraculous* (Cambridge, 1927), pp. 53–4.

2 *David Hume and the Miraculous*, p. 53.
3 Peter Jones, *Hume's Sentiments: Their Ciceronian and French Context* (Edinburgh, 1982), pp. 11–19.
4 See the Fourth Meditation, *Meditations on First Philosophy*, first published 1641.
5 See Norman Kemp Smith, "The Naturalism of Hume," *Mind* 14 (1905): 149–73, 335–47, and *The Philosophy of David Hume* (London, 1941). See also Barry Stroud, *Hume* (London, 1977), chap. 1.
6 I have discussed this issue more fully in my "Hume's Skepticism and the Dialogues," in *McGill Hume Studies*, ed. David Fate Norton, Nicholas Capaldi, and Wade L. Robison (San Diego, 1979), pp. 253–78.
7 This is what separates him so clearly from the common-sense school. On this point, see David Fate Norton, "Hume and His Scottish Critics," in *McGill Hume Studies*, pp. 309–24, and chap. 5 of his *David Hume: Common-Sense Moralist, Sceptical Metaphysician* (Princeton, 1982).
8 What follows here is not an attempt at the impossible feat of summarizing Book 2 in a few paragraphs, but an attempt to indicate the most important parts of its argument for the assessment of Hume's alternative to rationalism in moral psychology. I give a somewhat more detailed treatment in chapter 5 of my *Hume* (London, 1975). The clearest account of Book 2 is still that of Páll S. Árdal, *Passion and Value in Hume's* Treatise (Edinburgh, 1966). Important recent discussions are to be found in Nicholas Capaldi, *Hume's Place in Moral Philosophy* (New York, 1989), especially chap. 5; and Annette C. Baier, *A Progress of Sentiments: Reflections on Hume's* Treatise (Cambridge, Mass., 1991), especially chaps. 6 and 7.
9 This remark is probably intended to avoid the appearance of psychological hedonism that could be left by the earlier classification. Kemp Smith and Árdal have said that the passions Hume refers to here should be classified separately as primary, rather than direct, but I cannot follow up the merits of this suggestion here.
10 I have tried to distinguish what Hume means here from what analytical philosophers have intended by these terms in my *Hume*, chap. 5.
11 We owe the clear understanding of Hume's distinction between calm and violent passions to Árdal. See his *Passion and Value in Hume's* Treatise, pp. 95ff.
12 I use here the terminology that Hume presents later in Section 4 of the *Enquiry concerning Human Understanding*. It is clear that the same distinction is intended in this passage in T 2.3.3.
13 For important further discussion of these very complicated questions, see Norton, *David Hume*, chap. 3, and Baier, *A Progress of Sentiments*, chap. 7. An older but very shrewd discussion is to be found in Rachel

M. Kydd, *Reason and Conduct in Hume's* Treatise (Oxford, 1964), chap. 5.

14 Hume's views are anticipated by Thomas Hobbes in chap. 21 of *Leviathan*, first published in 1651.

15 The best-known case is Gilbert Ryle in *The Concept of Mind* (London, 1949), chap. 3.

16 I have briefly discussed Hume's views on this in my *Hume*, pp. 111–17. For a fuller treatment, see John Bricke, "Hume's Volitions," in *Philosophers of the Scottish Enlightenment*, ed. Vincent Hope (Edinburgh, 1984), pp. 70–90.

17 Butler does avoid explicit commitment on whether conscience is best described as a rational power or as a moral sense. See his comments in his *Dissertation on Virtue*, vol. 2 of *The Works of Bishop Butler*, ed. J. H. Bernard (London, 1900), p. 287. But it seems clear that the role Butler ascribes to conscience is one for which Hume feels he must find an alternative consistent with his own science of man.

18 Sympathy seems to drop out of sight in the second *Enquiry*, and it has been a matter of considerable controversy whether this shows Hume to have abandoned it or not. For an argument that he has not, see the appendix to John B. Stewart, *The Moral and Political Philosophy of David Hume* (New York, 1963). For an argument that he has, see Capaldi, *Hume's Place in Moral Philosophy*, chap. 7.

19 For additional discussions of Hume on justice, see David Fate Norton, "Hume, Human Nature, and the Foundations of Morality," Part IV, this volume; and Knud Haakonssen, "The Structure of Hume's Political Theory," Part III, this volume.

20 In this respect, I am in agreement with David Norton's position in his *David Hume*.

21 Butler's arguments on this are found in the first, second, and third of his *Sermons at Rolls Chapel*, *Works*, I, 25–57.

22 One recalls here the definition of a virtue in Aquinas: "a good disposition of the mind, by which we live righteously, of which no one can make bad use" (*Summa Theologica*, 1a 2ae, 55, 4).

23 The two fundamental essays on this theme are Robert Paul Wolff, "Hume's Theory of Mental Activity", *Philosophical Review* 69 (1960): 289–310; and Fred Wilson, "Hume's Theory of Mental Activity," in *McGill Hume Studies*, pp. 101–20.

24 On this complicated topic, see the essay by John Biro in this volume; Nelson Pike, "Hume's Bundle Theory of the Self: A Limited Defense," *American Philosophical Quarterly* 4 (1967): 159–65; and my "Hume's Theory of the Self Revisited," *Dialogue* 14 (1975): 389–409.

25 For a classic discussion of this notion, see R. M. Chisholm, "Freedom and Action," in *Freedom and Determinism*, ed. Keith Lehrer (New York, 1966), pp. 11–44.

26 It is given its due place in Baier's *A Progess of Sentiments*, especially chap. 7.

27 *A Progress of Sentiments*, p. 136.

6 Hume, human nature, and the foundations of morality

> I found that the moral Philosophy transmitted to us by Antiquity, labor'd under the same Inconvenience that has been found in their natural Philosophy, of being entirely Hypothetical, & depending more upon Invention than Experience. Every one consulted his Fancy in erecting Schemes of Virtue & of Happiness, without regarding human Nature, upon which every moral Conclusion must depend. This therefore I resolved to make my principal Study, & the Source from which I wou'd derive every Truth in Criticism as well as Morality.   (KHL)

Of "late years" there has been, Hume wrote in his *Treatise of Human Nature*, a controversy that has "so much excited the curiosity of the publick, *whether these moral distinctions be founded on natural and original principles, or arise from interest and education.*" Those who adopted the second of these views – those who traced the alleged distinction between virtue and vice to self-interest and education – had claimed, as Hume puts it, that morality itself has "no foundation in nature" but is, rather, founded merely on the pain or pleasure that arises from considerations of self-interest. In contrast, those who ranged themselves on the other side of this issue – those who said that moral distinctions are founded on natural and original principles – claimed that "morality is something real, essential, and founded on nature" (T 2.1.7, 295–6).

Hume does not say what he means by "late years." He may have had in mind only the preceding quarter century, in which case the principal players alluded to will have been Bernard Mandeville and

I wish to thank J. C. A. Gaskin, Terence Penelhum, and Robert Shaver for helpful comments on an earlier version of this essay.

Francis Hutcheson, and such lesser-known writers as William Wollaston, Gilbert Burnet, John Balguy, and Archibald Campbell. But
the controversy to which Hume refers was well under way a century
earlier, and we can be sure that he was familiar with the contributions made to it by such writers as Hugo Grotius, Thomas Hobbes,
Samuel Pufendorf, and Ralph Cudworth. To understand Hume's
moral theory requires that we see him as not only fulfilling his
promise to examine these competing hypotheses, but as joining in,
and hoping to resolve, the controversy over the foundations of morality. Hume himself, as we shall see, argues that morality has a firm
foundation in nature – in *human* nature.

I. BACKGROUND

The early-modern version of the debate over the foundations of morality was doubtless occasioned by a number of those complex phenomena associated with the general cultural and intellectual up-
heaval Europe experienced during the Renaissance: the revival of
interest in classical learning, the European voyages to the Far East
and to the Americas, the Protestant Reformation with its attendant
wars and debates, and the rise of the experimental method and the
new science, to mention some of the most obvious and familiar. Just
as these events appear to explain the renewal of philosophical
scepticism (of generalized doubts about claims to know, and especially about claims to know the real nature of things), so, too, do
they appear to explain the rise of a protracted debate about the foundation of the moral distinctions we claim to make. Certainly Montaigne, the paradigm sceptic of the sixteenth century, was already
explicitly drawing attention to this issue.

The problem is more clearly delineated, however, by Hugo Grotius, who begins his famous *Of the Rights of War and Peace* (1625)
by noting the claims of those who, both in the past and in his own
age, treated morality "as if it were nothing but an empty Name." It
would be pointless, Grotius realizes, to undertake a treatise on right
if there is really no such thing, and thus he sets out to establish the
existence of right "on solid foundations."[1]

According to Grotius, the moral sceptics argue that laws were
instituted merely out of self-interest, and that self-interest is the
only motivation of human action. Those who held this view, and

who also assumed that moral distinctions depend on differences of motivation, concluded that there are no real moral distinctions. Justice and natural right, they said, are at best, "mere Chimera," and, at worst, foolish: "Nature prompts all Men, and in general all Animals, to seek their own particular Advantage: So that either there is no Justice at all, or if there is any, it is extreme Folly, because it engages us to procure the Good of others, to our own Prejudice." In opposition to this moral scepticism, Grotius offers no fewer than four foundations of right or morality: humanity's unique sociability, the human understanding or reason, the covenants obliging individuals to society or to any particular course of action, and the free will of God.

Grotius grants that humans are not the only animals that live in groups and show a concern for their young and even for other members of their species. But humans are different in so far as they have not only an inherent desire for society, but also a further unique faculty of knowing and acting according to general principles. In short, humans have, taking these abilities together, a unique "Social Faculty" that gives them a "Care of maintaining Society in a Manner conformable to the Light of human Understanding." This social faculty serves as perhaps the most important foundation of morality by giving rise to those rules (the Laws of Nature) that operate in well-regulated communities, while the keeping or not keeping of these rules is the source of the distinction we make between justice and injustice. Second, humans are endowed with the ability to judge which things are, or will be, pleasant or hurtful, and from this further fact we can see that it is natural and agreeable for us to follow the dictates of this judgement or reason. In doing so, we avoid the mistakes to which we would be led if we were to be guided only by fear or present pleasure or blind passion. Moreover, whatever is contrary to this discerning reason will prove to be contrary to the laws of nature that derive from the exercise of our social faculty. Third, covenants, whether expressly or tacitly made, also provide a foundation for morality, for it is on them that the civil law and its obligations depend.

Right and wrong and justice and injustice are so well anchored in the nature of things, Grotius supposes, that the laws of nature would arise and have force even though there were no deity: "all we have now said would take place, though we should even grant, what without the greatest Wickedness cannot be granted, that there is no God, or that he takes no Care of human Affairs." Nonetheless, knowing as we do that there is a deity, and that to him our creator we owe all that we have, including our very existence, we find in the "free Will of God" a further foundation of morality. Our judgement, operating on the principle that the acts of a supreme benefactor create unquestionable and unceasing obligations, shows us that the deity "ought to be obeyed by us in all Things without exception, especially since he has so many Ways shewn his infinite Goodness and Almighty Power."

These considerations led Grotius to the conclusion that the sceptical claim that justice and right are founded only on self-interest is mistaken. Justice and right are the necessary result of the operation of dispositions inherent in human nature. These dispositions unfailingly give rise to social organizations in which distinctions between right and wrong or justice and injustice are found, and are found to be of fundamental importance. The rules and distinctions they produce, far from being the merely conventional products of an isolated and transient self-interest, are the products of nature, of human nature, itself.

In contrast to Grotius, Thomas Hobbes was widely perceived as having put the case for moral scepticism. Deeply impressed with the findings of the new science, Hobbes rejected the medieval view that nature itself incorporates intrinsic values, in so far as natural things strive to fulfil qualitative goals, and then went on to argue that all phenomena, moral and physical, are to be explained by the same mechanical principles. There are no values in nature, and there is no foundation of morality in nature.[2] Humans are essentially amoral. There is no social faculty, nor is there any morally significant difference among human motivations. Each of us acts from self-interested motives and only from these motives. Granted, we routinely appear to make moral distinctions, to call some persons or actions "good" and others "evil," but analysis shows that there is no substantive foundation for these moral distinctions. "Good" refers to that which gives pleasure, "evil" to that which gives pain, while those things that give rise to pleasure and pain are a function of transient and idiosyncratic appetites or desires that are themselves merely mechanical responses to physical stimuli. Consequently, all allegedly moral terms are meaningful only "with relation to the person that useth them: there being nothing simply and absolutely [good or evil]; nor any common rule of good and evil, to be taken from the nature of the objects themselves."[3]

Samuel Pufendorf shared with Hobbes the view that nature is devoid of value and that morality has no foundation in nature. To be sure, Pufendorf grants that each individual thing includes a set of properties and dispositions that has come to be called its nature. But he offers a *voluntarist* account of this fact: natures have been both constituted and produced by a free act of the Divine Creator, and this act of creation is at least logically distinct from further acts that create certain "moral Entities."[4] Assuming that these logically distinct acts were also temporally distinct, we see that the deity first created nature, and that then, by separate and equally free acts of the will, imposed moral distinctions on nature. Thus, although lesser intelligent creatures can also impose moral distinctions, it is to the deity that moral distinctions are ultimately to be traced. Moreover, as God has created the world, he is seen to have the right to demand of any creature that it conform its behaviour to his impositions, and the further right to punish any creature that fails so to conform. The foundation of morality is not in nature, but in the omnipotence of a deity who voluntarily and at his own pleasure determines what shall be right and wrong by demanding that lesser and otherwise amoral agents act as he bids.

Ralph Cudworth thought Hobbes and Pufendorf guilty of fundamental errors; each in his own way had launched a dangerous assault on morality. According to Cudworth, moral distinctions are reflections of fixed and immutable features of reality. Hobbes, like Protagoras and other moral sceptics in ancient times, claims that justice and injustice are merely "*Factitious* or Artificial things," mere conventions, there being in this view nothing "Real or Natural but *Atoms* and *Vacuum*." The voluntarists would also have us believe that there is nothing really good or just. On their theory, those things that we call evil or believe to be unjust could equally well have been made, by the unconstrained power of the deity, good and just.[5] To meet the threat of these mistaken and dangerous views, Cudworth turned to what he called the true atomical philosophy, or the new science correctly understood. As befits an avowed Platonist, he rejected the view that nature itself is a mere jumble of conglomerates accidentally or arbitrarily composed. This cannot be the case, the Platonist argument runs, if we have knowledge, even incomplete knowledge, of nature. Knowledge, after all, is immutable: it is of things as they are and would not be *knowledge* of them if they could be other than they are: the knowledge of a thing always entails knowing the nature of the thing, so that if there is knowledge, there must be a nature to know.[6]

This general conception of knowledge is directly relevant to Cudworth's moral concerns. Knowledge, even knowledge of physical objects, presupposes both that there are real and enduring natures to be known, and that our minds are fitted with innate ideas that enable us to recognize these natures. But if there are such things as bodies and causes and triangles, and if we have innately the conceptions of these things as well as the ability to match these conceptions to corresponding aspects of the world, why should we doubt that there are real and enduring moral natures – real and enduring good or justice, for example – and why should we doubt that we possess innately such moral conceptions as virtue, honesty, and justice. In Cudworth's view, we should not so doubt. We do have these conceptions, and we do have the ability to match them to aspects of the world. As much as some things partake of triangularity, so some actions partake of justice; and just as it is true to say of certain things that they are triangular and not round, so is it true to say of certain actions that they are just and not unjust. Moreover, triangularity is triangularity, and justice is justice, quite independently of desires, conventions, or the pronouncements of even the most powerful being.[7] Hobbes was wrong to reduce morality to the commands of the sovereign; Pufendorf was wrong to reduce it to the commands of the deity. Even God commands – and commends – what is just because, of itself and prior to any command, it is just.

The debate over the foundations of morality simmered on through the turn of the eighteenth century. Samuel Clarke, John Balguy, and other *rationalists* argued, as Balguy put it, that "the Foundations of Morality must be laid either in the Truth or Nature of Things themselves, or in the Divine Ideas, which comes to the same thing," and that actions are right in so far as they bring about relations that conform to the real relations holding between these immutable natures. Thus, for example, a person receiving a benefit "acts *rightly* and *reasonably*" when his actions conform to, or mirror, the "Relation of Gratitude between him and his Benefactor."[8] In contrast,

Lord Shaftesbury sought to show that virtue is "really something in itself, and in the nature of things" by means of a careful study of human nature itself. This study led him to the conclusion that, contrary to the claims of Hobbes and the other sceptical, "selfish" moralists, humans have a *moral sense*: a natural moral character that includes a genuinely unselfish concern for others and the facility to recognize objectively founded moral distinctions.[9]

The controversy boiled over again following the publication, in 1723, of an expanded version of Bernard Mandeville's *The Fable of the Bees*. Mandeville paid virtually no attention to the epistemological aspects of Shaftesbury's theory, but he attacked what he perceived to be the excessive optimism of a theory that represented humanity as fundamentally unselfish, and he trenchantly restated moral scepticism in the form of an artifice theory: from a moral perspective, human actions are all essentially alike because all are motivated by self-interest. But a clever and manipulating few, seeing that a widespread *belief* that there are well-founded moral distinctions would make others governable, invented morality and then duped these others into supposing it genuine. "Moral Virtues," runs Mandeville's notorious conclusion, are nothing more than "the Political Offspring which Flattery begot upon Pride."[10]

Among the many replies to this new manifestation of moral scepticism, Francis Hutcheson's was uniquely a defence and a further development of the views of Shaftesbury. Hutcheson also emphasizes the importance of the study of human nature. When we undertake this study we find that our perceptions of good are considerably more complex than either the moral sceptics or the rationalists have imagined. An inanimate object affects us differently than does the free action of a rational agent. Two men may perform precisely the same action, resulting in precisely the same advantage to us. But if we see that one man is constrained or that he is motivated by self-interest, while the other is motivated by a concern for us, we find that our reactions are very different. These examples show that our reactions, our affections or feelings, are not shaped entirely by self-interest. Other examples show that humans do sometimes act altruistically, and that this is in fact a normal or natural mode of behaviour. Once facts of this sort have been established, Hutcheson goes on to ask "what *Senses*, *Instincts*, or *Affections*" must necessarily be presupposed to account for them. Neither self-interest nor reason are adequate to the task.[11] These facts of human experience can only be explained if we suppose humanity equipped with a moral sense – with a sense that motivates us to useful and kindly actions, and that also approves actions of this sort. Moral distinctions have their foundation in human nature.

II. CRITICISM

Hume's examination of the controversy regarding the foundations of morality is found principally in two works, the *Treatise of Human Nature*, and *An Enquiry concerning the Principles of Morals*. These works show Hume to have thought that what he and others of his period called moral scepticism – the view that alleged moral distinctions have no other foundation than idiosyncratic and subjective preferences – is mistaken. As noted, Hobbes had been perceived as denying that there is any independent or objective foundation for the moral distinctions we appear to make. To many, it seemed that he had come to this conclusion because he was convinced that all actions are motivated by self-interest, and hence are morally indistinguishable. Hume accepts one premise of this argument, the claim that motives play a pre-eminent role in the determination of virtue, but he rejects as ill-founded the claim that all our motives are self-interested. Humans may well be predominantly self-interested, but an accurate review of their behaviour reveals "instances, in which private interest was separate from public; in which it was even contrary," and in which the *publicly* interested act was the one performed. On other occasions, private and public interest concur and thereby work together to produce a regard for the public good greater than that which would have been produced by self-interest alone. Faced with facts of this kind, "we must," Hume says, "renounce the theory, which accounts for every moral sentiment by the principle of self-love" (EPM 5.1–2, 215–19; see also E-DM).[12]

Mandeville's artifice theory is shown to be equally unsatisfactory. Some philosophers, Hume says, "have represented all moral distinctions as the effect of artifice and education, when skilful politicians endeavour'd to restrain the turbulent passions of men, and make them operate to the public good, by the notions of honour and shame." This theory is simply "not consistent with experience." First, there are virtues and vices that have nothing to do with public good. These virtues Mandeville's theory fails entirely to explain. Second, if we had no *natural* moral sentiments, no politician, however skilful, could excite moral reactions in us by artifice or teach us that use of language which characterizes the moral domain. Not only do we respond differently to different kinds of behaviour, but we also, even according to Mandeville, competently use a moral vocabulary – we consistently denominate some things honourable, others dishonourable, and so forth. But on Mandeville's account the existence and use of this vocabulary must be traced to those skilful politicians he hypothesizes. Such an explanation, Hume suggests, is simply unbelievable, analogous to claiming that skilful opticians could teach a sightless species to use, competently, a vocabulary of colour terms. Had nature not made moral distinctions "founded on the original constitution of the mind, the words, *honourable* and *shameful*, *lovely* and *odious*, *noble* and *despicable*, had never had place in any language; nor could politicians, had they invented these terms, ever have been able to render them intelligible, or make them convey any idea to the audience" (T 3.2.2, 500; 3.3.1, 578; EPM 5.1, 214).

Hume also rejected the efforts of the rationalists and voluntarists to give morality a supranatural foundation. The moral rationalists claimed, for example, that moral distinctions are based on transcendental principles and immutable relations that oblige all rational creatures and that can only be discerned by the use of reason. The facts, according to Hume, are very different. As far as any of us knows or can know, morality has to do only with human beings and human affairs. We do not know what is expected of higher beings; our reason cannot reach to such heights. But, if this transcendental realm is beyond our reach, we need not suppose that reason provides the foundation of morality. An exaggerated view of the power of reason leads the rationalist to suppose that reason can pierce its way into the realm of transcendental values. Once we see that reason lacks entirely this extraordinary power, we can conclude that morality does not depend exclusively on reason.

In addition, rationalists tell us that there are immutable principles of the form: parents are always to be obeyed and venerated, or siblings must never interact sexually. In other words, there is no doubt but that parricide and incest are taken to be immoral. But the rationalists seem not to have noticed that these principles are constantly

violated in nature, and violated without any thought that these violations are immoral. No rationalist has yet chastised a tree for over-
growing and thereby killing its parent tree; no cats from the same
litter have yet been pronounced morally reprehensible for interbreed-
ing. Not even the rationalists, then, suppose morality to derive entirely from abstract relations and the conformity or nonconformity
of actions to these relations. If the rationalist attempts to counter
this objection by saying that trees are not guilty of parricide because
they lack a will and choice, he will in effect have abandoned his
theory in favour of one that derives moral differences from the
causes of actions, not merely from conformity or nonconformity to
abstract relations. And finally, even if we did know the abstract
principles to which the rationalists allude, these principles would
not provide an adequate foundation for morals. Morality is a practical affair, one that involves volitions and actions. Neither abstract
rational principles nor reason is capable of providing the motivational force that is essential to morality (T 3.1.1, 455–70).[13]

One solution to the motivational issue was provided by Pufendorf
and other voluntarists. These theorists trace morality to, ultimately,
the unconstrained will of an omnipotent deity who is said to have a
detailed concern for, and knowledge of, each of his creatures. The
deity lays down laws, thus establishing morality, and then provides
sanctions, in the form of eternal rewards and punishments, that
motivate humans to conform their behaviour to these laws.[14] Hume
was, understandably, unimpressed with this approach to the matter.
Voluntarists, in his view, had misunderstood the nature of morality
and its relationship to religion and religious belief. They suppose
that a person who acts as she is told to act because she fears she will
be punished if she fails to do so is nonetheless a virtuous or morally
good person. Hume, on the contrary, supposed that a person's motives play an important role in determining her moral character and
the moral character of her actions. Perhaps some actions performed
from a motive of fear (an obviously self-interested motive) will
count as virtuous actions, but the voluntarists are wrong to suppose
that all morality is reducible to self-interest. These voluntarists may
be right about the foundations of religion or religious practice, but
they have failed to explain the foundations of morality.[15]

Hume argues, then, that neither the remote, philosophical deity of
Cudworth, nor the personal, awe-inspiring deity of Pufendorf pro-

vides a proper foundation for morality. And he meant that these arguments should provide a general conclusion: morality can no more be traced to the transcendental or the supranatural than to bodies, forces, and motions. But if founded neither on rules or forces that transcend nature, nor on features of physical nature, where may the foundations of morality lie? In human nature, said Hume, echoing Grotius, Shaftesbury, and Hutcheson.

III. FUNDAMENTAL FEATURES OF HUME'S THEORY

Although the accounts of morality found in the *Treatise* and the second *Enquiry* are fundamentally consistent with one another, there are noticeable differences between them. In due course we will need to give separate consideration to these two versions of Hume's theory, but in the meantime we can consider some fundamental features that they share.

Human nature as a primitive element

To say that morality is founded on human nature is to suggest that, with respect to morals, human nature is a primitive element, an ultimate fact, beyond which explanation cannot go. Hume begins the *Treatise* by suggesting that all the sciences, morals included, rest on human nature, and that it would be a poor philosophy indeed that attempted to carry the explanation of human nature to unobserved principles or causes allegedly more ultimate than this nature as it is observed (T Intro, xvi–xix). Elsewhere he argues that there are in the "mental world" effects as extraordinary as in the physical, and that the causes of these effects "are mostly unknown, and must be resolv'd into *original* qualities of human nature, which I pretend not to explain" (T 1.1.4, 13). Near the end of the *Treatise* he refers to "particular *original* principles of human nature, which cannot be accounted for" (T 3.3.1, 590), while in the *Enquiry concerning the Principles of Morals* he is equally explicit:

It is needless to push our researches so far as to ask, why we have humanity or a fellow-feeling with others. It is sufficient, that this is experienced to be a principle in human nature. We must stop somewhere in our examination of causes; and there are, in every science, some general principles, beyond

which we cannot hope to find any principle more general. No man is absolutely indifferent to the happiness and misery of others. The first has a
natural tendency to give pleasure; the second, pain. This every one may find
in himself. It is not probable, that these principles can be resolved into
principles more simple and universal, whatever attempts may have been
made to that purpose. But if it were possible, it belongs not to the present
subject; and we may here safely consider these principles as original: happy,
if we can render all the consequences sufficiently plain and perspicuous!

(EPM 5.2, 219–20n)[16]

The unalterability of human nature

To rest morality on human nature is also to suggest that, for a start,
this nature provides a stable base for morality. For Hume, this base is
not merely stable, but also unalterable. If "we cast our eye upon
human nature," we will discover "that in all nations and ages" the
same kinds of things cause pride or humility, and so much so that we
can predict with considerable accuracy the reactions of a stranger. If
we do perceive "any variation in this particular, it proceeds from
nothing but a difference in the tempers and complexions of men;
and is besides very inconsiderable. Can we imagine it possible, that
while human nature remains the same, men will ever become entirely indifferent to their power, riches, beauty or personal merit,
and that their pride and vanity will not be affected by these advantages?" (T 2.1.3, 280–1).[17] The "different stations of life," Hume
argues, "arise necessarily, because uniformly, from the necessary
and uniform principles of human nature. Men cannot live without
society, and cannot be associated without government" (T 2.3.1,
402). Should a traveller tell us that he had discovered a country
whose inhabitants exactly resembled "those in *Plato's Republic* on
the one hand, or those in *Hobbes's Leviathan* on the other," few
would be so credulous as to believe him, for there is "a general
course of nature in human actions, as well as in the operations of the
sun and the climate." Although so explicit a claim about the unalter-
ability of human nature is missing from the second *Enquiry*, Hume
does there speak of the "necessary and infallible consequences of the
general principles of human nature," while the *Enquiry concerning
Human Understanding* repeats exactly the position taken in the
Treatise (T 2.3.1, 402–3; EPM 5.2, 230; EHU 8.1, 84).

A distinction of motives

To rest morality on human nature is also to suggest that it exhibits certain substantive features which, in conjunction with other circumstances of human life, operate to produce moral experience and moral distinctions. That Hume supposed that humans are typically able to act from significantly different motives is clear from his criticism of the selfish theory.[18] But he also argues that specific distinctions of motive lead directly to moral distinctions.

Philosophers on both sides of the foundations controversy had argued that distinctions of motive underlie, and give rise to, whatever genuine moral distinctions we may make. Among Hume's more immediate predecessors, Richard Blackmore had said that the "necessary intrinsick Principle which constitutes a moral Action" is the end or purpose for which it is done, so that what "distinguishes a good Action from an evil one is a right End, which excites the Will to chuse it, and to which it is directed in the Intention of the Agent."[19] According to Mandeville, "it is impossible to judge of a Man's Performance, unless we are th[o]roughly acquainted with the Principle and Motive from which he acts." When we are so acquainted, we discover that apparently virtuous actions, however useful they may be, are without moral merit because they are done from self-interest. Thus, for example, whoever acts from pity, says Mandeville,

> what good soever he may bring to the Society, has nothing to boast of but that he has indulged a Passion that has happened to be beneficial to the Publick. There is no Merit in saving an innocent Babe ready to drop into the Fire: The Action is neither good nor bad, and what Benefit soever the Infant received, we only obliged our selves; for to have seen it fall, and not strove to hinder it, would have caused a Pain, which Self-preservation compell'd us to prevent.[20]

Hutcheson discusses at length the motives underlying actions and concludes that even those "Actions which in Fact are exceedingly useful, shall appear void of *moral Beauty*, if we know they proceeded from no kind Intentions towards others."[21]

Hume himself argues that we appear to be well- or ill-disposed toward a person in accordance with the pleasure or pain he or she causes us. On closer inspection, however, we discover that the person in question must not only cause us pleasure or pain, but also must do so from some "durable" feature of mind: he must either act "knowingly, and with a particular design and intention," or from a settled character.[22] Generally speaking, a person who "harms us by accident, becomes not our enemy upon that account, nor do we think ourselves bound by any ties of gratitude to one, who does us any service after the same manner. By the intention we judge of the actions, and according as that is good or bad, they become causes of love or hatred." The principal exception to this rule arises from character: a person who exhibits "constant and inherent" qualities is esteemed or hated in proportion to the pleasure or pain these qualities cause, independently of any intention (T 2.2.3, 348).

The moral significance of these distinctions of motive is revealed when we find Hume repeating with approval the view that distinctions of motive underlie, and give rise to, whatever genuine moral distinctions we may make. In a letter to Hutcheson written while he was making his final set of revisions to Book 3 of the *Treatise*, Hume wrote, "Actions are not virtuous nor vicious; but only so far as they are proofs of certain Qualitys or durable Principles in the Mind" (HL 1: 34). In the *Treatise* itself he maintains that when we appear to direct moral praise or blame to actions we are in fact only considering "the motives that produced them, and consider the actions as signs or indications of certain principles in the mind and temper," and "that all virtuous actions derive their merit only from virtuous motives, and are consider'd merely as signs of those motives" (T 3.2.1, 477–8). Just in case this is not clear enough, he later says that "If any *action* be either virtuous or vicious, 'tis only as a sign of some quality or character. It must depend upon durable principles of the mind, which extend over the whole conduct, and enter into the personal character" (T. 3.3.1, 575).

The second *Enquiry* contains no comparable general discussion of the relation of motive to moral merit, but Hume does there repeatedly insist that humans act from motives of significantly different kinds, and that this difference underlies morality itself. Humans sometimes act from benevolent motives, and this in itself is sufficient to make a person virtuous: "it seems undeniable," he writes, "*that* nothing can bestow more merit on any human creature than the sentiment of benevolence in an eminent degree" (EPM 2.2, 181). To this he adds that "It is sufficient for our present purpose, if it be allowed, what surely, without the greatest absurdity cannot be disputed, that there is some benevolence, however small, infused into our bosom; some spark of friendship for human kind; some particle of the dove kneaded into our frame, along with the elements of the wolf and serpent" (EPM 9.1, 271).[23] Moreover, humans as presently constituted are unavoidably concerned with the well- or ill-being of their fellow creatures, and thus at times when our own interests are not involved we find that what promotes the happiness of these fellows "is good, what tends to their misery is evil, without any farther regard or consideration. Here then are the faint rudiments, at least, or outlines, of a *general* distinction between actions" (EPM 5.2, 230).

A moral sensibility

Hume also believes that humans come equipped with a moral sensibility and, consequently, that the moral qualities of human agents – their relevantly different motivations – occasion in us distinct and peculiar feelings that reflect these different motives. When in the *Treatise* he first raises the issue of the foundation of morals, he goes on to say that the "most probable hypothesis, which has been advanc'd to explain the distinction betwixt vice and virtue, and the origin of moral rights and obligations," is that a fundamental feature of our nature causes us to experience pleasure or pain upon the observation of certain "characters and passions" or motives (T 2.1.7, 296).[24] In *Treatise* 3.1.2, he argues that because reason alone is unable to locate or distinguish virtue or vice, it "must be by means of some impression or sentiment they occasion, that we are able to mark the difference betwixt them" (470).

As we have noted, the second *Enquiry* suggests that our propensity to feel approbation in response to benevolence provides the rudimentary framework on which morality depends. The benevolence in question may be weak, too weak by itself to motivate us. Nonetheless, it produces a preference for what is useful to humankind, and from this "A *moral distinction*, therefore, immediately arises; a general sentiment of blame and approbation; a tendency, however faint, to the objects of the one, and a proportionable aversion to those of the other" (EPM 9.1, 271). And how does this happen? By the operation of the relevant durable principles of mind (an intention, for example) on our moral sensibility. Virtue, says Hume, is "*whatever mental action or quality*" of the agent that "*gives to a spectator the pleasing sentiment of approbation.*" Vice has the contrary effect on the same sensibility (EPM App 1, 289).[25]

An instrumental reason

On Hume's reading of the evidence, there is no guise in which reason alone can serve as the foundation of morality. Reason is unable to grasp moral differences; such differences, as we have seen, engender responses that are sensed or felt. And, while morality by its very nature involves active agents, reason is "perfectly inert" and quite unable to motivate agents to act. In addition, Hume strikingly proclaims: "Reason is, and ought only to be the slave of the passions." It does not follow, however, that Hume thought reason has no important role to play in morality. Reason may be subservient to the passions, but the service it offers is essential to morality. Our desires, we might say, give us certain goals, but reason, because only it can inform us of the relations of causes to effects, is required to direct these desires to their goals. On other occasions, however, reason informs us that our desired end is unattainable or would be harmful. In these latter cases, "our passions yield to our reason without any opposition" (T 3.1.1, 458; 2.3.3, 415–16). The significance of these facts to the foundations of morality is succinctly stated in the second *Enquiry*:

One principal foundation of moral praise being supposed to lie in the usefulness of any quality or action, it is evident that *reason* must enter for a considerable share in all decisions of this kind; since nothing but that faculty can instruct us in the tendency of qualities and actions, and point out their beneficial consequences to society and to their possessor. . . . But though reason, when fully assisted and improved, be sufficient to instruct us in the pernicious or useful tendency of qualities and actions; it is not alone sufficient to produce any moral blame or approbation. . . . [R]eason instructs us in the several tendencies of actions, and [the sentiment of] *humanity* makes a distinction in favour of those which are useful and beneficial.   (EPM App. 1, 285–6)

IV. *A TREATISE OF HUMAN NATURE*

Of Morals, the final book of Hume's *Treatise*, addresses itself directly to the dispute regarding the foundations of morals. The work begins with a discussion showing that reason is not, and that sentiment or feeling is, the means by which we are able to mark the distinction between virtue and vice. Hume defends, in effect, a causal theory of moral perception, one in which an impartial consideration of intention, motive, or character (the relevant durable principles of mind) are said to give rise to *"peculiar"* pleasures and pains, the unique moral sentiments. The "moral deformity" of an action (and actions themselves are, morally speaking, only signs of the motives that produce them) is "felt by an internal sense, and by means of some sentiment, which the reflecting on such an action naturally occasions" (T 3.1.2, 472; 3.1.1, 466).

Having settled this apparently epistemological issue, Hume restates the question he had first raised in his earlier discussion of the passions: Are virtue and vice founded on natural and original principles, or do they arise merely from such other principles as interest and education? He returns a cautious response. The answer to this question depends on what is meant by those decidedly ambiguous terms, *nature* and *natural*. If *natural* is understood to contrast with *miraculous*, then "the distinction betwixt vice and virtue is natural." If *natural* is contrasted with *rare* or *unusual*, then we can conclude that there is nothing more natural than our moral sentiments. But *nature* may also be contrasted with *artifice*; we may contrast what is done instinctively or automatically with what is invented or contrived. According to Hume, some moral distinctions, some virtues, are in this third sense *natural*, while others are *artificial*, the result of human contrivance (T 3.1.2, 474–5).

The natural virtues

In saying that some virtues are natural, Hume is claiming that some of the human characteristics – he mentions, among others, love of one's children, beneficence, generosity, clemency, moderation, temperance, and frugality – to which we respond with approbation are embedded as fundamental propensities of human nature itself. The evidence suggests that every human being, from the most primitive times to the present, has been motivated by these inherent virtues. It is not Hume's view that these virtues are especially powerful and able invariably to overcome the additional, self-regarding instincts that also characterize humankind. Our natural generosity, for example, seldom extends its motivational effect beyond our immediate circle of family and friends; beyond that point our typical mode is a selfish one. But there are natural virtues; we sometimes desire no more than the good of another or the restraint of our own excesses.

Even more important, those who observe the effects of the natural virtues experience, as it were, the pleasure of those who benefit from such virtues. This displaced pleasure or approbation is made possible by the operation of sympathy, a principle of communication. Human beings, Hume suggests, resonate among themselves like strings of the same length wound to the same tension. Consequently, when one of us observes a quality or character that has a tendency to the good of other individuals or of humanity itself, and whose operation produces, or may be expected to produce, pleasure in others, we ourselves resonate with the pleasure of those others. We ourselves neither receive nor expect to receive any direct benefit from the observed quality, but our sympathetic link to it causes us to approve it: by means of sympathy we feel approbation. This approbation – suitably qualified by considerations of impartiality, generality, and distance in time and place – turns out to be nothing else than the unique moral sentiment by which we mark the presence of virtue; disapprobation, *mutatis mutandis*, is the sentiment by which we mark the presence of vice (T 3.3.1, 579; see also E-OC 479–80).

The artificial virtues

In contrast to the natural virtues there are others – justice, fidelity, and allegiance are examples – that are not as such embedded in human nature. These, the artificial virtues, have evolved. They have, gradually and over a long period of time, developed on the base of human nature as humans interact with one another and their environment.[26] It is Hume's view that even the most primitive people, organized into the smallest viable human unit, the family, could have been and were moved to act generously toward one another, but that such peoples, in such units, had no need for the rules of justice. In Hume's system, justice is concerned entirely with property arrangements.[27] When the social unit was the family, there was no more need for a system governing private property than there is for "mine" and "thine" between husband and wife. It was only as societies grew larger and more complex, and as certain goods came to be in short supply, that a system of justice was developed.

How is it, Hume asks, that *"the rules of justice are establish'd by the artifice of men"*? In response to his own question, he emphasizes humanity's natively perilous condition: "Of all the animals, with which this globe is peopled, there is none towards whom nature seems, at first sight, to have exercis'd more cruelty than towards man." It is only by banding together in societies that humanity was able to overcome these natural disadvantages: society enables those in it to increase their force, their abilities, and their safety. Hume goes on to suggest that while society (a social unit governed by the rules of justice) itself was not entirely natural – society was not an original feature of the human condition – its development, fortunately, was natural. Certain features of human nature and of our environment have led us beyond the most primitive social unit, the extended family, to the larger units of true societies (T 3.2.2, 484–5).

If nature led the way to this development, there were nonetheless natural obstacles to it. There was first the natural human temper, with a significant tendency towards a disruptive selfishness. There is the further fact that possessions acquired by industry or good fortune can be stripped from us and are in such short supply that violent dispossessions are a likely feature of our primitive state. We need society in order to increase our abilities, strength, and safety; yet in this primitive state, no such rule-governed social state was to be found. The idea of justice "wou'd never have been dream'd of" among the rude and savage, for their conduct was ruled by natural partiality. The remedy came when even the earliest humans saw that their interests would be served by a form of co-operation that led to the development of conventions that had the effect of curbing their heedless natural partiality, thereby bestowing a beneficial stability of possession to scarce external goods.[28] In time, this insight was developed to the point that enlightened self-interest was able to bring heedless self-interest under control. In this way, justice, and with it society, came into being (T 3.2.2, 488–9).

Hume's account of justice is complicated by the fact that he begins it by reminding us that the motive from which an action is done determines the moral character of that action: "all virtuous actions derive their merit only from virtuous motives, and are consider'd merely as signs of those motives." If the conventions and practice of justice derive from motives of self-interest, how can justice or its practice be any kind of virtue? Hume shows that he is well aware of this difficulty when he goes on to consider a second question about justice: What are *"the reasons, which determine us to attribute to the observance or neglect of these rules a moral beauty and deformity,"* or, why do *"we annex the idea of virtue to justice, and of vice to injustice"* (T 3.2.1–2, 478, 484, 498). In answering this second question, Hume tells us, in effect, how justice is moralized. He tells us how it is that we come to attach *moral* significance to what is apparently a self-interested concern that the rules of justice be maintained.

In the normal and slowly developing course of events, the societies that were made possible once heedless self-interest was brought under the control of enlightened self-interest increased in size. As they did so, it became more difficult for individuals to see how their private interest was being served by adherence to the established rules of justice, and consequently some individuals broke these rules – they acted unjustly – perhaps without even noticing that they were doing so. Others, however, invariably noticed when these rules were broken and they themselves were thereby harmed, just as we still notice such harmful transgressions. Moreover, even when the injustices perpetrated by others are so remote as not to harm us or to affect our interest, we are nonetheless displeased because we find such behaviour "prejudicial to human society, and pernicious to every one that approaches the person guilty of it" (T 3.2.2, 499). In short, what began as a purely self-interested concern that the rules of justice be maintained becomes in addition an other-regarding concern that these rules be followed. Furthermore, this additional concern develops to the extent that individuals who contravene the rules of justice are made uneasy by their very own contraventions and declare even these to be vicious.

Two features of human nature make this development possible. The first is our tendency to establish general rules, and to give to these rules an inflexibility that can withstand even the pressures of self-interest. Once we have established rules that are to govern the possession and exchange of property, we find our sentiments are influenced by these rules even when their use is contrary to our self-interest. Rules with that kind of continuing force exercise at least a partial check on self-interest. Second, the principle of sympathy is again at work. Any individual act of justice may be contrary to the public good, so that it is "only the concurrence of mankind, in a general scheme or system of action, which is advantageous," but sympathy is equal to the task (T 3.3.1, 579). Unaffected by our narrowly selfish interests, sympathy causes us to feel approbation in response to actions that maintain the system of justice and, by extension, the public interest, and disapprobation in response to those that fail to give such support: it is because sympathy causes us to share the approbation or uneasiness of others that "the sense of moral good and evil follows upon justice and injustice. . . . [S]elf-interest is the original motive to the *establishment* of justice: but a sympathy with *public* interest is the source of the *moral* approbation which attends that virtue" (T 3.2.2, 499–500; italics as at 670). The net result is that justice, because it comes to have a second foundation in human nature, does eventually evolve into a full-fledged moral virtue. In Hume's own words:

> Upon the whole, then, we are to consider this distinction betwixt justice and injustice, as having two different foundations, *viz.* that of *self-interest*, when men observe, that 'tis impossible to live in society without restraining themselves by certain rules; and that of *morality*, when this interest is once observ'd to be common to all mankind, and men receive a pleasure from the view of such actions as tend to the peace of society, and an uneasiness from such as are contrary to it. 'Tis the voluntary convention and artifice of men, which makes the first interest take place; and therefore those laws of justice are so far to be consider'd as *artificial*. After that interest is once establish'd and acknowledg'd, the sense of morality in the observance of these rules follows *naturally*, and of itself.
>
> (T 3.2.6, 533)[29]

Duty and obligation

Hume does not provide us with a systematic account of how it is that duty or obligation arise – of how it is that individuals come to be obliged. In fact, in one of the most widely discussed paragraphs in the *Treatise*, Hume criticizes virtually all his predecessors for deriving propositions expressing obligation from purely factual premises. This may lead some to suppose that Hume is arguing that all moral imperatives (all propositions of the form, "X ought to do Y" or "X ought to have done Y") are unfounded, and that he is inconsistent when he later suggests that humans do in fact have both natural and moral duties or obligations. Such a reading would be a mistake.

Hume's argument is found at the end of his critique of the rationalist account of the foundations of morality and buttresses that critique by showing again "that the distinction of vice and virtue is not founded merely on the relations of objects, nor . . . perceiv'd by reason." His argument as stated is of very limited scope. He argues only that it is "altogether inconceivable" that a proposition containing the modal term "ought" can be *deduced* from other propositions that contain no such term (T 3.1.1, 469–70). He argues, that is, that those who suppose they have rationally deduced obligations from merely factual premises have committed a logical blunder, but he does not claim that obligation itself is inexplicable or an illicit, meaningless concept.

What account of obligation or duty can be derived from the text of the *Treatise*? Human nature is again the key. Because human nature is uniform, human action generally follows certain patterns: there is a natural or usual course of behaviour that corresponds to the passions or motivating principles that constitute human nature (T 3.2.1, 483). Consequently, we expect behaviour to conform to these patterns. When it fails to do so, our expectations are disappointed, and we respond with feelings of disapprobation or blame. We then say that the individual who is blamed has failed to act rightly or has failed to do his duty. As Hume describes such ascriptions of blame, the charge we make may either amount to the claim that the failure in question is fundamentally a failure of motive, or only to the simpler claim that an expected action or pattern of behaviour is missing. "We blame a father for neglecting his child," he says, "because it shews a want of natural affection, which is the duty of every parent." He then goes on to suggest that, were not *natural* affection for children a standard feature of human nature, the care of children would not be *expected* of parents, and consequently, it would be impossible for parents to have a *sense of duty* regarding the care of their children. As he later says, "A father knows it to be his duty to take care of his children: But he has also a natural inclination to it. And if no human creature had that inclination, no one cou'd lie under any such obligation" (T 3.2.1, 478; 3.2.5, 518–19).

This understanding of Hume's position is consistent with his further claim that taking any action to be a duty presupposes that there is, "distinct from a sense of duty," a prior motive to perform that action. Moreover, he explicitly claims that this prior motive must be a part of human nature itself: *"no action can be virtuous, or morally good, unless there be in human nature some motive to produce it, distinct from the sense of its morality."* The interpretation is also consistent with his claim that a man may perform certain actions merely from a "sense of duty" (when lacking, that is, the separate, natural motive "common in human nature"), and thus *suppose*, mistakenly, that "he has, by that means, fulfill'd his duty." That is, he may suppose that he has been virtuous even though he lacks the very feature that is genuinely virtuous, namely, a virtuous or other-regarding motive. In one literal sense, then, duty for Hume is what is *expected* of individuals. But he clearly insists that individuals may perform in the expected manner from one of two kinds of motive: because of a morally meritorious, first-order motive (regard for another), in which case one is really virtuous; or from a morally empty, second-order motive (the sense that one ought to conform one's behaviour to expectations), in which case one only appears to be virtuous. In cases of the second sort, the sense of duty enables the individual to mask and to neutralize the fact that he or she is not really virtuous (T 3.2.1, 478–9).

Hume's admittedly meagre remarks suggest that our idea or concept of duty is the consequence of an experiential process that is structurally similar to the process that gives rise to the idea of necessary connection. The idea of necessary connection derives, according to Hume, from the impression of expectation that arises on the occasion of the experience of a particular event of type *A* after events of type *B* have been repeatedly experienced to follow closely the experience of *A*'s. Hume's remarks about duty suggest that a similar impression of expectation underlies our idea of moral obligation, as well as that of blame, and at least some forms of approbation. "Our sense of duty always follows the common and natural course of our passions," he says (T 3.2.1, 484). From this common course of human nature comes the expectation that certain actions will be performed. When those actions fail to be performed, we feel disappointment or disapproval just when, if the actions had been carried out, we would have been pleased or approving. Feelings of disapproval of just this particular type (feelings that are distinctive at least in so far as they arise in just these circumstances), copied in one of the several ways in which ideas copy impressions, become the idea of blame, or the idea that an individual *ought* to have acted in some particular way. Blame, generalized, to apply to all who ought so to act, becomes the concept of duty. The *idea* of duty is derived from the impression of expectation; the *sense* of duty is just that impression when it is associated with this generalized concept of blame. Duty or obligation cannot be deduced from factual premises, but they are derived from the facts of human experience.

V. *AN ENQUIRY CONCERNING THE PRINCIPLES OF MORALS*

An Enquiry concerning the Principles of Morals was first published in 1751. Of all his writings, Hume thought this second *Enquiry* "incomparably the best," but as he also claimed that it and *An Enquiry concerning Human Understanding* represented attempts to recast the substance of the *Treatise* into clearer and more palatable forms, we can assume that Hume thought the second *Enquiry* to be essentially consistent with the *Treatise*, and to improve on this earlier work principally by simplifying and clarifying the views found there (MOL). Whether or not this assumption is correct, it is clear that on moral perception and sympathy the *Enquiry* has decidedly less to say than does the *Treatise*, and that the later work makes no use of the language of "natural" and "artificial" virtues.

At the outset of the *Enquiry*, Hume gives short shrift to those disingenuous controversialists "who have denied the reality of moral distinctions." It is scarcely conceivable that anyone could believe so sceptical a hypothesis, and clearly impossible that such a scepticism could be consistently lived; we need not waste our time on the disputes of these would-be moral sceptics. But Hume does again turn to the controversy "concerning the general foundation of Morals; whether they be derived from Reason, or from Sentiment." Granting that there are sound arguments to support the claims of both reason and sentiment, he proposes to settle the question of the true origin or foundation of morals by following a simpler and less abstract method. He will "analyse that complication of mental qualities, which form what, in common life, we call Personal Merit." He will, that is, survey those mental qualities, the possession of which causes us to praise or blame the possessor. Such an analysis should be relatively easy to complete. As every language includes a set of terms by which we express such praise or blame, we can expect language itself to give us reliable guidance. All that we need is to discover the circumstances that govern the use of the terms by which we express our praise or blame; we need only discover the common feature(s) of the qualities that are esteemed or blamed. This, Hume insists, is "a question of fact, not of abstract science," and consequently, provided only that we follow the "experimental method [of] deducing general maxims from a comparison of particular instances," we can expect our enquiry to be successful (EPM 1, 169–74).

The particulars on which Hume first focuses are those relating to two social virtues, benevolence and justice. It is obvious, he says, that our benevolent qualities are esteemed. To say of a person that he or she is *"sociable, good-natured, humane, merciful, grateful, friendly, generous, beneficent,* or their equivalents" is to "express the highest merit, which *human nature* is capable of attaining." The esteem that we accord these qualities arises in large part because of their "tendency to promote the interests of our species, and bestow happiness on human society." The usefulness of these forms of benevolence is at least a necessary condition of the esteem we give to them, a conclusion that is confirmed by the fact that, once acts of a particular type cease to be useful, they cease to be esteemed (EPM 2.1, 176, 181). Hume's analysis of justice leads him to say that the origin of justice (and such similar virtues as allegiance) can be traced entirely to their general usefulness, and their existence depends upon the particular circumstances of humankind. Alter these circumstances – provide an abundance of all our necessities, or make such items so scarce that it is impossible to give an adequate share to all who have need – and the conventions of justice would never arise. Had one of these conditions prevailed at the beginning of society, the rules for the distribution of property would never have arisen; should one prevail in the future, our present rules, proving useless, would atrophy, disappear. It is in this sense, then, that "the necessity of justice to the support of society is the sole foundation of that virtue," and it is this "circumstance of usefulness" that causes us to praise those actions and qualities that contribute to a well-ordered society (EPM 3.1, 183–204, esp. 203–4).

But why, Hume goes on to ask, does this usefulness please us?

Why is it that we esteem those qualities that are beneficial to society? Before answering the question, he notes that it does not concern inanimate objects. We obviously find many such objects to be useful, but that is no reason to suppose that we are to call them virtuous, nor do we, except in odd, non-moral ways, attribute virtues to them: "The sentiments, excited by utility, are, in the two cases, very different." Those sentiments directed toward "thinking rational beings" include esteem or approbation, while the sentiments directed toward mere things are clearly very different. Our concern, then, is with our approbation of those distinctly human acts that benefit (or harm) humans and society (EPM 5.1, 213n).

Hume supposes that two answers have been given to his question, Why does utility please? Some have said that acts useful to society receive our approbation because, and only because, we see them as benefitting ourselves personally. Others believe that these acts receive our approbation on some or even many occasions because, although they give us no personal benefit, human beings, constituted as they are, recognize the acts as beneficial to others and take pleasure in the experience or thought of such benefits. As we know, Hume aligns himself with the second group. He grants that human nature is marked by a strong tendency towards self-interest, and that the claim that we support the principles of morality and social order only because of this interest has creditable supporters. It is here that Hume shows that the selfish theory cannot be correct because it cannot account for crucial aspects of our experience. The selfish theory cannot account for our competent use of moral language or the fact that we give our approbation to actions remote from us or clearly contrary to our interests. Utility pleases us because, finally, we are to some degree other-regarding beings, and utility contributes to the good of others (EPM 5.1, 214–15).

In the following sections of the second *Enquiry*, Hume focuses his attention on some of the non-social virtues and thereby expands his account of the qualities that constitute personal merit in such a way that the claims of the selfish theory are further weakened. In Section 6, he takes up those qualities which, while useful to their possessors and approved of by those others who recognize them, are of no benefit to these approving non-possessors. Such qualities as discretion, industry, frugality, prudence, and discernment (the "selfish virtues") tend only to the usefulness of their possessors, and yet we praise them and their possessors, a fact entirely inexplicable by the selfish hypothesis. Section 7 treats of qualities immediately agreeable to ourselves, and Section 8 of those immediately agreeable to others. It is important to note that to each of the latter two kinds of qualities our response is immediate. Thus, prior to any calculation regarding usefulness or useful tendencies, we praise such qualities as cheerfulness, greatness of mind, dignity, and tranquillity, or wit, politeness, eloquence, decency, and cleanliness. These qualities are approved of by those who observe them in others; even those who only hear of a person endowed with such qualities find themselves responding with approbation. There is, then, further evidence that some approvals are not determined by self-interest.

Although Hume suggests that these conclusions may have a certain *philosophical* novelty, it is difficult for him to resist the view that they are obvious and obviously correct. It is surely surprising, he says, that anyone would think it necessary to prove that "Personal Merit consists altogether in the possession of mental qualities, *useful* or *agreeable* to the *person himself* or to *others.*" Fortunately, although "systems and hypotheses have perverted our natural understanding," or at least that of philosophers, ordinary individuals accept implicitly the view of merit that has been sketched (EPM 9.1, 268–70).

Hume's analysis is not quite complete. He undertakes to show how this finding about personal merit, obvious and important though it may be, provides us with a *foundation* for morality. To this end, he focuses on a factual concomitant of the account of personal merit he has provided: humans are not entirely selfish creatures. As we have seen, "there is some benevolence, however small, infused into our bosom; some spark of friendship for human kind." Weak though these generous inclinations may be, they are strong enough to cause us to prefer that which is "useful and serviceable to mankind, above what is pernicious and dangerous" (EPM 9.1, 271). Moral distinctions are founded on this fact, the fact that we desire, however weakly, what is beneficial to our fellow humans, and on the further fact that we respond with approval or disapproval to the qualities or actions of others. There are genuine and significant differences between characters and the actions resulting from them. Some are beneficial to mankind, and some are pernicious. Witnessing these actions and characters, we respond with approbation or disapprobation. In doing so, we make moral distinctions: we ca *morally good* those actions or characters that result in public benefit; those intending injury we call *morally evil*.

This way of putting the matter is, Hume points out immediately, too general. It is not enough that we respond to the actions and characters of others with approval or disapproval. Some responses – those directed by the passions of avarice, ambition, vanity, and the like – "are here excluded from our theory concerning the origin of morals" because they "have not a proper direction for that purpose." The very idea of morality presupposes a "sentiment common to all mankind, which recommends the same object to general approbation," a sentiment "so universal and comprehensive" as to extend even to those persons the most remote from any given moral assessor. This sentiment, derived from a "universal principle of the human frame," is, of all our sentiments, the only one capable of providing "the foundation of any general system and established theory of blame or approbation" or "the foundation of morals." Why? Because the sentiments that derive from this principle: (a) are the same for all humans; (b) produce in each of us the same moral assessments; (c) have as their scope all humans; and (d) produce moral assessments, in each of us, of all other humans (EPM 9.1, 271–3).[30]

If in all this Hume seems to presage the concern with universalizability that has been a prominent feature of ethics since Kant, he also seems to echo his own *Treatise*, wherein he insists that only the judicious or impartial observer can expect to experience *moral* sentiments, and also the writings of Shaftesbury, where one finds the suggestion that humankind is characterized by a *sensus communis* or sense of commonality and community. Surely, however, Hume has significantly underestimated the difficulty we have in distinguishing our uniquely moral sentiments from those arising from self-interest, given what we can only suppose to be our more realistic and sophisticated understanding of the way that interest affects perception. Two centuries later, we find it difficult to credit his claim that this distinction is "so great and evident" that language itself must be moulded by it and made into an instrument enabling us to "express those universal sentiments of censure or approbation, which arise from humanity," so that "Virtue and Vice become then known." In fact, even Hume's assurance gave way to doubt. The natural philosophers, he notes, have measured the earth, accounted for the tides, ordered the heavens, and even calculated the infinite, and yet there is still dispute regarding the foundation of morals. "When I reflect on this," he says, "I fall back into diffidence and scepticism, and suspect that an hypothesis, so obvious, had it been a true one, would, long ere now, have been received by the unanimous suffrage and consent of mankind" (EPM 9.1, 274, 278). In the twenty-five years during which Hume could follow the reception of *An Enquiry concerning the Principles of Morals* he would have gained ample evidence that his hypothesis was not unanimously received; indeed, it was seldom understood. Nonetheless, he retained enough confidence in his conclusions to encourage their regular republication, and it was just before his death that he said that of all his works this *Enquiry* seemed to him the best. This mixture of doubt and assurance is typical of Hume.

NOTES

1 *The Rights of War and Peace [De jure belli ac pacis]* (London, 1738), The Preliminary Discourse. All quotations from Grotius are from this discourse.

2 For a fuller account of these developments, see my *David Hume: Common-Sense Moralist; Sceptical Metaphysician* (Princeton, 1982), pp. 21–26.

3 *Leviathan*, ed. M. Oakeshott (Oxford, 1960), Part 1, chap. 6; see also chaps. 10, 11, 13. *Leviathan* was first published in 1651. Although in the seventeenth and eighteenth centuries Hobbes was virtually always read as offering a sceptical and reductivist analysis of morality, he is now sometimes viewed as offering a more positive analysis, or, at least, a worst-case scenario – even if there are no values in nature and humans are motivated only by self-interest, morality can be developed and maintained on the foundation of this pervasive self-interest. As will be apparent below, Hume did not view Hobbes in this more positive way but saw him as a moral sceptic who had attempted to undercut the foundations of morality. A helpful introduction to Hobbes is Richard Tuck, *Hobbes* (Oxford, 1989).

4 Speaking generally of moral entities, Pufendorf says: "As the original Way of producing natural Entities is by *Creation*, so the Manner of framing moral Entities cannot be better expressed than by the Term of *Imposition*. For these [moral entities] do not proceed from Principles ingrafted in the Substance of Things, but are added, at the Pleasure of intelligent Creatures, to Beings already perfect in their Nature, and to

the real Productions of those Beings; and consequently [they] obtain their whole Existence from the Determination of their Authors. The same Power assigns them such and such Effects, which, when it sees convenient, it can destroy, without causing any natural Alteration in the Subject to which they were apply'd." *Of the Law of Nature and Nations [De jure naturae et gentium]*, trans. B. Kennet (London, 1729), p. 3. This work was first published in 1672. Helpful introductions to Pufendorf are Michael Seidler, "Introductory Essay," *Samuel Pufendorf's On the Natural State of Men* (Lewiston, 1990); and James Tully, "Introduction," *On the Duty of Man and Citizen According to Natural Law* (Cambridge, 1991).

5 Ralph Cudworth, *A Treatise concerning Eternal and Immutable Morality* (London, 1731; facsimile reprint, New York, 1976), pp. 4, 9–10. If, as the voluntarists claim, the unconstrained will of the deity is the source of moral distinctions, and if the deity stands to the moral domain as omnipotent creator to creation, and is himself "devoid of all Essential and Natural Justice," then it follows that he could at any time alter his moral impositions in any way he chooses. It also follows, then, "that nothing can be imagined so grossly wicked, or so fouly unjust or dishonest, but if it were supposed to be commanded by this Omnipotent Deity, [it] must needs upon that Hypothesis forthwith become Holy, Just and Righteous."

6 *A Treatise concerning Eternal and Immutable Morality*, pp. 55–74.

7 *A Treatise concerning Eternal and Immutable Morality*, Book 4, chaps. 3–6; see especially pp. 286–88.

8 John Balguy, *The Foundation of Moral Goodness* (London, 1728; facsimile reprint, New York, 1976), pp. 31, 37.

9 Anthony Ashley Cooper, Lord Shaftesbury, *The Moralists*, in *Characteristics of Men, Manners, Opinions, Times*, ed. J. M. Robertson, 2 vols. (Indianapolis, 1964), 2: 53. For further discussion of Shaftesbury's response to Hobbes, see my *David Hume*, pp. 33–43.

10 *An Enquiry into the Origin of Moral Virtue*, in *The Fable of the Bees*, ed. F. B. Kaye, 2 vols. (Oxford, 1966), 1: 51.

11 *An Essay on the Nature and Conduct of the Passions and Affections, with Illustrations on the Moral Sense* (London, 1742), pp. 209–10. This work was first published in 1728. See also Hutcheson's *An Inquiry into the Original of our Ideas of Beauty and Virtue* (London, 1725), Treatise 2, *Concerning Moral Good and Evil*.

12 Hume says that the most obvious objection to "the selfish hypothesis" (which he attributes to Hobbes and Locke) is that it does not conform to the obvious facts (EPM App 2, 298).

13 I have sketched only a part of Hume's criticism of the rationalists.

14 Pufendorf does not suppose that it is only the deity who provides the sanctions essential to morality. The state or other institutions may also do so by establishing temporal sanctions.

15 Hume, in contrast to most moralists of his time, supposed that religious belief was in general a threat to, not a support of, society and morality. His view is perhaps most obvious in his *The Natural History of Religion*. For further discussion of this point, see the essays in this volume by Knud Haakonssen and John Gaskin, and my "Hume, Atheism, and the Autonomy of Morals," *Hume's Philosophy of Religion*, ed. M. Hester (Winston-Salem, 1986), pp. 97–144.

16 This passage from the second *Enquiry* has been taken to be evidence of a major change in Hume's position: the substitution of the principle of humanity or fellow-feeling for the principle of sympathy that is central to the theory presented in the *Treatise*. This may well be the correct inference to draw from the passage, but Hume's strategy remains unchanged. Whatever may be the ultimate, observable principles of human nature, it is with these original principles that our investigations must end. On the question of Hume's (possibly) changing view of sympathy, see John B. Stewart, *The Moral and Political Philosophy of David Hume* (New York, 1963) pp. 329–37; and Nicholas Capaldi, *Hume's Place in Moral Philosophy* (New York, 1989), pp. 195–248.

17 Hume argues that the "inconstancy" which is a noticeable feature of human behaviour also has its source in the structure of human nature (see, for example, T 2.1.4, 284; 2.3.1, 402; 3.2.9, 551, 553, and note 29 here).

18 Of the selfish theory, Hume says: "There is another principle, somewhat resembling the former; which has been much insisted on by philosophers, and has been the foundation of many a system; that, whatever affection one may feel, or imagine he feels for others, no passion is, or can be disinterested; that the most generous friendship, however sincere, is a modification of self-love; and that, even unknown to ourselves, we seek only our own gratification, while we appear the most deeply engaged in schemes for the liberty and happiness of mankind. By a turn of imagination, by a refinement of reflection, by an enthusiasm of passion, we seem to take part in the interests of others, and imagine ourselves divested of all selfish considerations: but, at bottom, the most generous patriot and most niggardly miser, the bravest hero and most abject coward, have, in every action, an equal regard to their own happiness and welfare" (EPM App 2, 296).

19 "An Essay upon False Vertue," in *Essays upon Several Subjects* (London, 1716), pp. 243–4.

20 Mandeville, *An Enquiry into the Origin of Moral Virtue*, in *The Fable of the Bees*, 1: 56.

21 Francis Hutcheson, *An Inquiry concerning the Original of our Ideas of Beauty and Virtue*, 4th ed. (London, 1738; facsimile reprint, 1969), p. 167; see also pp. 132–99.

22 Hume's formulation allows for "a particular design and intention" and "a settled character" to be logically distinct. Thus, while my settled character could be formed (in large part) by the sum of my particular designs and intentions, and could in many instances effectively determine my particular designs and intentions, I could nonetheless on some occasions form particular designs that run counter to my settled character. Hume must certainly think this is possible, for he supposes that moral reform is possible (see T 2.3.2, 412).

23 Apparently deaf to Mandeville's cynicism, Hume also says: "What [self-] interest can a fond mother have in view, who loses her health by assiduous attendance on her sick child, and afterwards languishes and dies of grief, when freed, by its death, from the slavery of that attendance? . . . These and a thousand other instances are marks of a general benevolence in human nature, where no *real* interest binds us to the object" (EPM App 2, 300).

24 Hume goes on here to say that the "uneasiness and satisfaction" (the pleasure and pain) we feel in response to the relevant characters and passions "are not only inseparable from vice and virtue, but constitute their very nature and essence." A careful study of Hume reveals that in saying some feature X constitutes "the very essence" of some other item Y, he invariably appears to mean only that X is an essential, or necessary, condition of Y. This interpretation appears to be supported by Hume's own revised version of his text, found in the *Dissertation on the Passions*: "The uneasiness and satisfaction, produced in the spectator, are essential to vice and virtue. To approve of a character, is to feel a delight upon its appearance. To disapprove of it, is to be sensible of an uneasiness. The pain and pleasure, therefore, being, in a manner, the primary source of blame or praise, must also be the causes of all their effects; and consequently, the causes of pride and humility, which are the unavoidable attendants of that distinction" (DP 2.6, 4: 147). For present purposes, however, it is enough to note that in his more detailed discussion of the moral sense Hume claims only that the feelings in question constitute not virtue and vice, but "our praise or admiration," and then adds: "We do not infer a character to be virtuous, because it pleases: But in feeling that it pleases after such a particular manner, we in effect feel that it is virtuous" (T 3.1.2, 471).

25 Elsewhere Hume says that humans, "where everything else is equal," make a "choice or distinction between what is useful, and what is pernicious. Now this distinction is the same in all its parts, with the *moral distinction*, whose foundation has been so often, and so much in vain, enquired after. The same endowments of the mind, in every circumstance, are agreeable to the sentiment of morals and to that of humanity. . . . By all the rules of philosophy, therefore, we must conclude, that these sentiments are originally the same; since, in each particular, even the most minute, they are governed by the same laws, and are moved by the same objects" (EPM 6.1, 235–6).

26 Hume emphasizes that, in denying justice to be a natural virtue, he does not mean to say that it is arbitrary or unnatural; the rules of justice are conventions, but they too have a foundation in human nature (T 3.2.1, 484).

27 For additional discussions of Hume on justice, see Terence Penelhum, "Hume's Moral Psychology," Part VI, this volume; and Knud Haakonssen, "The Structure of Hume's Political Theory," Part III, this volume.

28 To say that early humans *saw* that their interests would be served by cooperation is not to say that they at once articulated this insight, or found it necessary to articulate it before they could act on it. "Two men, who pull the oars of a boat, do it by an agreement or convention, tho' they have never given promises to each other" (T 3.2.2, 490). It is also conceivable that individuals could begin to cooperate in the matter of property arrangements without having expressed the conventions that govern their behaviour.

29 Hume adds that this artifice is augmented by "the public instructions of politicians, and the private education of parents" (533–4), but he twice (T 3.2.2, 500; 3.3.1, 578) criticizes those who overstate the role of politicians. Their artifices are also dependent on the natural foundation provided by human nature.

30 It is necessary to close this account without discussing other important issues raised by Hume. For example, in Part II of his "Conclusion" to the *Enquiry*, Hume takes up the important question of "our interested *obligation*" to virtue, or the question "whether every man, who has any regard to his own happiness and welfare, will not best find his account in the practice of every moral duty." He concludes that on the whole (matters of justice providing the notable exception), it is both in our interest, and compatible with our natures, to be virtuous (EPM 9.2, 278–84). In "A Dialogue," a short work generally published along with *An Enquiry concerning the Principles of Morals*, Hume argues that the great diversity of moral custom is consistent with his claim that the principles

upon which morality is founded are constant. Just as one river flows north, another south, although both are "actuated, in their opposite directions, by the *same* principle of gravity," so are the differences of moral practice to be accounted for "from the most universal, established principles of morals" (D, 333–34).

7 The structure of Hume's political theory

David Hume believed that most of the views about society and politics prevalent in his day had roots in one or another of "two species of false religion," *superstition* and *enthusiasm*. Both were developments of conflicting theological doctrines that appealed to two different types of personalities. Both had come to be associated with opposing political interests. Both sprang from ignorance. And, while the two species had been universally present in society and in individuals in varying degrees throughout history, the peculiarity of modern post-Reformation Europe was the violent oscillation between them, as evidenced by the many wars of religion. Their more extreme adherents were also, not least, responsible for the plight of modern Britain, both north and south. One of the tasks of the philosophical historian, Hume believed, was to explain the preponderance at particular times of one or the other of these persuasions. The task he set for his political theory was to explain why both were philosophically misconceived, empirically untenable, and, in their extreme forms, politically dangerous.

I. THE POLITICS OF RELIGION

One part of humanity, Hume notes, has a tendency to "weakness, fear, [and] melancholy, together with ignorance." In this state, the imagination conjures up forces operating under the surface, and the mind is prone to grasp methods of influencing these forces by "ceremonies, observances, mortifications, sacrifices, presents, or [by] any practice, however absurd or frivolous which either folly or knavery recommends to a blind and terrified credulity." This condition and these practices Hume calls *superstition*. In religion, priests, church establishments, and rituals are used to mediate between the individual and these forces. In society and in politics, the superstitious person is disposed to accept established forms and powers as inherent in the nature of things and to see society as a hierarchical structure with a monarch as the unitary source of authority and sovereignty as a divine right (E-SE, 74).

In contrast, another part of humanity has a tendency to "hope, pride, presumption, [and] a warm imagination, together with ignorance." In this state, which Hume calls *enthusiasm*, individuals take flights of fancy from the real world, presume direct rapport with higher powers, and incline towards ungovernable self-assertion. In religion, priests, church establishments, and rituals are rejected. In society and politics, enthusiasts assert the rights of the individual. They often incline to forceful remodelling of authority and generally see self-government as the only proper government, at least in principle. Enthusiasts favour contractualist accounts of such authority as they will accept and insist on the protection of individual civil liberties (E-SE, 74).[1]

Hume's political theory is more than an outright rejection of such received ideas as those associated with superstition and enthusiasm. He meant his political writings to be also political *acts*, shaping the opinions or beliefs that in turn shaped politics and society. To achieve this end, he sought to provide a theory of the nature of social and political phenomena different from those that served to reinforce superstition and enthusiasm. He proceeds, on the one hand, by analyzing those beliefs which in recent history had tended to modify the ideal types of superstition and enthusiasm; on the other hand, he argues that such analysis in itself forms a set of opinions or beliefs with direct and beneficial political consequences. Speaking in the idiom of the time, he showed how his principles led him to take one or the other side in current debates. Often, of course, his topical conclusions obscured the theoretical premises, not only for his contemporaries but for subsequent generations of interpreters. The main problem in explaining Hume's political thought has always been how to provide a clear understanding of the close coherence between the general and the particular and the theoretical and the historical. His theory of the nature of social and political phenomena is mainly to be found in the third book of the *Treatise* and in the second *Enquiry*, while the particulars of the historically contingent situation of modern Britain and Europe are analyzed in many of his *Essays* and in the *History of England*. In order to understand either, we have to grasp the sense in which basic social and political institutions are, according to Hume, *artificial*. This can best be achieved by looking at the *philosophical* ideas underpinning superstition and enthusiasm. Elsewhere this might have been called his metaphysics of politics; Hume's aim was to unmask the politics of religious metaphysics.

II. MORALS — FOUND OR CONSTRUCTED

Hume was keenly aware of the continuing influence of ideas derived from Aristotle and mediated by scholastic tradition. From this perspective, social forms (such as property and contract) and political roles (such as magistracy) have their foundation in essences, in inherent structures found in nature itself. On such a theory, specific actions are only property-holding, contracting, or governing in so far as they are an attempt to actualize the inherent meaning or the essence signified by these words. Moral, social, and political relations between people are not constructed by the individuals involved; such relations are established with reference to something over and above the persons concerned, namely, an objective structure of reality and meaning on which individuals try to draw. Hume saw these ideas as the philosophical equivalent of the religious hocus-pocus of superstition (transubstantiation, for example). Like most such ideas, this philosophy supported the need for authoritative interpreters of the meanings supposedly inherent in, or essential to, life in society. It was, in other words, the philosophy behind Catholicism, High Church Anglicanism, old-fashioned Toryism, absolutism, and divine-right monarchism.

The reactions in post-Reformation Europe to these directions in religion and politics were, as Hume realized more clearly than most, immensely complex and often contradictory. It was possible, however, to discern some of the philosophical ideas which were basic to much Reformation thought, and which were eventually spelled out with great clarity by natural law philosophers such as Hugo Grotius, Thomas Hobbes, Samuel Pufendorf, and John Locke. With the partial exception of Grotius, these writers held that there were no moral or political meanings inherent in the structure of things. All meaning, or value, is willed or constructed and imposed upon a natural world that *in itself* is amoral and apolitical. The basic act of will is that of God who, in choosing the particular human nature He did, delegated to humans the task of creating moral and political forms which would make possible the culture of humanity. According to most protestant natural law thinkers, human reason could, unaided by revelation, derive from the *character* of human nature and the human position in the world a certain guidance in morals and politics, and this is what they called the law of nature. Generally speaking, the basic law of nature held that, since people were sociable and, indeed, had to be sociable in order to exist at all, various measures had to be taken. These measures were contained in derivative laws of nature which specified the creation of moral and political institutions ranging from marriage and property to civil government and the law of nations. A few thinkers, notably Grotius and Hobbes, tried to formulate a theory which dispensed with natural law as a guide for the human will. On this view, social and political forms are settlements negotiated between individuals with often conflicting claims and intentions, or *rights*. Natural law in this scheme is simply the lessons learned from such settlements, not the prescription for how to make them in the first place.[2]

The division between a natural law direction and a natural rights direction in protestant natural law theory was of fundamental importance for the further development of political thought, as we shall see. For the moment, however, the significant point is that both forms of natural law theory apparently subscribed to the view that the institutions of moral and political life are contractually constructed by individuals.

These ideas of personal autonomy, of individual rights, of the absence of mediating factors between God and man, and the consequent construction of morals and politics according to our own lights – ideas identified since with "constructivists" – these parts of the philosophical argument could be taken to the extremes of enthusiasm in religion and fanatical factionalism in politics. This had happened repeatedly in many parts of Europe, in Hume's opinion, but never with more devastating effects than in seventeenth-century Britain, marked as it was by religious strife and civil warfare. Even in his own time the political effects of the enthusiastic cast of mind remained a danger to be guarded against; as Hume grew older, he sometimes feared that the battle against it might yet be lost.[3]

III. HUME ON JUSTICE

The theory of social artifice presented in the third Book of the *Treatise* is an attempt to formulate a position mediating the two philosophical traditions briefly outlined in the preceding section. Hume, of course, has no time for scholastic essences, and his naturalism precludes any role for the divine voluntarism of most protestant natural law. Hume's individuals can expect neither inherent structures nor transcendent guidance. Only Hobbes had isolated humanity metaphysically and religiously as completely as Hume, yet the two thinkers reach very different conclusions about the human condition. It is not only that Hume gives a good deal more credit to the generous side of human nature. He also gives an account of the social relations between individuals which, while sharing the individualistic naturalism of Hobbes, is profoundly un-Hobbesian.

The actions that spring from the *natural virtues* and vices (beneficence, clemency, moderation, and their opposites, for example) are, according to Hume, "entirely natural, and have no dependance on the artifice and contrivance of men." Each of these actions is a simple or self-contained act that establishes relations between particular agents and particular patients (T 3.3.1, 578, 574). An act of benevolence, or its opposite, is completed as one act or one occasion when that virtue, or vice, is being expressed, for example, by the giving of a gift or the denial of a service. Such an activity may stretch over time, but it is nevertheless in a significant sense one act. Acts of benevolence may of course prompt reactions, such as gratitude, but these reactions are clearly *other* acts. Acts that result from natural virtue and vice are coherent and self-contained because they have a point or a meaning when taken *in isolation* – even when seen as nothing more than relations between specific individuals, a point Hume emphasizes by noting that we value each performance of a natural virtue (T 3.3.1, 579).

The natural virtues, "commonly denominated the *social* virtues, to mark their tendency to the good of society," provide the basis for family life and intimate circles of friendship, but social life at large requires something else entirely, namely, a set of *artificial virtues* (T 3.3.1, 578; 3.2.2, 486–7). When I as agent abstain from taking the fruit of my neighbour's pear tree, pay my landlord his rent, or answer the government's military call-up, my actions cannot be understood *in isolation* as mere expressions of inherent features of my nature. These actions have reference to something else, to something beyond the other person or persons, the patient(s) affected by them. This patient may be unknown to the agent or may have been undeserving of the agent's behaviour: the neighbour may never harvest his fruit, the landlord may be excessively rich and grasping, the government may be conducting an unjust war. In such cases an agent's behaviour can only have meaning and only be evaluated through its relation to some additional factor beyond both the agent(s) and patient(s) involved. It has meaning only within a framework which is in an important sense objective and distinct from individuals and their qualities. The relations between people who hold property to the exclusion of others, who contract for exchange of goods or services, and who owe allegiance or support of some sort – these relations can only be established because the people involved have something other than each other's intentions to refer to, something which can shape their intentions. My giving money to another person does not constitute "paying rent" merely because we have, respectively, intentions of giving and receiving. The transaction is given its particular meaning because it involves a social practice or institution, in this case a special form of contract. In other words, individual actions of this sort are not self-contained and complete. We cannot see their point and evaluate them without invoking the social practice to which they relate or on which they rely. Individual actions can be approved of as instances of such institutionalized practices as holding private property, keeping promises and contracts, paying allegiance, and the like, *because* such practices already exist and are approved of. This peculiar circumstance is, as Hume explains, well illustrated by actions which seem absurd when taken in isolation, but which acquire meaning and can be evaluated once we assume their reference to a social practice of the sort mentioned. Consequently, when we see a poor person paying money to a rich one, we assume that a loan is being settled or goods paid for (T 3.2.1, 480–1).

Hume's analysis of the nature of social actions is a thorough rejection of will theories, such as contract theories. That is, he rejects theories according to which such social actions as respecting property claims acquire meaning because they derive from acts of will of the participating individuals. Like thinkers in the Aristotelian and Thomistic tradition, Hume holds that acts of will can only establish social relations *outside intimate groups* if these acts are given meaning by something over and above themselves.[4] In contrast to that tradition, however, Hume rejected the view that there are fixed and essential meanings for such social institutions as property and contract. Such institutions are no more than practices, a fact he signals by calling them and their associated virtues and vices – justice and injustice, for example – artificial (T 3.2.1, 483–4). They are artificial because they are human creations. At the same time, Hume has deprived himself of the simple contractualist account of these institutions as expressions of will. On his account, property and contract must exist as social practices prior to any acts of will relating to them. Hume has thus saddled himself with a genetic problem, namely, how to account for the origins of the social practices that constitute basic social institutions.

The solution Hume suggests involves luck, moderate foresight, and imitative behaviour (T 3.2.2, 484–501). We inevitably live in family units, and while this is largely a response to natural passions and natural virtues, as well as to "the numberless wants and necessities" with which nature has lumbered human beings, it provides some experience with relative divisions into *mine* and *thine* and with trust. It requires only modest luck and prudence to attempt to imitate this in relations with people outside the family group. The scarcity of goods and abilities, in relation to needs and desires, puts a premium on making a success of such attempts. It is therefore easy to see how it may become common practice to respect people possessing, transferring, and exchanging things that in one way or another are associated with them, and then coming to trust each other's word about future actions. The general pattern of such practices may be explained by the way the imagination works along empirically established associative lines (T 3.2.3–5, 501–25).

It is a question of how such practices gain sufficient strength to withstand the pressure of conflict, for instance, in situations of social expansion and scarcity. The two basic requirements are that each practice should come to be valued independently of its individual instantiations and should be seen as binding or obligatory upon the individual. Rather than being just the sum total of what people do, social practices have to become independent rules specifying what is good and to be done.

Hume here offers a radical solution to what had proved to be one of the most intractable problems in moral philosophy, the relationship between *goodness* and *obligation*. At one extreme were those who thought that human nature had been so impaired by original sin that humankind had no insight into moral goodness and could be directed and governed only by being obliged to certain forms of behaviour. The obliging wills might be those of a hierarchy of authorities, terminating in God, as in much Lutheran thought; or they might be those of each individual, reflecting directly the will of God, as in much Calvinist thought. Either way, we have a will theory of morals and politics of the sort Hume thought impossible, and we do not have an account which makes any necessary link between moral goodness and being obliged. In contrast to this line of thought were a wide variety of theories which all allowed that even in its fallen state, humanity was left with some natural capacity for moral insight. In Hume's recent past, they ranged from Cambridge Platonism and the rationalism of Samuel Clarke to the moral sense theories of Shaftesbury and Hutcheson. The proponents of such theories all had the task of explaining whether and how insight into moral goodness had implications for moral obligation. They all thought it did, and they all had extreme difficulty in accounting for it.

The problem was a serious theological one. If each person had a natural moral faculty which could bring moral understanding, and if such understanding imposed a moral obligation, then God's moral role in human life was severely curtailed. The morally good person would not need God, whose moral function would be reduced to that of policing the morally wayward. This was clearly unacceptable, for it would make morals ideally independent of God. Accordingly, in all these theories we find some residual element of divine voluntarism. Generally speaking, a way out was sought in some variation on the following theme. Since the relationship in God's nature between moral insight and moral will is unbroken – whatever account of the relationship theologians may give – and since humans to some extent share in the moral insight, a pale reflection of this relationship may be established in human nature if men and women can partake in God's will and in some measure make it their own. The chief way of accounting for this without resort to revelation was teleological. The particular and confined moral good which each person and community is able to effect may be understood as a contribution to the overall good of the moral universe of all moral agents past, present, and future. This universal good is understood to be the intention of the divinity as shown in the purposefulness of creation. Consequently, our particular will to do the particular good in our power is part of God's general will for the moral creation as a whole. If on occasion we lack that particular will, or if it is weak and undecided, the thought of the teleological arrangement, that is, of God's will, is able to supply the want. We are then acting out of a sense of obligation.

This type of teleology and the associated "Christian utilitarianism," as it is now often called, was probably the most pervasive style of moral and political thought in the eighteenth century.[5] An early formulation by Richard Cumberland had some influence, but the most important version was undoubtedly Francis Hutcheson's.[6] This line of argument provided the basis for the empirical "science of morals" which characterized a great deal of Enlightenment social thought. Since so much depended upon the teleological arrangement of the universe, an important task of the science of morals was to provide a map of the moral world showing how its various components ideally fitted together. The popular science of morals was thus a description of the proper working of the moral institutions currently making up society – *proper* being defined in terms of making social life possible as a contribution to the general happiness of humankind.

Hume matched this agenda point for point. Once such forms of behaviour as respect for the possessions of others and keeping of promises have become fairly common, it will be evident to all that they are socially useful by allowing things to be done collaboratively which otherwise could not be done. This social utility, or public good, is merely the outcome of individual actions, but it appears as though it were the result of a shared design. Consequently, individuals are inclined to approve of the behaviour that brings about the public good, for it appears as though this behaviour were aimed at this outcome, and contrariwise, to disapprove of behaviour having contrary effects. In this way, the basic rules of justice pertaining to property and contract come to be accepted as moral rules. In short, while the purposefulness of certain general patterns of behaviour is only apparent, the perception of this apparent purposefulness, or teleology, in itself becomes an independent cause of such behaviour in the future.

The problem is that not every *application* of the rules of justice produces good results for all the individuals concerned, or in extreme cases, for any individuals. Nonetheless, because of their general public utility, we still think that the rules should be kept, or that they are obligatory. While the popular moral philosophy sketched here invoked what we may call the internalization of God's will in order to account for obligation, Hume suggests instead that we internalize a social "will." In a social group where just behaviour is generally approved as good because it produces social utility, people who in a particular case lack any motive for justice – perhaps because neither they nor any other assignable person stand to gain anything from the action in question – will tend to have a motive supplied. Because everyone generally approves of just behaviour *as if* it sprang from a separate laudable motive, people lacking such a motive will feel morally deficient as compared with their surroundings and will come to disapprove of or hate themselves on that account. In this they will be reinforced by the disapproval of their fellows. This self-loathing becomes the motive or the will by which people act justly as a matter of obligation.

We may also say that just behaviour has become an artificial accretion on the natural person. We disapprove of deficiencies – a lack of a certain degree of benevolence, for example – in the natural moral qualities and see it as an obligation to re-instate benevolence to its "natural" place amongst our motives. In the same manner, we have learned to see the failure to have a motive to be just to constitute a deficiency. Since there is no motive to be re-instated in this case, we have to "invent" one, namely, the will to be full moral characters like other people in our society. A crucial concept in Hume's analysis of obligation is thus that of character. Part of our moral character is natural, part of it derives from social living. Deficiencies in the former evoke a natural, in the latter, a socially induced, desire to repair our character. These desires are, respectively, our obligation to the natural and to the artificial virtues.[7] This causal account of the moral obligation to pursue the artificial virtues, typified by justice, is the crowning effort in Hume's subversion of the reigning paradigms of moral and political philosophy. It had a number of no less subversive repercussions.

IV. THE BASIS FOR AUTHORITY

The rules of justice form the basis of any significant scale of organized social living. Yet the obligation to obey the rules of justice depends on nothing more than each person's perception of the general social *opinion* of these rules. Although the formation of such opinion is a strong and universal tendency in human life, it is clearly subject to severe disruption and fluctuation. People accordingly seek to protect the rules of justice by the institution of government (T 3.2.8, 543). But then one must ask, what is the basis for the authority of government to administer justice or to do anything else? Or in Hume's language, what is the source of allegiance to government? In answering this question, he follows a pattern similar to that employed in his analysis of the rules of justice.

The traditional Tory notion that authority is inherent in the social world in the form of a divine right has to be rejected because it invokes forces about which humans can know nothing. The traditional Whig notion that authority derives from contractual arrangements is, Hume argues, empirically false and conceptually confused.[8] The essential feature of a contractual arrangement is that it involves *choosing* whether or not to enter into the arrangement: but a choice that is unknown to a chooser is not a choice. It seems impossible to identify any contract by virtue of which any group living under a particular government owes allegiance to that government. The generality of humankind knows nothing of such a contract, and even if there had been some contract in the past, it would not carry authority beyond the original contractors. Hume thus finds incoherent the common suggestion that there is a "tacit" contract, a contract about which a people does not know or think. Furthermore, individuals on the whole have no choice. We are generally born into societies that are already subject to government and find ourselves obliged to obey the laws of that government. People of a particularly enthusiastic cast may, of course, say that they always have the choice of dying rather than living with what they consider a tyrannical government. These are exactly the people Hume fears most of all because in their fanaticism they could destroy existing government, and their wildness of temper could never sustain a lasting government (T 3.2.7–9, 534–50).

The contract theory of allegiance to government is in any case muddled in exactly the same way as the contractual account of property. It tries to reduce allegiance to acts of will by individuals, but in doing so it *presupposes* that there is a government, that is, an authority with some claim to allegiance to which individuals pledge that allegiance. Individual acts of obedience, in the form of promises, for instance, can only be recognized as expressions of allegiance if the object of such behaviour is the sort of person or group of persons to whom allegiance is due. Governmental authority must therefore rest on something existing prior to any such promise of allegiance. In the terms used in the account of property, we can see that the subjects of government must have an interest in government distinct from their interest in keeping their pledge of allegiance. The interest in question is, in general terms, an interest in external and internal protection and, especially, in the administration of justice. To the extent that such interest establishes obedience as a general pattern of behaviour, allegiance becomes, like justice, another artificial accretion on the natural personality of those involved. Once this has happened, the absence of sentiments of allegiance is perceived as a personal deficiency. In this way, allegiance, like justice, becomes a matter of not only "the *natural* obligations of interest ... but also the *moral* obligations of honour and conscience" (T 3.2.8, 545).

Hume's idea of the obligation of allegiance has a certain similarity with a form of contract theory which had some currency in his time, but which he never mentions at all, namely, implied contract. In fact, in his rejection of tacit contract, he seems to suggest that he did not see any difference between these two theories. Those who did distinguish between tacit and implied contracts saw the former as a voluntary commitment signalled in a non-verbal way, but still as an identifiable behaviourial event. On the other hand, an implied contract does not arise from any particular event; there is no act of will. The commitment of an implied contract follows from, is implied by, what a person *is* or what position or office (spouse, child, doctor, neighbour, citizen, magistrate) he or she holds. This was a way of thinking about social relations which had partly Aristotelian, partly Stoic origins, and which had been translated into the common teleologically based systems of morals outlined here.[9] Hume, too, thought that duties arise from what a person is, but this could not be accounted for teleologically in terms of the over-all aim of the system of moral beings, nor, because there is no act of will involved, was there any reason to invoke "contract" to account for these duties.

Hume's theory of allegiance also saddles him with a genetic problem: how to account for the first origins of government. In his earlier works he is content to give a brief and bland explanation to the effect that, since government is superimposed upon social groups which already recognize the rules of justice, including the obligation to keep promises, it is possible to see the first institution of government as a matter of mutual promises. It is clear, however, that his concern is to discredit the idea that this has any implications for a continuing allegiance to government (T 3.2.8, 541–2; E-OC, 470–1). After a lifetime of reflecting on the problem and, doubtless, after discussing it with his friend Adam Smith, Hume altered his argument in the last essay he wrote, "Of the Origin of Government." In this essay he suggests that government has its origins in people's habit of submission to military leaders in time of war. Such leadership would naturally attract non-martial functions, for example, the administration of justice and the collection of revenue, and gradually become commonplace between bouts of warfare (E-OG, 39–40).[10]

V. OPINION AND THE SCIENCE OF POLITICS

Irrespective of the historical account of the origins of government, Hume always maintained his position that contract and consent are not, and cannot be, the basis for continued allegiance to governmental authority. The basis for government is a combination of the two factors discussed in the *Treatise* and noted in the preceding section: a people's perception of the public interest in protection, especially through enforcement of the rules of justice, and their perception of their obligation to allegiance. In the *Essays*, he provocatively formulates this view by saying that it is "on opinion only that government is founded." This "opinion is of two kinds, to wit, opinion of INTER-

EST, and opinion of RIGHT" (E-FP, 32–3). People are generally born
into, and continue to live in, societies that are under some form of
government. The opinions of these subjects that their government
can care for the public interest, and has the right to exercise authority, are the foundation of this government. Consequently, the central
task of the science of politics is to account for the formation and
transformation of these fundamental opinions.

Some of the causes of opinion are so universal that they can be
explained in completely general terms; they are operative in practically all circumstances of human life. This applies to beliefs concerning the interest and obligation upon which pre-governmental
institutions rest – the rules of justice pertaining to property and
contract – and to the beliefs underlying government itself. A few
additional features of politics may be explained in similarly general
terms, but it soon becomes necessary to draw on more particular
factors, factors that are more historically specific. While it is possible
to discuss in general terms the relationship between "liberty" and
"slavery" in government, one cannot introduce concepts like "parties" into one's account without drawing on the experience of particular forms of government. To so do requires knowledge of specific
events in individual countries. Consequently, Hume's science of politics ranges from a consideration of what some of his contemporaries
would have called the "natural history" of the human species, that
is, from his examination of human understanding and the principles
of morals, through historically based general maxims, to the civic
history of particular cultures and states. This entire range of material
is necessarily part of his *science* of politics because, even in the
explanation of the most specific event, there will be references to the
universal principles of human nature underlying all moral thought,
and to the institutions to which those principles have led. Only
rarely will our explanations depend on the idiosyncratic whims of
individuals. And even in those rare cases, as for example the extremes of enthusiastic madness, deviations from principle can only
be understood as such because we know the regularity that is being
broken. At the same time, the full range of explanations, from the
most general to the most specific, is part of a science of *politics*
because all explanations are concerned with the formation of those
opinions that support the institutions of society. The more general

part of politics explains that such institutions are the kind of things that must have a history, while the more specific parts reveal the history they have actually had. The general principles of politics teach us that political action must start from an understanding of the particular political conditions to which history has brought us. Hume's political theory is, in other words, an explanation of why political theorizing in abstraction from historical conditions is futile and often dangerous. Hume was acutely conscious of the fact that this was in itself a political opinion calculated to inform political conduct at a particular time and place. Indeed, this was undoubtedly part of the reason why he went to such lengths to popularize his theory by means of his *Essays* and the *History*. The formation of sound political opinions is the most basic political activity, and Hume's political theorizing was such an activity. There is often a sense of urgency in Hume's political writings, for he was always keenly aware that people's opinions are fickle. Under the influence of passions – of avarice, of factional or dynastic or confessional allegiances, of utopian dreams of perfection – our understanding of our situation and that of our society too often becomes clouded, particularly in situations of uncertainty and instability. When there is uncertainty about who has authority or about what those in authority may do, our habitual ways of thinking and behaving are broken. Under such circumstances opinions and actions are much more likely to be influenced by imagined situations than by actual conditions, and passionate flights of fancy tend to take over. Since opinions are formed by experience, we can only have empirically well-founded opinions about who is doing what in society if there is a certain regularity of behaviour. The message of Hume's theory concerning the basic features of society is that such regularity cannot come from individual minds and wills alone; it depends upon something outside the individual, namely regular or rule-bound institutions that can guide our behaviour and consequently our expectations of each other. If such institutions, once acquired, are lightly given up, we lose habit and regularity; we lose, that is, the most important means of orienting ourselves to others. Consequently we cannot know what we ourselves may do with success, and we will have lost our most elementary freedom. This is the rationale for the enormous emphasis Hume placed on institutional stability.

VI. THE DISTRIBUTION OF JUSTICE

Stability can be seen from two perspectives: the stability of what those in authority *do* and the stability of who they *are*. These two topics are fundamental to Hume's political thought.

The conduct of government is only stable and predictable if it follows publicly known general rules – only if it is government in accordance with law. Government must therefore be concerned with issues that are suitable subjects of law. These are primarily forms of behaviour that are in the public interest, but not necessarily in the interest of each individual concerned in the particular instance.

> We are, therefore, to look upon all the vast apparatus of our government, as having ultimately no other object or purpose but the *distribution of justice*, or, in other words, the support of the twelve judges. Kings and parliaments, fleets and armies, officers of the court and revenue, ambassadors, ministers, and privy-counsellors, are all subordinate in their end to this part of administration. Even the clergy, as their duty leads them to inculcate morality, may justly be thought, so far as regards this world, to have no other useful object of their institution.   (E-OG, 37–8; italics added)

While at first sight an example of the hyperbole to which Hume occasionally resorts in the *Essays*, this passage makes clear what carries most weight. Hume has no doubt about the necessity of a governmental agenda in defence and foreign affairs as well as in economics and culture, but he gives priority to maintaining those two basic institutions of justice – property and contract – which make social life possible. In so far as the populace has a clear opinion that this balance of priorities constitutes the public interest and that the government protects this interest as well as any possible government could, to that extent the government has a secure source of allegiance (E-FP, 33).

It follows from this that Hume must reject policies that significantly break the rules of justice. He rejects, for example, the suggestion that governments should treat individual citizens according to their natural merit. Such a policy would create the greatest uncertainty. Merit is so dependent on each particular situation that it is impossible to formulate general rules for it; consequently, no orderly allocation of goods could be based on it. The same criticism applies to all other schemes for the distribution of goods or status on the basis of alleged personal merits or virtues. Hume criticizes in particular the claims of those religious fanatics who say *"that dominion is founded on grace,* and *that saints alone inherit the earth,"* and points out that England had experienced such enthusiasm from the Puritans and from one of their political sub-sects, the Levellers, who claimed that there ought to be "an equal distribution of property" (EPM 3.2, 193).

Regarding the distribution of property, Hume adds some further considerations of importance. Even if we assume that equality of property could somehow be achieved, its maintenance would be "extremely *pernicious* to human society. Render possessions ever so equal, men's different degrees of art, care, and industry will immediately break that equality." In order to keep people equal in their possessions, these "virtues" would have to be controlled. To do so, would require a "most rigorous inquisition," would impoverish society, and would break down social subordination and order (EPM 3.2, 194). These remarks make it clear that Hume's notion of justice is not purely formal and procedural. The rule that everyone should have the same quantity of external possessions is as universal in form as Hume's rules concerning the allocation of property. But he rejects such a rule because it would require tyrannical interference with individuals' natural qualities – with their virtues and with their personal freedom. The object of just laws is thus individual liberty and, since the most obvious and most endangered expression of such liberty is the acquisition and use of property, justice is centrally concerned with property, and, it follows, with contracts.

This order of justification is noteworthy, for in the *Treatise* Hume has sometimes seemed to limit the object of the rules of justice to securing property per se. He there says that we have three "species of goods," the "internal satisfaction of our mind, the external advantages of our body, and the enjoyment of such possessions as we have acquir'd by our industry and good fortune." Of these, the first cannot be taken from us, and the second, while transferable, can be of no use to others. "The last only are both expos'd to the violence of others, and may be transferr'd without suffering any loss or alteration; while at the same time, there is not a sufficient quantity of them to supply every one's desires and necessities" (T 3.2.2, 487–8). External goods are, accordingly, the *direct* objects of justice. What the passages from the second *Enquiry* make clear is that through the protection of property the two other species of goods are being *indirectly* protected as well (3.2, 193–4).

VII. THE ROLE OF RIGHTS

Hume scarcely used the traditional notions of *rights* in his moral and political philosophy. Writers on these subjects commonly used a scheme based on materials from Roman law and developed by natural lawyers from Hugo Grotius onwards.[11] On this scheme, certain features were inherent in each person qua human being, while others were acquired and added to the person through his or her activity in life. The former were natural or innate rights and correspond roughly to Hume's natural virtues; the latter were adventitious or acquired rights and correspond roughly to Hume's artificial virtues. Some of the natural rights were "imperfect," others were "perfect," as were all acquired rights. Kindness, benevolence, gratitude, and the like could be claimed as rights only imperfectly because the qualities of the claimant that would justify the claim were too uncertain and variable to be the subject of law, and the moral urgency of claims for them was too limited to warrant the use of legal force to secure them. But the perfect natural rights, life, liberty, personal judgement – or bodily, behavioural, and mental integrity – and their adventitious or artificial extension of the person to property and contractual relations were sufficiently ascertainable to be regulated by law, and their protection by the force of law was deemed so important that it provided the main justification for the institution of government. The distinction between perfect and imperfect rights in respect of their certainty and enforceability sounds very much like Hume's distinction between artificial virtues such as justice and the natural virtues such as beneficence. Yet, as we saw at the end of the previous section, he recognized that in addition to property, certain natural qualities – the goods of mind and body – require the protection of law, and that they receive such protection when property is legally safeguarded. These natural qualities or goods are the areas of life that, in theories of natural law, are protected as perfect natural rights. In other words, in substance, Hume was in agreement with the popular natural law systems of morals, but he could not use the concept of rights to formulate his argument. When he does talk of rights, it is casually and in connection with property and contract, or it is in the context of authority – the right to govern.

Hume could not use the concept of rights because both of the rights traditions were unpalatable to him. On one view, rights were qualities of the person as a moral agent; they were the primary feature of all morals, and all moral institutions, such as rules of property or structures of authority, arose when individuals adapted their respective rights to each other. This view had received daring philosophical formulations by Grotius and Hobbes, for whom the qualities, or rights, in question were nothing more mysterious than the various claims of individuals on their surrounding world and on each other. In many respects this view was close to Hume's way of thinking, but there were two good reasons why he could not accept it. First, this form of rights argument led directly to the contractarian will theories of social institutions which we have seen him reject. Only if he had found a way of seeing the ascription of rights to individuals as part of the process of socialization could he have reconciled rights with his moral theory.[12] A second reason for rejecting this form of rights argument was probably that it was too readily associated with politico-religious enthusiasm and was politically dangerous. Religiously based claims to a freedom of the spirit to govern oneself were only too easily couched in terms of rights, or liberties.

On a second view, rights, far from being the primary moral feature of the person, were derivative from a natural law which ascribed duties and rights to individuals. This was by far the most pervasive view of the philosophical status of rights, based on traditional expositions of Christian notions of natural law, as well as on the ideas of Samuel Pufendorf, Richard Cumberland, and other modern natural lawyers.[13] One leading characteristic of this theory was that rights, and especially perfect rights, were dependent on duties; when one person has a right to something, others have a duty to abstain from it. This is similar to Hume's reasoning about the moral quality of the rules of justice. But if in these circumstances Hume had invoked a concept of rights, he would have been in great danger of being misunderstood. He had to avoid the traditional argument entirely because, as we have seen, the natural law involved was part of a teleological and providentialist scheme of justification.

In sum, there are very good reasons embedded in Hume's theory of morals and politics for rejecting both the common theories of rights. But this did not lead him to reject the entire jurisprudential approach to politics. His basic ideal of stable governmental action is couched in the juridical terms of the rules of justice, and these rules cover the central areas of private jurisprudence in the systems of natural law. They cover, that is, the protection of natural and adventitious rights, especially real and personal rights such as property, succession, contract, and delict.

This ideal of government, or "the rule of law," was, in the British political debate, associated with "free" governments, whether purely republican like those of the Italian city states and the United Provinces (Netherlands), or "mixed" like the British government. One of Hume's most provocative contributions to this debate was his partial divorce of the question of the nature and stability of government from that of the nature and stability of governmental action. He showed, first, that absolute monarchies like France were under certain circumstances perfectly able to adopt the rule of law and serve the public interest; and, second, that "free" governments like the British one harboured forces that tended towards anarchy, and thereby tyranny and the undermining of the public interest.

VIII. THE RIGHT TO GOVERN

Having seen what Hume meant by stability of governmental action, we are left with a second question about stability, the question of who governs. All governments, Hume says, are founded on two opinions, opinion of right and opinion of interest. We have discussed opinion of interest, or what Hume describes as the "sense of the general advantage which is reaped from government," in terms of the regular administration of justice as the ideal of what good government should do and what citizens should seek from their government. Opinion of right is concerned with who the people think should rule, and it is divided into two kinds: "right to POWER and right to PROPERTY" (E-FP, 33). A government generally held by the people to have a right to power and to serve the public interest will be stable, unless its constitution allows for some popular influence, as in a republican or mixed constitution. In these cases, people's opinion of the right to property normally includes the idea that there should be *some* proportionality between property and political influence. Hume remarks that a "noted author [James Harrington] has made property the foundation of all government; and most of our political writers seem inclined to follow him in that particular" (E-FP, 33–4).[14] But Hume rejects Harrington's claim that the balance of political power is directly dependent upon the balance of property. There is a certain tendency for power to gravitate towards the propertied, but this process is normally influenced by several other factors, such as reverence for settled constitutional forms – that is, it is influenced by the opinion of right to power. Otherwise the British government would have become republican, given the weight of the propertied gentry represented in the House of Commons. In constitutions where property can have influence, there is always a danger that this may conflict with beliefs about the right to power, and consequently there is a danger of instability. This is the framework for Hume's analysis of factionalism in "free" government in general and in that of Britain in particular. The danger of instability is not great in governments, such as absolute monarchies, that rest primarily on the opinion of right to power, but monarchies may be fraught with other dangers.

Hume's analysis of the opinion of a government's right to power is in accordance with his general views regarding the connections between habitual behaviour, the creation of expectations, and the making of moral judgements.[15] He suggests that the factors which form such opinion may be divided into five categories, *long possession, present possession, conquest, succession,* and *positive laws* (T 3.2.10, 556–63).

Long possession of power is the strongest and most common source of authority, as was dramatically demonstrated in Britain by the continuing influence of the Stuarts long after they had exhausted most other sources of authority, including that of present possession. *Present possession* of power will always influence people's opinion about to whom they owe allegiance, as is shown by the repeated changes of sovereignty in Britain during the seventeenth and early eighteenth centuries. *Conquest* is a particularly forceful demonstration of present possession and has been used efficiently throughout recorded history. In the eyes of some, the accession of William of Orange to the British throne was an example of conquest. By *succession,* Hume means a situation in which the son succeeds to the father's authority as if this authority were property even though such succession had not been long established. Finally, *positive laws* that regulate who should hold power will always have some impact upon a people's opinion of rightful authority, and this would undoubtedly be the case in Britain following the Act of Settlement (1701), which secured the Hanoverian succession to the thrones of England (after 1707, Great Britain) and Ireland. All these principles influence people's opinion of rightful authority, and if they all concur, the government has "the strongest title to sovereignty, and is justly regarded as sacred and inviolable." Often, of course, the principles do not point in the same direction, and there is no general principle that will effectively sort them out. In the end, all politics is "entirely subordinate to the interests of peace and liberty" (T 3.2.10, 562). Whatever the principles on which a government may try to rest its authority, if it too grossly invades these interests, the rationale for government has been removed. In that sense the people always have a right to resistance.

Whatever the principle or principles upon which a government bases its claim to sovereignty, the invocation of history will soon play a role. In monarchies, the importance of history is reflected in the weight laid on the hereditary principle. Elective monarchies tend to be unstable but often make up for it through the principle of succession. In republics and mixed governments, historical justification is sought in the ancient origins of the constitutional forms followed. These invocations of the past for the purposes of legitimation are often mere myths, of course, and Hume certainly rejected as pure fiction the various Whig ideas of an ancient English constitution.[16] He clearly took it as one of the hallmarks of modern civilization that such myths could be subject to criticism without endangering the stability of government. Much of his historical and political writing was meant to educate modern Britons in this regard. By giving a candid view of the past, Hume hoped to provide a realistic understanding of how the passage of time influences the present. "Time and custom give authority to all forms of government, and all successions of princes; and that power, which at first was founded only on injustice and violence, becomes in time legal and obligatory" (T 3.2.11, 566). This was crucially important in Britain. Even if the accession of William of Orange could be seen as usurpation in 1688, the course of history had lent legitimacy to the whole of the succession set in train then. It was the latter which was important for the allegiance of British subjects in the middle of the eighteenth century. The task of non-partisan, philosophical history in the service of the science of politics was to disregard factions and factional myths and explain the process by which the nation had arrived at its particular present: by this process the "interests of peace and liberty" had been shaped. It was necessary for the politically relevant part of the population to hold enlightened opinions about the government's rights on the basis of its present performance with regard to these interests. One of the most remarkable features of modern Europe was, Hume suggested, that this enlightenment was taking place not only within the mixed constitution of Britain, but also in the continental monarchies, or at least in France, the most modern of these.

Traditionally, monarchies had whenever necessary created suitable opinions of governmental authority through the tyrannical and arbitrary exercise of force. Among Britons, this was still the entrenched caricature of French "slavery," a caricature which Hume thought it was important to dislodge. France was in the vanguard of an entirely new species of monarchy, the civilized monarchy.[17] This admittedly did not have the dynamism to generate the central elements of civilization in the first place; it imitated free societies like Britain. Once adopted, however, civilized modes of life were fairly secure in a monarchy, in some respects perhaps even more secure than under a mixed constitution.

Hume's analysis of the process of civilization is subtle and rich and beyond easy summary. The three main foci are the expression of the human spirit in arts and sciences, the protection of the person by means of law, and the acquisition and exchange of the goods of the external world (see T 3.2.2, 487). In dealing with these three factors, Hume is showing the relationship between merely living and living well, to use the Aristotelian distinction. For a society to live at all, it needs, in addition to a government strong enough to protect it externally, a minimal system of justice and the wherewithal to feed itself. In a society where the government, for whatever reason, is restrained from doing much more than securing these things, a spirit of enterprise and individualism will tend to predominate. There will be a growth of knowledge arising from experiments in living and producing, and it is on this basis that a commercial society like the British emerges. By living at all, a free society comes to live well.

Intriguingly, monarchies can also become civilized by wanting to live equally well: in realizing this wish, they may adopt some of the basic features of a free society. Monarchies are characterized by a crust of nobility, whose status is dependent upon the good will of the monarch rather than their own enterprise, and whose life is guided by codes of honour and ritualized show. Such a class will feed off the arts and crafts developed in a free society and then will often outstrip that society in the finer arts, as exemplified by the superiority of French literature. Cocooned as they are within such a class of culture, monarchs are little inclined to take much interest in the life of society at large, and no social group is sufficiently propertied to make it necessary for them to do so. As long as the civil order is maintained by the enforcement of law, society can be left alone, and this freedom, combined with the need for foreign goods, eventually leads to the growth of commerce. This was the model of the modern civilized monarchy emerging in France, which Hume admired and about which he tried to enlighten his countrymen.

Despite his admiration for France, Hume never forgot that such a society enjoyed a regular administration of justice only by default. There were no constitutional guarantees because there was no constitutional counterweight to the crown. For all its freedom and civilization, modern monarchy had no political liberty. Hume thought social life with political liberty highly precarious, and in his more pessimistic periods, when faced with libertarian excesses such as the Wilkes riots in London in the 1760s, he thought a civilized monarchy the safest long-term solution. What he feared in a free constitution was its tendency to breed factions and the tendency of factionalism to degenerate into fanaticism, disorder, and anarchy, out of which would grow tyranny. In other words, the very engine of civilized living, namely, freedom under law, found its most refined protection in a system of political liberty which inevitably harboured forces which could become destructive of that engine. This was the situation in which contemporary Britain found itself, and the anatomy of factionalism was consequently a central concern in Hume's literary intervention in public life: his *Essays* and much of the *History*.

The new and difficult point Hume had to impress on his readers was that in a free constitution political differences could not be *about* the constitution; they had to be *within* the constitution. Factionalism as he knew it was inconsistent with this: "the influence of faction is directly contrary to that of laws" (E-PG, 55). The general danger in factionalism was that it would lead to fragmentation by pitting group interests against each other at the expense of the public interest. Even worse, it tended to transform the recurring question of who should discharge the offices of government into a question of the balance between the powers of the constitution itself. This was particularly dangerous in a mixed constitution such as the British, where the main factions naturally would form around two different principles of government, the monarchical and the republican. The extraordinary thing was that Britain, as Hume saw it, was in the process of breaking away from this division. But his contemporaries did not appreciate this and, by continuing the old factional rant, they endangered the precarious constitutional and political balance that was emerging. A readable analysis of factionalism was needed.

IX. ABOVE PARTIES

Factions, or parties – Hume often uses the two words interchangeably – fall into two broad categories, personal and real. Personal factions are held together by personal relations, normally extensive family ties. While such relations can play a role in any party, they most easily dominate politics as a whole in small republics, such as those of Italy. Real factions are the ones that can help us understand larger states, and especially Britain. "*Real* factions may be divided into those from *interest*, from *principle*, and from *affection*." Factions based upon *interest* typically arise when two different social groups, like the nobility and the common people, have, or think they have, opposing interests. Since interest is inevitably a driving force in all human endeavour, such factions "are the most reasonable, and the most excusable." In England it had often been thought that there was a fundamental opposition between the interests of "the *landed*" and those of the "*trading* part of the nation," and this belief was an important aspect of the division of the political nation into "court" and "country" factions. But the belief was simply not justified. If people are to avoid such false oppositions, they must be enlightened so that the pursuit of interest, which is constitutive of human behaviour, is guided by the belief that the public interest is also the most important private one (E-PG, 59–60).

In contrast, political factions inspired by *principle*, "especially abstract speculative principle, are known only to modern times, and are, perhaps, the most extraordinary and unaccountable *phaenomenon*, that has yet appeared in human affairs" (E-PG, 60). The key word here is "speculative." If division between factions is only concerned with differences of a speculative or theoretical sort, then there is no objective necessity for any division in political behaviour. That is to say, there is nothing outside the minds of those involved over which to divide. If the factional principles concerned things like power or goods which only one or other party could have, then there would be a *prima facie* case for division. In matters speculative, however, each mind could hold its own, were it not for a natural tendency to convince other minds to conform to one's own and thus to one's group. The factor that gave this natural tendency such sway in the modern world was, in Hume's opinion, the Christian religion. In its origins, Christianity, in contrast to most other religions, was not an establishment faith. It could only survive by developing a strong priesthood to protect the sect against secular power. The priesthood therefore had a vested interest in continuing to govern their flock in separation from the state and from other sects. In order to do so, they had to invent speculative principles around which to rally their followers, and in this the priests sought reinforcement from speculative philosophy. When the universal church broke up, the opposing forces burst upon modern Europe in the disastrous religious wars. "Such divisions, therefore, on the part of the people, may justly be esteemed factions of *principle*; but, on the part of the priests, who are the prime movers, they are really factions of *interest*" (E-PG, 62). The danger from the people is factions based on enthusiasm; from the priests, factions primed by superstition.

Hume feared factionalism based upon the opposing principles of superstition and enthusiasm most of all because of its rabble-rousing potential. Couching their rhetoric in whatever was the political jargon of the day, leaders could take to the streets and the meeting-houses and appeal to the large section of the population that was outside the reach of proper education. The only way to deal with such factionalism was to enlighten the potential leaders of the factions. To this purpose Hume supported every move that could secure the inclusion of the clergy in the world of letters. Clergymen of taste and learning would tend to see issues of doctrinal theology as matters for discussion amongst the educated rather than as reasons for social divisions, and they would see their role vis-à-vis their congregations as a moralizing and civilizing one rather than as a sectarian one.

The British political system, however, also bred leaders of secular faction who based their causes on "principle." In the wake of the constitutional settlement after the Revolution of 1688, members of the old Tory and Whig factions had been weaving a complicated (and shifting) patchwork, the main components of which were a government or court faction consisting largely of modern Whigs *and* a country opposition consisting of groups of Tories and old-fashioned Whigs who were only rarely able to act coherently as a group. Hume thought that this factionalism should be dealt with in two ways. At one level, the principles invoked by the factions should be criticized. At another level, this criticism should not take the usual form of political polemics but rather the detached form of polite literary debate. Politics had to be made polite and subject to civilized manners just like art and literature; it had to be written about according to literary standards – as in Hume's *Essays* and *History* – and not in the form of polemic or diatribe. The substantial criticism of factional principles Hume approached in a variety of ways. In the *Treatise*, the second *Enquiry*, and some of the *Essays*, he tried to show the untenability of the basic philosophical principles behind the factions which we considered at the beginning of this essay, that is, the ideas of natural hierarchy and authority, on one side, and will theories of contract, on the other. In the *History* and some of the *Essays* he rejected as spurious the historical authority invoked for party principles.[18] And in several of the *Essays* he argued that the factions were politically blind to the realities of the contemporary situation and therefore potentially disastrous. This was not least the case with factions arising from affection, as distinct from those from interest and from principle.

Factions from *affection* "are founded on the different attachments of men towards particular families and persons, whom they desire to rule over them" (E-PG, 63). Such factions were powerful forces in history, and Hume analyzed at some length the attachment of Englishmen and Scots to the Stuarts, and of the new breed of Britons to the Hanoverians, an issue that remained at the forefront of British politics until the defeat of the last Jacobite rising in 1745 (E-PS; E-

PGB, 71–2; HE 71, 6: 530–4). Political opposition based on such principles was irrational since it could seldom serve the real interests of those involved. The voice of reason could only try to persuade people of this and, more generally, try to show that it mattered less who governed than how they governed. The best constitution was one of such stable procedures that even poor rulers might govern in the public interest. At least in his more optimistic moments before the pessimism of the 1760s and 1770s set in, Hume thought that the British constitution was approaching, or could approach, such a stable and positive form. The problem was that factional cant was blinding Britons to this possibility.

X. THE STABILITY OF GREAT BRITAIN

The loudest charge against the British political system as it operated after the Revolution of 1688, and especially against the long regime of Sir Robert Walpole, was that of "corruption," by which was meant the manipulation of the House of Commons by the Crown and its ministers. Rejecting the use of such charged language, Hume pointed out that it was in fact a system of mutual dependence and the very thing that, however precariously, enabled political liberty to be combined with stability in a mixed constitution. The Crown was economically infinitely weaker than the property represented in the Commons taken as a whole, a state of affairs constitutionally ratified in the Crown's dependence upon Parliament for supply. In balance, the Crown had acquired a measure of control over parts of the lower house taken individually and in that way secured the stability of the policy pursued at any given time. This was possible because of the respect given to traditional constitutional forms and because the Crown was a great deal richer than any individual subject. Through distribution of offices in government and church, pensions and honours, procurement of secure parliamentary seats, and the like, the king and his ministers enrolled members of Parliament in support of court positions on decisive issues. The motives and indeed the characters of those involved might not stand the closest moral scrutiny, but that was not to be expected of people in power in any system. The point was that this system converted private – and not so private – vices into public interest.

The same could not, in Hume's eyes, be said about the other part of the charge of corruption, the undermining of the economy through public debt. The government increasingly financed its business, including successive large-scale wars, by means of public loans from the community, guaranteed by the public treasury. Trading in these bonds became a major part of the finance market. The stability of this whole system was assumed to depend upon the ability of the government to honour the loans, and as the public debt grew and grew, it seemed that the only barrier to national bankruptcy was trust in the future, which meant trust in the stability of the government to secure a future. Like many more traditional thinkers, Hume believed that landed property was a stabilizing influence on government. Since real estate could not be removed from the country, the landed interest was the interest of the country. But, in a commercial society where land itself was increasingly a commodity and subject to the fluctuations of financial exchange, even land did not provide a *terra firma* for a government engaged in loan financing on a large scale. The whole financial system appeared increasingly to be a mental construct of the players involved, a kind of economic superstition, with decreasing reference to anything objective and extramental. It was left to Hume's only peer in such matters, Adam Smith, to show that in this regard financial systems operated on rules not much different from the rules of justice, as Hume had expounded them. That such systems were useful and the result of choice distinguished them from those based on superstition.

XI. OPENING THE EYES OF THE PUBLIC: TWO CENTURIES OF READING HUME

In the Preface to the first edition of his *Essays* (1741), Hume sets his new literary effort into the context of the polite essays of the time, referring to Addison's and Steele's *The Spectator* and to *The Craftsman* in which Bolingbroke published some of his most important political writings (W 3:41–2). It is unclear, because unexamined, how much impact Hume's intervention had on the public debate in general or how far it compensated for the ineffectiveness of the *Treatise*. While Hume had clearly damned himself as an infidel who could not be appointed to a university chair in philosophy, he was probably of no great significance in the public discussion of morals and politics until he published his *Political Discourses* (1752) and, especially, the Stuart volume of his *History of England* (1754). In an age when the political battles of the present were habitually fought through the past, Hume judged correctly that history – English history – was the most effective medium for his political views. Yet effectiveness was bought at a price. The philosophically based attempt at impartiality and balance between Tory and Whig readings of the past only served to concentrate the public attention on the party-political issue, to the detriment of discussion of the underlying philosophical ideas. Despite private protestations and public pursuit of even finer balance in subsequent volumes of the *History*, the work effectively marked him out as a Tory apologist in his principles. The posthumous publication in 1702–4 of Clarendon's *History of the Rebellion* and a string of subsequent histories had so inured the British public to seeing their past and therefore their present in Tory–Whig terms that Hume's principles of impartiality had little chance of being perceived and, typically, it was primarily on the battleground of history that he had to be countered, for example in the monumental Whig history of Catherine Macaulay.[19]

Hume's *History* became the standard work of its kind for sixty or seventy years, until eventually overtaken by T. B. Macaulay's great work, which was explicitly designed as a Whig replacement. Thus, even in its demise, Hume's work served to maintain the narrow agenda of Tory versus Whig. Throughout the nineteenth and the first half of the present century Hume was rarely thought of as a political theorist at all, except occasionally on the issue of the social contract.[20] Not until the 1960s and, especially, the 1970s did Hume figure as much more than a Tory historian who rejected the original contract.

It was Duncan Forbes's detailed scholarship and J. G. A. Pocock's grand vision of Anglo-American political culture that effectively drew attention to Hume as a complex social and political theorist.[21] Forbes set in train the search for connections between Hume's purely philosophical principles, especially in the *Treatise*, and his application of these to formulate a "sceptical" or "scientific" Whiggism that not only cut across the old Tory–Whig divide but also, and much more importantly for our understanding of Hume's immediate situation, sorted out the division between court and country factions that had come to dominate British politics since 1688. The question of the coherence between Hume's philosophical endeavour in the *Treatise* and *An Enquiry concerning the Principles of Morals* and his political principles has subsequently been dominant in major studies of his political thought. In a particularly useful introduction to Hume's political philosophy, David Miller argues that there is a gap between Hume's general scepticism and his political conservatism and that this gap is filled by what he calls Hume's "ideology." This thesis has been rejected by John B. Stewart, who argues that Hume's view of practical knowledge led him to the principles of liberalism. In a book that presents the most detailed account of Hume's idea of the artificiality of sociopolitical institutions, Frederick Whelan argues for the coherence of Hume's political thought, and in an unusually wide-ranging interpretation of the Humean *oeuvre*, Donald Livingston tries to show that it is given coherence by Hume's adoption of a narrative approach, not only in his histories and essays but also in the more narrowly philosophical writings.[22]

The picture painted by Duncan Forbes was simultaneously and independently given depth and nuance by Pocock's evocative image of an Atlantic political debate centrally concerned with the civic-humanist values of classical republicanism that had been revived in the Italian city-states of the Renaissance. The ideal of a polity consisting of citizens of property sufficient to keep them independent and armed to protect their freedom was, it was suggested, the background against which we had to understand the post-1688 debates about the corrupting influence of transient commercial wealth, as opposed to permanent real estate; about civic or public virtue; about the virtues of a citizen militia and the dangers of a standing army; about the balance of the constitution between executive and citizenry and, consequently, about the duration and independence of Parliament.[23] When set against this general framework, Hume, it became clear, had a political agenda of hitherto unsuspected richness.

The notion of an Atlantic Machiavellian moment of neo-classical republicanism strengthened the attention to another public whose eyes Hume might have opened. In one of the periodic identity crises which seem to be among the most permanent features of American culture, American scholars have during the past twenty-five years rediscovered republicanism and its associated civic ethics as an alternative to Lockean liberalism in their attempts to understand the meaning of America.[24] This has again directed attention to the European, and especially the British, discussion of this republicanism in the period of the American founding. The general proposition is as follows.[25] In their search for principles in the light of which they could understand their problems and justify their solutions, the North American colonists were particularly receptive to the neo-republican and anti-court ideas of the country opposition in the mother country. But among the problems they faced after independence was the classical dogma that a republican form of government could exist only in a small country. The solution to this problem, as outlined by James Madison in *Federalist* No. 10, was, it was suggested, directly inspired by Hume's speculative "Idea of a Perfect Commonwealth."[26] Since then, Hume has become part of the much more general discussion about the role of the Scottish Enlightenment's ideas in America in the late eighteenth century.[27]

While the explosion of scholarly interest in the Scottish Enlightenment has benefited Hume scholarship generally,[28] his political (and moral) thought has been particularly well served by much new work on Adam Smith. The better we understand Smith's work, the better we may appreciate the sharpest reading Hume's politics has received. It was the publication of a new set of students' notes from Smith's lectures on jurisprudence, as part of the new collected edition of Smith's works, that began to open up the question of how Hume's theory of justice related to traditional theories of natural law.[29] Smith's theory was, it was suggested, in effect offering a Humean basis for a jurisprudential system that hitherto had rested on entirely different philosophical foundations.[30] The relationship between natural law and Hume's politics had already been put under debate by Duncan Forbes's pioneering sketches.[31] This and the new work on Smith inspired further work on natural law, and it soon became clear that the civic humanist republicanism sketched in this chapter lived side by side with a similarly ancient and revived natural jurisprudence.[32] If Hume's interventions in the public political debates around him have to be understood against the background of civic humanism, his underlying political philosophy has, among other things, to be appreciated in its relationship to natural law. Natural law dominated the Scots moral philosophy courses, at least in Glasgow and Edinburgh, as well as the teaching of law.[33] It was in many ways the systematic framework for a common social ethics which all of Hume's readers would have accepted as a matter of course.

Interest in the connections between Hume's science of politics and Adam Smith's incomplete science of a legislator meant that Hume became part of the explorations of the fate of the latter. As a result, we can now see that in the generation following his death Hume was not exclusively read as a Tory historian but also as a thinker of mixed political principles and as a pioneer in the empirico-historical study of politics.[34]

Hume's political writings opened eyes not only in Britain and across the Atlantic but also in continental Europe. What they saw is difficult to summarize, not only because it varied significantly from country to country, but also because it is quite unevenly explored. In a path-breaking study, Laurence Bongie showed how Hume's *History* had a profound impact on French political thought before, during, and after the Revolution, but there is no similar study of the role of Hume's political thought in general.[35] The *History* was also the dominant factor in the German eighteenth-century reception of Hume as a political thinker, although his other political writings were by no means as unknown as is sometimes assumed.[36] Once we go further afield, the study of how Hume's political thought was read in his own time becomes even more patchy. By contrast, there is now a modern literature on Hume, including his politics, in all the major and several of the minor languages.

NOTES

1 For examples of Hume's analysis of the origins of prominent modern forms of enthusiasm, namely, quakerism and congregationalism, see HE 62, 6: 142–6 and 57, 5: 441–3.

2 In addition, the law of nature was, of course, considered a positive law of God as revealed in His Word, but in this guise it could only be considered a law for those who received the Word, namely, Christian believers. The relationship between natural law and natural rights in Grotius and Hobbes is explained in detail in my "Hugo Grotius and the History of Political Thought," *Political Theory* 13 (1985): 239–65; and "Divine/Natural Law Theories in Ethics," *Cambridge History of Seventeenth-Century Philosophy*, ed. M. Ayers and D. Garber (Cambridge, forthcoming), chap. 7, sec. 4; and in Richard Tuck, *Natural Rights Theories* (Cambridge, 1979), esp. chaps. 3 and 6; and *Hobbes* (New York, 1989).

3 In a number of letters in the late 1760s and early 1770s, Hume expressed
   his fear and loathing for the London mobs rioting in support of the re-
   election to Parliament of the outlawed John Wilkes. Hume saw it as a
   degeneration of the demand for liberty to a senseless fanaticism which
   English freedom allowed to feed on itself, thus creating factionalism and
   "barbarism" of a sort that could endanger this very freedom. See HL 2:
   180–1, 191–2, 209–11, 212–13, 216, 261; NHL 196, 199.

4 The scholastic theory of contract derives from Aquinas's theory of promises in *Summa Theologica*, 2.2.88. The late scholastics, especially in the
   Spanish schools, made a sophisticated combination of this doctrine and
   the Roman law on contracts. This combination had an enormous influence through the seventeenth and eighteenth centuries – even on the
   natural lawyers who helped undermine the philosophical basis for the
   doctrine – and we find it in civilian lawyers like Jean Domat and Robert-
   Joseph Pothier who influenced the French *Code Civil* (1804). See Domat,
   Les loix civiles dans leur ordre naturel (Paris, 1689), Bk. 1; Pothier,
   Traité des obligations (Paris-Orléans, 1761–4). The modern alternative
   to the Aristotelian–Thomistic idea of contracts as the actualization of
   the inherent essence of contracting was commonly seen to be the combination of nominalistic definitions and will theories in thinkers like
   Hobbes and Locke. See Hobbes, *Leviathan*, ed. Richard Tuck (Cambridge, 1991), pp. 94–5; Locke, *An Essay concerning Human Understanding*, ed. P. H. Nidditch (Oxford, 1975), 1.3, 2.28, 4.4; see also Locke,
   Two Treatises of Government, ed. Peter Laslett (Cambridge, 1960), 2.81.
   It must be stressed, however, that the scholastic form of teleology was
   widely replaced by the teleological scheme of natural religion, and the
   latter was not much more suited to support pure will theories of promising and contracting than its predecessor. Eighteenth-century theories of
   promise and contract – legal as well as political – are therefore mostly
   complicated and confused, a circumstance that makes Hume's theoretical clarification the more remarkable.

5 See J. E. Crimmins, "John Brown and the Theological Tradition of Utilitarian Ethics," *History of Political Thought* 4 (1983): 523–50.

6 This is documented in my "The Character and Obligation of Natural
   Law according to Richard Cumberland," *Studies in Seventeenth-
   Century Philosophy*, ed. M. A. Stewart (Oxford, 1993); and "Natural
   Law and Moral Realism: The Scottish Synthesis," *Studies in the Phi-
   losophy of the Scottish Enlightenment*, ed. M. A. Stewart (Oxford,
   1990), pp. 61–85.

7 See T 3.2.1, 478–9; 3.2.2, 498–501; 3.2.5, 517–19, 522–3; 3.2.8, 545;
   3.3.1, 574–91; 3.3.3, 602–3. For further discussions of Hume's theory of
   obligation, see my *The Science of a Legislator. The Natural Jurispru-*

dence of David Hume and Adam Smith (Cambridge, 1981), pp. 30–5;
and, in this volume, Terence Penelhum, "Hume's Moral Psychology,"
Part V, and David Fate Norton, "Hume, Human Nature, and the Foundations of Morality," Part IV.

8 Hume explains the labels "Whig" and "Tory" in HE 68, 6: 381, and
accounts for the emergence of the Whig and Tory parties at the Revolution of 1688–9 in HE 71, 6: 523–34. The basic party principles and their
connection with the later division between court and country interests
are laid out in E-PGB, 69–72, and E-CP. Pre-Revolution Tory ideas of
divine right to rule owed a great deal to Robert Filmer's *Patriarcha* of
1680; see *Patriarcha and Other Writings*, ed. J. P. Sommerville (Cambridge, 1991); among many post-Revolution restatements, Charles Leslie's voluminous output is representative, for example, *The Constitution, Laws, and Government of England Vindicated* (London, 1709) and
The Finishing Stroke (London, 1711). The role of John Locke's *Second
Treatise of Government* (1689) – in *Two Treatises of Government* – for
the formation of Whig principles continues to be a matter of dispute, as
does the significance of radical contractarianism in general. Representative examples of the sort of Whiggism Hume has in mind are the anonymous *Vox Populi, Vox Dei: Being True Maxims of Government* (London,
1709); Daniel Defoe, *The Original Power of the Collective Body of the
People of England, Examined and Asserted* (London, 1702); and Benjamin Hoadly, *The Original and Institution of Civil Government Discuss'd* (London, 1710), esp. pt. 2.

9 For the notion of implied contract, see my "From Natural Law to the
Rights of Man: A European Perspective on American Debates," *A Culture of Rights. The Bill of Rights in Philosophy, Politics and Law, 1791
and 1991*, ed. Knud Haakonssen and Michael Lacey (Cambridge, 1991),
pp. 35–42.

10 See Adam Smith, *Lectures on Jurisprudence*, ed. R. L. Meek, D. D. Raphael, P. G. Stein (Oxford, 1978), Report of 1762–3, 5: 114–19, 127–8,
134–8; Report of 1766: 15–18, 93–6. On Smith, see my *The Science of a
Legislator*, pp. 129–31. For a further discussion of Hume's view, see
Duncan Forbes, *Hume's Philosophical Politics* (Cambridge, 1975), p. 76.

11 Concerning the concept of rights in early modern natural law theory, see
my "Divine/Natural Law Theories in Ethics."

12 This was one of the most significant philosophical achievements of
Adam Smith, who explained justice in terms of rights, rights in terms of
injury, and injury in terms of the reactions of spectators (ideal or actual).
See Smith, *Lectures on Jurisprudence*, Report of 1762–3, 1.1, 9–25; Re-
port of 1766: 5–11. For detailed exposition, see my *The Science of a
Legislator*, pp. 99–104.

13 See Samuel von Pufendorf, *The Law of Nature and Nations*, ed. J. Barbeyrac, trans. B. Kennett, 5th ed. (London, 1749), 1.6, esp. secs. 3, 4, and 15 and the notes thereon by Jean Barbeyrac; Richard Cumberland, *A Treatise of the Laws of Nature*, trans. J. Maxwell (London, 1727), chap. 1, secs. 22, 27–35. For a comprehensive overview of various forms of Christian natural law, see H.-P. Schneider, *Justitia Universalis. Quellenstudien zur Geschichte des "Christlichen Naturrechts" bei Gottfried Wilhelm Leibniz* (Frankfurt a.M., 1967).

14 Hume is referring to one of the central theses of James Harrington in such works as *Oceana* and *The Prerogative of Popular Government*. See Harrington, *The Political Works*, ed. J. G. A. Pocock (Cambridge, 1977), pp. 163–5, 181–2, 231ff., 404ff., 458ff. Hume discusses Harrington in E-BG, 47–8, and E-IPC, 514–16, 522–3.

15 This process is outlined in connection with the obligation to justice in Part III of this chapter.

16 For further discussion of this topic, see David Wootton, "David Hume,'the historian'," Part IV, this volume.

17 Hume's analysis of modern monarchy in general and of that of France in particular is scattered through the *Essays*. The most important passages upon which the present discussion is based are E-LP, 10–11; E-PR, 22–4; E-CL; E-RP, 113–19, 124–33; E-OC, 485–6. The issue is discussed in Forbes, *Hume's Philosophical Politics*, pp. 152–60; and Nicholas Phillipson, *Hume* (London, 1989) pp. 61–70.

18 As David Wootton shows in his essay in this volume.

19 Earl of Clarendon (Edward Hyde), *The True Historical Narrative of the Rebellion and Civil Wars in England*, 3 vols. (London, 1702–4); Catharine Macaulay, *History of England from the Accession of James I to that of the Brunswick Line*, 8 vols. (London, 1763–83). The histories *post* Clarendon, which helped create the climate in which Hume's efforts at political-philosophical history have to be understood include, Laurence Echard, *History of England from Julius Caesar to 1689*, 3 vols. (London, 1707–18); White Kennett, *Complete History of England* (London, 1706) and *A Compassionate Enquiry into the Causes of the Civil War* (London, 1708); Viscount Bolingbroke (Henry St. John), *Remarks on the History of England* (London, [1743]); Paul de Rapin-Thoyras, *Histoire d'Angleterre*, 10 vols. (The Hague, 1723–7; English trans., London 1726–31); John Oldmixon, *Critical History of England*, 2 vols. (London, 1724–6) and *History of England during the Reigns of the Royal House of Stuart* (London, 1730); Daniel Neal, *The History of the Puritans*, 4 vols. (London, 1732–8); James Ralph, *The History of England during the Reigns of King William, Queen Anne, and King George I; With an Introductory Review of the Reigns of the Royal Brothers Charles and James* (London,

1744); William Guthrie, *History of England from the Invasion of Julius Caesar to 1688*, 4 vols. (London, 1744–51); Thomas Carte, *A General History of England*, 4 vols. (London, 1747–55).

20 See, for example, Ernest Barker's *Social Contract. Essays by Locke, Hume, and Rousseau* (Oxford, 1947), political philosophy's answer to the Locke–Berkeley–Hume view of epistemology.

21 The most central works are Duncan Forbes, *Hume's Philosophical Politics* (Cambridge, 1975); "Sceptical Whiggism, Commerce, and Liberty," in *Essays on Adam Smith*, ed. A. S. Skinner and T. Wilson (Oxford, 1975), pp. 179–201; and "Hume's Science of Politics," in *David Hume. Bicentenary Papers*, ed. G. P. Morice (Edinburgh, 1977), pp. 39–50. J. G. A. Pocock, *The Machiavellian Moment. Florentine Political Thought and the Atlantic Republican Tradition* (Princeton, 1975) and "Hume and the American Revolution: The Dying Thoughts of a North Briton," in *McGill Hume Studies*, ed. David Fate Norton, Nicholas Capaldi, and Wade Robison (San Diego, 1979), pp. 325–43, now republished in Pocock, *Virtue, Commerce, and History* (Cambridge, 1985), pp. 125–41, a work that further deepens Pocock's interpretation. See also the Introduction to *Wealth and Virtue: The Shaping of Political Economy in the Scottish Enlightenment*, ed. Istvan Hont and Michael Ignatieff (Cambridge, 1983). The point made in the text is not meant to imply that there were no valuable contributions to scholarship on Hume's politics prior to these, but only that none were particularly effective in creating a broader view of Hume's politics in the scholarly debate. See, for example, G. Vlachos, *Essai sur la politique de Hume* (Athens, 1955); L. Wenzel, *David Humes politische Philosophie in ihrem Zusammenhang mit seiner gesamten Lehre* (Cologne, 1959); G. Giarrizzo, *David Hume, politico e storico* (Turin, 1962); A. Schaefer, *David Hume. Philosophie und Politik* (Meisenheim, 1963); J. B. Stewart, *The Moral and Political Philosophy of David Hume* (New York, 1963). F. A. von Hayek's attempts to establish the complex paternity for his own brand of liberalism yielded a scholarly offspring of interest and some influence, "The Legal and Political Philosophy of David Hume," *Il Politico* 28 (1963): 691–704, republished in Hayek, *Studies in Philosophy, Politics and Economics* (London, 1967), pp. 106–21.

22 David Miller, *Philosophy and Ideology in Hume's Political Philosophy* (Oxford, 1981); John B. Stewart, *Opinion and Reform in Hume's Political Philosophy* (Princeton, 1992); Frederick Whelan, *Order and Artifice in Hume's Political Philosophy* (Princeton, 1984); Donald W. Livingston, *Hume's Philosophy of Common Life* (Chicago, 1984). Other studies include Christopher Berry, *Hume, Hegel and Human Nature* (The Hague, 1982); Stephen Buckle, *Natural Law and the Theory of Property. Grotius*

to *Hume* (Oxford, 1991); Nicholas Capaldi, *Hume's Place in Moral Philosophy* (New York, 1989); Antony Flew, *David Hume: Philosopher of Moral Science* (Oxford, 1986); Jonathan Harrison, *Hume's Theory of Justice* (Oxford, 1981); David R. Raynor, Introduction to *Sister Peg. A Pamphlet Hitherto Unknown by David Hume,* ed. D. R. Raynor (Cambridge, 1982), pp. 1–37; Richard F. Teichgraeber III, *"Free Trade" and Moral Philosophy. Rethinking the Sources of Adam Smith's* Wealth of Nations (Durham, N.C., 1986), chap. 3. The studies of Hume's *History* are also of relevance to his politics; see V. Wexler, *David Hume and the History of England* (Philadelphia, 1979); Nicholas Phillipson, *Hume* (London, 1989); N. Capaldi and D. Livingston, ed., *Liberty in Hume's "History of England"* (Dordrecht, 1990).

23 Concerning Hume and the militia issue, see John Robertson, *The Scottish Enlightenment and the Militia Issue* (Edinburgh, 1985), esp. chap. 3.

24 The literature on this topic is now extensive. The pioneering studies were Bernard Bailyn, *The Ideological Origins of the American Revolution* (Cambridge, Mass., 1967); and Gordon S. Wood, *The Creation of the American Republic 1776–1787* (Chapel Hill, 1969). Useful surveys of the literature are R. E. Shalhope, "Toward a Republican Synthesis: The Emergence of an Understanding of Republicanism in American Historiography," *William and Mary Quarterly,* 3d ser., 29 (1972): 49–80, and "Republicanism and Early American Historiography," *William and Mary Quarterly,* 3d ser., 39 (1982): 334–56; J. T. Kloppenberg, "The Virtues of Liberalism: Christianity, Republicanism and Ethics in Early American Political Discourse," *Journal of American History* 74 (1987): 9–33; Peter S. Onuf, "Reflections on the Founding: Constitutional Historiography in Bicentennial Perspective," *William and Mary Quarterly,* 3d ser., 46 (1989): 341–75.

25 Again, Pocock's work was the most important in clearing the ground; see esp. *The Machiavellian Moment,* chap. 15, and *Virtue, Commerce, and History,* pp. 160–8, 183–8, 263–76.

26 This particular problem was studied early in an article that has become a classic, Douglas Adair, "'That Politics May Be Reduced to a Science': David Hume, James Madison and the Tenth *Federalist,*" *Huntington Library Quarterly* 20 (1957): 343–60; republished in Adair, *Fame and the Founding Fathers: Essays by Douglas Adair,* ed. T. Colbourn (New York, 1974), pp. 93–106.

27 Here, too, the literature is formidable. Particularly influential and controversial has been Garry Wills, *Inventing America. Jefferson's Declaration of Independence* (New York, 1978), which discusses Hume extensively. Recent contributions include my "From Natural Law to the Rights of Man: A European Perspective on American Debates," in *A*

Culture of Rights. The Bill of Rights in Philosophy, Politics, and Law, 1791 and 1991, ed. M. Lacey and K. Haakonssen (Cambridge, 1991), pp. 19–61; Scotland and America in the Age of the Enlightenment, ed. R. B. Sher and J. R. Smitten (Princeton, 1990), which includes a comprehensive survey of the literature by R. B. Sher, pp. 1–27; D. W. Howe, "Why the Scottish Enlightenment Was Useful to the Framers of the American Constitution," Comparative Studies in Society and History 31 (1989): 572–87.

28 The most comprehensive bibliographic survey of the Scottish Enlightenment is R. B. Sher, Church and University in the Scottish Enlightenment. The Moderate Literati of Edinburgh (Edinburgh, 1985), pp. 329–76.

29 Adam Smith, Lectures on Jurisprudence, ed. R. L. Meek, D. D. Raphael, and P. G. Stein (Oxford, 1978), part of The Glasgow Edition of the Works of Adam Smith, 6 vols. (Oxford, 1976–83).

30 See my The Science of a Legislator; this work should be seen against the background of the most valuable study of Smith's general politics, Donald Winch, Adam Smith's Politics. An Essay in Historiographical Revision (Cambridge, 1978), which includes important discussions of Hume.

31 Forbes, Hume's Philosophical Politics, chaps. 1–2, and "Natural Law and the Scottish Enlightenment," The Origins and Nature of the Scottish Enlightenment, ed. R. H. Campbell and A. S. Skinner (Edinburgh, 1982), pp. 186–204.

32 The relationship between republicanism and natural law is discussed by J. G. A. Pocock, "Cambridge Paradigms and Scotch Philosophers: A Study of the Relations between the Civic Humanist and the Civil Jurisprudential Interpretation of Eighteenth-Century Social Thought," in Wealth and Virtue, pp. 235–52; and in my essays, "Natural Jurisprudence in the Scottish Enlightenment: Summary of an Interpretation," in Enlightenment, Rights and Revolution, ed. D. N. MacCormick and Z. Bankowski (Aberdeen, 1989), pp. 36–49 and "Natural Law and Moral Realism: The Scottish Synthesis."

33 In addition to my "Natural Jurisprudence in the Scottish Enlightenment" and the literature discussed there (see esp. note 5), see my Introduction to Thomas Reid, Practical Ethics. Being Lectures and Papers on Natural Theology, Self-Government, Natural Jurisprudence and the Law of Nations, ed. K. Haakonssen (Princeton, 1990).

34 See esp. Stefan Collini, Donald Winch, and John Burrow, That Noble Science of Politics. A Study in Nineteenth-Century Intellectual History (Cambridge, 1983), chaps. 1–2; Biancamaria Fontana, Rethinking the Politics of Commercial Society: The "Edinburgh Review" 1802–1832 (Cambridge, U.K., 1985), esp. chap. 3; see also my "From Moral Philoso-

phy to Political Economy: The Contribution of Dugald Stewart," in *Philosophers of the Scottish Enlightenment*, ed. Vincent Hope (Edinburgh, 1984), pp. 211–32; "The Science of a Legislator in James Mackintosh's Moral Philosophy," *History of Political Thought*, 5 (1984): 233–66; "John Millar and the Science of a Legislator," *Juridical Review*, June 1985, pp. 41–68; and "James Mill and Scottish Moral Philosophy," *Political Studies*, 33 (1985): 628–41; Donald Winch, "Science and the Legislator; Adam Smith and After," *Economic Journal*, 93 (1983): 501–20; and "Adam Smith: Scottish Moral Philosopher as Political Economist," *Historical Journal* 35 (1992): 91–113. For the Smithian background, see also T. D. Campbell, *Adam Smith's Science of Morals* (London, 1971); and A. S. Skinner, *A System of Social Science. Papers Relating to Adam Smith* (Oxford, 1979) – both with extensive discussions of Hume – and D. D. Raphael, "Adam Smith: Philosophy, Science, and Social Science," in *Philosophers of the Enlightenment*, ed. S. C. Brown (Brighton, 1979), pp. 77–93.

35 Laurence L. Bongie, *David Hume. Prophet of the Counter-Revolution* (Oxford, 1965).

36 For a brief overview, see G. Gawlick and L. Kreimendahl, *Hume in der deutschen Aufklärung. Umrisse einer Rezeptionsgeschichte* (Stuttgart-Bad Cannstatt, 1987), esp. pp. 67ff., 112ff., and 160–7. Hume is also discussed in a useful study of Hegel's attitude toward the Scottish Enlightenment: N. Waszek, *The Scottish Enlightenment and Hegel's Account of "Civil Society"* (Dordrecht, 1988). Both of these works have extensive bibliographies. For Hume's reception in Italy, see Marialuisa Baldi, *David Hume nel settecento italiano: filosofia ed economica* (Florence, 1983).

8 David Hume: Principles of political economy

David Hume's essays were "the cradle of economics," suggested John Hill Burton, in the first important biography of Hume.[1] Although this may be a biographer's exaggeration, there can be no doubt that Hume's work provides an important contribution to economics as a discipline together with a significant critique of the types of policy recommendations which are associated with the mercantilist position.

I. ECONOMICS: THE BACKGROUND

Mercantilism is difficult to define. It has been aptly described as "a shifting combination of tendencies which, although directed to a common aim – the increase of national power – seldom possessed a unified system of policy, or even a harmonious set of doctrines. It was a very complicated web of which the threads mingled inextricably."[2] Hume, unlike Adam Smith, made no attempt to treat mercantilism as a *system*, but he did identify a number of "threads" in the literature.

First, Hume drew attention to the position that foreign trade is more important than domestic, a point of view which is admirably summarised by the title of Thomas Munn's *England's Treasure by Forraign Trade. Or, The Ballance of our Forraign Trade is the Rule of our Treasure* (1630).[3] Second, he identified the associated concern with the determinants of the rate of interest when he examined the view that interest was determined by the quantity of money. Third, he considered the claim that industry "would not emerge *spontaneously*, it would have to be *induced* by legislation,"[4] a point which is neatly caught in William Petyt's *Britannia Languens* (1680). "Noth-

222

ing," Petyt noted, "can so effectually and certainly secure the peace of the Nation, as the Regulating of our Trade, since it will set all Mens heads and hands at work in all manner of Innocent and Profitable Imployments, and introduce a general satisfaction and Harmony."[5] Finally, Hume examined the claim that low wages were an incentive to industry – the utility of poverty argument.[6]

It would be wrong, however, to suggest that the mercantilists among Hume's predecessors provide an adequate expression of the nature of economic theory at the time Hume was composing his essays. In the seventeenth century, speculation on economic questions was beginning to follow a distinctive methodology.[7] A striking example of this methodological revolution is provided by William Petty (1690), a founding member of the Royal Society:

The method I take . . . is not very usual; for instead of using only comparative and superlative words, and intellectual arguments, I have taken the course (as a specimen of the political arithmetic I have long aimed at) to express myself in terms of number, weight, or measure; to use only arguments of sense, and to consider only such causes, as have visible foundations in nature; leaving those that depend upon the mutable minds, opinions, appetites, and passions of particular men, to the consideration of others.[8]

Another example of the new method is provided by Gregory King's posthumously published *Political Arithmetic*. The manuscript of this work may have had a profound influence on Charles Davenant's classic works, *An Essay on the East India Trade* (1697) and *Discourses upon the Public Revenue and Trade* (1698). Pioneering work on population statistics was done by Petty's friend, John Graunt, whose *Political Observations on the Bills of Mortality* appeared in 1662. Edmund Halley further advanced population studies in his *Degrees of Mortality of Mankind* (1693).

An additional remarkable example, but this time in a Cartesian mode, is provided by Sir Dudley North's *Discourses upon Trade* (1691). North, like Davenant, was an advocate of free trade. In the Preface to this work, Roger North acknowledged the debt of Sir Dudley, his brother, to Descartes, whose *"excellent" Discourse on Method* is *"so much approved and accepted in our Ages."* Of his brother's work, North remarks: *"I find Trade here Treated at another rate, than usually hath been; I mean Philosophically: for the ordinary and vulgar conceits, being meer Husk and Rubbish, are waived; and he begins at the quick, from Principles indisputably true; and so proceeding with like care, comes to a Judgment of the nicest Disputes and Questions concerning Trade."* To this he added: *"And hence it is, that Knowledge in great measure is become Mechanical; which word I need not interpret farther, than by noting, it here means, built upon clear and evident Truths."*[9]

It is tempting to see subsequent developments in economics as involving a combination of two different methodological approaches. In his *Principles of Political Oeconomy* (1767), Sir James Steuart explicitly adopted the techniques of both induction and deduction while making a formal approach to the construction of theory. But there were other, and earlier, examples – notably Henry Martyn's *Considerations on the East India Trade* (1701). In his prefatory remarks to this work, Martyn notes that he "has endeavour'd after the manner of the *Political Arithmetick*, to express himself in Terms of Number, Weight, and Measure; and he hopes, he shall not be thought to speak with confidence, of any thing that is not as certain as the very Principles of *Geometry*."[10]

There were still further developments which could have attracted Hume's attention. Especially important were the works of those who placed emphasis on the economic consequences of the fundamental principles of human nature, and, more particularly, on the important role played by self-interest. The first and most obvious of these writers was Bernard Mandeville, author of *The Fable of the Bees* (1705–23), whose influence Hume acknowledges in his *A Treatise of Human Nature* (T Intro, xvii). Less obvious is Pierre de Boisguilbert, whose *Detail de la France* (1695) places self-interest at centre stage and also gives prominence to issues that Hume was later to emphasize, namely, the interdependence of economic phenomena and the operation of the circular flow. Isaac Gervaise, less interventionist than Boisguilbert, attempted to put the case for the freedom of trade on scientific grounds, and successfully articulated the concept of the balance of trade, a concept later emphasized by Hume.[11] Jacob Vanderlint's contribution, *Money Answers All Things, or an Essay to make Money Plentiful . . . and increase our Foreign and Domestick Trade* (1734), advanced theses similar to those we will find Hume to have adumbrated, and further anticipated the role of self-regulating mechanisms in international trade. Dugald Stewart was to compare

Vanderlint with Hume "in point of good sense and liberality," while Marx was to charge that Hume followed Vanderlint's work "step by step."[12]

While Stewart identified a *parallel* between Hume and Vanderlint, *debts* are more difficult to establish. But Burton has drawn attention to Hume's knowledge of Sebastian Vauban, marshall of France, whose *Dixme Royale* (1701) is remarkable for its empirical content and for the analysis of taxation – another important strand in Hume's essays. Burton has also reminded us of Hume's debt to Montesquieu.[13] Given that Hume read some of Josiah Tucker's work in manuscript and corresponded with him,[14] it is likely that he was familiar with the latter's *Essay on Trade* (1749), a work which also emphasized the need to place economic studies on a scientific basis. Hume also cites Jean-François Melon, *Essai politique sur le commerce* (1734), Dutot's *Reflections politiques sur le commerce et les finances* (1738), and Joseph Paris-Duverney's commentary (1740) on the latter's work (E-Mo, 287–8).

Hume's knowledge of the work of Francis Hutcheson opens up intriguing possibilities even if it is likely that the shape which Hutcheson gave to the study of economics had a greater influence on his student, Adam Smith, than it did on Hume.[15] Like Hume (and later Smith), Hutcheson treated questions of political economy as integral with issues in ethics and jurisprudence.[16] We are thus reminded of another, distinctive, approach to the study of political economy, one which took its origins, in part, from the work of Grotius and Pufendorf, and which was further stimulated by philosophical considerations.[17] But the path Hume was to follow was largely his own. It differs from that of Hutcheson and also from that of John Locke, another major philosopher of an earlier age who made a significant contribution to the development of scientific economics.[18]

II. FUNDAMENTAL PRINCIPLES OF HUME'S ECONOMICS

Psychology

In his valuable introduction to *David Hume: Writings on Economics*,[19] Eugene Rotwein reminds us that Hume's discussion of economic issues relies heavily on principles elaborated in his *Treatise of Human Nature*. Rotwein notes especially Hume's conviction that "all the sciences have a relation, greater or less, to human nature; and that however wide any of them may seem to run from it, they still return back by one passage or another. Even *Mathematics, Natural Philosophy, and Natural Religion*, are in some measure dependent on the science of Man; since they lie under the cognizance of men, and are judged of by their powers and faculties" (T Intro, xv).

Hume was also convinced that the science of man itself must be founded "on experience and observation." But, because this science cannot make experiments purposely, he concluded that we

must therefore glean up our experiments in this science from a cautious observation of human life, and take them as they appear in the common course of the world, by men's behaviour in company, in affairs, and in their pleasures. Where experiments of this kind are judiciously collected and compared, we may hope to establish on them a science, which will not be inferior in certainty, and will be much superior in utility to any other of human comprehension.   (T Intro, xvi, xix)

This approach to his subject gives Hume grounds for maintaining a point of view that was to prove profoundly influential in the eighteenth century, namely, that both human nature, and, to a lesser extent, human behaviour, are uniform – that, as he was to put it in *An Enquiry concerning Human Understanding*, "there is a great uniformity among the actions of men, in all nations and ages, and that human nature remains still the same, in its principles and operations" (EHU 8.1, 83).

Among the constant principles Hume identified as essential to human happiness are "action, pleasure, and indolence" (E-RA, 269). In practice, he placed the most emphasis on the first of these. "There is," he said, "no craving or demand of the human mind more constant and insatiable than that for exercise and employment; and this desire seems the foundation of most of our passions and pursuits" (E-In, 300). He makes a direct application of this need for action to the sphere of economics: "In times when industry and the arts flourish, men are kept in perpetual occupation, and enjoy, as their reward, the occupation itself, as well as those pleasures which are the fruit of their labour" (E-RA, 270; see also T 2.3.10, 450–1).

Self-interest and the pursuit of gain

In addition to isolating the importance of the love of action, Hume also calls attention to the desire for gain: "Avarice, or the desire of gain, is an universal passion, which operates at all times, in all places, and upon all persons" (E-RP, 113). This desire is linked to vanity and pride: "We found a vanity upon houses, gardens, equipages, as well as upon personal merit and accomplishments," but the most common of these sources of vanity is property (T 2.1.9, 303; 2.1.10, 309). Indeed, "riches are to be consider'd as the power of acquiring the property of what pleases," and the "very essence of riches consists in the power of procuring the pleasures and conveniences of life. The very essence of this power consists in the probability of its exercise, and in its causing us to anticipate, by a *true* or *false* reasoning, the real existence of the pleasure" (T 2.1.10, 311, 315).

Hume used this argument to throw important light on what Adam Smith was later to describe as man's drive to better his condition, and in so doing anticipated Smith's claim that this drive has generally a social reference in as much as it is rooted in the desire for approbation. As Hume put it: "There are few persons, that are satisfy'd with their own character, or genius, or fortune, who are not desirous of shewing themselves to the world, and of acquiring the love and approbation of mankind" (T 2.2.1, 331–2). This position he elaborated by arguing that the

satisfaction we take in the riches of others, and the *esteem* we have for the possessors may be ascrib'd to three different causes. *First*, To the objects they possess; such as houses, gardens, equipages; which, being agreeable in themselves, necessarily produce a sentiment of pleasure in every one, that either considers or surveys them. *Secondly*, To the expectation of advantage from the rich and powerful by our sharing their possessions. *Thirdly*, To sympathy, which makes us partake of the satisfaction of every one, that approaches us.   (T 2.2.5, 357–8)

Hume placed the most emphasis on the third of these causes, *sympathy*, saying that "the pleasure of a stranger, for whom we have no friendship, pleases us only by sympathy. To this principle, therefore, is owing the beauty, which we find in every thing that is useful. . . . Wherever an object has a tendency to produce pleasure in the possessor, or in other words, is the proper *cause* of pleasure, it is sure to please the spectator, by a delicate sympathy with the possessor" (T 3.3.1, 576–7).[20]

Self-interest and constraint

Hume drew attention to a problem created by the active pursuit of gain, namely, the problem of maintaining social order. Our avidity to acquire "goods and possessions for ourselves and our nearest friends," he writes, "is insatiable, perpetual, universal, and directly destructive of society," and our natural benevolence to strangers is too weak a passion to "counter-balance the love of gain." In fact, we find that our natural self-interest can only be constrained by itself and redirected to constructive ends: "There is no passion, therefore, capable of controlling the interested affection, but the very affection itself, by an alteration of its direction." This redirection, or "alteration" as Hume calls it, "must necessarily take place upon the least reflection; since 'tis evident, that the passion is much better satisfy'd by its restraint, than by its liberty, and that by preserving society, we make much greater advances in the acquiring possessions, than by running into the solitary and forlorn condition, which must follow upon violence and an universal licence" (T 3.2.2, 492).

We see, then, the importance of society – and of the conventions of justice on which society is founded – as basic pre-conditions of the social order we find beneficial and prize. Justice itself originates, Hume writes, "*from the selfishness and confin'd generosity of men, along with the scanty provision nature has made for his wants*" (T 3.2.2, 495). Having observed "that 'tis impossible to live in society without restraining themselves by certain rules," human beings have (perhaps without conscious forethought) devised the needed rules. But, once the rules are in place, it happens that we "receive a pleasure from the view of such actions as tend to the peace of society, and an uneasiness from such as are contrary to it." This fact and "the public instructions of politicians, and the private education of parents, contribute to the giving us a sense of honour and duty in the strict regulation of our actions with regard to the properties of others" (T 3.2.6, 533–4).[21] As the reference to politicians perhaps indicates, the final condition for social order, and one

which is essential to the conduct of economic affairs, is some system of government. Given that we as individuals "are, in a great
measure, govern'd by interest," it is obvious that we need to institu-
tionalize some form of control over these individual interests. We
need to "change our circumstances and situation, and render the
observance of the laws of justice our nearest interest, and their
violation our most remote." This we have done by establishing a
relatively few persons as magistrates or "governors and rulers."
These are individuals who are meant to "have no interest, or but a
remote one, in any act of injustice; and being satisfied with their
present condition, and with their part in society, have an immediate interest in every execution of justice, which is so necessary to
the upholding of society. . . . These persons, then, are not only
induc'd to observe those rules in their own conduct, but also to
constrain others to a like regularity, and inforce the dictates of
equity thro' the whole society" (T 3.2.7, 534–7).

The use of history

The student of Hume's writings on economics should be aware that
the great bulk of his published work was historical, and that he
believed "history is not only a valuable part of knowledge, but opens
the door to many other parts, and affords materials to most of the
sciences." It is an invention which "extends our experience to all
past ages, and to the most distant nations" (E-SH, 566). Looked at in
this way, historical studies afford invaluable information with regard to the principles of human nature and to the fact that the
expression of these principles would be profoundly affected by the
socio-economic environment which may happen to exist and by
changes in habits, customs, and manners.

To the economist, the most interesting parts of Hume's *History of
England* may initially be the appendices and reports of miscella-
neous transactions introduced throughout the work. These answered to Hume's desire to "take a general survey of the age, so far
as regards manners, finances, arms, commerce, arts and sciences.
The chief use of history is, that it affords materials for disquisitions
of this nature; and it seems the duty of an historian to point out the
proper inferences and conclusions" (HE 62, 6: 140).

Hume applies this procedure to his account of the entire range of

English history, from the time of Julius Caesar to the Revolution of 1688.[22] Quite apart from the intrinsic value of the material, Hume's accounts are informed by an attempt to understand specific policies in their institutional, economic, and political settings, with the importance of economic liberty emphasized throughout. Thus, for example, in his discussion of the ecclesiastical affairs under Henry VIII, Hume remarks that "most of the arts and professions in a state are of such a nature, that, while they promote the interest of the society, they are also useful or agreeable to some individuals; and in that case, the constant rule of the magistrate, except, perhaps, on the first introduction of any art, is, to leave the profession to itself, and trust its encouragement to those who reap the benefit of it."[23] Unless the process is "disturbed by any injudicious tampering, the commodity is always sure to be at all times nearly proportioned to the demand" (HE 29, 3: 135). The same emphasis is apparent in the treatment of the regulation of interest, wages, and the prohibitions on the export of specie and, above all, in the context of international trade: "It is evident, that these matters ought always to be left free, and be entrusted to the common course of business and commerce" (HE 26, 3: 78).

At the same time, it has to be recognized that the *History* was primarily concerned with the broader theme of the study of civilization and with the interconnections between the growth of commerce, the changing forms of government, and liberty. In short, Hume's concern was with the origins and nature of the present establishments in Europe, where the economic dimension was only one part of a wider whole. Hume's perception of the interplay between economic growth and liberty moved Adam Smith to remark:

Commerce and manufactures gradually introduced order and good government, and with them, the liberty and security of individuals, among the inhabitants of the country, who had before lived almost in a continual state of war with their neighbours, and of servile dependency upon their superiors. This, though it has been the least observed, is by far the most important of all their effects. Mr. Hume is the only writer who, so far as I know, has hitherto taken notice of it.[24]

The relevance of these positions for the contemporary understanding of Hume's treatment of economic theory and policy will be readily apparent.[25]

III. THE "ECONOMIC" ESSAYS

It is usual to identify nine of Hume's essays as the economic essays; eight of these were first published in 1752 and the ninth in 1758.[26] These are *essays*, rather than a treatise or a work that addresses separate subjects from one point of view. Yet Hume believed economic questions to be amenable to scientific treatment largely as a result of his belief in the constant principles of human nature and the emphasis which he gave to self-interest. In a famous passage, he asserted that "it is certain, that general principles, if just and sound, must always prevail in the general course of things, though they may fail in particular cases; and it is the chief business of philosophers to regard the general course of things" (E-Co, 254).

Hume also noted that there are areas of experience about which generalization is difficult: "*What depends upon a few persons is, in a great measure, to be ascribed to chance, or secret and unknown causes: What arises from a great number, may often be accounted for by determinate and known causes.*" From this principle he concludes that the "domestic and the gradual revolutions of a state must be a more proper subject of reasoning and observation, than the foreign and the violent." He also concludes that it is easier to "account for the rise and progress of commerce in any kingdom, than for that of learning; and a state, which should apply itself to the encouragement of the one, would be more assured of success, than one which should cultivate the other" (E-RP, 112–13).

It should also be observed that the separate essays show a unity of purpose.[27] All of them illustrate the fundamental propositions outlined earlier. This unity of purpose and method enables us to identify three major strands in Hume's discussion: historical dynamics, or the process of historical change; the use of the historical method; and the use of both of these perspectives in the treatment of international trade.

Historical dynamics and the exchange economy

"As soon as men quit their savage state, where they live chiefly by hunting and fishing," Hume suggests in "Of Commerce," they become farmers or manufacturers, "though the arts of agriculture employ *at first* the most numerous part of the society" (E-Co, 256). In an early anticipation of the theory that humanity has passed, by stages, from hunting and gathering to the commercial society of eighteenth-century Europe, Hume noted that where there is little stimulus to change, "people must apply themselves to agriculture." Because they cannot exchange any surplus for other commodities, humans in this situation have no temptation to "encrease their skill and industry." As a result, the "greater part of the land lies uncultivated. What is cultivated, yields not its utmost for want of skill and assiduity in the farmers" (E-Co, 260–1).

In contrast, Hume continued, "When a nation abounds in manufactures and mechanic arts, the proprietors of land, as well as the farmers, study agriculture as a science, and redouble their industry and attention. The superfluity, which arises from their labour, is not lost; but is exchanged with manufactures for those commodities, which men's luxury now makes them covet" (E-Co, 261). In short, Hume suggests that there is likely to be a gradual progression toward the interdependence of the two main sectors of activity. Playing an important supporting role are the merchants, "one of the most useful races of men, who serve as agents between those parts of the state, that are wholly unacquainted, and are ignorant of each other's necessities" (E-In, 300).

Hume's argument has it roots in his deployment of a favourite thesis of the eighteenth century, namely that men have natural wants which gradually extend in a self-sustaining spiral. "Every thing in the world is purchased by labour; and our passions are the only causes of labour" (E-Co, 261). It was this thesis which Mandeville addressed with such amusing consequences in *The Fable of the Bees*, and which drew from Hume the comment that to "imagine, that the gratifying of any sense, or the indulging of any delicacy in meat, drink, or apparel, is of itself a vice, can never enter into a head, that is not disordered by the frenzies of enthusiasm" (E-RA, 268).

But there is more to the thesis than a concentration on a gradual institutional change; it is also a part of Hume's argument that the emergence of what came to be known as the *stage of commerce* would induce an accelerating rate of change owing to changes in habits and manners – notably by encouraging the desire for gain and by giving progressively increasing scope to man's active disposition.[28] The historical process of economic development had been stimulated by the discovery of gold, for example, and this had been a factor, Hume thought, in the rapid rate of economic growth during the reign of Charles I and during the period from the Restoration to the Revolution of 1688 (E-Mo, 286; HE 62, 6: 148; 71, 6: 537).

Hume went on to observe that "industry and arts and trade encrease the power of the sovereign as well as the happiness of the subjects" in so far as they "store up so much labour, and that of a kind to which the public may lay claim" through taxation. Here again the modern commercial state has an advantage, for "when the riches are dispersed among multitudes, the burthen feels light on every shoulder" (E-Co, 260, 262, 265). He warned against such arbitrary impositions as a poll tax, expressing a strong preference for taxes on consumption in order to minimize disincentives:

The best taxes are such as are levied upon consumptions, especially those of luxury; because such taxes are least felt by the people. They seem, in some measure, voluntary; since a man may chuse how far he will use the commodity which is taxed: They are paid gradually and insensibly: They naturally produce sobriety and frugality, if judiciously imposed: And being confounded with the natural price of the commodity, they are scarcely perceived by the consumers. Their only disadvantage is, that they are expensive in the levying.   (E-Ta, 345–6)

Indeed, Hume even contended that taxation *could* prove an *encouragement* to industry: "Where taxes are moderate, are laid on gradually, and affect not the necessaries of life," he writes, they "often serve to excite the industry of a people, and render them more opulent and laborious, than others, who enjoy the greatest advantages" (E-Ta, 343).[29]

The modern state has a further advantage in that it can borrow present resources through the sale of securities which "are with us become a kind of money," a development which encourages "a set of men, who are half merchants, half stock-holders" and who are willing to trade in securities for small profits. Consequently, more individuals, those "with large stocks and incomes, may naturally be supposed to continue in trade, where there are public debts; and this, it must be owned, is of some advantage to commerce, by diminishing its profits, promoting circulation, and encouraging industry" (E-PC, 353–4).[30]

The essays are also remarkable for the emphasis which Hume

gave to the other, non-economic advantages which accrue from the process of historical development: "The minds of men, being once roused from their lethargy, and put into a fermentation, turn themselves on all sides, and carry improvements into every art and science. Profound ignorance is totally banished, and men enjoy the privilege of rational creatures, to think as well as to act, to cultivate the pleasures of the mind as well as those of the body." He noted that the "more these refined arts advance, the more sociable men become"; they "flock into cities; love to receive and communicate knowledge" (E-RA, 271). He also emphasized sociological and political developments in a notable passage in the *History*. During the reign of Henry VII, he writes,

The common people, no longer maintained in vicious idleness by their superiors, were obliged to learn some calling or industry, and became useful both to themselves and to others. And it must be acknowledged, in spite of those who declaim so violently against refinement in the arts, or what they are pleased to call luxury, that, as much as an industrious tradesman is both a better man and a better citizen than one of those idle retainers, who formerly depended on the great families; so much is the life of a modern nobleman more laudable than that of an ancient baron.   (HE 26, 3:76)

This theme is elaborated in "Of Refinement in the Arts." Where "luxury nourishes commerce and industry," Hume writes, "the peasants, by a proper cultivation of the land, become rich and independent; while the tradesmen and merchants acquire a share of the property, and draw authority and consideration to that middling rank of men, who are the best and firmest basis of public liberty." This development brought about major constitutional changes, at least in England, where the "lower house is the support of our popular government; and all the world acknowledges, that it owed its chief influence and consideration to the encrease of commerce, which threw such a balance of property into the hands of the commons. How inconsistent then is it to blame so violently a refinement in the arts, and to represent it as the bane of liberty and public spirit!" (E-RA, 277–8).

This dynamic environment, buttressed by "equal laws," further enhances the possibilities for economic growth.[31] But it is important to note here that Hume also offered a sharp critique of egalitarianism: however attractive and compelling the "ideas of *perfect* equality may seem, they are really, at bottom, *impracticable*; and were they not so, would be extremely *pernicious* to human society. Render possessions ever so equal, men's different degrees of art, care, and industry will immediately break that equality" (EPM 3.2, 194).

The historical or institutional method

Hume's interest in the historical process led him quite naturally to develop a distinctive technique for dealing with purely economic questions, a technique which led him to give prominence to institutions, and in particular to the role of customs and manners. While this technique shapes all the essays, three in particular stand out in this regard: the essays on population, money, and interest.

In the long essay "Of the Populousness of Ancient Nations," a work which has scarcely received the attention it deserves, Hume addressed a proposition advanced by Robert Wallace in his *Dissertation on the Numbers of Mankind in Ancient and Modern Times* (1753). Wallace maintained that population levels had been higher in ancient than in modern days.[32] In response, Hume argued that "there is in all men, both male and female, a desire and power of generation, more active than is ever universally exerted." Consequently, in addressing the question at issue, it is necessary to know the "situation of society" and to compare "both the *domestic* and *political* situation of these two periods, in order to judge of the facts by their moral causes" (E-PA, 381, 383).

In arguing that modern society was the more populous one, Hume pointed out that the use of slavery in ancient times had been "in general disadvantageous both to the happiness and populousness of mankind" (E-PA, 396). He also pointed out that ancient times had been characterized by a relatively high incidence of military conflict and by political instability. But perhaps the most striking aspect of his argument is his claim that "trade, manufactures, industry, were no where, in former ages, so flourishing as they are at present in EUROPE" (E-PA, 416). In short, Hume saw that population is ultimately limited not just by political factors, but also by the food supply, and this in turn is affected by the type of economic organization prevailing.

Hume granted "that agriculture is the species of industry chiefly requisite to the subsistence of multitudes; and it is possible, that this industry may flourish, even where manufactures and other arts are unknown and neglected." But, he added,

The most natural way, surely, of encouraging husbandry, is, first, to excite other kinds of industry, and thereby afford the labourer a ready market for his commodities, and a return of such goods as may contribute to his plea-sure and enjoyment. This method is infallible and universal; and, as it prevails more in modern government than in the ancient, it affords a pre-sumption of the superior populousness of the former.   (E-PA, 419–20)

It is clear, then, that Hume saw no simple relationship between population and the food supply. Much depends on the form of eco-nomic organization, on the degree to which sectors of activity are interdependent, and on the degree to which men are motivated by the desire for gain.

The same basic view informs "Of Money." There Hume rejects the conventional wisdom that money can be regarded as wealth and describes the relationship between changes in the money supply and the general price level: "If we consider any one kingdom by itself, it is evident, that the greater or less plenty of money is of no conse-quence; since the prices of commodities are always proportioned to the plenty of money" (E-Mo, 281).[33] Less familiar is the fact that Hume consistently contrasted the situation of a primitive economy with a more sophisticated version. In a primitive economy, "we must consider, that, in the first and more uncultivated ages of any state, ere fancy has confounded her wants with those of nature, men, content with the produce of their own fields, or with those rude improvements which they themselves can work upon them, have little occasion for exchange, at least for money, which, by agree-ment, is the common measure of exchange." In a more advanced state of society, "great undertakers, and manufacturers, and mer-chants, arise in every commodity; and these can conveniently deal in nothing but in specie. And consequently, in this situation of soci-ety, the coin enters into many more contracts, and by that means is much more employed than in the former" (E-Mo, 290–1).

The changed form of economic organization heralds a change in manners by giving greater scope to individual effort and must there-fore massively increase the supply of commodities which are subject to exchange. Hume thus concluded that although prices in Europe had risen since the discovery of gold in the New World, these prices were in fact much lower than the increase in the money supply itself might suggest:

And no other satisfactory reason can be given, why all prices have not risen to a much more exorbitant height, except that which is derived from a change of customs and manners. Besides that more commodities are produced by additional industry, the same commodities come more to market, after men depart from their ancient simplicity of manners. And though this encrease has not been equal to that of money, it has, however, been considerable, and has preserved the proportion between coin and commodities nearer the ancient standard.   (E-Mo, 292–3)

The essay "Of Interest" discusses an instance of the fallacy of taking "a collateral effect . . . for a cause." A lowered rate of interest "is ascribed to the plenty of money; though it be really owing to a change in the manners and customs of the people" (E-Mo, 294). The contention is that high interest rates arise from three circumstances: "A great demand for borrowing; little riches to supply that demand, and great profits arising from commerce," while a low rate of interest will reflect the contrary circumstances (E-In, 297).

In a primitive economy, the essay goes on, there will be little evidence of frugality, but often a considerable demand for borrowing for the purpose of consumption. This state of habits or manners is consistent with high rates of interest. In the modern economy there will be high levels of demand for funds to be used for productive purposes, but also an enhanced supply of such funds because

commerce encreases industry, by conveying it readily from one member of the state to another, and allowing none of it to perish or become useless. It encreases frugality, by giving occupation to men, and employing them in the arts of gain, which soon engage their affection, and remove all relish for pleasure and expence. It is an infallible consequence of all industrious professions, to beget frugality, and make the love of gain prevail over the love of pleasure.   (E-In, 301)

In short, the increase of commerce "by a necessary consequence, raises a great number of lenders, and by that means produces lowness of interest." This result is accompanied by a further tendency to reduce the rate of profit: "when commerce has become extensive, and employs large stocks, there must arise rivalships among the merchants, which diminish the profits of trade." Hume thus concluded that the most important single factor was not simply the supply of money, but a change in manners and in the form of economic organization. Interest, he wrote, is "the barometer of the state, and its lowness is a sign almost infallible of the flourishing condition of a people" (E-In, 302–3).[34]

The technique just considered counsels caution in offering generalizations in economics. The way in which economic relationships develop will necessarily be affected by manners and by the prevailing institutional structures. It is therefore important to note Hume's awareness of a further fact, namely, that economic relationships will be affected by the condition of an economy even where the institutional structure is stable. He makes this point regularly, but aptly illustrated it in "Of Money": "It seems a maxim almost self-evident, that the prices of every thing depend on the proportion between commodities and money, and that any considerable alteration on either has the same effect, either of heightening or lowering the price. Encrease the commodities, they become cheaper; encrease the money, they rise in their value" (E-Mo, 290).

This statement seems clearly to mean that an increase in the money supply will generate a change in the price level in cases where resources are fully employed, while a similar change in the supply of money could be expected to result in an increase in the supply of commodities if there are unemployed resources. Hume's analysis of the process by virtue of which changes in the money supply affect the economy embraces both results and at the same time takes the argument a step further.

Here are a set of manufacturers or merchants, we shall suppose, who have received returns of gold and silver for goods which they sent to CADIZ. They are thereby enabled to employ more workmen than formerly, who never dream of demanding higher wages, but are glad of employment from such good paymasters. If workmen become scarce, the manufacturer gives higher wages, but at first requires an encrease of labour; and this is willingly submitted to by the artisan, who can now eat and drink better, to compensate his additional toil and fatigue. He carries his money to market, where he finds every thing at the same price as formerly, but returns with greater quantity and of better kinds, for the use of his family. The farmer and gardener, finding, that all their commodities are taken off, apply themselves with alacrity to the raising more; and at the same time can afford to take better and more cloths from their tradesmen, whose price is the same as formerly, and their industry only whetted by so much new gain. It is easy to trace the money in its progress through the whole commonwealth; where we shall find, that it must first quicken the diligence of every individual, before it encrease the price of labour.   (E-Mo, 286–7)

This reasoning, Hume added, leads us to the conclusion that the domestic happiness of a country is entirely independent of the size of the supply of money. All that matters – what constitutes "good policy of the magistrate" – is that the supply of money continually increase. If the magistrate can achieve that goal, "he keeps alive a spirit of industry in the nation, and encreases the stock of labour, in which consists all real power and riches" (E-Mo, 288). But, as we shall see, a rather different appreciation of this matter was to emerge in the course of Hume's discussion of international trade.

International trade

In discussing the problem of international trade, Hume again proceeds at a number of levels. He first draws attention to the general benefits of foreign trade. In "Of Commerce," for example, he points out that if "we consult history, we shall find, that, in most nations, foreign trade has preceded any refinement in home manufactures, and given birth to domestic luxury" (E-Co, 263). In the same essay, he makes the further point, as Smith was later to put it, that imitation leads domestic manufactures to emulate the improvements of foreign ones.[35] Hume repeats this claim in "Of the Jealousy of Trade," asking us there to compare "the situation of GREAT BRITAIN at present, with what it was two centuries ago. All the arts both of agriculture and manufactures were then extremely rude and imperfect. Every improvement, which we have since made, has arisen from our imitation of foreigners; and we ought so far to esteem it happy, that they had previously made advances in arts and ingenuity" (E-JT, 328).

This sentiment sets the tone of this particular essay, which explicitly criticizes what Hume took to be a characteristic feature of mercantilist policy, namely, an unfounded jealousy or suspicion of the commercial success of other nations. "Nothing is more usual, among states which have made some advances in commerce," he wrote,

than to look on the progress of their neighbours with a suspicious eye, to consider all trading states as their rivals, and to suppose that it is impossible for any of them to flourish, but at their expence. In opposition to this narrow and malignant opinion, I will venture to assert, that the encrease of riches and commerce in any one nation, instead of hurting, commonly promotes the riches and commerce of all its neighbours; and that a state can scarcely carry its trade and industry very far, where all the surrounding states are buried in ignorance, sloth, and barbarism.   (E-JT, 327–8)

In a passage which may well have struck a chord with the French economist J. B. Say, who first formulated his famous law while discussing exactly this topic, Hume continued:[36]

The encrease of domestic industry lays the foundation of foreign commerce. Where a great number of commodities are raised and perfected for the home-market, there will always be found some which can be exported with advantage. But if our neighbours have no art or cultivation, they cannot take them; because they will have nothing to give in exchange. In this respect, states are in the same condition as individuals. A single man can scarcely be industrious, where all his fellow-citizens are idle. . . . Nor needs any state entertain apprehensions, that their neighbours will improve to such a degree in every art and manufacture, as to have no demand from them. Nature, by giving a diversity of geniuses, climates, and soils, to different nations, has secured their mutual intercourse and commerce, as long as they all remain industrious and civilized.   (E-JT, 329)

And he closed the essay with a passage which must have attracted the attention of Adam Smith:

I shall therefore venture to acknowledge, that, not only as a man, but as a BRITISH subject, I pray for the flourishing commerce of GERMANY, SPAIN, ITALY, and even FRANCE itself. I am at least certain, that GREAT BRITAIN, and all those nations, would flourish more, did their sovereigns and ministers adopt such enlarged and benevolent sentiments towards each other.   (E-JT, 331)

The second aspect of Hume's analysis supports this attitude towards foreign commerce on grounds that are essentially technical. Building on the analysis found in "Of Money," Hume examines the case of two or more economies with no unemployed resources with a view to demonstrating the futility of the mercantilist preoccupation with a positive balance of trade. Against this mercantilist concern, Hume contends that a net inflow of gold would inevitably raise prices in the domestic economy, while the loss of gold from the foreign economies would reduce the general price level in them. The net result would be an increase in the competitiveness of the foreign economy and a decrease in the competitiveness of the domestic economy. In "Of the Balance of Trade," Hume had pointed out that "money, in spite of the absurd jealousy of princes and states, has brought itself nearly to a level," just as "all water, wherever it communicates, remains always at a level" (E-BT, 314, 312). In "Of the Jealousy of Trade" he continues:

> From these principles we may learn what judgment we ought to form of those numberless bars, obstructions, and imposts, which all nations of EUROPE, and none more than ENGLAND, have put upon trade; from an exorbitant desire of amassing money, which never will heap up beyond its level, while it circulates; or from an ill-grounded apprehension of losing their specie, which never will sink below it. Could any thing scatter our riches, it would be such impolitic contrivances.   (E-JT, 324)

The third dimension of Hume's treatment of foreign trade is more complex. The basic premise here – that countries have different characteristics and different rates of growth – opens up a distinctive policy position as compared to those so far considered.

The *presence* of an argument reflecting a judgement that economic conditions are likely to be diverse is not perhaps surprising in a writer such as Hume. As Richard Teichgraeber has recently pointed out, Hume's perspective was Euro-centric, rather than Anglo-centric.[37] While critical of Montesquieu's claim that manners and customs depend on physical factors, Hume was nonetheless conscious of the fact that countries could have distinctive physical endowments and was clearly aware that climate could have some influence upon economic activity (E-Co, 267; see also E-NC).

Note that the use of the historical method involves the comparison of economic types, while emphasis on the dynamic element draws attention to the importance of individual effort and to an accelerating rate of change as institutions and manners themselves change. On the one hand, the reader is reminded of the importance of a "diversity of geniuses, climates, and soils"; on the other hand, emphasis is placed on the fact that the extent to which men make use of "art, care, and industry" may vary in one society over time, and between different societies at any given time. Other factors which will affect the rate of growth and cause variations in rates of growth in particular communities include the form of government and the degree to which public policies such as trade regulations, taxes. and debt are deployed with intelligence.

Hume illustrated this new aspect of the problem by referring to the issue of regional imbalance (a concern which he shared with Josiah Tucker), citing the case of London and Yorkshire (E-PC, 354–5). In his early essay, "That Politics May be Reduced to a Science," he made the interesting further claim that, "though free governments have been commonly the most happy for those who partake of their freedom; yet are they the most ruinous and oppressive to their provinces" (E-PR, 18–9). This regional dimension is as relevant to the rich country–poor country debate (can a poor country hope to catch and overtake a rich country?) as is the international dimension, although it was upon the latter that Hume chose to place most emphasis.

Hume's treatment of the performance of the modern economy, especially in "Of Money" and "Of Interest," implies that an increase in productivity may give the developed economy an advantage in terms of the price of manufactures. He also recognized that an inflow of gold into a growing economy need not generate adverse price effects. As he observed in a letter to James Oswald: "I never meant to say that money, in all countries which communicate, must necessarily be on a level, but only on a level proportioned to their people, industry, and commodities." To this he added, "I agree with you, that the increase of money, if not too sudden, naturally increases people and industry" (HL 1:142–3). Looked at from this point of view, Hume might have agreed with Tucker that "the poor country, according to my apprehension, can never overtake the rich, unless it be through the fault and mismanagement of the latter"[38]

In "Of Money" Hume had already noted that where "one nation has gotten the start of another in trade, it is very difficult for the latter to regain the ground it has lost; because of the superior industry and skill of the former, and the greater stocks, of which its merchants are possessed, and which enable them to trade on so much smaller profits" (E-Mo, 283). But he observed that the historical increase in the quantity of money which quickened diligence could also result in a general increase in the price level, an increase that would be disadvantageous in the context of international trade. The advantages enjoyed by a relatively advanced economy, he continued,

are compensated, in some measure, by the low price of labour in every nation which has not an extensive commerce, and does not much abound in gold and silver. Manufactures, therefore gradually shift their places, leaving those countries and provinces which they have already enriched, and flying to others, whither they are allured by the cheapness of provisions and labour; till they have enriched these also, and are again banished by the same causes. And, in general, we may observe, that the dearness of every thing, from plenty of money, is a disadvantage, which attends an established commerce, and sets bounds to it in every country, by enabling the poorer states to undersel[l] the richer in all foreign markets.   (E-Mo, 283–4)

Hume clearly felt that these trends were beginning to manifest themselves in England. There, "some disadvantages in foreign trade by the high price of labour, which is in part the effect of the riches of their artisans, as well as of the plenty of money," were already being felt (E-Co, 265). The position which he was striving to formulate was well put in a letter to Lord Kames in the course of a discussion of advantages enjoyed by rich countries:

The question is, whether these advantages can go on, increasing trade *in infinitum*, or whether they do not at last come to a *ne plus ultra*, and check themselves, by begetting disadvantages, which at first retard, and at last finally stop their progress. . . . It was never surely the intention of Providence, that any one nation should be a monopoliser of wealth: and the growth of all bodies, artificial as well as natural, is stopped by internal causes, derived from their enormous size and greatness. Great empires, great cities, great commerce, all of them receive a check, not from accidental events, but necessary principles.   (HL 1:271–2)

These sentiments expand on a point which had already been made in "Of Money," where Hume had said that there "seems to be a happy concurrence of causes in human affairs, which checks the growth of trade and riches, and hinders them from being confined entirely to one people" (E-Mo, 283).[39]

The possibilities which Hume outlined are not without their implications for economic policy. A relatively backward economy, for example, might find it advantageous to adopt a policy of protection for infant industries. More advanced economies confronting a general loss of markets might have to adopt a policy of protection in order to sustain the level of employment. Hume regarded the possibility of such a response with some equanimity, noting that "as foreign trade is not the most material circumstance, it is not to be put in competition with the happiness of so many millions" who might otherwise find themselves unemployed (E-Co, 265). Thus, while there is in Hume's writings a marked presumption in favour of free trade, he also recognized that government intervention may be beneficial. But any policies so instituted must always be consistent with the prevailing circumstances. This perspective is itself entirely consistent with that which Hume adopted when dealing with questions of a more purely theoretical nature.

Hume's concern with policy serves to remind us of other aspects of his contribution to economic theory. As we saw when discussing *historical dynamics*, Hume's tone is thoroughly optimistic in the sense that he saw economic change as resulting from a series of institutional changes whose net result is to give increasing scope to humanity's active disposition, and in particular to the pursuit of riches. This vision of the future is, however, qualified by the introduction of the classical thesis of growth and decay, a thesis that manifests itself in Hume's belief that mature economies will eventually and necessarily confront constraints to their further development.

A further qualification of Hume's optimism emerges from his discussion of what he believed to be a characteristic feature of the modern state, namely, public credit. In this modern institution Hume saw several dangers. First, "national debts cause a mighty confluence of people and riches to the capital, by the great sums, levied in the provinces to pay the interest." Second, public stocks "being a kind of paper-credit, have all the disadvantages attending that species of money" (E-PC, 354–5).[40] Third, holders of this kind of stock "have no connexions with the state" and can "enjoy their revenue in any part of the globe"; they are a group liable to "sink into the lethargy of a stupid and pampered luxury, without spirit, ambition, or enjoyment." Fourth, this form of wealth conveys "no hereditary authority or credit to the possessor; and by this means, the several ranks of men, which form a kind of independent magistracy in a state, instituted by the hand of nature, are entirely lost; and every man in authority derives his influence from the commission alone of the sovereign." Hume concluded that the modern state relying on public credit could be affected by those circumstances which would offset the political and constitutional advantages that had been emphasized in "Of Refinement in the Arts": "No expedient remains for preventing or suppressing insurrections, but mercenary armies: No expedient at all remains for resisting tyranny: Elections are swayed by bribery and corruption alone: And the middle power between king and people being totally removed, a grievous despotism must infallibly prevail" (E-PC, 357–8).

IV. CONCLUSION

The major Scottish figures who contributed to the development of political economy in the two decades following the publication of the *Political Discourses* were Sir James Steuart and Adam Smith. These two men could hardly have been more different. Steuart had been a committed Jacobite whereas Smith was a Whig. As an economist, the former was, seemingly, an advocate of interventionism, while the latter is now regarded as a leading advocate of economic liberalism. Yet Steuart and Smith had two things in common; both were profoundly influenced by Hume's economic essays, and both enjoyed his close friendship.

From a biographical point of view, Steuart's known links with Hume are few. We do know that Hume visited Steuart in his ancestral home of Coltness, in Lanarkshire, on a number of occasions, during at least one of which the two men discussed Hume's *History*. Steuart's *Principles of Political Oeconomy* (1767) also figures in a long letter he wrote to Hume (the only surviving letter from Steuart to Hume) – a letter which is remarkable for its good humour and familiarity and which attests the "many proofs you have given me of your friendship." Hume had probably given some assistance in the vexed question of a pardon for Steuart's Jacobite activities but had also read the *Principles* in draft. In a letter dated March 11, 1766, Professor Rouet wrote to Baron Mure that "George Scott and David Hume have looked into our friend's manuscript and are exceedingly pleased with it," although Hume was later said to have been critical of its "form and style."[41]

It is not difficult to see why Hume might have approved at least of the structure of the *Principles*. The book parallels Hume's preoccupation with the social and political implications of economic growth and places a similar emphasis on the role of natural wants. In it, too, there are discussions, similar to those found in Hume, of the theory of population and of the nature of the exchange economy. Indeed, it could be claimed that Steuart carried Hume's argument further in the sense that he addressed the problems which could be faced by an economy in the process of transition from an advanced agrarian stage to a primitive stage of the exchange economy. Steuart also went further than Hume in addressing the issues presented by variations in rates of growth both regionally and internationally, an analysis which resulted in a generalized statement of the three stages of trade: infant, foreign, and inland.[42]

If Sir James Steuart offered a legitimate development of Hume's treatment of political economy, it is equally true that Adam Smith more fully comprehended the latter's views as to the appropriate shape and scope of this discipline. It is now a commonplace that Smith endeavoured to link philosophy, history, and economics as part of a grand plan which was announced in the closing pages of the first edition of *The Theory of Moral Sentiments* and repeated in the advertisement to the sixth and last edition of that work. But when we take the *Treatise of Human Nature* in conjunction with the *Essays, Moral, Political, and Literary*, it becomes apparent that the outlines of the model had already been established by Hume. It was Hume who saw the close relationship between the "*understanding and passions*," the subjects of the first two books of the *Treatise*, and "*morals, politics* and *criticism*," the remaining subjects he projected as part of a five-volume *Treatise of Human Nature* (T Adv, [xii]).

It is important to note that Adam Smith had a close knowledge of Hume's philosophy, so close that Dugald Stewart would conclude that the "Political Discourses of Mr Hume were evidently of greater use to Mr Smith, than any other book that had appeared prior to his lectures."[43] It is equally noteworthy that Smith acknowledged Hume's historical analysis of the links between commerce and liberty. Smith would have agreed with the view that Hume "deserves to be remembered . . . for his more fundamental attempt to incorporate economics into a broader science of human experience."[44]

But Smith's formal economic analysis differs from that of Hume (and of Steuart) partly because it followed in the wake of some of the great systematic performances of the period. Notable among these is Richard Cantillon's *Essai sur la nature du commerce en general*, written in the 1730s but not published until 1755. Cantillon's teaching was disseminated, in part, by the Marquis de Mirabeau in the *Ami des hommes* (1756) and probably had a profound influence on the Physiocrats.[45] The most notable of this group include François

Quesnay, whose *Tableau economique* (1757) provided a coherent account of a macro-economic model, and Turgot, whose *Reflections on the Formation and Distribution of Riches* dates from 1766.[46]

Adam Smith was to object that the members of the Physiocratic school "all follow implicitly, and without any sensible variation, the doctrine of Mr. Quesnai."[47] Perhaps with this in mind, Hume in 1769 wrote to the Abbé Morellet: "I hope that in your work you will thunder them [the Physiocrats], and crush them, and pound them, and reduce them to dust and ashes! They are, indeed, the set of men the most chimerical and most arrogant that now exist, since the annihilation of the Sorbonne. I ask your pardon for saying so, as I know you belong to that venerable body. I wonder what could engage our friend, M. Turgot, to herd among them; I mean, among the economists" (HL 2: 205).

But the truth is that writers such as Quesnay and Turgot produced a model of a capital-using system wherein all magnitudes were dated and in which a number of sectors of activity were featured. In addition, socio-economic groups were presented as being fully interdependent. Adam Smith knew of this work, and it seems to have influenced the macro analysis of Book 2 of the *Wealth of Nations*.[48] Hume's essays, most of them written by 1752, are innocent of a model of this kind – and so, too, was Steuart's *Principles*, the first two books of which were completed in the isolation of Tubingen early in 1759. Hume's economic essays do not compare with the great systematic treatises of his friends, different as they were in character, or to the analytical contributions of the Physiocrats.

That being said, it must be noted that Hume made significant contributions to the study of population and of money, especially to the development of the quantity theory and to the analysis of specie flow. There, his work "remained substantially unchallenged until the twenties of this century."[49] Hume also succeeded in establishing that there is a relationship between the production of commodities and the level of aggregate demand, a relationship more commonly associated with the work of J. B. Say. Certainly, Hume's analysis of the sectoral division of labour, his treatment of the theory of population, and his consideration of international trade separately and severally prompt a conclusion which, in the words of Say, "may at first sight appear paradoxical; viz. that it is production which opens a demand for products."[50]

If Hume's essays do not constitute a single coherent treatise, they do, as this essay has endeavoured to show, disclose evidence of systematic treatment. Perhaps the most important single feature of this treatment is to be found in the use of history and of the historical method: Hume consistently sought to link economic *relationships* with the environment and the state of manners. This position was to find later expression in the work of the German Historical school and of the American Institutionalists.[51] But it is important to note that Hume's historical technique is different from that later adopted by Adam Smith. In Smith's hands, the history of civil society is essential for our understanding of the exchange economy and of the social and political environment which it may produce. But in Smith, history is the *preface* to political economy rather than integral to the treatment. In fact, it has been said that Smith did *not* use the *historical method* in dealing with economic questions:

One may say that, despite its pronounced emphasis on economic development, Smith's approach to its more general aspects is less basically genetic or evolutionary than Hume's . . . . With regard particularly to his treatment of the theoretical issues of political economy, Smith clearly exhibits the tendency to abstract from historical influences which was so characteristic of Ricardo and the later classical economists.[52]

A further point of interest to the modern economist is Hume's systematic comparison of different economic stages and his concern with the process of transition between them. This procedure throws important light on the problems of economic and social development. So, too, does his concern with international trade between economies with different characteristics and different rates of growth. Hume's argument effectively introduced the "rich country – poor country" debate which was also addressed by, among others, Tucker, Wallace, and Steuart. Such a perspective means that *policy* recommendations must always be related to the circumstances which prevail. Joseph Schumpeter's description of the work done by the contemporary Italian economist Ferdinando Galiani thus applies, despite Hume's belief in the uniformity of human nature, equally to Hume:

One point about his thought must be emphasised . . . he was the one eighteenth-century economist who always insisted on the variability of man and on the relativity, to time and place, of all policies; the one who was completely free from the paralysing belief – that then crept over the intellectual life of Europe – in practical principles that claim universal validity; who saw that a policy that was rational in France at a given time might be quite irrational, at the same time, in Naples.[53]

The analytical success of the *Wealth of Nations* in the first two decades of the nineteenth century had some unfortunate results.[54] The dominant classical orthodoxy made it possible to think of economics as quite separate from ethics and history, thus obscuring the true purposes of Smith and Hume. In referring to these problems, Hutchison was moved to remark, in a telling passage, that Smith was unwittingly led by an invisible hand to promote an end no part of his intention, that "of establishing political economy as a separate autonomous discipline."[55]

The dominance of a version of Smith's economic system in the nineteenth century led to the belief that the history of the subject dated from 1776, thus detracting attention, temporarily at least, from the contributions of Smith's predecessors – English, French, Italian, and Scottish. The acceptance of Smith's account of the mercantile system also caused advocates of intervention, such as Steuart, to be regarded as mercantilists on this ground alone, and sometimes to cause commentators to view with mild embarrassment the occasional departures of the enlightened Hume, not from the *principle*, but from the *application*, of a policy of free trade.

NOTES

1 *Life and Correspondence of David Hume*, 2 vols. (Edinburgh, 1846), 1: 354.

2 P. J. Thomas, *Mercantilism and the East India Trade* (London, 1926), p. 3. The classic authorities on the mercantile system include Gustav von Schmoller, *The Mercantile System and Its Historical Significance* (London, 1896); Edgar S. Furniss, *The Position of the Labourer in a System of Nationalism* (Boston, 1920); Jacob Viner, "English Theories of Foreign Trade before Adam Smith," *Journal of Political Economy* 38 (1930): 249–301, 404–57; P. W. Buck, *The Politics of Mercantilism* (New York, 1942); Joseph A. Schumpeter, *History of Economic Analysis* (London, 1954), pp. 335–76; Eli Heckscher, *Mercantilism* (London, 1955).

3 Munn's *England's Treasure* is reprinted in *A Select Collection of Early*

English Tracts on Commerce, ed. J. R. McCulloch (London, 1856), pp. 115–209. McCulloch's collection includes eight texts first published between 1621 and 1701.

4 E. A. G. Johnson, "Unemployment and Consumption: The Mercantilist View." *Quarterly Journal of Economics* 46 (1932): 700.

5 *Britannia Languens, or a Discourse of Trade: Shewing the Grounds and Reasons of the Increase and Decay of Land-Rents, National Wealth and Strength*, cited from *Early English Tracts*, ed. J. R. McCulloch, p. 501. McCulloch suggests there is no evidence for George Chalmers's claim that Petyt, who "published some political writings," wrote *Britannia Languens* (p. x).

6 See Furniss, *Position of the Labourer*, esp. chap. 4; and Johnson, "Unemployment and Consumption," 698–719.

7 Writers who review the "main actors" in the drama include Schumpeter, *History of Economic Analysis*; and E. A. G. Johnson, *Predecessors of Adam Smith. The Growth of British Economic Thought* (New York, 1937); William Letwin, *The Origins of Scientific Economics: English Economic Thought, 1660–1776* (London, 1963); and Terence W. Hutchison, *Before Adam Smith: The Emergence of Political Economy, 1622–1776* (Oxford, 1988). My debts to these works, and especially to that of Hutchison, will be evident in what follows in this section. Douglas Vickers, *Studies in the Theory of Money, 1690–1776* (London, 1959), remains the classic account of monetary theory in the period, and is highly recommended.

8 *Political Arithmetic* (London, 1690), quoted from Hutchison, *Before Adam Smith*, p. 37.

9 Cited from McCulloch, *Early English Tracts*, pp. [514–15].

10 On Steuart, see *Sir James Steuart, Principles of Political Oeconomy*, ed. Andrew Skinner (Edinburgh, 1966), pp. lx–lxii. Martyn's *Considerations* is reprinted in McCulloch, *Early English Tracts*, pp. 541–629.

11 Hutchison, *Before Adam Smith*, pp. 126–9.

12 *The New Palgrave: A Dictionary of Economics*, s.v. "Vanderlint, Jacob."

13 *Life and Correspondence*, 1: 92, 304–5.

14 See HL 1: 270–2; 2: 180, 182, 205.

15 W. R. Scott, *Francis Hutcheson* (Cambridge, 1900), pp. 230–43; see also W. L. Taylor, *Francis Hutcheson and David Hume as Predecessors of Adam Smith* (Durham, N.C., 1965), pp. 12–28; and *The New Palgrave: A Dictionary of Economics*, s.v. "Hutcheson, Francis."

16 Richard F. Teichgraeber III, *"Free Trade" and Moral Philosophy: Rethinking the Sources of Adam Smith's* Wealth of Nations (Durham, N.C., 1986).

17 Schumpeter, *History of F   nomic Analysis*, chap. 2.

18 See, for example, Locke's *Consequence of the Lowering of Interest* (1691), and *Further Considerations concerning the Raising of the Value of Money* (1695).

19 (Edinburgh, 1955). Professor Rotwein has provided the most important commentary on Hume's economic writings thus far published. His edition incorporates correspondence between Hume; Charles de Secondat, Baron Montesquieu; James Oswald of Dunnikier; Henry Home, Lord Kames; Anne-Robert-Jacques Turgot; and the Abbé Morellet, 1740–76.

20 Adam Smith was critical of Hume's contention that the "same principle produces, in many instances, our sentiments of morals, as well as those of beauty" (T 3.3.1, 577). Smith's criticism is found in *The Theory of Moral Sentiments*, ed. D. D. Raphael and A. L. Macfie (Oxford, 1976), pt. 4, pp. 179–93; this work was first published in 1759. But Smith accepted, and indeed elaborated upon, Hume's use of sympathy to explain economic phenomena.

21 For further discussion of these points, see the essay by David Fate Norton in this volume, "Hume, Human Nature, and the Foundations of Morality."

22 For the titles of the several volumes of *The History of England*, and information about the order in which the volumes appeared, see Part I of the bibliography in this volume.

23 This is a preamble to Hume's argument in favour of an established church. Such an institution, he argues, curbs the "pernicious" and "interested diligence of the clergy" (HE 29, 3:135).

24 *An Inquiry into the Causes of the Wealth of Nations*, ed. R. H. Campbell, A. S. Skinner, and W. B. Todd (Oxford, 1976), 3.4.4 (1: 412). This work was first published in 1776.

25 Duncan Forbes suggests that the essay "Of Refinement in the Arts" is an abridged version of those aspects of the *History* briefly touched upon here. *Hume, The History of Great Britain*, ed. Duncan Forbes (Harmondsworth, 1970), p. 297.

26 The nine essays are "Of Commerce," "Of Refinement in the Arts," "Of Money," "Of Interest," "Of the Balance of Trade," "Of the Jealousy of Trade," "Of Taxes," "Of Public Credit," and "Of the Populousness of Ancient Nations." Those published in 1752 were a part of the immediately successful *Political Discourses*. "Of the Jealousy of Trade" was published in 1758.

27 This point has been made by Rotwein, *Hume: Writings on Economics*, p. cv.

28 Rotwein, *Hume: Writings on Economics*, p. 19, suggests that the historical variability of moral standards is a theme of Hume's "A Dialogue," a work routinely published at the end of *An Enquiry concerning the Princi-*

ples of Morals. For Smith's views, see *The Theory of Moral Sentiments*, 5.2 (pp. 194–211).

29 See M. Arkin. "The Economic Writings of David Hume – a Reassessment," *South African Journal of Economics* 24 (1956): 204–20. Hume corresponded with Turgot on the subject of taxation; see especially Turgot to Hume, 7 September 1766 and 25 March 1767 (Rotwein, pp. 206–7; 210–13), and Hume to Turgot, September 1766 (HL 2: 93–5).

30 Hume was for some years convinced that government borrowing served to reduce interest rates. From 1752 to 1764, "Of Public Credit" included a note reading: "On this head, I shall observe, without interrupting the thread of the argument, that the multiplicity of our public debts serves rather to sink the interest, and that the more government borrows, the cheaper they may expect to borrow; contrary to first appearance, and contrary to common opinion. The profits of trade have an influence on interest" (E, 637).

31 In "Of Commerce," Hume says that "every person, if possible, ought to enjoy the fruits of his labour, in a full possession of all the necessaries, and many of the conveniencies of life." He went on to note that "in this circumstance consists the great advantage of ENGLAND above any nation at present in the world, or that appears in the records of any story" (265). The link between commerce and liberty is one of the themes developed in "Of Civil Liberty."

32 Wallace's work was not published until after Hume's, but Hume had seen the manuscript, and apparently encouraged Wallace to publish it. See Rotwein, *Hume: Writings on Economics*, p. 184. Hume also cites Montesquieu with whom he corresponded on the subject (E-PA 379–80). For a summary of the theory of population in this period, see Schumpeter, *History of Economic Analysis*, pp. 250–8.

33 Hume's initial statement of this relationship occurs in a letter of 10 April 1749, to Montesquieu (HL 1: 136–8). For a summary of treatments of the quantity theory of money, see Schumpeter, *History of Economic Analysis*, pp. 311–17.

34 For additional information about eighteenth-century views of interest rates, see Rotwein, *Hume: Writings on Economics*, pp. xiv–xvi; Schumpeter, *History of Economic Analysis*, pp. 327–34; and Hutchison, *Before Adam Smith, passim.*

35 *Wealth of Nations*, 3.3.19 (p. 408). See also HE 33, 3: 328.

36 Say's law is that supply creates its own demand. On the origin of this law, see my "Say's Law: Origins and Content," *Economica* 34 (1967): 153–66.

37 Teichgraeber, *"Free Trade" and Moral Philosophy*, p. 106.

38 Quoted from Rotwein, *Hume: Writings on Economics*, p. 205.

39 The rich country–poor country issue was the subject of considerable debate. See, for example, James Oswald to Hume, 10 October 1749 (Rotwein, pp. 190–6), where it is argued, among other things, that rich countries are likely to enjoy continuing advantages. Hume took issue with this position in a letter to Oswald dated 1 November 1750 (HL 1: 142–4). The topic is also addressed in correspondence between Hume and Kames (HL 1: 270–1) and Josiah Tucker and Kames (Rotwein, pp. 202–4). On this debate, see also Istvan Hont, "The 'Rich Country–Poor Country' Debate in Scottish Classical Political Economy," in *Wealth and Virtue: The Shaping of Political Economy in the Scottish Enlightenment*, ed. Istvan Hont and Michael Ignatieff (Cambridge, 1983), pp. 271–315.

40 See also "Of Money" (p. 284) and "Of the Balance of Trade" (p. 317). These concerns reflect the doubts raised by John Law, *Money and Trade Considered* (1705), whose position was echoed in part by George Berkeley in his *Querist* (1735–7). It is interesting to note that both these writers were concerned with the problems of underdeveloped economies; see Hutchison, p. 184.

41 Skinner, *Sir James Steuart*, pp. xlv–xlvi.

42 See my "David Hume: Precursor of Sir James Steuart," *Discussion Papers in Economics* (University of Glasgow), no. 9003; and "The Shaping of Political Economy in the Enlightenment," *Scottish Journal of Political Economy* 37 (1990): 145–65.

43 Dugald Stewart, "Account of the Life and Writings of Adam Smith," *Essays on Philosophical Subjects* (Oxford, 1980), pp. 320–1.

44 Rotwein, *Hume: Writings on Economics*, p. cxi.

45 Richard Cantillon, *Essai sur la nature du commerce en general*, ed. Henry Higgs (London, 1931); Henry Higgs, *The Physiocrats; Six Lectures on the French Economistes of the 18th Century* (London, 1897); Ronald L. Meek, *The Economics of Physiocracy* (London, 1962). For a brief discussion of the views of the Physiocrats, see *The New Palgrave: A Dictionary of Economics*, s.v. "Physiocracy."

46 The latter work is included in *Turgot on Progress, Sociology and Economics*, ed. and trans. Ronald L. Meek (Cambridge, 1973).

47 *Wealth of Nations*, 4.9.38 (2: 678–9).

48 See my *A System of Social Science* (Oxford, 1979), chap. 5.

49 Schumpeter, *History of Economic Analysis*, p. 367; see also Vickers, *Theory of Money*, pp. 217–39.

50 Quoted from my, "Say's Law: Origins and Content," p. 159.

51 Leo Rogin, *The Meaning and Validity of Economic Theory; a Historical Approach* (New York, 1956), pp. 1–13.

52 Rotwein, *Hume: Writings on Economics*, pp. cix–cx; see also Hutchison, *Before Adam Smith*, pp. 213–14.

53 Schumpeter, *History of Economic Analysis*, pp. 293–4.
54 Richard F. Teichgraeber III, "'Less abused than I had reason to expect': The Reception of *The Wealth of Nations* in Britain, 1776–90," *Historical Journal* 30 (1987): 337–66.
55 Hutchison, *Before Adam Smith*, p. 355.

9 Hume's literary and aesthetic theory

Hume's observations on art are set in the framework of social life, which is why he considers both the making of, and response to, works of art as human actions subject to the analysis he has offered of other human actions. Although he never published his intended treatise on "criticism" (T Adv [xii]) and no explicit theories of beauty, art, or criticism are to be found in his works, by bringing together his scattered remarks on these subjects, and by looking at his general aims and the context in which he wrote, we can identify his principal views on these topics.

I. CONTEXT

In establishing Hume's views on what today we call aesthetics, it is important to note their date and their context, and also to recognize that his experiences and references, in almost every respect except the crucial one of classical literature, were narrower than those of an informed modern reader. Concepts of, and attitudes to, the different arts in the 1740s differed from ours, as did artistic practices and expectations; access to the arts and the availability of them were limited. Hume always claimed to base his tenets on experience, and it is therefore doubly important to understand the intellectual environment in which he wrote. Most of his observations were made within a thirty-year period beginning in the late 1720s, at the outset of the social and intellectual revolutions that were to gain rapid momentum in the second half of the eighteenth century and to transform Europe. Aesthetics achieved its modern forms only after his death, and its development is inseparable from many intellectual, social, political, and economic factors – such as the spread of wealth and the increase of leisure among the middle classes; greater ease of travel, and the beginning of public concerts and public museums (in which works would be removed from their original contexts); the decline of individual patronage, with the corresponding freedom for artists to satisfy a growing market or to do what they wanted; the beginning of the formal study of the arts, especially literature, by non-practitioners and non-owners in colleges and universities; a greater availability of books and illustrations as secondary sources of information about the arts; the increasing influence of critics, through journals – factors which greatly enlarged the audience for the arts. At the same time, the distinctions between the arts and sciences hardened.

Hume's references to arts other than literature are infrequent and fleeting. He almost never refers to music or to sculpture, his asides on painting are inconsequential, and architecture gains more than a passing mention only in his letters from Europe in 1748; what little theoretical or philosophical writing was available to him on these arts gets almost no mention.[1] His critical views seem to have been formed with mainly poetry and drama in mind, although it was commonplace in his day to compare and even identify poetry with painting, as Dryden had done in his preface to the translation of C.A. du Fresnoy's poem *De Arte Graphica* (The art of painting), entitled *A Parallel betwixt Painting and Poetry* (1695), which Hume could have seen as a student.[2] Hume accepted the standard view of his time that paintings were often able to convey a narrative or act as an historical record or symbol, but he more often regarded them as essentially pieces of decorative furniture on a par with small-scale replicas or copies of classical sculptures, which were fashionable in his time. Of course, the painter Allan Ramsay was a close friend, and Hume had access to Border houses and even the best houses in Rheims, when studying there in the 1730s (see HL 1: 5, 12), but he would have seen few paintings other than portraits until he accompanied General St. Clair to Vienna and Northern Italy in 1748 (see HL 1:64), and we should remember that the label "portrait" covered fanciful historical likenesses as well as "faces" of actual sitters. Until after the mid-century there were few collectors in Scotland, and even in England the market and audience for painting, together with critical debate, had not developed to the extent Hume later observed in Paris in the 1760s. There were, of course, illustrated books and engravings, but their scale and content encouraged a literary approach. Unlike George Turnbull in his *Treatise on Ancient Painting* (1740), Alexander Gerard in his *Essay on Taste* (1759), or even Lord Kames in his later *Elements of Criticism* (1762,) Hume makes no reference to the influential ideas of Roger de Piles, Charles Alphonse du Fresnoy, or André Félibien; and of Jonathan Richardson, whose challenging writings first appear in 1715, there is not a word.[3] There is ample textual evidence, nevertheless, that Hume derived much of his critical theory from French writers, and we now know that he owned, at some stage, a significant selection of the most important French texts.[4]

Hume displays no knowledge of music, but he was not without opportunity to learn, because the Edinburgh Musical Society had flourished since the 1690s, although it was formally constituted only in 1728; there was also a strong tradition of dance and folksong, and English opera arrived in Edinburgh in 1751. There was almost no theoretical discussion of music outside France, however, and Hume refers to no one other than Jean-Baptiste Dubos, although later he may have heard about the dispute between Jean Jacques Rousseau and Jean Philippe Rameau.

It would be natural for architecture, rather than painting or music, to capture the attention of someone engrossed, as Hume was, in the debate on the relative merits of ancient and modern learning and culture. He owned at least three of the major volumes which addressed this debate between the Ancients and Moderns.[5] He comments on it in letters written during his Viennese mission and in 1767 expresses pride in the architectural achievement of Robert Adam (HL 1: 118–127; 2: 173). He refers to, and thus presumably had seen, the beautifully illustrated translations of Andrea Palladio that were available from the 1720s; and he quotes a significant passage from Claude Perrault's influential commentary on the Roman writer Marcus Vitruvius Pollio (EPM App 1, 292).[6] But what else had he read? There was remarkably little on architecture of a philosophical or theoretical nature in either France or England before the 1760s; there were practical handbooks for builders, of course, and what were essentially pattern books, but there is no reason to think that they were of interest to Hume.[7] Vitruvius, Leon Battista Alberti, Palladio, Sebastiano Serlio, Vincenzo Scamozzi, Giacome Barozzi da Vignola were all available in English, and Hume could readily have consulted the work of Fréart de Chambray, as well as that of Perrault.[8] But if 1757, and the appearance of the essay on taste, is taken as the last date for influencing Hume's published philosophical thoughts on the arts, Marc-Antoine Laugier's (as then anonymous) An Essay on Architecture (1753, Eng. trans., 1755) is available, but Sir William Chambers's A Treatise on Civil Architecture (1759) is ruled out. There were also the articles on architectural matters in the early volumes of the famed Encyclopédie, and several works by Robert Morris, but Hume refers to these no more than to the others.[9]

London witnessed a huge building program throughout the eighteenth-century, and the increased wealth of English patrons provided opportunities for designers such as Chippendale, who were quick to publicize their work. But Hume saw little of this until after he had written the Treatise and early Essays, and he died before more than a handful of elegant houses had appeared in Edinburgh's New Town.[10] Thirty years earlier, in the Treatise, he had stated that buildings, furniture, and utensils are made to fulfil specific functions, and that their beauty derives largely from their success in this regard: "Most of the works of art are esteem'd beautiful, in proportion to their fitness for the use of man," and the beauty of "tables, chairs, scritoires, chimneys, coaches, sadles, ploughs," and indeed "every work of art" is "chiefly deriv'd from their utility" (T 3.3.1, 577; 2.2.5, 364).[11]

Hume always proclaimed that literature was his principal passion. He was widely read in classical, English, French, and Italian authors and frequently alludes to them. But we must recognize that for him literature was a very general category which included history and philosophy. This explains why he assesses literature, of almost any kind, as the coherent expression of thought. Moreover, the notion of judgement, which became associated with that of critic, involved a decision on the appropriateness of expression to the state of the speaker's mind, the intended listener's own capacities, and the particular context. Eighteenth-century British and French writers alike claimed Joseph Addison's eleven papers, "On the Pleasures of the Imagination," for the Spectator of 1712, as a significant source of their theoretical ideas. Hume admired Addison's skill and success as a popular essayist and of course refers to these papers, but he could see that the gesture towards an acknowledged Lockean account of the imagination failed to explain the philosophical issues raised; Addison's arguments were altogether too slight. And the insights Hume adopted from Jean de La Bruyère, Nicolas Boileau-Despréaux, or Bernard le Bovier de Fontenelle needed a more substantial grounding than could be provided by the passing reflections of Anthony Ashley Cooper, third Earl of Shaftesbury, or his avowed champion Francis Hutcheson.[12] Hume found much of what he needed in a book that for at least fifty years was the most influential work of its kind throughout Europe, although in this case, too, his task was to provide a stronger philosophical underpinning by reference to a comprehensive theory of human nature.

The Abbé Jean-Baptiste Dubos was secretary of the French Academy from 1723 until his death in 1742; he had been a friend of the Huguenot scholar Pierre Bayle, whose philosophical scepticism he found increasingly congenial and who greatly inspired Hume. Dubos had also helped to publicize *An Essay concerning Human Understanding* of his friend John Locke, in Pierre Coste's French translation, at the beginning of the century. Like Fontenelle, whose work he admired, Dubos was a learned and cultured man, and his volumes abound in references to ancient and modern works, and in allusions to recent scientific discoveries. Nowhere is this more apparent than in *Réflexions critiques sur la poésie et sur la peinture*, which appeared first in 1719, went through several editions, and was translated into English in 1748. Hume referred to it in his "Early Memoranda" (of the early 1730s), and its impact is discernible both in the *Essays, Moral and Political* of 1741–2, especially when the topic is art, and most dramatically in his "Of the Standard of Taste" of 1757.[13] (Adam Smith, in the 1780s, also adopted from Dubos a significant portion of his ideas about the arts.) Like many influential writers, Dubos was not in fact very original in any of the particular tenets he espoused; his skill lay in synthesizing to a remarkable degree many of the critical ideas "in the air," and in the range of issues he identified as calling for analysis and reflection.

The *Réflexions* is, among other things, a contribution to the debate between the Ancients and Moderns, Hume's interest in which is everywhere apparent in the 1741 *Essays*. Writers in England had imported this debate from France, and by the early 1700s several issues were being discussed, including the nature of judgements of taste and the influence of history and society on such judgements; the limits of criticism and the role of rules in it; the nature of beauty and the respective roles of experts and the public in its determination; the particular stature of Homer, who was taken to represent the essence of ancient literary achievement; and the nature of progress, particularly as revealed in modern institutions and practices, and in relation to Christianity. Hume expressed views on all these matters, and although his hero was in most things Cicero, his admiration for recent political progress and material advance, together with his refusal to appeal to authority or to Christianity, aligned him with the Moderns. Moreover, Hume's debt to Dubos goes some way to explain why almost all of his own remarks on the arts are set in the framework of our social life.

Hume's own artistic preferences and critical observations on particular works are entirely orthodox for the age, and like those of his friend Adam Smith, are rather uninteresting. They are securely anchored in classical, and modern neo-classical, works. On his journey to Paris in 1763, he carried with him the works of Virgil, Horace, Tasso, and Tacitus – his Homer was too large (HL 1: 401). In 1741, he claims Virgil and Racine as representing the peaks of ancient and modern literary achievement, and France as possibly surpassing ancient Greece in artistic merit. At the same date, he objects to anything the eighteenth century branded as "Gothic" and to any excess ornament (E-SR, 193; E-CL, 91). In 1757 he objects to Homer on account of the moral attitudes represented (E-ST, 246), and at about the same time he declares that Donne is guilty of the "most uncouth expression" and that Shakespeare, although a genius, is too often tasteless (HE App 4, 5: 151–2). These rather flat and official verdicts, which appear in his History of England, of the late 1750s, should be juxtaposed, however, with his patriotic and romantic enthusiasm for John Home's Douglas (1755) and, initially, for James Macpherson's putative translations of Gaelic poetry in the 1760s. But Hume's broad notion of literature must be underlined, since he never displayed as much interest in poetry and drama as in history and philosophy. His proposed treatise on "criticism" would have been part of his overall account of the science of man and would not have taken its departure from particular concern with one or more of the arts themselves.

II. BEAUTY AND JUDGEMENTS OF BEAUTY

In *A Treatise of Human Nature*, Hume hardly mentions the arts, but he attempts to mark out the domain of reason and sentiment in matters of beauty. Although his remarks on beauty are strictly subordinate to other, usually moral, concerns, they are relevant to his later reflections on the arts because of his observations on judgement in general, and disinterested evaluation in particular.

In outline, his view is that beauty is an indefinable "power" in objects which causes a pleasurable sentiment (T 2.1.8, 299); beauty is not itself a sentiment, nor even a property discernible by the five senses, but rather a property whose presence is *felt* (by a sixth or even seventh sense, as Dubos and Hutcheson, respectively, said) only when objects with certain detectable properties causally interact, under specifiable conditions, with minds having certain properties (E-Sc, 164–6; EPM App 1, 292).[14] Discussion can focus on the object in which a person takes delight, and by altering his perceptions of it, can set off a new causal chain which results in a new sentiment.

Although Hume distinguishes beauty, perception of beauty, and judgements of beauty, he concentrates on the last, further distinguishing, in line with Shaftesbury, between beauty of form, of interest, and of species.[15] Hume gives two closely related examples of intrinsic beauty, perception of which is barely, if at all, mediated by conceptual judgement. He says we might attend to the beauty of the "form" of "some senseless inanimate piece of matter" (T 2.2.5, 363–4); or we might find that "some species of beauty, especially the natural kinds, on their first appearance, command our affection and approbation" (EPM 1, 173).[16]

Two important principles operate in judgements of beauty: comparison and sympathy. The first functions in our classification of objects: "We judge more of objects by comparison, than by their intrinsic worth and value" (T 3.3.2, 593; 2.2.8, 372). Sympathy operates whenever we think of objects in association with people; thus, our sympathy with the owner of a house enables *us* to derive pleasure from the "convenience" of *his* house (T 2.2.5, 364).

The justification of judgements of beauty depends on the species and nature of the object to which it is attributed; beauty of utility is relative to species, whether the utility benefits the animal itself, or the owner of an object; it also varies between cultures (T 2.1.8, 299; 3.2.1, 483; 3.3.5, 615). Although it is detected by a sentiment, beauty is as "real" as colour and other allegedly secondary qualities, and discussion of it can be objective, however difficult to achieve this may be. Three factors are necessary to the objectivity of such judgements: the conventions of language, the universal psychological make-up of human beings, and the possibility of publicly shareable viewpoints.

Everyone acknowledged that reference to utility required the exercise of judgement, and Hume emphasizes the importance of both the kind of beauty in question, and the kind of thing that is said to be beautiful. Every community, Hume thinks, agrees on the descriptions of whatever most concerns it; no special mystery surrounds the conventions governing such discourse, although their historical and psychological origins may be obscure; but within the social group deviation from the conventions calls for explanation. Thus, what counts as a beautiful plain depends on a particular community's notion of a plain, and in Hume's context a plain cannot be both "overgrown" and "beautiful": "a plain, overgrown with furze and broom, may be, in itself, as beautiful as a hill cover'd with vines or olive-trees; tho' it will never appear so to one, who is acquainted with the value of each. But this is a beauty merely of imagination, and has no foundation in what appears to the senses" (T 2.2.5, 364). We could attend merely to some aspect of its form, say its colour, or consider the area under a description other than "plain," and one might then be able to *think* of it as beautiful, although not, presumably, to *feel* it to be so. Such beauty, however, would be "merely of imagination." There are other cases in which Hume considers the imagination to operate. We may justifiably describe as beautiful an uninhabited but fertile land, or an imprisoned athlete, because "where any object, in all its parts, is fitted to attain any agreeable end, it naturally gives us pleasure, and is esteem'd beautiful, even tho' some external circumstances be wanting to render it altogether effectual." Here, "the imagination adheres to the *general* views of things," so that "the *seeming tendencies* of objects affect the mind" (T 3.3.1, 584–7; see also 2.1.10, 311).

Hume argues that for the required causal interaction to occur between observer and observed, for our judgements to be objective, and for social communication to take place at all, it is necessary to establish and agree upon appropriate viewpoints. The metaphorical notion of viewpoint here covers the descriptions under which an object is considered, as well as the observers' beliefs, attitudes, and interests.

It is central to Hume's position that " 'tis impossible men cou'd ever agree in their sentiments and judgments, unless they chose some common point of view, from which they might survey their object, and which might cause it to appear the same to all of them" (T 3.3.1, 591). This general viewpoint is the source of the "general inalterable standard, by which we may approve or disapprove of characters and manners. And tho' the *heart* does not always take part with those general notions, or regulate its love and hatred by them, yet are they sufficient for discourse, and serve all our purposes in company, in the pulpit, on the theatre, and in the schools" (T 3.3.3, 603). Such standards are revisable, because they serve the needs of the community, and those needs may change (EPM 5.2, 229). Moreover, "*general rules* are often extended beyond the principle whence they first arise; and this in all matters of taste and sentiment" (EPM 4, 207; T 2.2.5, 362); only close attention to the context will enable us to distinguish between the origins of a principle and its present foundations (E-OC, 469). It is contingent, of course, which standards are accepted within a particular context, since the judgement is made on grounds of utility, but it is necessary that there are some standards.

We can adopt the required "*general* points of view" only "in our thoughts," but they are necessary to all social life: " 'twere impossible we cou'd ever make use of language, or communicate our sentiments to one another, did we not correct the momentary appearances of things, and overlook our present situation." Strictly speaking, the adoption of a "general" viewpoint enables us to correct our language rather than our sentiments; first, because "our passions do not readily follow the determination of our judgment," and change more slowly than the operations of the imagination; second, because our sentiments are not influenced immediately, but only mediately by judgements (T 3.3.1, 581–3).

Such passages support the view that Hume is one of the first British writers to emphasize the central importance of *context* to our critical judgements. "The passion, in pronouncing its verdict, considers not the object simply, as it is in itself, but surveys it with all the circumstances, which attend it" (E-Sc, 172), while "in many orders of beauty, particularly those of the finer arts, it is requisite to employ much reasoning, in order to feel the proper sentiment" (EPM 1, 173). We may have to learn what complexities need to be considered, but discussion can change how we think of something, and thereby set off a new causal sequence ending in new sentiments and verdicts.

III. EARLY ESSAYS

In the *Essays* of 1741–2, there are several discussions of the origins and social development of the arts, and Hume frequently follows Dubos closely. Hume agrees with Dubos that the fine arts can develop only when groups or societies exist beyond the conditions of bare subsistence, and indeed only when production of the necessities of life exceeds demand. (Contemporaries of Hume never considered the choices of colour, size, shape, and decoration or texture of containers or dwellings among so-called early peoples as art or incipient art.) Like Dubos, Hume claims that the arts and sciences arise only among peoples who have what he calls a "free government," and some measure of security; moreover, strong rival states stimulate invention whilst also curbing territorial expansion. The arts, which require patronage, are likely to flourish best in a civilized monarchy, and the sciences in a republic, but perfection in either domain is necessarily followed by cyclical decline. From the individual standpoint, Hume holds that nothing can be done to alter our inner constitution, although it exerts a crucial influence over our taste. But reasoning also has important roles to play, not least in modifying the ways we perceive and describe things. Dubos had shown how physical and physiological factors, such as ageing, affect our critical judgements; by contrast, Hume emphasizes social or "moral" factors. He argues that happiness – consisting in a balance between action, pleasure, and indolence – is necessary to the physical well-being of individuals, as well as to the political health of society.

Dubos argued that works of art raise artificial, not natural, passions, and that everyone except fellow artists and scholars reads works of art for pleasure. The contrast between artists and scholars, on the one hand, and spectators, on the other, is important; fellow-artists are interested in the techniques and know-how, but as rival craftsmen and potential competitors for attention, they cannot, in that frame of mind, adopt a properly disinterested attitude (Dubos may have been the first to use this notion in an exclusively aesthetic context). Dubos insists that we can derive sustained pleasure from a work only if we understand it in some way, and the minimal requirement is for *ordre* – which might be translated as "discernible structure." The "public," and not the self-proclaimed professional critics, are the proper judges of art because, having no self-interest in the transaction, they can more easily answer the primary question of whether they have been moved or affected by a work – and that question is not the task of reason but of an internal sense called *sentiment*.[17] The role of reason is to identify the features of a work which cause us pleasure; in this way reason justifies the verdict of sentiment. The tasks of identification and justification typically belong to the critic. There is a contrast, therefore, between the artist who makes, the spectator who responds, and the critic who explains. The "public," it should be added, turns out to be a privileged group which has learned through experience to exercise comparative taste; they are the "true amateurs," because the learned are in danger of losing touch with the very point of the arts, which is to please.

Dubos influenced Hume not only in his reflections on the physical, social, and political conditions of the arts, but also when he came to consider the conditions for the proper responses to them. This will become apparent in the next section. Before examining Hume's most important essay on matters of criticism, however, we should briefly look at a short essay he published at the same time, under the title "Of Tragedy." There Hume takes up the fashionable topic of why spectators should derive pleasure from representations of tragic events which in real life they would abhor. Most well-known writers in France and Britain had something to say on the subject, including Addison, Dubos, and Lord Kames. Hume combines the views of Dubos and Fontenelle, and augments them.[18] He agrees with them that we never fail to know that we are in a theatre, that almost any passion is better than none, and that almost any form of imitation or representation arrests our attention and pleases us. The clue, he thinks, lies in the mastery of language and presentation, which allows one of the conflicting passions to become dominant over the other. The intense horror we experience from the story is itself converted to something pleasing by the overwhelming plea-sure of the beauty with which it is presented. The conversion can only occur when the story is fictional, or at least narrated about the past. Hume does not mention the notion of sympathy, perhaps be-cause it would diminish pleasure to the extent that it induced identi-fication with the sufferers (E-Tr, 216–25).

IV. "OF THE STANDARD OF TASTE"

In 1755 The Edinburgh Society for Encouraging Arts, Sciences, Manufactures, and Agriculture in Scotland had proposed, but failed, to award a medal for "the best essay on taste." Adam Smith and Hume were members of the society, as was Allan Ramsay, who had just published his own "A Dialogue on Taste." The society renewed its proposal in 1756 and awarded a gold medal to Alexander Gerard. His expanded submission was published, at Hume's urging, in 1759 as *An Essay on Taste*, together with "three dissertations on the same subject," by Voltaire, d'Alembert, and Montesquieu; these last were, in fact, unacknowledged translations from entries under "Goût" in volume 7 of the *Encyclopédie*. Meanwhile, in 1757, Hume had pub-lished (in *Four Dissertations*) an essay of his own, "Of the Standard of Taste," together with "Of Tragedy" and two other essays; he told a correspondent that his essay on taste was a substitute for one on geometry which Lord Stanhope persuaded him to withdraw. Ram-say, like Hume, cites Shaftesbury as a point of departure when dis-cussing whether there could be a standard of taste and offers a socio-logical explanation of changes in fashion, placing great weight on habit and social status. Hume's own essay is condensed, and heavily derivative from the Abbé Dubos, but to a degree rests on the compre-hensive philosophical system he had already worked out. Indeed, he seeks to find in human nature, as well as in social practices, a resolu-tion for the problem Ramsay located only in social practices. Ge-rard's much longer book takes its departure from a Humean position and discusses many of the same issues: the need for attention and comparison in order to establish the ends and merit of a work; the need for good sense, reasoning, and models; the parallels between taste and virtue; the need to ground our conclusions in experience.

In his essay Hume, in effect, extends his reflections from *An En-quiry concerning the Principles of Morals* on the respective roles of reason and sentiment in the realm of values. Some so-called judgements of taste are, he believes, palpably foolish and indefensible; "the taste of all individuals is not upon an equal footing," and we should not give unrestricted license to the claim that it is "fruitless to dispute concerning tastes" (E-ST, 242, 230). He recognizes that those who introduce sentiment into the analysis must nevertheless avoid claiming that everyone is equally right in matters of sentiment. Indeed, if rational discourse is even to be possible, there must be some "standard," "rule," or "criterion" by which disputes can be resolved (E-ST, 229). Consequently, Hume hopes to show that criticism is a factually based, rational, social activity, capable of being integrated into the rest of intelligible human discourse, and he attempts to establish that sentiment can be a criterion. Of course, if there are "rules," whether of composition or criticism, they must not be thought of as "fixed by reasonings *a priori*, or . . . be esteemed abstract conclusions of the understanding" (E-ST, 231).

Hume holds that to discern the subtle or the defining properties of something, a purely passive attitude is not enough. The observer must self-consciously attend to the object in question and, moreover, be in a proper state of mind when doing so; a merely causal reaction will be replaced by an appropriate causal interaction, to which the observer significantly contributes. Following Dubos, Hume states that three traits are needed: "A perfect serenity of mind, a recollection of thought, a due attention to the object" (E-ST, 232). In art, the problem is complex: "In order to judge aright of a composition of genius, there are so many views to be taken in, so many circumstances to be compared, and such a knowledge of human nature requisite, that no man, who is not possessed of the soundest judgment, will ever make a tolerable critic in such performances" (E-DT, 6). Hume lists three main "causes" why people do not respond properly to works of art, and each one is derived *verbatim* from Dubos: a person may lack delicacy, may lack good sense, or may suffer from prejudice. These are all transliterated seventeenth-century French technical terms, essentially Cartesian, familiar to all of Hume's learned contemporaries (E-ST, 234, 239–40). Hume holds that delicacy of feeling enables one to "be sensibly touched with every part of" a work (E-DT, 4), and there can be no doubt that such discriminating perception requires judgement of some kind. The Cartesians had defined good sense as true judgement of sensible things, its role being to guard against false judgement, or prejudice. Hume accepts the point: "reason, if not an essential part of taste [not, that is, the defining element], is at least requisite to the operations" of it (E-ST, 240). "To form a true judgment" a critic "must place himself in the same situation" as the audience for whom the work was conceived, and to whom it was originally addressed (E-ST, 239). Good sense attends to four features of the context: the ends for which a work has been calculated, the effectiveness of the means to those ends, the mutual relations of the parts and of the parts to the whole, and the intelligibility of the whole. For example, "the object of eloquence is to persuade, of history to instruct, of poetry to please by means of the passions and the imagination. These ends we must carry constantly in our view, when we peruse any performance." In addition, "every kind of composition, even the most poetical, is nothing but a chain of propositions and reasonings," so that intelligibility is central (E-ST, 240).

To overcome failures caused by prejudice or the lack of delicacy and good sense, two steps are necessary (again from Dubos): practice and comparison. *Practice* is necessary to overcome superficial first impressions, since any "very individual performance" should be "more than once perused by us, and be surveyed in different lights with attention and deliberation." Only in this way can we determine "the relation of the parts" and their respective merits. Likewise, *comparison* "between the several species and degrees of excellence" is essential, since someone "who has had no opportunity of comparing the different kinds of beauty, is indeed totally unqualified to pronounce an opinion with regard to any object presented to him. By comparison alone we fix the epithets of praise or blame, and learn how to assign the due degree of each." A prejudiced critic fails to place "himself in that point of view, which the performance supposes," and "obstinately maintains his natural position." Hume insists that "every work of art, in order to produce its due effect on the mind, must be surveyed in a certain point of view, and cannot be fully relished by persons, whose situation, real or imaginary, is not conformable to that which is required by the performance" (E-ST, 237–9). We see here Hume's view that a work of art is an intentional act, calling for self-conscious mental action on the part of the spectator.

Although he rarely uses the term, Hume is clearly concerned with the nature and conditions of "interpretation" which leads to an un-

derstanding of a work (see EPM 9.1, 271); practice is needed in order
to achieve discrimination, and comparison in order to place a work
in its proper categories. A long footnote to Section 3 of *Philosophical
Essays concerning Human Understanding* of 1748 (later retitled as
An Enquiry . . .), a footnote sometimes omitted in later editions
(including that cited in this volume), is here significant. There
Hume argues that the principles of human agency are themselves
represented in, or at least leave traces in, what we do and underlie
the spectator's acts of interpretation. That is why he says, in 1757,
"the same address and dexterity, which practice gives to the execution of any work, is also acquired by the same means, in the judging
of it" (E-ST, 237). For Hume, our capacity to understand the world
depends on our capacity to understand the causes in operation. In *An
Enquiry concerning Human Understanding*, he asks causal questions about each of the issues he raises later in "Of the Standard of
Taste": the artist and the conditions of creation, the art product
which results, and the audience and the conditions of response.
Moreover, like Dubos, Hume's interest centres on broadly representational works of art, and he asks causal questions about the things
or events represented, in order to determine the consistency and
intelligibility of the work's content. His internal questions about
the consistency of the work itself presuppose answers to the external matter of the proper viewpoint, and the relations between the
work and other things – such as society at large, or morality. He
declares that,

as man is a reasonable being . . . he seldom acts or speaks or thinks without
a purpose and intention. . . . In all compositions of genius, therefore, 'tis
requisite that the writer have some plan or object . . . there must appear
some aim or intention in his first setting out, if not in the composition of
the whole work. A production without a design would resemble more the
ravings of a madman, than the sober efforts of genius and learning.

(EHU 3, in W 4: 19)

In "narrative compositions," it is a rule that "admits of no exception," that the narrated events "must be connected together, by
some bond or tye," must "form a kind of *Unity*, which may bring
them under one plan or view, and which may be the object or end of
the writer in his first undertaking." Again, in epic and narrative
poetry, it "is incumbent on every writer, to form some plan or de-

sign, before he enter on any discourse or narration, and to comprehend his subject in some general aspect or united view, which may be the constant object of his attention." Above all, it is necessary that such works "have a sufficient unity to make them be comprehended" (EHU 3, in W 4: 19–23).

In the *Treatise*, Hume argued that consistency of ideas ensures their "easy transition," together with "the emotions or impressions, attending the ideas"; the natural requirement for such easy transitions lies behind demands for consistency of treatment and tone in literature, and for balanced figures in painting and statuary (T 2.2.8, 379–80; 2.2.5, 364; EPM 6.2, 245). "The designs, and projects, and views of men are principles as necessary in their operation as heat and cold, moist and dry" (T 3.1.2, 474); they are, in brief, the conditions of human agency, and a knowledge of them is a condition of understanding what a man does.

It is precisely because art is a human activity that we require it to be intelligible; "durable" pleasure, indeed, is dependent upon understanding in the relevant ways (T 2.2.4, 353; see also 2.3.10, 451). Our affections are aroused, or at least sustained, it might be said, only if the actions of our fellows display what might be called a certain *transparency*.

Even if, as Hume maintained in the second *Enquiry*, the "final sentence depends on some internal sense or feeling, which nature has made universal in the whole species" (EPM 1, 173), a "judgment on any work" involves more than a mere report of such a feeling (E-ST, 241). Judgement involves identifying the causes of the pleasurable sentiment, and these causes are to be found among the properties of the work itself, although they are detectable only from certain viewpoints. Like Sancho's kinsmen, in Cervantes's *Don Quixote* (2.13), who were vindicated by the discovery of the leather thong (Hume gets the story slightly wrong), a critic who identifies the causes of his sentiment will have "justified the verdict" (E-ST, 235); he will have established its appropriateness by establishing its repeatable causal conditions. Dubos had claimed, in 1719, that the role of reason was to justify the judgement that sentiment had already made (*justifier le jugement que le sentiment a porté*), by determining the "causes" of our pleasure; critics, indeed, can tell us the cause of an effect one has already felt (*la cause d'un effet qu'on sentait déjà*) only if, on Hume's view, the antecedent is identifiable, and the relation repeatable.[19] "Reason," therefore – that is, induc-tive, experimental reasoning – is "requisite to the operations" of taste (E-ST, 240) because the proper sentiment depends on the proper discernment, which in turn involves thinking of the work in particu-lar, determinate, ways. "Critics can reason and dispute more plausi-bly than cooks" (E-Sc, 163) because cooks are concerned solely with the physical causes of sensations, require minimal mental contribu-tion from the customer, and the dishes they create are not bearers of meaning; critics, on the other hand, require sound judgement in order to discern the consistency and meaning of an intentional hu-man performance, and in order to understand it. It must be stressed, nevertheless, that a genuine man of taste must experience a pleasur-able sentiment when he attends to a work in specified ways, because that is the sentiment whose cause and justification he wishes to locate in the work itself. In brief, the "proper sentiment" is a com-plex response to a work, involving causal interaction between it and a spectator who attends to it in specifiable ways; a critic's task includes the determination of the spectator's viewpoint, and he justi-fies his verdicts by bringing others to perceive and think of the work in the way he has.

When discussing the causes of failure to feel the proper sentiment, Hume raises two important questions, although he directly answers only one of them. First, he asks how we should "silence the bad critic" who insists on his sentiment in the face of counter-evidence to his causal claims (E-ST, 236). Hume's answer is that we must appeal to parallel cases whose relevance the bad critic acknowl-edges. Hume's view is that in the absence of established models and general principles, time and the facts will ultimately vindicate any critical judgement; someone with unusual powers of discrimination may fail to convince his peers, but it is to be hoped that truth will triumph in the end. He would admit, however, that even if an estab-lished critic can convince his audience about a new case, we are left in ignorance as individuals or as unestablished critics, because self-doubt will typically accompany our failure to convince others. This point leads to the second issue: In the context of art criticism, how can pretenders be detected? In contrast to the bad critic, who insists on his own sentiment, the pretender says what others do say or are willing to say, but either experiences no pleasure, or derives it from properties other than those he claims to be the cause of the pleasure.

Hume's question about pretenders is a legacy of the search for a criterion of knowledge, and of debates about genuine faith in religion. The question forces us to clarify the role of the calm passions in his theory. If, as is possible, a pretender's judgements eventually gain acceptance, they do so in the absence of sentiments in him similar to those felt by other people. What matters to those others is not what he personally feels, although they happen to be deceived about that, but the identification of the viewpoints from and through which properties of the work can be discerned. We all begin by learning what to say from others, and no one can begin by being a pretender; pretence is parasitic upon some knowledge. Hume has already emphasized that it is by comparison that "we learn how to" assign the epithets of praise and blame (E-ST, 238). Even the eventual pretender, at first, must learn the same conventions as his peers, in order to be able to communicate at all. In the *Treatise*, Hume observed that "in changing the point of view, tho' the object may remain the same, its proportion to ourselves entirely alters" (T 2.2.10, 390); and later he noted that "a very small variation of the object, even where the same qualities are preserved, will destroy a sentiment" (EPM 5.1, 213n). So disagreements in judgements may have their source in variations between the observers, or in the objects observed, or in the viewpoints adopted. But Hume never doubts the possibility of reaching agreement on descriptions of states of affairs, although it is an empirical fact whether a particular community possesses adequate conventions to achieve them.

What sort of person is a pretender? If inner sentiments play no role in discussions of public objects, a pretender must be someone who wants to be admired for his judgements on those things, even though he knows he lacks the normal pleasurable sentiments derived from attending to them. There are many possible motives for wanting to deceive others about our internal states. Hume believes that men want to agree primarily because they are social beings; the bond of social sympathy is so strong that we can rarely hold out against the general opinion of others (T 3.3.2, 592; DP 2.10, 4: 152; see also T 2.1.11, 316). Moreover, as members of a community we begin by being told what to say, and only subsequently discover any internal accompaniments to our utterances. Someone thrust into a new culture and society, as Shaftesbury and others recognized, would not know what judgements it was appropriate to make, and at first would not even know how to describe the matters in hand. Of course, as Hume often states, education can lead to purely mechanical reactions, which, in this case, might mean judgements made in the absence of the inner sentiments which are their ground (EPM 5.1, 214; 3.2, 202). A man can become a pretender only when he discovers that his internal life differs from those of his peers, but by then he may well have established alternative associations which act as cues. Hume's pretender in criticism, indeed, has much in common with a colour-blind man. Both, for the most part, can get by with their learned responses; both, in his view, suffer from a defect in their mental constitution, as a result of which they are lacking in certain basically natural reactions (E-Ep, 140); neither, once we know their handicap, is to be relied upon as our guide.

In the concluding pages of the essay, Hume continues to follow Dubos. Psychological facts about individuals, and social facts about communities, explain residual variations within otherwise agreed judgements. Thus, Ovid, Horace, and Tacitus are all worthy of esteem, although at different times of his life a man may prefer one above another. Such preferences are "innocent," because "it is almost impossible not to feel a predilection for that which suits our particular turn and disposition" (E-ST, 244; see also EPM 5.2, 222). It often requires "some effort" to judge the works of other ages and cultures, but adverse verdicts should be restricted to those which confound the boundaries of vice and virtue (E-ST, 246–7). It is possible that Hume intended to mark a moral distinction between a bad critic and a pretender, because in the worst cases, a pretender, setting out to deceive, may elicit approval of what is really reprehensible.

For Hume, the notions of mistake, error, falsity, are associated with a critic's failure to convince a suitable peer group, over a suitable period of time, about the alleged facts; the possibility of mistakes entails the possibility of correction, and a bad critic is one who persists in his mistakes. It is a question of fact who the arbiters of taste are at any particular time, and how they gain recognition, although Hume believes that most of us "are apt to receive a man for whatever he has a mind to put himself off for" (E-IM, 553). On this view he could claim that most critics are self-proclaiming. Few people are properly qualified to be critics, however, because it is rare to find the combination of "strong sense" and "delicate sentiment, improved by practice, perfected by comparison, and cleared of all prejudice" (E-ST, 241).

Some modern commentators have alleged that Hume's account is entirely circular: the standard of taste is established by, or recognized in, the true critics; and the true critics are recognized by adherence to the standard of taste.[20] But this is not Hume's position. He holds that when learning social practices, and the conventions that govern them, we learn at the same time who currently count as the experts, and what are accepted as the best examples. But if this is true when a practice is already established, it does not explain how the first experts in a given field gain recognition, or how established judgements are modified or, exceptionally, overturned. Hume cannot appeal solely to the passing of time since, by itself, that does nothing to establish either correctness or appropriateness; and it is useless as a criterion in the present. He admits that eighteenth-century responses to Homer and the Greek tragedians differ from those of their own time, but he also holds that, once prejudices are removed, audiences can perceive the lasting and true beauties of the works. Yet once the properties of a work are truly discerned, the endorsement of later times does little more than clarify which works should function as models at different stages in a tradition. Hume does not raise the question of whether long-admired works either are or must be understood differently at different times; nor whether some works admit of significantly varying interpretations. Since, at least in 1741, he canvassed a cyclical view of the progress of the arts, it is surprising that he did not directly analyze the factors in changing tastes. If every individual is constrained in his judgements by the traditions he has inherited, he is unlikely to witness the vindication of any large-scale reassessments he may attempt. And since Hume also holds that whatever pleases cannot be a fault (E-ST, 232), it may be asked whether someone might not derive greater pleasure from a work which, in the view of experts, he has misunderstood or misperceived.

At the end of the essay, having conceded that the expression of merely personal likes and dislikes admits of no worthwhile discussion, Hume asserts that the overall merit of a work stands or falls on an estimate of its moral stance, if there is one. Three kinds of observation can be made by a critic, therefore: "I like the work," "The work is good of its kind," "The work is morally praiseworthy."

Reference to the standard of taste covers the conditions for establishing what something is, the models against which it is to be measured, and the true moral standards. Hume is quite clear that, even if pleasure is the occasion of sustained attention to a work, the critic's task is to concentrate on the work, not on himself. In the *Treatise*, he stated that "our approbation is imply'd in the immediate pleasure" (T 3.1.2, 471), and in this sense a man himself needs no justification for the pleasures he experiences. But as a social being he wishes to communicate that pleasure, and to seek reassurance that he does not deviate markedly from his peers. This he can do only by getting agreement from others over the causes of shareable pleasures. Hume himself, for example, admits distress at being unable to change his sentiments to accord with those of men he respects; he hopes that the long-term verdict of posterity will vindicate him (HL 2: 133). In another letter, he remarked that we often conceal our dislike of something because of our inability to give reasons for our verdict (HL 1: 30). To express our dislike is often to publicize our deviation from the accepted evaluation and, as such, our judgement calls for explanation. We can retreat, of course, in the direction of our psychological idiosyncrasies, but to do so is to withdraw our original verdict from public discussion. If we advance towards a viewpoint available to others, however, we advance towards objective verdicts.

Hume nowhere discusses questions about the *meaning* of works of art, even though he was entirely familiar with long-running battles over the interpretation of biblical and other historical texts. This is partly because he believes that in the general context of communication, any distortion of the "natural meaning" of terms is socially irresponsible. It should also be noted that, compared with the absolute necessities of life, art is one of life's "superfluities"; this aside, the habit of conversing together, and of contributing to each other's pleasures, increases the level of both knowledge and humanity (E-RA, 272).

The overall view can be outlined as follows. Someone becomes conscious of pleasure in a certain object. He needs only a vague awareness of its properties to be able to concentrate more fully, and to render his first "obscure and confused" sentiment "clear and distinct" (E-ST, 237; T 2.3.9, 441). But it is not, strictly, the original sentiment that becomes clear. Attention requires the fullest perceptual and intellectual effort, and the spectator naturally seeks a state of equilibrium and consistency. If the spectator can make sense, in some way, of what he perceives, he will experience new sentiments, which will temporally succeed his earlier ones, and may loosely be described as enhancing them. To determine the focus of his pleasures he must appeal to publicly discernible things, using the conventions of his community, and these conventions secure all the objectivity we need for our judgements and verdicts. Moreover, as a social being, a spectator wishes to reassure himself that his responses resemble those of his neighbours, and to share with them what he enjoys.

V. CONCLUSION

This essay began with the suggestion that Hume's observations on art are set in the framework of social life, and that this is why he considers both the making of, and the response to, works of art as human actions subject to the analysis he has offered of other human actions. In the broadest sense, works of art are pleasurable means of communication between human beings, and so the pre-conditions of effective communication apply to art as much as to other means. Certain works please us because of the particular properties they possess; one of our tasks is to identify these causes in order to enable others to share in our enjoyment. We cannot comprehend a work of art merely by being in its presence, however. Two properties which belong to human actions, and which are goals of our comprehension, are meaning and value: neither is discernible by the five ordinary senses alone. The mind must be actively involved. Just as inference beyond the present data is necessary for all factual reasoning, so interpretation is necessary to establish the meaning of what another has done. Hume's commitment to classical learning, and in particular to the views of Cicero, explains his interest in the practice and theory of rhetoric. From that domain he derived the view that one can, and should, ask a set of questions of any text in order to grasp its meaning: Who wrote it? For whom? About what? How? When? Where? Why? He did not sufficiently consider, however, how complex or difficult these questions might be.

Neither Hume nor anyone else in the first part of the eighteenth century envisaged the multiple interpretations of works of art which, in the late twentieth century, are a commonplace of critical theory. His emphasis is primarily on the *context* in which works are encountered. The great danger, as Dubos saw, is that the critic may become a parasite; a disengaged non-practitioner who passes judgement and exercises authority over the lives of both makers and spectators, and who transforms the critical role from that of a dispensable intermediary to that of an indispensable oracle. At that stage, criticism has assumed autonomy as a practice in its own right, but one which fundamentally depends on the agency of others.

Hume's views were discussed by his immediate contemporaries such as Lord Kames, Adam Smith, Alexander Gerard, Thomas Reid, George Campbell, and Hugh Blair. Hume's close friend Adam Smith accepted most of his views on the arts, and those of Dubos, but underlined the implication of Hume's emphasis on context by stressing that our overriding concern is with the meaning of works.[21] Immanuel Kant undoubtedly conceived the first part of his *Critique of Judgment* as a response to Hume, whose essay on taste was translated by Sulzer for him. After a gap of almost 200 years, interest in that same essay has been renewed among Western philosophers working in aesthetics.[22]

The precise nature of the context in which Hume was writing, and its profound differences from our own, are usually ignored, however, and most modern commentators on Hume see no need to anchor their reflections in practical knowledge of one or more of the arts. To those who find aspects of a Kantian aesthetics convincing, a major challenge raised by Hume is whether an empiricist aesthetics is possible. The roles of imagination and the emotions, in both creation and response, which Hume did not explore in detail, still require satisfactory analysis; the issues of interpretation and meaning occupy many modern theorists of language and criticism, as do the complex social contexts in which works of art are made, recognized, and assessed.

NOTES

1 The musical scene in eighteenth-century Scotland is explored in David Johnson, *Music and Society in Lowland Scotland in the Eighteenth Century* (Oxford, 1972). The contexts of painting and architecture in Britain are analyzed in: John Summerson, *Georgian London* (London,

1945); Iain Pears, *The Discovery of Painting: The Growth of Interest in the Arts in England, 1680–1768* (Yale, 1988). The French context for architecture, painting, and criticism is examined in Joseph Rykwert, *The First Moderns* (London, 1980); Thomas E. Crow, *Painters and Public Life in 18th-Century Paris* (Yale, 1985). See also J. Paul Hunter, *Before Novels: The Cultural Contexts of Eighteenth-Century English Fiction* (New York, 1990).

2 John Dryden, *A Parallel betwixt Painting and Poetry*, in *De Arte Graphica. The Art of Painting*, by C. A. du Fresnoy (London, 1695). On the list of books in the library organized by Professor Robert Steuart in 1724, called the Physiological Library, and to which Hume had access as a student, see Michael Barfoot, "Hume and the Culture of Science in the Early Eighteenth Century," in *Studies in the Philosophy of the Scottish Enlightenment*, ed. M. A. Stewart (Oxford, 1990), pp. 151–90. For a study of comparisons between poetry and painting, see R. W. Lee, *Ut Pictura Poesis: The Humanistic Theory of Painting* (New York, 1967).

3 George Turnbull, *A Treatise on Ancient Painting* (London, 1740): Alexander Gerard, *An Essay on Taste* (London, 1759); Henry Home, Lord Kames, *Elements of Criticism* (London, 1762). Roger de Piles, *Conversations sur la connoissance de la peinture et sur le jugement qu'on doit faire des tableaux* (n.p., 1677); Charles Alphonse du Fresnoy, *De Arte Graphica* (Paris, 1668); André Félibien, *L'Idée du peintre parfait* (Paris, 1707); Jonathan Richardson, *Two Discourses. I. An Essay on the whole Art of Criticism as it relates to Painting. II. An Argument in behalf of the Science of a Connoisseur* (London, 1719).

4 For a detailed analysis of Hume's views on the arts and criticism see my *Hume's Sentiments: Their Ciceronian and French Context* (Edinburgh, 1982). I discuss the possible influence on Hume of Ephraim Chambers, *Cyclopaedia: Or an Universal Dictionary of Arts and Sciences* (London, 1727) in "Hume and the Beginnings of Modern Aesthetics," *The Science of Man in the Scottish Enlightenment*, ed. Peter Jones (Edinburgh, 1989). Information regarding the Hume Library is taken from David Fate Norton and Mary J. Norton, "New Light on the Hume Library," an unpublished paper presented to the bibliographical societies of Edinburgh and Oxford. Earlier studies on Hume and his context include T. Brunius, *David Hume on Criticism* (Stockholm, 1951); W. J. Hipple, Jr., *The Beautiful, the Sublime, and the Picturesque in Eighteenth-Century British Aesthetic Theory* (Carbondale, 1957).

5 According to the library list compiled by Norton and Norton, the following editions were in the Hume Library: Charles Perrault, *Parallèles des anciens et des modernes* (Amsterdam, 1693; 1st ed. 1688); William Wotton, *Reflections upon Ancient and Modern Learning* (London,

1694); Jean-Baptiste Dubos, *Réflexions Critiques sur la poésie et sur la peinture* (Utrecht, 1732; 1st. ed. 1719). Hume later owned Louis Dutens, *Recherches sur l'origine des découvertes attribuées aux modernes* (Paris, 1766). Hume was also familiar with the important discussions of the issue in Bernard le Bovier de Fontenelle, *Digression sur les anciens et les modernes* (Paris, 1688), and *Dialogues des morts* (Paris, 1683).

6 On Robert Adam, see John Fleming, *Robert Adam and his Circle* (London, 1962); Geoffrey Beard, *The Work of Robert Adam* (Edinburgh, 1978); Joseph and Anne Rykwert, *The Brothers Adam* (London, 1985). Claude Perrault, *Les Dix Livres d'architecture de Vitruve* (Paris, 1673). Professor Steuart's class library list of 1724 cites a copy of Perrault's *Abrégé* of Vitruvius, along with works on the construction and geometry of fortifications.

7 The definitive reference is Eileen Harris, *British Architectural Books and Writers, 1556–1785* (London, 1990).

8 Marcus Vitruvius Pollio, *The Ten Books of Architecture* (1st Eng. trans. of Perrault's *Abridgement* 1692); Leon Battista Alberti, *De Re Aedificatoria* (Florence, 1485; 1st complete Eng. trans. 1726); Andrea Palladio, *I Quattro libri dell'architettura* (Venice, 1570; 1st complete Eng. trans. 1715); Sebastiano Serlio, *Architettura* (Venice and Paris, 1537–47; 1st Eng. trans. 1611); Vincenzo Scamozzi, *L'Idea della architettura universale* (Venice, 1615; 1st Eng. trans. 1676); Giacome Barozzi da Vignola, *Regole delle cinque ordini d'architettura* (Rome, 1563; 1st Eng. trans. 1655); Roland Fréart, Sieur de Chambray, *Parallèle de l'architecture antique et de la moderne* (Paris, 1650; 1st Eng. trans. 1664).

9 Marc-Antoine Laugier, *An Essay on Architecture* (London, 1755); William Chambers, *A Treatise on Civil Architecture* (London, 1759); Robert Morris, *Lectures on Architecture* (London, 1734, 1736). On the *Encyclopédie*, see Kevin Harrington, *Changing Ideas on Architecture in the Encyclopédie, 1750–1776* (Ann Arbor, 1985).

10 Hume's own more modest New Town house, situated on what is now called St. David Street, at the southwest corner of St. Andrew Square, was built for him in 1770–1. For further details, and speculation about the naming of St. David Street, see Ernest Campbell Mossner, *The Life of David Hume* (Edinburgh, 1954), 562–6.

11 "Art" meant "skill," and the phrase "work of art" was used well into the 1750s to mean any works involving skill; the term was not synonymous with "the fine arts," which denoted painting and the decorative arts.

12 Jean de La Bruyère, *Les Caractères* (Paris, 1688); Nicolas Boileau-Despréaux, *Oeuvres diverses* (Paris, 1701); Bernard le Bovier de Fontenelle, *Oeuvres diverses* (La Haye, 1728). Anthony Ashley Cooper, third Earl of Shaftesbury, *Characteristicks of Men, Manners, Opinions, Times*

(London, 1711); Francis Hutcheson, *An Inquiry into the Original of Our Ideas of Beauty and Virtue*, Treatise I, *Concerning Beauty, Order, Harmony, Design* (London, 1725).

13 See Ernest Campbell Mossner, "Hume's Early Memoranda, 1729–1740," *Journal of the History of Ideas* 9 (1948): 492–518, esp. p. 500. For a full discussion of Hume's debts to Dubos, and the debate between the Ancients and Moderns, see my *Hume's Sentiments*.

14 Dubos probably derived his notion of a sixth sense (Dubos 2.22) from Fontenelle, *Entretiens sur la pluralité des mondes* 3 (1688), but it was commonplace to cite Cicero (*De Oratore* 3.1.195) as the classical source of the idea. On Hutcheson, see Peter Kivy, *The Seventh Sense* (New York, 1976).

15 Shaftesbury, *Characteristics*, ed. J. M. Robertson, 2. vols. (Indianapolis, 1964), 2: 136–8.

16 The references here to natural kinds are echoed later in Immanuel Kant, *The Critique of Judgement* (1790), trans. J. C. Meredith (Oxford, 1952), pp. 154–5. Kant maintained that "the empirical interest in the beautiful exists only in *society*," and that interest can combine with a judgement of taste only "after it has once been posited as a pure aesthetic judgment." Hume would probably reply that his own agreement with the former point was part of his attempt to avoid anything like the latter.

17 It should be emphasized that the ambiguity in the French term *sentiment*, deplored by French and English writers alike, is precisely mirrored in Hume's term "sentiment," by which he sometimes means "emotion, passion," and sometimes "judgement, opinion"; indeed, for him, the term treacherously covers both feeling and thought. Adam Smith, in 1762, used the term to mean "moral observations"; see his *Lectures on Rhetoric and Belles Lettres*, ed. J. C. Bryce (Oxford, 1983), Lecture 11, p. 58.

18 Addison, *Spectator*, 418; Dubos, *Réflexions critiques*, 1.1; 1.44; Henry Home, Lord Kames, *Essays on the Principles of Morality and Natural Religion* (Edinburgh, 1751), 1.1; Fontenelle, *Réflexions sur la poétique*, 36.

19 Dubos, *Réflexions critiques*, 2.22, 32.

20 Peter Kivy, "Hume's Standard of Taste: Breaking the Circle," *British Journal of Aesthetics* 7 (1967): 57–66.

21 For an analysis of Smith's views, see my "The Aesthetics of Adam Smith," in *Adam Smith Reviewed*, ed. Peter Jones and Andrew S. Skinner (Edinburgh, 1992), pp. 56–78.

22 For example, Mary Mothersill, *Beauty Restored* (Oxford, 1984); George Dickie, *Evaluating Art* (Philadelphia, 1988).

10   David Hume, "the historian"

The first volume of Hume's *History of England*, dealing with the early Stuarts, appeared in 1754. The final volumes, covering the period from the invasion of Julius Caesar to 1485, appeared in 1762, although Hume was occupied with revisions of the whole work until his death.[1] In writing history, Hume was partly creating, partly responding to, a new market. In 1757, he thought history "the most popular kind of writing of any" (HL 1: 244). In 1770, he wrote, "I believe this is the historical Age and this [Scotland] the historical Nation" (HL 2: 230). He knew of no less than eight histories that were currently being written. The year before, in England, he had declared, "History, I think, is the Favourite Reading" (HL 2: 196). Hume and his friend William Robertson were in large part responsible for this new popularity of history, much of it written by Scotsmen for English readers.[2] Hume himself had received unprecedented payments for his *History* (for which he sold the copyright on each volume, rather than collecting royalties): he made at least £3,200 on the whole, at a time when a friend of his could consider himself well to do on £80 per annum (HL 1: 193, 255, 266, 314). Although in practice his *History* seems to have sold less well during his lifetime than the various volumes of his *Essays*, Hume was consistently of the opinion that this was his bookseller's fault. The market for history books was potentially far larger (HL 2: 106, 229, 233, 242).

I. THE HISTORICAL AGE

Hume was the beneficiary of an immense expansion in the reading public that took place in the mid-eighteenth century.[3] Much of that public was middle-class and female, and perhaps its favourite reading was the new genre that seems to have been invented especially for it, the novel: Richardson's *Pamela* appeared in 1740; *Clarissa* in 1748.[4] As early as 1741, however, Hume had felt that the history book could supplant the novel. "There is nothing which I would recommend more earnestly to my female readers than the study of history," he wrote, "as an occupation, of all others, the best suited both to their sex and education, much more instructive than their ordinary books of amusement, and more entertaining than those serious compositions, which are usually to be found in their closets" (E-SH, 563). Only a woman who was acquainted with the history of her own country, and with those of Greece and Rome, could engage in conversation which "can afford any entertainment to men of sense and reflection." Moreover, history provided the best way of becoming "acquainted with human affairs, without diminishing in the least from the most delicate sentiments of virtue" (E-SH, 566–7). The same could not be said for the actual "practice of the world," or for poetry, since poets "often become advocates for vice." Philosophy, for its part, could rarely move the passions; it is historians who are "the true friends of virtue" (E-SH, 567).

It was as a friend of virtue, one writing in competition with novelists, that Hume deliberately sought to move his audience to tears by his account of the execution of Charles I (HL 1: 210, 222, also 344; MOL).[5] He was certainly successful: indeed, we have letters from female admirers testifying to how his history had moved their passions. One of them told him that she had never had such a good opinion of herself as when reading his history: evidently Hume had inspired virtuous sentiments in her, and thereby made her feel virtuous and admirable (HL 2: 347, 366–7).[6]

Hume thus early saw a central role for history in contemporary culture. He had himself long thought of writing history, and he was evidently spurred on by the conviction that "there is no post of honour in the English Parnassus more vacant than that of History." Previous historians – even Paul de Rapin-Thoyras, the most widely admired of them – had lacked "style, judgement, impartiality, care" (HL 1: 170).[7] Only a contemporary historian could hope to meet the first test. In 1741 Hume was able to write: "The first polite prose we have, was writ by a man [Swift] who is still alive" (E-CL, 91). Since there were no contemporary British historians of note, Hume had to look abroad for his models. Horace Walpole thought Hume's style was influenced by Voltaire, but Voltaire's *Siècle de Louis XIV* did not appear until 1751.[8] The models Hume himself refers to were more distant in time. He tells us he was writing "after the manner of the Ancients," at least in that he was writing a concise narrative (HL 1: 170). The *Annals of Imperial Rome* (c. A.D. 117) by Gaius Cornelius Tacitus were soon to be his model for working backwards rather than forwards in time (HL 1: 251), and it is probably from Tacitus that he took his habit of explaining what different types of people thought about events at particular moments of crisis: Hume thus took over a version of the fictitious speeches beloved of ancient historians.

In 1758, Hume apologized to Walpole for not having provided footnote references to his sources in the volumes on the Stuarts: it was a defect he was to remedy when he revised them (HL 1: 316, 379). His apology provides us with the best guide to his more recent models: "I was seduc'd by the example of all the best historians even among the moderns, such as Matchiavel, Fra paolo, Davila, Bentivoglio; without considering that that practice [of providing references] was more modern than their time, and having been once introduc'd, ought to be follow'd by every writer" (HL 1: 284).[9] (Machiavelli, the oldest, was born in 1469; Bentivoglio, the youngest, died in 1644.) Fra Paolo Sarpi (1552–1623) in particular was singled out for praise in the *History*: his account of the Council of Trent was an admirable example of historical writing, so effective that the Roman Catholic church would, Hume thought, never dare call another general council while there was a prospect of such a historian being alive to write about it (HE 39, 4: 388–9, note F). Sarpi had thus single-handedly changed the course of history: Hume could hope no more of his own undertaking.[10]

Niccolò Machiavelli, Sarpi, Enrico Davila (author of the *Historia delle guerre civili di Francia* [1630]), and Guido Bentivoglio (author of *Della guerra di Fiandra* [1632–9]) have more in common than that they are all sixteenth-century Italians, and all influenced by Tacitus. They had all taken an active part in political life, and had written about events within the memory of their contemporaries. For them, history was a practical account of how power politics functioned, and an indispensable education for those who planned to participate in political life. Their natural audience was composed of the members of the political elite – all, of course, men. In order to make himself like such men, Hume had set out in 1748 to acquire a knowledge of courts and camps by entering the service of General St. Clair (HL 1: 109; see also NHL, 23). But Hume's *History*, as it was finally written, places little emphasis upon court intrigues and military prowess. It sees events, above all, from the point of view of the intelligent spectator, not the participant, just as its readers are expected to be spectators: Addison's *Spectator* had provided the model for some of Hume's moral and political essays, and had done much to educate the new polite public that Hume sought to address. If Hume had a model amongst historians it is likely, once again, to have been Sarpi: for if the audience to which Sarpi directed his *History of the Inquisition* was one of Venetian politicians, the intended audience of the *History of the Council of Trent* (1619) was much wider. He made the notion that a general council expressed the will of God incredible to an educated public who did not participate in church politics but wished merely to decide what to believe about the church.

Hume's *History* sought to address a new audience: an audience neither of politicians nor antiquarians, but of those who aspired to participate in polite conversation. This gave history a new role: that of retelling a story already told. We take it for granted that there will be more than one history dealing with a particular subject, but to those living in the eighteenth century there was something novel about this idea. As Hume set to work on the *History*, Charles Rollin had recently published his *Histoire Romaine* (1738–41): this was the first attempt to retell the history of ancient Rome for a modern audience.[11] Until then it had always been assumed that those who wanted to learn about Roman history would do so through a direct reading of the great historians of ancient Rome, Gaius Sallustius Crispus (Sallust: c. 86–35 B.C.), Titus Livius (Livy: c. 59 B.C.–A.D. 17) and Tacitus (c. A.D. 56–120). This assumption was also held about English history. In the same letter to Walpole, Hume defended himself against a view which he felt Walpole "rather insinuated than advanc'd; as if it were superfluous to re-write the English history, or publish on that subject any thing which has ever before in any shape appeard in print." Hume insisted, first, that there was too much material for anyone but a professional to come to grips with it all. "The original books, which instruct us in the reign of Q. Elizabeth alone, would require six months reading at the rate of ten hours a day" (HL 1: 285). The historian thus, in part, provided a précis, and it was partly as a précis of English history that Hume's volumes had such astounding success: seven complete editions during his lifetime, and one hundred and seventy-five in the century after his death.[12] Why, though, beyond the fact that Hume was more concise, read Hume on the Civil War rather than the great historian and statesman, Edward Hyde, Earl of Clarendon (1609–74)? It was Clarendon, not Hume, who embodied the traditional ideal of the historian: an intelligent participant in the events he himself described. Hume's response was that most people who read the original sources "wou'd attain but a very confus'd idea of the transactions of that period." The problem was not merely the abundance of material, but the difficulty of making sense of it. "To allege therefore the number of historical monuments against composing a history seems not much better founded, than if one shoud give it as a reason for not building a house, that he lay near a quarry" (HL 1: 285). Thus the accounts of contemporaries were no longer to be regarded as self-sufficient narratives, but to be treated as mere sources, a quarry for the modern historian. It was wrong to think that history, once written, need never be re-written. At the heart of Hume's undertaking was, therefore, a novel, and largely unstated, conception of progress in historical knowledge.

Hume turned to the writing of history partly in deliberate pursuit of literary fame, though, despite what he says in his autobiography, this can scarcely have been his overriding motive, for his *Essays* had already won him renown. Just as important was his desire to explore, through the writing of a historical narrative, philosophical, political, and moral questions that lay at the heart of his previous enquiries.[13]

II. HISTORICAL CRITICISM

What did Hume have to tell his readers that was new? Before we look at the substantive content of the history, we need to understand in what sense Hume was a "philosophical" historian.[14] One Hume scholar has rashly claimed that there was no philosophy of history in the eighteenth century.[15] In fact, there was a well-established literature on historical methodology, one that dealt with philosophical problems central to Hume's own interests. The founding text for this literature was the *La logique, ou l'art de penser*, commonly known as *The Port-Royal Logic*, written by two Jansenist theologians, Antoine Arnauld and Pierre Nicole, and first published in 1662.[16] In that work Arnauld (for he seems to have been primarily responsible for the chapters of interest to us) had invented modern probability theory by arguing that a number of different activities – games of chance, the authentication of legal documents, belief in miracles – were philosophically related because they all involved judgements of probability. Courts had established rules to determine which documents could be admitted in a trial because they wanted to minimize the chance of fraud, misrepresentation, and error. Historians, when they reported that Augustine had witnessed a miracle, were agreeing to give credence to Augustine's testimony despite the inherent improbability of the events described: Augustine's good character and intelligence eliminated the possibility of fraud, misrepresentation, or error.

Arnauld thus sought to formulate the rules that should govern the criticism of sources by applying probability theory. Crucially, he separated judgement of the actual likelihood of an event in itself (he agreed miracles were improbable in themselves) from judgement of the quality of the testimony (good testimony could make an improbable event likely). From this analysis there derived a series of works which sought to formulate the rules that should be employed in assessing historical testimony, and which insisted that several independent witnesses should be given credence if they contradicted one isolated individual, and that direct participants and eyewitnesses were to be believed when they contradicted those who relied upon second-hand information.[17] An immediate consequence of this was a downgrading of the reliability of oral tradition: a point made with particular force by Protestants such as John Locke, since it undermined the Catholic claim that theological truths are based in traditional knowledge.[18]

The new (largely French) literature on historical source criticism threw up a number of key problems, all of which Hume sought to address. First of all, how could we claim to have first-hand knowledge of the existence of Julius Caesar when the sources we relied on were in fact copies of copies? *De bello Gallico* was only in appearance a primary source: such a work was in fact a secondary authority, since the reader had to trust in the fidelity of generations of printers, and, before them, of scribes. For ancient history there were, on this view, virtually no primary sources at all. In the *Treatise*, Hume insisted that this sceptical argument was specious: scribes and printers were generally to be trusted (T 1.3.13, 145). The most important theorist in this field (and one who was almost certainly known to Hume) was Nicolas Fréret, whose *Réflexions sur l'étude des anciennes histoires et sur le degré de certitude de leurs preuves* (1729) was a response to the sceptical arguments of J. Lévesque de Pouilly's *A Dissertation upon the Uncertainty of the History of the first four ages of Rome*.[19] Fréret argued that we could trust historians like Livy when they reported events that we could no longer confirm by appealing to independent sources, for they had access to sources now lost to us.[20] There was nothing inherently impossible about knowledge of the past.

To make this claim, Fréret had to justify a critical reading of Livy. Livy freely reported natural prodigies and even miracles. Fréret argued that we could be sceptical of the first and incredulous with regard to the second, but still trust Livy's accounts of military and political conflicts. In "Of Miracles," Hume set out to justify a systematic scepticism with regard to all reports of miraculous events through a novel application of probability theory. Originally intended for publication in the *Treatise*, this essay would have balanced his defence of the reliability of our sources for the knowledge of ancient history, paralleling Fréret's treatment of the subject. His argument (which was eventually published in the *Enquiry concerning Human Understanding*) proceeded by imagining a miracle for which there was apparently unimpeachable testimony. Yet one would have to balance this testimony against the inherent unlikelihood of an event contrary to the constant course of nature. Thus "external" and "internal" evidence would seem almost perfectly balanced. Take into account, though, the fact that those who advocated a belief in miracles were self-interested witnesses who were trying to win adherents to their own cause, and at once it becomes clear that their testimony must not be taken at face value. The "internal" evidence must always outweigh the "external," and one could only properly believe in a miracle if the testimony in favour of it were so strong that it would take a miracle for it to be false – that is, only if the alternative to belief in a miracle was belief in a greater miracle.

In his long and brilliant essay "Of the Populousness of Ancient Nations" (first published in 1752), Hume presented a tour de force in the criticism of sources. Regularly, one found apparently reliable ancient sources reporting cities with enormous populations and battles involving armies of extraordinary size: it was easy to conclude that the ancient world was far more populous than the modern. Hume set out to show that these claims were inherently implausible: slaves had few opportunities to breed and raise children; massacres and destructive wars were common; the small physical space that cities occupied was irreconcilable with the claims made for their populations; and high interest rates were infallible evidence of primitive economies, economies consequently incapable of supporting dense populations. Thus by drawing together different types of evidence from an immense range of sources, Hume showed that ancient claims with regard to population sizes were completely unreliable; round numbers, like reports of miracles, represented a special category of evidence to be treated with extreme scepticism. Hume's detailed and technical argument was not of merely antiquarian importance: it provided decisive evidence for the claim that modern civilization was superior to ancient. Hume emerged victorious from a debate with Robert Wallace, one of the last major battles in the long-running war between those who saw history as a record of decline from ancient glory, and those who saw it in terms of an (at least temporary) progress towards modern sophistication.[21]

In *The History of England*, source criticism also had a central role to play, for factual claims about the past were crucial to contemporary debates between Whigs and Tories, and between Protestants and Catholics. One of Hume's central purposes was to expose party myths: parties, like religions, depended upon historical claims that could be subjected to impartial criticism. Detailed historical enquiry into such claims could lead one to conclusions that no reasonable person would question and could in the process provide evidence that decisively undermined the rhetoric of political extremists. Hume identified three episodes that played a crucial role in contemporary historical mythologies, and it was no little part of his purpose in the *History* to show how historians could separate fact from myth with regard to episodes such as these:

There are indeed three events in our history, which may be regarded as touchstones of partymen. An English Whig, who asserts the reality of the popish plot, an Irish Catholic, who denies the massacre in 1641, and a Scotch Jacobite, who maintains the innocence of queen Mary, must [in the light of Hume's *History*] be considered as men beyond the reach of argument or reason, and must be left to their prejudices.   (HE 39, 4: 395, note M)[22]

Hume's position on these questions inevitably involved him in controversy, even with those, such as Robertson, whose judgement he usually respected. In his view, one side was obviously right, the other wrong. This was not the case with an equally vexed question, that of the authorship of the *Eikon Basilike*. This work, supposedly by Charles I and published immediately after his execution, was undoubtedly the most successful piece of political propaganda in English history. It portrayed the king as pious, honest, and as concerned with the welfare of his subjects. Its popular success played a major part in preparing the way for the Restoration. But did it really provide an insight into the king's secret thoughts, or was it, as many claimed, the hypocritical concoction of a royalist chaplain, Dr. Gauden? Hume, who wanted to defend Charles's good character, had an interest in finding the book to be by Charles himself, but he did not in any way understate the difficulty of reaching a decision:

The proofs brought to evince, that this work is or is not the king's, are so convincing, that, if an impartial reader peruse any one side apart, he will think it impossible, that arguments could be produced, sufficient to counter-balance so strong an evidence: And when he compares both sides, he will be some time at a loss to fix any determination. Should an absolute suspence of judgment be found difficult or disagreeable in so interesting a question, I must confess, that I much incline to give the preference to the arguments of the royalists. The testimonies, which prove that performance to be the king's, are more numerous, certain, and direct, than those on the other side [though Hume added a footnote admitting this might be an over-statement]. This is the case, even if we consider the external evidence: But when we weigh the internal, derived from the style and composition, there is no manner of comparison. These meditations . . . are so unlike the bombast, perplexed, rhetorical, and corrupt style of Dr. Gauden, to whom they are ascribed, that no human testimony seems sufficient to convince us, that he was the author.   (HE 59, 5: 547–8)

Here Hume had found a real case that appeared at first sight to correspond to the hypothetical case he had discussed in "Of Miracles," one where two bodies of evidence are in perfect balance. As in the case of "Of Miracles," Hume goes on to insist on the superiority of internal over external evidence: in the one case, the inherent improbability of an event contrary to the laws of nature; in the other, the inherent improbability of Dr. Gauden's prose being transformed. Such evidence could be so strong that no testimony could serve to contradict it: the case against Dr. Gauden's authorship was precisely as strong as the case against miracles.

Hume had argued that unskilled individuals, even if they could spare the time and energy to study the monuments of the past, would not necessarily know what to make of them. Conflicting claims regarding the casket letters, supposedly written by Mary Queen of Scots (in Hume's view her authorship could be demonstrated), or the authorship of *Eikon Basilike*, could only breed confusion unless one had an adequate training in historical method and understood the philosophical principles involved in the assessment of testimony.

III. HISTORICAL ARCHITECTURE

When we speak nowadays of the philosophy of history we sometimes mean to refer to the detailed philosophical analysis of the nature of historical evidence, and sometimes to large-scale theories that claim to identify a pattern or a meaning in the course of history. Hume was familiar with both sorts of philosophy of history. He would not have thought it unreasonable to regard his history as a test of the large-scale theories of James Harrington (1611–77), Charles-Louis de Secondat, baron de Montesquieu (1689–1755), and Anne-Robert-Jacques Turgot, baron de l'Aulne (1727–81), who would have been in his eyes the most important exponents of the second sort of philosophy of history.

Harrington was an important figure for the analysis of English politics for four reasons: first, he had in *Oceana* (1656) given an account of an ideal commonwealth, laying down principles according to which a free state ought to be established, and providing a standard by which the eighteenth-century English constitution could be measured. Second, Harrington believed that, by grounding his ideal state in the principle of self-interest, he had constructed a new science of politics, although he acknowledged that in this respect he was indebted to

Machiavelli and to Thomas Hobbes. Third, he had provided an account of English history according to which the mid-seventeenth-century political crisis was the inevitable outcome of a long period of social change. Fourth, his followers after the Restoration had mounted a sustained attack on two contemporary developments that they believed had shifted the balance of power in favour of the monarchy: the development of a professional or "standing" army, and the growth of royal revenue and royal bureaucracy to the point that the king could significantly influence the political process by the offer of places and pensions, by bribery and corruption.

Hume engaged with all four aspects of the Harringtonian and neo-Harringtonian position.[23] In the "Idea of a Perfect Commonwealth," he largely approved of Harrington's ideal model of a republic, while offering some improvements. Second, in "That Politics may be reduced to a Science" and in "The Independency of Parliament," he accepted the Harringtonian position that political institutions created a framework within which people pursued their interests; and that it was therefore possible to predict how they would behave. Such predictions must be based on the assumption that people would act selfishly: although in fact not everyone was selfish, enough people were to undermine any institution that relied upon men acting selflessly. The key to politics was thus the study of institutions, not men; good institutions would cause men to act as if they themselves were good. Third, in "Of the Protestant Succession," he by and large accepted the Harringtonian account of the social changes that had made an increase in the power of the Commons inevitable in the mid-seventeenth century. In "The Independency of Parliament," however, he sought to show that Harrington was wrong to conclude from this that the monarchy was bound to be abolished. Finally, in "Whether the British Government inclines more to Absolute Monarchy, or to a Republic," he accepted the neo-Harringtonian account of the rising power of the Crown.

Hume is never uncritical in his attitude to Harrington, but he is always a friendly, never a hostile, critic (see, for example, "Of the First Principles of Government"). Harrington had constructed the first determinist account of history: he had argued that the distribution of landed property determined the distribution of military strength, and that this in turn must predetermine the outcome of political conflict. All one had to do was to extend his definition of property to include commercial wealth to have a species of economic determinism. If one then argued that commercial activity had civilizing consequences, one would have a new economic explanation for the progress of liberty. Adam Smith believed one could find this argument in Hume's *History*. He wrote in *The Wealth of Nations*:

Commerce and manufactures gradually introduced order and good government, and with them, the liberty and security of individuals, among the inhabitants of the country, who had before lived almost in a continual state of war with their neighbours, and of servile dependency upon their superiors. This, though it has been the least observed, is by far the most important of all their effects. Mr. Hume is the only writer who, so far as I know, has hitherto taken notice of it.[24]

Hume would certainly have agreed with Smith that the subject had hitherto been ignored. In 1741 he had written:

Trade was never esteemed an affair of state till the last century; and there scarcely is any ancient writer on politics, who has made mention of it. Even the ITALIANS have kept a profound silence with regard to it, though it has now engaged the chief attention, as well of ministers of state, as of speculative reasoners. The great opulence, grandeur, and military atchievements of the two maritime powers [England and Holland] seem first to have instructed mankind in the importance of an extensive commerce.   (E-CL, 88–9)

Thus, writing a century after Harrington, Hume was bound to give much more importance to commerce than Harrington had done. A major purpose of a history of England must be to trace the role of commercial expansion in the country's rise to opulence and grandeur. What was not to be expected was that Hume, instead of treating political liberty as a cause of commercial expansion, as he often had done in the *Essays* (92–3, 113, 265), would reverse the order of causation and insist that commerce, in England at least, had caused the appearance and expansion of liberty. It was in the towns that political liberty had first existed; it was the development of the money economy that made serfdom an anachronism which the lords saw no need to preserve; and the rise of personal freedom "paved the way for the increase of political or civil liberty." Hume did not offer a "four stages theory of history" that explained historical change in terms of the development of the means of production: this was to come later, in Smith and his associates.[25] But he certainly had provided a new type of economic explanation of history, which we may term a commercialized Harringtonianism.

Hume, like Harrington, saw in the rise of the gentry the profound cause of the shift in the balance of power that undermined the monarchy in the early seventeenth century. If the Harringtonian character of his analysis is not always obvious, it is because Hume saw in the rise of the gentry the explanation, not of the Civil War, but of the constitutional revolution that preceded the Civil War itself. Social change (combined with the fact that Parliament provided an institutional context within which that change could find political expression) might explain the events of 1640–1; only religious enthusiasm could explain Parliament's inability to come to terms with the king. Harrington saw the execution of the king as the natural outcome of the political process he had traced; Hume saw the mixed constitution of the early eighteenth century as its natural outcome. For the aberration of the Cromwellian regime, other explanations were necessary. Harrington had failed to take account of the fact that "though men be much governed by interest; yet even interest itself, and all human affairs, are entirely governed by *opinion*" (E-BG, 51).

It is much harder to be sure about Montesquieu's influence upon Hume than it is about Harrington's, for the simple reason that Hume's thinking seems to parallel Montesquieu's before as well as after the publication of *De l'Esprit des lois* (1748). On one key issue he certainly disagreed with Montesquieu: "Of National Characters" (1748) reads as a refutation of Montesquieu's account of the role of climate in shaping political and cultural life. It is not impossible that this is exactly what it is, for Hume may have known something of the arguments of *De l'Esprit des lois* prior to their publication.[26]

In other respects, Hume's thinking is so close to Montesquieu's that reading Montesquieu can help in the interpretation of Hume's *History*.[27] Montesquieu and Hume both work with a threefold typology of regimes: despotisms, civilized monarchies, and constitutions based on liberty, such as the English. England is for both of them the most singular example of liberty the world has seen. Both use the word "liberty" in several distinct senses, but both are primarily concerned with one which commentators sometimes call "private" or "civil" liberty, and for which representative government served as merely a means.[28] Montesquieu defined "political liberty" as "that tranquillity of spirit which comes from the opinion that each one has of his security, and in order for him to have this liberty the government must be such that one citizen cannot fear another citizen."[29] Hume, in a posthumously published essay, stressed (surely following Montesquieu on the division of powers) the need for citizens to have no cause to fear, not only each other, but also their government.

> The government, which, in common appellation, receives the appellation of free, is that which admits of a partition of power among several members, whose united authority is no less, or is commonly greater than that of any monarch; but who, in the usual course of administration, must act by general and equal laws, that are previously known to all the members and to all their subjects. In this sense, it must be owned, that liberty is the perfection of civil society.   (E-OG, 40–1)

Thus both see the key to English liberty as lying in the establishment of a division of powers between legislative and executive, but both regard other constitutional developments as indispensable: the jury system, *habeas corpus*, an independent judiciary, and the freedom of the press are pillars of liberty. Both believe that the competing interests of legislative and executive must necessarily create conflicting parties in support of these different interests, and that these parties will inevitably re-write history to justify their policies.[30] Finally, both believe that the essential pattern of the evolution of English history since the Norman Conquest has been one of feudal anarchy, which gave way to despotism, which itself gave way to the liberty of a mixed constitution. Both agree that there never has been a civilized monarchy in England, partly because such an institution depends on a strong nobility, while the English nobility was fatally weakened before the emergence of a strong monarchy.

Finally, Montesquieu's *De l'Esprit des lois* forcefully reminds us of a central problem that faced Hume as he wrote the *History*. The classical models for historical writing were all almost entirely narrative in form. Montesquieu, however, showed that one could analyze a constitution and a culture at a moment in time, presenting it as an ideal type. Indeed, one needed to do this if one was to grasp the logic of events. Hume therefore committed himself to extended digressions explaining the character of the constitution at different times, and surveying events (for example, developments in the arts and sciences) that did not fit comfortably within a narrative framework. Nevertheless, these digressions seemed to him at odds with the narrative form proper to historical writing, and in later editions of the *History* he moved parts of them into notes (HL 1: 294).³¹ Moreover, although Hume clearly felt that constitutional institutions and practices were crucial to the explanation of political events, he resisted following Montesquieu so far as trying to establish a close relationship between developments in a nation's culture and those in its political life: Hume never claimed to identify a single *esprit* running through all aspects of the life of an epoch.

Turgot, unlike Harrington and Montesquieu, had little influence on Hume, but his views provide a helpful contrast to Hume's own. It is not possible to determine when Hume first read Turgot's "On Universal History" (1751), which argues that all history is the history of progress. In 1768, full of pessimism over the demands for "liberty" made by Wilkes, Hume pointed to events in England as a refutation of Turgot's views: "I know you are one of those, who entertain the agreeable and laudable, if not too sanguine hope, that human Society is capable of perpetual Progress towards Perfection. . . . Pray, do not the late Events in this Country appear a little contrary to your System?" Hume was convinced that dangerous policies – above all the growth of the national debt – could endanger civilization. He was not even persuaded by Turgot's view that "since the Discovery of Printing we need no longer Dread the usual Returns of Barbarism and Ignorance" (HL 2: 180). On the contrary, reading the first volume of Edward Gibbon's *Decline and Fall of the Roman Empire* (1776) made him remark on the "marks of Decline" in England, where "the Prevalence of Superstition . . . prognosticates the Fall of Philosophy and Decay of Taste" (HL 2: 310). He foresaw "a new and a sudden Inroad of Ignorance, Superstition and Barbarism" (NHL, 199). Turgot's confidence that progress was guaranteed by providence must indeed have seemed to Hume to be itself a sophisticated superstition. He was much happier with Voltaire's *Candide, ou l'optimisme* (1759): "It is full of Sprightliness & Impiety, & is indeed a Satyre upon Providence, under Pretext of criticizing the Leibnitian System" (NHL, 53). History itself, in Hume's view, provided no grounds for any faith in providence, even in the secularized form of a belief in the inevitability of progress.

IV. WHIGS AND TORIES

We come now to the central, and most difficult, question in the assessment of Hume as a historian: that of the politics of the *History*.[32] Scholars have adopted a number of views on this question, and Hume's own explicit descriptions of the political significance of the *History* in his letters are open to more than one interpretation. For some, the *History* presents a conservative view of politics: it reflects the growing conservatism of Hume's views after the Jacobite uprising of 1745 and was revised further in a conservative direction after Hume responded with hostility to the "Wilkes and Liberty" campaigns. It is thus essentially a "Tory" history.[33] According to another view, the whole point of the *History* is its impartiality: Hume presents the views of the different parties involved in English politics and admits that all have a certain justification.[34] However, on this view Hume held that past practice was almost the only basis for establishing whether a government was legitimate. Hume's declared support for the Revolution of 1688 in the *Treatise* and the *History* involved him, it is argued, in no little inconsistency. A third view is that Hume wrote to defend the existing constitution, and that he approved those men and measures that brought it about, even though they could only be seen to have been admirable with the advantage of hindsight and had no proper idea of what they were doing at the time.[35] Hume certainly describes in the *Treatise* the psychological process that causes one to make retrospective judgements in the light of the outcome of events (T 3.2.10, 566–7), but a history written from such a point of view would fail in what was for Hume its essential purpose, that of distinguishing virtue from vice: to do this the historian would have to give up the advantage of hindsight. A fourth view holds that Hume thought that the contemporary absolutist monarchies of Europe were superior to the mixed monarchy of England; that he not only hoped to see absolutism established in England in his own day, but regretted the failure of the Stuarts to establish it in the seventeenth century.[36] Beyond Hume's insistence that civilized absolutist governments are legitimate where they are already established, this view seems to me to have little evidence to support it. I must admit to a certain sympathy with a fifth view, namely, that the *History* is informed throughout by Hume's love of liberty, although it would be quite wrong to equate liberty, as Hume under-stood the term, with democracy.[37]

There is no doubt that the first volume of the *History* was well received in France partly because it gave the Stuart monarchy a sympathetic treatment. During the reaction to the French Revolution, Hume's hostility to the execution of Charles I made him seem the first counter-revolutionary historian, a precursor of Burke.[38] Louis XVI's own response to the news of his death sentence was to set about re-reading Hume's account of Charles's execution.[39] Even before the French Revolution, the anti-Wilkes reaction had in-creased Hume's popularity in England. He wrote in 1768:

Licentiousness, or rather the frenzy of liberty, has taken possession of us, and is throwing everything into confusion. How happy do I esteem it, that in all my writings I have always kept at a proper distance from that tempting extreme, and have maintained a due regard to magistracy and established government, suitably to the character of an historian and a philosopher! I find on that account my authority growing daily; and indeed have now no reason to complain of the public.   (HL 2: 191–2)

Such readings, however, ignore important aspects of Hume's argu-ment, aspects that survived his many revisions of his work, all of which, he said, favoured the Tories. He described the 1770 revisions as follows: "I am running over again the last Edition of my History in order to correct it still farther. I either soften or expunge many villanous seditious Whig Strokes, which had crept into it. I wish that my Indignation at the present Madness, encourag'd by Lyes, Calum-nies, Imposture, and every infamous Art usual among popular Lead-ers, may not throw me into the opposite Extreme. I am, however, sensible that the first Editions were too full of those foolish English Prejudices, which all Nations and all Ages disavow" (HL 2: 216). It would be wrong, however, to overestimate Hume's conservatism, even towards the end of his life. Not only was he, as he put it, "an American in my Principles" (HL 2: 303), unconditionally supporting American independence from an early date, but he was also happy to say bluntly that the French monarchy would have to be overthrown so that the French people could escape the burden of the government debt (HL 2: 242). Indeed, it gave Hume great pleasure to think people would have trouble categorizing him: "Whether am I Whig or Tory? Protestant or Papist? Scotch or English? I hope you do not all agree on this head; & that there [are] disputes among you about my principles" (HL 1: 196). Clearly he would delight in the continuing disputes over how to categorize him.

To make sense of Hume's *History*, we must take more seriously than commentators usually do the fact that his is a narrative history describing changing social and political circumstances. Hume's emphasis on change was, indeed, one of the most original aspects of his history. Tory historians before 1688, such as Robert Brady, the first volume of whose *Complete History of England* appeared in 1685, and Jacobite historians, such as Thomas Carte, author of *A General History of England* (1747–55), had insisted that the ancient constitution of England was that of divine-right monarchy: the revolutions of 1642 and 1688 were scarcely forgivable from this point of view, and the mid-eighteenth-century constitution an outrage. Whig historians before 1714 had argued the opposite case: the ancient constitution of England was one that guaranteed the liberties of the subject. On this view, which was supported by James Tyrrell in his *General History of England* (1696–1704), and later by Rapin, Parliament, including the House of Commons, was an institution of Saxon origin, and one with an unbroken history. The Stuarts had sought to undermine this ancient constitution; the Revolution of 1688 had restored it. In Hume's day, elements of this view were adopted by Tory opponents of the court, such as Henry Saint-John, viscount Bolingbroke.[40] This country opposition attacked the court for corruption, and attacked the Whig government, particularly Walpole in the period immediately before his fall, for extending executive power. The reply of the court Whigs to this assault was a novel one. Lord Hervey, for example, argued that there had been no ancient constitution.[41] The constitution of England had been constantly in flux. There had been no secure liberty before 1688. The present administration should be judged not by its fidelity to a mythical set of constitutional principles, but by its ability to preserve effective and beneficent government.

Placed in this context, there is no doubt that Hume, for all his claims to impartiality, effectively ended up supporting the argument of the court Whigs. The first volume he wrote was the volume on the early Stuarts. Although in writing that volume he came increasingly to suspect that traditional Whig history was deficient, and although he defended at length the character and motives of Charles

I, he still tended to the Whig view that the Stuarts were innovating
to the detriment of Parliament. Once he had worked on the Tudor
period, he became convinced that Tudor rule had been despotic and
revised his account of Stuart aspirations accordingly.[42] Hume's revisions of his *History* may have been hostile to Whig prejudices, but
they brought him closer to the court Whig position.

In Hume's view, the barbarism of the Middle Ages and the despotism of the Tudors were not surprising: they were precisely what one
would expect to find in a primitive society. A vast gulf separated us
from the world of our ancestors. In place of traditional Tory and
Whig arguments, which stressed constitutional continuity and paid
little attention to social change, Hume stressed the distance at
which we stood from both the social and the political life of our
ancestors: he attacked, alongside the Whig myth of the ancient constitution, the myth of the Roast Beef of Old England. A poor diet and
a despotic government were intimately related. In correspondence
he explained his view bluntly:

> My Notion is, that the uncultivated Nations are not only inferior to civiliz'd
> in Government, civil, military, and eclesiastical; but also in Morals; and
> that their whole manner of Life is disagreeable and uneligible to the last
> Degree. I hope it will give no Offence (and whether it do or not, I must say it)
> if I declare my Opinion, that the English, till near the beginning of the last
> Century, are very much to be regarded as an uncultivated Nation; and that
> even *When good Queen Elizabeth sat on the Throne*, there was very little
> good Roast Beef in it, and no Liberty at all. The Castle of the Earl of North-
> umberland, and no doubt that of the Earl of Warwick, the *King Maker* and
> others, was no better than a Dungeon: No Chimney to let out the Smoak; no
> Glass Windows to keep out the Air; a glimmering Candle here and there,
> which coud scarce keep their Ragamuffins of Servants and Retainers from
> breaking their Shins or running foul of each other: No Diet but salt Beef and
> Mutton for nine Months of the Year, without Vegetables of any kind: Few
> Fires and these very poor ones. . . . When Queen Catherine of Arragon had a
> Fancy to eat a Sallad, she coud not find one in all England, she was obligd to
> send a Messenger to the Low Countries for that Purpose: And I suppose
> when her Tyrant of a Husband [Henry VIII] thought she was with Child, and
> that the Life of his royal Issue depended upon it, he woud indulge her in that
> Caprice.   (NHL, 198)

Hume himself came from what had long been, by his description,
"the rudest, perhaps, of all European Nations; the most necessitous,

the most turbulent, and the most unsettled" (HL 2: 310). The extraordinary rapidity of social change in the Scotland of his day made him, along with the rest of the enlightened Scots, acutely sensitive to the social evolution which had taken place in the past; the continuing backwardness of the Highlands must have provided them with a vivid picture of medieval life in France or England.

Nevertheless, Hume was prepared to find even in the Middle Ages the stirrings of modern liberty. Although he insisted on placing the Magna Carta, the great charter of liberties of 1215, in a feudal and baronial context, he was also prepared to see in it statements of principle that would have met with the approval of a Locke or a Sidney:

It must be confessed, that the former articles of the Great Charter contain such mitigations and explanations of the feudal law as are reasonable and equitable; and that the latter involve all the chief outlines of a legal government, and provide for the equal distribution of justice, and free enjoyment of property; the great objects for which political society was at first founded by men, which the people have a perpetual and unalienable right to recal, and which no time, nor precedent, nor statute, nor positive institution, ought to deter them from keeping ever uppermost in their thoughts and attention.
(HE 11, 1: 445)

This is hardly the language of the thirteenth century, and it comes perilously close to approving views that Hume had attacked in his essay "Of the Original Contract."[43] When he describes the execution of Algernon Sidney (d. 1683), who had been convicted because he had defended, in a private manuscript, views such as these, Hume, far from attacking contractarianism, cautiously defends it: Sidney "had maintained principles, favourable indeed to liberty, but such as the best and most dutiful subjects in all ages have been known to embrace; the original contract, the source of power from a consent of the people, the lawfulness of resisting tyrants, the preference of liberty to the government of a single person" (HE 69, 6: 436). Though he had indeed been involved in a conspiracy against Charles II, his conviction was contrary to law, his sentence iniquitous.

Such passages, taken in isolation, would appear to justify a court Whig reading of Hume: although liberty had not been long established, the principles of liberty had always been admirable. Hume himself insisted: "My views of *things* are more conformable to Whig principles; my representations of *persons* to Tory prejudices. Nothing can so much prove that men commonly regard more persons than things, as to find that I am commonly numbered among the Tories" (HL 1: 237). Duncan Forbes, whose study of *Hume's Philosophical Politics* is the most influential account of Hume's historical thought, prefers to emphasize Hume's own claims to impartiality, and dismisses this particular remark as superficial: Hume had no commitment to Whig principles.[44] But Hume's claims to impartiality are also misleading unless one notes that Hume claims to support Whigs and Tories *alternately*: in other words, he is always partial, even if he is not always on the same side (HL 1: 179, 369). The key to the volume on the early Stuarts lies, in fact, in the following description: "I am not surely unfavorable to the Parliament. Till they push'd their Advantages so far as to excite a civil War, so dangerous & unnecessary, I esteem their Conduct laudable; & to this Extremity nothing carry'd them but their furious Zeal for Presbytery: A low Bigotry, with which they sully'd a noble Cause" (HL 1: 222). Indeed, Hume's *History* is Parliamentary, not Royalist, in its account of the period from 1604 to 1641, and Parliamentary again in its account of the period from 1681 to 1688.

There is nothing arbitrary about this changing of sides: in Hume's view, it was a characteristic of English history that the "disinterested" (that is to say, the impartial) "fluctuated between the factions; and gave the superiority sometimes to the court, sometimes to the opposition" (HE 66, 6: 307–8). The history was written from the point of view of such disinterested individuals, whose concern was with the public good. Such people, Hume believed, supported Parliament until the end of 1641, until the Grand Remonstrance made war inevitable. They ought to have admired John Pym and John Hampden, Parliament's leading spokesmen, and approved the Petition of Right of 1628 and the constitutional revolution of 1640 and 1641, which had established the principles of the mixed constitution. They should have continued to support Parliament despite the execution in 1641 of Thomas Wentworth, Earl of Strafford, the king's chief minister, an event which foreshadowed the trial of Charles himself. But thereafter it was Parliament, not the king, that endangered stability (despite, for example, the king's attempt to arrest the leaders of the Commons, including Pym and Hampden, in 1642). The king had accepted that his was a limited monarchy, and there was nothing in his character to suggest that he could not be trusted. Only their "low Bigotry" drove men on to resistance, while those who were not bigots rallied to the royalist side.

The true heroes of Hume's account were thus the men who had known when to change sides, Clarendon and Lucius Carey, viscount Falkland, who had joined the king in 1642.[45] He willingly echoes Clarendon's praise of Falkland, attributing to him the authorship of the king's reply to the Parliament, *His Majesties Answer to the Nineteen Propositions* (June 1642), in which for the first time the principles of the modern English constitution were described and defended. Falkland, who died in battle in 1643, was the epitome of Hume's conception of virtue:

> devoted to the pursuits of learning, and to the society of all the polite and elegant, [he] had enjoyed himself in every pleasure, which a fine genius, a generous disposition, and an opulent fortune could afford. Called into public life, he stood foremost in all attacks on the high prerogatives of the crown; and displayed that masculine eloquence, and undaunted love of liberty, which, from his intimate acquaintance with the sublime spirits of antiquity, he had greedily imbibed. When civil convulsions proceeded to extremities, and it became requisite for him to chuse his side; he tempered the ardour of his zeal, and embraced the defence of those limited powers, which remained to monarchy, and which he deemed necessary for the support of the English constitution. Still anxious, however, for his country, he seems to have dreaded the too prosperous success of his own party as much as of the enemy; and, among his intimate friends, often after a deep silence, and frequent sighs, he would, with a sad accent, re-iterate the word, *Peace*.
>
> (HE 56, 5: 416–17)

Once we see Hume changing sides, we can recognize that, whether he writes in favour of king or Parliament, he always gives his support to the mixed constitution. For those who favoured such a constitution the key question at the end of 1641 was, he believed, "Can the king be trusted?" Hence the importance of Hume's account of Charles's character, and the strategic significance of his claim that the arguments of the royalists in 1642 were strongest when discussing not principle, but the past behaviour of the king. Similarly, between the Exclusion Crisis and 1688, the key question is the behaviour of James II. Hume refuses to take sides between the Whigs who trumped up the charges against Tories during the Popish Plot (1678), and the Tories who led the witch-hunt against Whigs after the Rye House plot (1683).[46] But from 1682 James's behaviour towards Scotland was unambiguous. He sought to execute men guilty only of having conversed with others who were suspected of having been rebels. Two women were tied to stakes and slowly drowned by a rising tide because they refused to take an oath of loyalty. James himself was believed to have participated in the torturing of suspects. If Clarendon represents the reasonable men and women who converted to Royalism before the outbreak of the Civil War, Archibald Campbell, ninth earl of Argyll, represents the loyal subjects who were forced to turn against James. Tried for his life because of his loyalty to Protestantism and the constitution, he was driven into exile late in 1682: from this moment, conspiracy against James was justified.

There was, of course, an important difference between 1642 and 1682: after the Restoration, Charles II and James II had no excuse for failing to recognize that England was now a limited monarchy. As Hume had argued in the *Treatise*, in any limited monarchy there must be a right of rebellion in defence of the constitution, for otherwise there will be no effective limits upon royal power. If Hume had good reason to defend rebellion in 1688, even on his own conservative principles, one is bound to ask on what grounds he could justify Parliamentary innovation in 1641? Perhaps, in the words of the *Treatise*, nothing is more essential to the public interest than the preservation of public liberty (T 3.2.10, 564), but what right can the public claim to construct public liberty where there has been none before? Even if they know that liberty will benefit society, how can they be confident that the attempt to establish it will not fatally undermine authority, and that innovation will not cause more harm than good?

In attempting to answer this question, the first thing to note is that England under the Tudors did not have what Hume termed a "civilized monarchy" (E-RP, 125). It suffered under a species of despotism. Thus, under Henry VIII the English were so thoroughly subdued that, "like eastern slaves, they were inclined to admire those acts of violence and tyranny, which were exercised over themselves, and at their own expence" (HE 33, 3: 323). Under Elizabeth, the government of England bore "some resemblance to that of Turkey at present: The sovereign possessed every power, except that of imposing taxes" (HE App 3, 4: 360). This limitation, as in Turkey (E-TA, 347–8), could only have pernicious consequences while the monarch sought to exercise absolute power. In England, it meant that the Crown had recourse to forced loans, or rather arbitrary confiscations, and to the sale of monopolies and privileges. Over time, the first practice would have destroyed all security of property, while the second would have destroyed all trade, reducing English society to the poverty of Turkish. An absolute government in which the monarch could levy taxes would have been preferable, for then the monarchy would have had an interest in the wealth of its subjects. Tudor despotism was thus dangerous to civil liberty and economic prosperity: it was in the public interest that such despotism should give way, either to civilized absolutism or to a mixed constitution.

In his Appendix to the reign of Elizabeth, Hume says that one should generally limit one's questions about constitutions to questions about the facts: to finding what has in practice been established.

> If any other rule than established practice be followed, factions and dissentions must multiply without end: And though many constitutions, and none more than the British, have been improved even by violent innovations, the praise, bestowed on those patriots, to whom the nation has been indebted for its privileges, ought to be given with some reserve, and surely without the least rancour against those who adhered to the ancient [that is, established] constitution.   (HE App 3, 4: 355; see also 23, 2: 514)

When Hume first wrote the *History*, he thought that in the early seventeenth century both Royalists and Parliamentarians had sought to undermine the existing constitution. In time, he came more and more to believe that many of the rights claimed by the Stuarts were established in previous practice; nevertheless, they could not be cleared of the charge of trying to innovate by making the king master of taxation. Since Parliament refused to finance the government adequately, such innovation might be justifiable, but, alas, the result would have been not a civilized absolutism, but an almost unparalleled concentration of power.

Hume thought that most supposedly absolute governments were in fact limited. As he put it in "Of the Origin of Government," "The sultan is master of the life and fortune of any individual; but will not be permitted to impose new taxes on his subjects: a French monarch can impose taxes at pleasure; but would find it dangerous to attempt the lives and fortunes of individuals" (E-OG, 40). Charles I, however, was able both to tax and to imprison at will. In many countries, Hume says, religion acts as a restraint on power, and indeed in his account of the "eleven years' tyranny" (1629–40), Hume says that the Church of England was the only effective restraint on royal authority (HE 53, 5: 250). The comment was deliberately ironical, for this was the church of Laud, a church which preached unrestricted divine-right monarchy.

In France, as Montesquieu had stressed, the power of the nobility provided a practical restraint on the king's will; in England, by contrast, the nobility had declined in the fifteenth century, creating a power vacuum that the monarchy had sought to fill. In France, the Parlements provided a guarantee of due process in law; in England, the Star Chamber could circumvent the normal processes of law; even common law judges served at the royal pleasure; and juries were easy to intimidate (HE App 3, 4: 356–60). In France, the church was in large measure independent of the Crown; in England, it was entirely under royal control. Such comparisons, implicit rather than explicit in Hume's *History*, could alone justify the innovations to which the Long Parliament resorted in its first sessions. Hume was thus able to conclude his account of the Tudors:

On the whole, the English have no reason, from the example of their ancestors, to be in love with the picture of absolute monarchy; or to prefer the unlimited authority of the prince and his unbounded prerogatives, to that noble liberty, that sweet equality, and that happy security, by which they are at present distinguished above all nations in the universe.   (HE App. 3, 4: 370)

The key to English liberty, equality, and security did not lie, however, as we might think, in representative government. Representative government was not on its own a guarantee of freedom, for elections provided scope for the Crown to bring its influence to bear, and the small number of members of Parliament made it possible for it to make full use of its powers of patronage. Hume would, in principle, have preferred more decisions to be taken, either by the electorate as a whole, or by much larger representative bodies. Liberty derived, in fact, from the constant effort to restrict royal authority within the mixed constitution. It was this that had given birth to institutions that were, in Hume's eyes, unprecedented advances towards civil liberty. First amongst these was *habeas corpus*, unique to England, of which he wrote: "as it has not place in any other form of government, this consideration alone may induce us to prefer our present constitution to all others" (HE 67, 6: 367). Second was the liberty of the press, also unique to England, of which he was prepared to claim (until the disadvantages of too much liberty became apparent to him during the Wilkes and Liberty crisis): "this liberty is attended with so few inconveniencies, that it may be claimed as the common right of mankind, and ought to be indulged them almost in every government" (E-LP, 604).[47]

Hume's support for Parliament under the early Stuarts thus rests, not on any principled commitment to representative government, but on the conviction that only the gentry, represented in Parliament and given a political voice by it, were in a position to control what showed every sign of becoming a tyrannical power. Fortunately, the spread of learning had ensured that many of the gentry entertained noble ambitions: "A familiar acquaintance with the precious remains of antiquity excited in every generous breast a passion for a limited constitution, and begat an emulation of those manly virtues, which the Greek and Roman authors, by such animating examples, as well as pathetic expressions, recommend to us" (HE 45, 5: 18–19). The House of Commons was the only potential restraint on royal power, and Hampden and his associates were right to rally to its defence. The success of the Parliamentary cause, however, owed more to bigotry than to good judgement and noble sentiment. "Though it was justly apprehended, that such precedents [as the imprisonment of Hampden], if patiently submitted to, would end in a total disuse of parliaments, and in the establishment of arbitrary authority; Charles dreaded no opposition from the people, who are not commonly much affected with consequences, and require some striking motive, to engage them in a resistance of established government" (HE 53, 5: 249–50). It was an irony that without religious bigotry (which was to provide the "striking motive"), liberty might never have been established in England in 1640, and that, without the invasion of William of Orange in 1688, it might never have been secured. Recognition of such ironies was, Hume believed, one of the pleasures of historical study (HE 23, 2: 518).

Hume thus writes in favour of the mixed constitution to which both moderate Parliamentarians and Royalists aspired in 1641, and which was finally established in 1688. Towards the end of the *History*, he tells us that the English have established "the most entire system of liberty, that ever was known amongst mankind" (HE 71, 6: 531), and, in one of the volumes written last, he claims that the main utility of history lies in instructing us to cherish the present constitution (HE 23, 2: 525). Earlier he had written of "*that singular* and happy *Government which we enjoy at present.*" In 1772, in a fit of "Spleen and Indignation," he struck out the words "*and happy,*" but his considered opinion was that they should be restored, for "the English Government is certainly happy, though probably not calculated for Duration, by reason of its excessive Liberty" (HL 2: 260–1). Thus, the English had established more liberty than had ever existed at any other time or in any other place; too much liberty, perhaps, for the stability of their political system, but not too much for the philosopher or the historian as he sought to go about his business. Hume, in impartially weighing the merits of Whig and Tory principles, was taking full advantage of that liberty of the press which was unique to England. The conclusion to the *History* might well have been the same as the epigraph to the *Treatise*, a famous sentence from Tacitus: *Rara temporum felicitas, ubi sentire, quae velis; & quae sentias, dicere licet* (Happy the times, when one can think what one likes, and say what one thinks). Hume may have been increasingly unsure how much liberty was compatible with stability; he never doubted that it was "the perfection of civil society."

NOTES

1 My essay title comes from the entry for our David Hume in the British Library catalogue, which, to the puzzlement of generations of philosophers, distinguishes him from others of the same name by identifying him as "the historian."

2 Robertson's *History of Scotland* appeared in 1759. For a recent discussion of Robertson, see M. Fearnley-Sander, "Philosophical History and the Scottish Reformation," *Historical Journal* 33 (1990): 323–38. Hume and Robertson had a low opinion of their chief English competitor, Tobias Smollett, whose *History of England* appeared in 1757 (HL 1: 302). When Gibbon published the *Decline and Fall*, Hume expressed surprise that an Englishman could have been capable of such a work. He expected Gibbon to understand that it was the highest of compliments to say that the book had been well received by "all the Men of Letters in this Place [Edinburgh]" (HL 2: 309–12).

3 Jerome Christensen, *Practicing Enlightenment: Hume and the Formation of a Literary Career* (Madison, 1987).
4 We do not know what Hume thought of Richardson. In 1773 he thought Laurence Sterne's *Tristram Shandy* the "best Book, that has been writ by any Englishman these thirty Years" (HL 2: 269).
5 J. C. Hilson, "Hume: the Historian as Man of Feeling," in *Augustan Worlds*, ed. J. C. Hilson, M. M. B. Jones, and J. R. Watson (Leicester, 1978), pp. 205–22.
6 Hume's *History of England* was translated into French by Octavie Guichard, Madame Belot, and published in Amsterdam in 1763. The leading Whig reply to his *History* was Catherine Macaulay's eight-volume *History of England from the Accession of James I to that of the Brunswick Line* (1763–83); see NHL, 80–2. Hume and Macaulay are compared in Natalie Zemon Davis, "History's Two Bodies," *American Historical Review* 93 (1988): 1–30.
7 The first volume of Rapin's *Histoire d'Angleterre* appeared in 1724, followed by an English translation in 1725.
8 "In this Countrey, they call me his Pupil, and think that my History is an Imitation of his Siecle de Louis XIV. This Opinion flatters very much my Vanity; but the Truth is, that my History was plan'd, & in a great measure compos'd, before the Appearance of that agreeable Work" (HL 1: 226).
9 The striking peculiarity amongst this list of "the moderns" is the omission of Francesco Guicciardini, Machiavelli's contemporary, and his superior as a historian. But Hume was familiar with Guicciardini's work, and mentions him on three separate occasions in *An Enquiry concerning the Principles of Morals*.
10 On Sarpi, see my *Paolo Sarpi: Between Renaissance and Enlightenment* (Cambridge, 1983). Those, such as Richard H. Popkin, who think that one of Hume's major achievements was to break with providentialist and prophetic history, attribute to Hume a transformation that Hume himself would probably have attributed to late Renaissance Italy. See "Hume: Philosophical versus Prophetic Historian," *David Hume, Many-sided Genius*, ed. Kenneth R. Merrill and Robert Shahan (Norman, 1976). The standard work on the subject is E. Cochrane, *Historians and Historiography in the Italian Renaissance* (Chicago, 1981).
11 An English translation began to appear in 1739.
12 David Berman, "David Hume on the 1641 Rebellion in Ireland," *Studies: An Irish Quarterly Review* 65 (1976): 101–12, at p. 110; David Fate Norton and Richard H. Popkin, eds., *David Hume, Philosophical Historian* (Indianapolis, 1965), pp. 109, 413–17.
13 The point is well made in David Fate Norton, "History and Philosophy

in Hume's Thought," in *David Hume, Philosophical Historian* (Indianapolis, 1965), pp. xxxii–l, which is particularly helpful on the links between Hume's scepticism and historical study.

14 "Philosophical history" is sometimes identified with "conjectural history," a term invented by Dugald Stewart (1753–1828), and one which he took to be identical with Hume's term "natural history" as used in *The Natural History of Religion*. Since this work lies outside the scope of the present chapter, I have not discussed conjectural history here. See, for example, H. H. Hopfl, "From Savage to Scotsman: Conjectural History in the Scottish Enlightenment," *Journal of British Studies* 17 (1978): 19–40. I also do not discuss here the view that Hume's insistence in the *Treatise* on the uniformity of human nature meant that his outlook was fundamentally ahistorical: see, for example, L. Pompa, *Human Nature and Historical Knowledge: Hume, Hegel, and Vico* (Cambridge, 1990). Pompa is remarkable for failing to grasp that Hume's concept of historical knowledge is intended to be a response to sceptical arguments (pp. 28–9, 33), and for failing to consider Hume's actual practice as a historian.

15 Donald W. Livingston, *Hume's Philosophy of Common Life* (Chicago, 1984), p. 211. It may be admitted that there was little philosophy of history in English: characteristically indifferent to philosophical questions is [P. Whalley], *An Essay on the Manner of Writing History* (London, 1746). A good guide to the way in which historical writing was conceived when Hume was writing the *History* are lectures 17–20 of Adam Smith's *Lectures on Rhetoric and Belles Lettres* (1762–3), ed. J. C. Bryce (Oxford, 1983). Smith, who was a close friend of Hume's, was aware that modern history was different from ancient history because it was preoccupied with proving matters of fact, but disapproved of this because it interrupted the narrative (p. 102). He also continued to think that the best historians were generally those who wrote about events of which they had personal experience (pp. 93–4).

16 On the significance of this work for Hume's philosophy of history, see my "Hume's 'Of Miracles': Probability and Irreligion," in *Studies in the Philosophy of the Scottish Enlightenment*, ed. M. A. Stewart (Oxford, 1990), pp. 191–229.

17 C. Borghero, *La certezza e la storia* (Milan, 1983) gives an excellent account of late-seventeenth and early-eighteenth century philosophies of history.

18 Daniel Woolf, "The 'Common Voice': History, Folklore and Oral Tradition in Early Modern England," *Past and Present* 120 (1988): 26–52; and my "Hume's 'Of Miracles'," pp. 198, 222–3.

19 Ian Ross tells me that it was probably Adam Smith who arranged for de

Pouilly's essay, which first appeared in French in 1729, to be published in English, in *The Philological Miscellany* (1761)

20 See my "Hume's 'Of Miracles'," pp. 200–3.

21 See Peter Jones's essay in this volume, and, for the seventeenth-century origins of the controversy, R. F. Jones, *Ancients and Moderns*, 2d ed. (Berkeley, 1965).

22 Hume's choice of three events in particular is presumably governed by his desire to have one each from English, Irish, and Scottish history. The reality of the Popish Plot – a supposed plot to assassinate the king and impose Catholicism on England by force – was firmly asserted by Shaftesbury in 1678, and it was the campaign to hunt down the plotters that brought the Whig party into existence. Numerous Protestants were murdered in an Irish Catholic uprising in 1641: this provided the justification for Cromwell's savage campaign against the Irish. Queen Mary of Scotland, the mother of James I of England, was complicit in the murder of her husband, Darnley: this was held to justify her expulsion from the throne, a precedent for the expulsion of James II in 1688, the legitimacy of which was denied by Jacobites.

23 James Moore, "Hume's Political Science and the Classical Republican Tradition," *Canadian Journal of Political Science* 10 (1977): 809–39.

24 *An Inquiry into the Causes of the Wealth of Nations*, ed. R. H. Campbell, A. S. Skinner, and W. B. Todd (Oxford, 1976), 3.4.4 (1: 412); C. N. Stockton, "Economics and the Mechanism of Historical Progress in Hume's *History*," in *Hume: A Re-evaluation*, ed. Donald W. Livingston and James T. King (New York, 1976), pp. 296–320.

25 See Andrew Skinner's essay in this volume, and R. L. Meek, "Smith, Turgot and the 'Four Stages' Theory," *History of Political Economy* 3–4 (1971–2): 9–27.

26 P. E. Chamley, "The Conflict between Montesquieu and Hume," in *Essays on Adam Smith*, ed. Andrew S. Skinner and T. Wilson (Oxford, 1975), pp. 274–305.

27 Montesquieu, *The Spirit of the Laws*, trans. and ed. A. M. Cohler and others (Cambridge, 1989), esp. pp. 18, 22, 156–66, 197, 325–33, 388, 456, 608.

28 David Miller, *Philosophy and Ideology in Hume's Political Thought* (Oxford, 1981), pp. 148–9; Duncan Forbes, *Hume's Philosophical Politics* (Cambridge, 1975), chap. 5. A classic text for the understanding of the Enlightenment definition of "liberty" is the article "la liberté politique" in *Encyclopédie*, ed. Denis Diderot and Jean Le Rond d'Alembert, 17 vols. (Paris and "Neufchastel," 1751–65).

29 Montesquieu, *Spirit of the Laws*, p. xli. Montesquieu writes, "I have had new ideas; new words have had to be found or new meanings given to

old ones." Hume: "I wish, that People do not take a Disgust at Liberty; a
word, that has been so much profand by these polluted Mouths [the
supporters of Wilkes], that men of Sense are sick at the very mention of
it. I hope a new term will be invented to express so valuable and good a
thing" (NHL, 196).

30 Hume thought (letter to Montesquieu) that Montesquieu somewhat underestimated the dangers of constitutional conflict (HL 1: 138).

31 Hume was obviously happier with another type of digression: the discussion of an individual's character. This was necessary, both to evoke the
readers' sympathies and passions, and to make it possible for them to
make moral judgements. In Hume's view, it is character rather than
individual actions that ought to be judged when assessing the moral
value of a person.

32 For Hume's own summary account of party politics in England, and his
explanation of terms such as "court" and "country," "Whig" and
"Tory," see E-PGB, 64–72.

33 Giuseppe Giarrizzo, David Hume politico e storico (Turin, 1962), and
"Ancora su Hume storico," Rivista storica italiana 83 (1971): 429–49.

34 Duncan Forbes, "Politics and History in David Hume," Historical Journal 6 (1963): 280–95; Hume's Philosophical Politics; and his introduction to Hume's History, a reprint of the first edition of the early Stuart
volume (Harmondsworth, 1970).

35 Livingston, Hume's Philosophy of Common Life, pp. 257–8.

36 Nicholas Phillipson, Hume (New York, 1989).

37 J. V. Price, "Hume's Concept of Liberty and The History of England,"
Studies in Romanticism 5 (1966): 139–57. Liberty in Hume's History of
England, ed. Nicholas Capaldi and Donald W. Livingston (Dordrecht,
1990), collects a number of essays which defend this view. David Miller,
Philosophy and Ideology, provides a balanced assessment. The most
recent contribution to this debate is John B. Stewart, Opinion and Reform in Hume's Political Philosophy (Princeton, 1992).

38 Laurence L. Bongie, David Hume: Prophet of the Counter-Revolution
(Oxford, 1965).

39 Livingston, Hume's Philosophy of Common Life, p. 317.

40 Bolingbroke was the author of "A Dissertation upon Parties" (1733–4)
and of Letters on the Study and Use of History, 2 vols. (London, 1752).
For a selection of Bolingbroke's works, see Historical Writings, ed. I.
Kramnick (Chicago, 1972).

41 John, Baron Hervey, Ancient and Modern Liberty Stated and Compared
(London, 1734). Hume did not share the court Whigs' favourable assessment of Walpole (E-CR, 574–6).

42 The full extent of Rapin's deficiency was obviously not apparent in

1753: HL 1: 170; contrast HL 1: 258. For the comparison between the
Tudors and the Stuarts, HL 1: 264, 461. For later revisions: HL 1: 379;
HL 2: 216, 260–1; NHL, 69–71. For Hume's views in 1758, E-CP, 493–
501. For an analysis, see E. C. Mossner, "Was Hume a Tory Historian?"
Journal of the History of Ideas 2 (1941): 225–36.

43 On which, see Knud Haakonssen's essay in this volume.

44 Forbes, *Hume's Philosophical Politics*, p. 292.

45 It is worth noting, however, that Hume regarded Bulstrode Whitelocke
as a more impartial historian than Clarendon (HE 64, 6: 215). Since
Whitelocke supported Parliament while Clarendon supported the king,
this judgement scarcely accords with a view of Hume as a Tory historian. Hume's judgement derives, presumably, from John Oldmixon, *Clarendon and Whitlock compar'd* (London, 1727).

46 The Rye House plot was a plot by leading Whigs, including Algernon
Sidney, to assassinate Charles II and his brother James.

47 The only exception Hume recognized was ecclesiastical government,
which he took to be incompatible with freedom of discussion.

11 Hume on religion

Hume's critique of religion and religious belief is, as a whole, subtle, profound, and damaging to religion in ways which have no philosophical antecedents and few successors. Some of the damage and a little of the subtlety will, I trust, become evident in Part II of this essay, where Hume's seminal discussions of the design argument for the existence of God, miracles, morality, and natural belief are examined. Before this, however, certain preliminaries need attention. First, there is the difficulty caused by the old-fashioned or unfamiliar terminology used by Hume and his commentators in describing and assessing what he has to say. Second, although the scale of Hume's writing on religion is reasonably obvious (it exceeds his output concerning any other subject except history), the fact that it is dispersed over a number of publications and partly embedded (sometimes none too clearly) in several more, as well as having to be drawn from essays, letters, and minor writings, needs to be understood before any informed discussion is possible. Third, there is the problem of seeing what he wrote not as ad hoc criticisms turned out piecemeal, but as a comprehensive critical strategy. Finally, a problem of interpretation results from Hume's "abundant prudence" in covering his real opinions with ambiguous irony and even, on occasions, with denials of his own apparent conclusions.

I shall attempt some clarification of these four preliminary issues in Part I of this essay, beginning with the terminology, a matter which infects and informs all else that can be said.

I. TEXT AND CONTEXT

Terminology

A basic classification of religious information according to its source in reason or in historically particular disclosures has long been established in the contrast between *natural theology* or *natural religion*, on the one hand, and *revelation* or *revealed religion*, on the other. *Natural religion* (the phrase usually does duty in the eighteenth century for the now more common term *natural theology*) is the system of conclusions about God's (or the gods') existence and nature supposedly attainable from evidence and by reasoning accessible to any intelligent person irrespective of any special information conveyed in the Bible, Koran, or other revelatory source. For example, the conclusion that a designing agent, not chance, is needed to explain the order of the cosmos is part of natural not revealed religion. *Revelation* or *revealed religion*, on the other hand, is the body of alleged truths about the divine which can only be obtained from particular historical and supposedly inspired sources such as the Bible or Koran. For example, the claims that an individual human person can expect resurrection after death, or that God once sent his son into the world, are parts of a revelation. A distinction is sometimes made between *particular revelation* and *general revelation*. *Particular revelation* is revelation as just described. *General revelation* is the supposed general experience of the presence of God in the religious life of each believer.

Within natural religion, two types of argument in various versions are, and always have been, conspicuous. Hume (and some others who use the pre-Kantian terminology) calls these *the argument a posteriori* and *the argument a priori*, respectively. *The argument a posteriori* is the phrase by which Hume usually refers to versions of what we would normally call the design argument, that is, the argument that God exists because His creative intelligence can be observed in the order or purposiveness to be found in the natural world (DNR 2, 143; 9, 188, for example). *The argument a priori*, in Hume's usage (DNR 9, 188), refers to his paraphrase of the particular cosmological argument to be found in Samuel Clarke's Boyle Lectures for 1704, later published as *A Discourse concerning the Being and Attributes of God*. The argument in Hume's words begins "Whatever exists must have a cause or reason of its existence" and concludes with the claim, "We must, therefore, have recourse to a necessarily existent Being, who carries the REASON of his existence in himself; and who cannot be supposed not to exist without an express contradiction" (DNR 9, 188–9).

Both the positive rejection of revelation as a source of religious knowledge and one of the possible conclusions attainable from the arguments and evidence of natural religion can be referred to as *deism*. Thus, the term *deism* was widely used in the eighteenth century, but with vague meaning, to indicate a view of religion which held that our reliable knowledge of God is based upon reason alone (that is to say, upon natural religion and not upon revelation). The term is not much used by Hume except to reject its application to himself.[1] It is also a term used to indicate belief (arrived at from reasoning alone) in a god who set the universe in motion or caused the universe to exist and then left it alone. Another way of expressing this limited view is to say that deism is the claim to rationally substantiated belief in a god lacking *providence*. *Providence*, while sometimes used as a synonym for God, is more particularly used to refer to that aspect of God's (or the gods') nature which consists in exerting control, guidance, or forethought in the moral affairs of mankind or the physical processes of the world. Hume uses *providence* in just this sense in Section 9 of the *Enquiry concerning Human Understanding*, where he argues that there is no evidence for God's providence.

When the God (either on the evidence of revelation or natural religion, or in some other way) is held to be a single and eternal God who created all things (possibly *ex nihilo*) and continues to sustain and work within his creation (that is, to exercise providence), the belief is usually called *theism*. Thus, the common root of the Judaic, Christian, and Islamic religions is theism.

Two corruptions of religion were of great concern to Hume and other eighteenth-century writers. These corruptions were *superstition*, usually associated with idolatry and with the Church of Rome, and *enthusiasm*, usually associated with the newly converted and with extreme Protestant sects. *Superstition* is the state in which "unknown evils are dreaded from unknown agents." Its source is "weakness, fear, melancholy, together with ignorance," and it manifests itself in "ceremonies, observances, mortifications, sacrifices, presents" directed towards the unknown agent. *Enthusiasm* is religion corrupted by emotional fanaticism or religious mania: "raptures, transports, and surprising flights of fancy" that are "attributed to the immediate inspiration of that Divine Being, who is the object of devotion" (E-SE, 73–4).[2]

An attitude to religion often associated in the late seventeenth and eighteenth centuries with enthusiasm, but also having a pedigree which includes Tertullian, Pascal, and possibly St. Paul, was sometimes referred to by Hume's near contemporaries as "implicit belief" or "blind belief" or "the submission of reason to faith." In the nineteenth century, this attitude was developed into the position known since about 1870 as *fideism*. This is the view, argued by some Christian apologists to be reinforced by Hume's scepticism, that religious belief is justified by faith alone, quite apart from reasons or evidence, because *all* knowledge rests upon premises accepted by faith.

Finally there are two confusing terms which both contain the word *natural*, but which are used in different senses: the eighteenth-century term *natural history* and the twentieth-century term *natural belief*. *Natural history* (as in Hume's *Natural History of Religion*) indicates an account of something as a natural phenomenon. In the title of Hume's work, the account is of the cause and conditions which "naturally" produce religion (as, for example, the presence of air and water "naturally" produce rust on iron) without reference to any reasons which can be produced in favour of or against the religion in question. The phrase *natural belief*, on the other hand, is not to be found in Hume's own writings. It was introduced by Norman Kemp Smith,[3] and has been much used since, to indicate basic or indispensable beliefs.

The works

Hume's two main works directly on religion are the *Natural History of Religion* (1757) and the *Dialogues concerning Natural Religion* (1779, but first written in the 1750s). The former deals with religion's natural origins in human nature and society – its causes. The latter examines the supposed rational grounds for belief in God or gods – its reasons. Parts of the latter examination had already been given a preliminary run in Section 11 of the *Enquiry concerning*

Human Understanding (1748), in which there also appeared the chapter "Of Miracles," Hume's celebrated onslaught on the credentials of the Christian revelation. But the *Enquiry* as a whole also develops an epistemological attack on metaphysics and "philosophical religion" whose final outcome is not unlike the conclusions of twentieth-century logical positivism (EHU 12.3, 165). Less obviously, the second *Enquiry*, the *Enquiry concerning The Principles of Morals* (1751) is also concerned with religion. In it, Hume gives an account of a morality in which what is added by religion to the secular core all too often amounts to spurious virtues and imaginary crimes which result in cruel, bigoted, and anti-utilitarian interferences in human affairs. Some of these interferences are chronicled in his *History of England* (published between 1754 and 1762).

Among Hume's fifty or so individual essays, there are numerous reflections on religion. These range from the lengthy footnote on the hypocrisy of the clergy, which is attached to "Of National Characters," to the damaging duality developed in "Of Superstition and Enthusiasm." This duality would seem to leave little of true religion once the corruptions of religion have been understood. But by far the most important essays are the two which ought to have appeared in 1757 along with the *Natural History of Religion*. These are "Of Suicide" (which argues that suicide is neither immoral nor irreligious) and "Of the Immortality of the Soul" (which argues that there is good evidence for man's mortality). Both essays were withdrawn by Hume before publication after threats against him or his publisher, although copies of both survived to be reprinted in modern editions.

Finally, letters and short documents apart, there is the *Treatise of Human Nature* (1739–40). The *Treatise*, Hume's first work, is, to our eyes, not overtly concerned with religion. Part of the reason for this is that Hume excised some of its "nobler parts" before publication, including some version of "Of Miracles" (which could have been located in Book 1, Part 3, between sections 13 and 14),[4] and possibly some version of "Of the Immortality of the Soul" (which could have formed the concluding pages to the section of Book 1 entitled "Of the Immateriality of the Soul"). But a more important reason that the *Treatise* as published does not seem to us much concerned with religion is that our sensitivities to what would constitute an attack upon religion are much weaker than those of

Hume's contemporaries. The nature of their sensitivities is illumi-
nated by the pamphlet *A Letter from a Gentleman*. The text is
drawn from a letter by Hume and was rushed into print on his behalf
in 1745 when he was a candidate for the Chair of Moral Philosophy
at Edinburgh University. In it, Hume is defended against six
"charges" that the *Treatise* subverts religion. To us, the most obvious charge is that some of his arguments about causation (particularly the section in Book 1 entitled "*Why a cause is always necessary*") constitute a significant criticism of the *a priori* argument for
God's existence.

The structure of Hume's critique

Suppose we put the fundamental question thus: Why does anyone
believe in God or gods, or cleave to the teachings of such theistic
religions as Christianity or Islam? The answer may be given (non-
exclusively) in terms of either reasons or causes, and it is under this
division that Hume's examination of religion begins to look like a
comprehensive critique rather than a collection of challenging but
discrete sections.

In traditional (and particularly eighteenth-century) religious apologetics, the reasons for belief in God usually took the form of appeals
to arguments and revelation. The appeal to revelation was neither to
the general revelation associated with dedicated religious practice
nor to individual claims to have direct information about the Divine, but specifically to the particular revelation of Christianity as
set out in the New Testament. This, it was supposed, carried with it
certain guarantees of its own authenticity. These guarantees were
that the revelation fulfilled prophecy and was attended with miracles. Miracles could only be brought about by God (and not any god,
but the one true God). Therefore a rational man had *grounds* for
accepting the Christian revelation as genuine. It is, of course, precisely these grounds which Hume set out to undermine in Section
10 of the first *Enquiry*, where, incidentally, he treats fulfilled prophecy as a species of miracle (EHU 10.2, 130).

The appeal to arguments to support belief in God was most commonly an appeal to those types of argument which Hume calls the
argument *a priori* (cosmological arguments) and the argument *a posteriori* (design arguments). These were the traditional core of natural

religion. The former is dismantled by Hume in the *Treatise*, the first *Enquiry*, and again in Part 9 of the *Dialogues*. The latter is subjected to a uniquely thorough and hostile examination in Section 11 of the first *Enquiry* and again throughout the *Dialogues*.

But if, as Hume contends, the arguments of natural religion do not establish the existence of any deity which could be an object of religious belief, and if revelation is not authenticated in any way which could convince a rational man, then it might seem that the only answer which can be given to the question "Why does anyone believe in God or gods?" is that the belief has natural *causes*. An investigation of these is Hume's subject in the *Natural History of Religion*. At the heart of his analysis is the contention that the origin of belief in gods is to be found in fear of the unknown causes of the sometimes malevolent, sometimes benevolent, and frequently capricious events which govern human life.

That, I think, is the main structure of Hume's critique of religion, but its details extend vastly further: to a "mitigated scepticism" (carefully developed in the first *Enquiry*) which would put religious metaphysics beyond our understanding; to a sharpened theological dilemma (EHU 8) between God's omniscience and man's moral answerability; to an analytic separation of morality and religion (implied in the *Treatise* and emphasized by the second *Enquiry*) with comments on particular issues such as suicide; to a philosophical account of personal identity and of the soul (T 1.4.5–6), which invites the rejection of immortality contained in "Of the Immortality of the Soul"; to an exposé in the *History of England* of the misery produced by religious fanaticism and superstition; and on to letters which contain all manner of detailed comments and criticisms (note, for example, his remarks on the psychology of worship and the inappropriateness of prayer in NHL, 13).

Hume's stance and the problem of interpretation

The problem with Hume's interpretation is that, although his actual arguments and the facts he adduces are regularly highly critical of religion and damaging to any belief in the divine, his affirmations (and sometimes the conclusions which he seems to draw) do not always look like the real outcome of his criticisms. Thus, for example, the *Natural History of Religion* reads like a reduction of religion to its causes in human nature, but in his brief "Introduction" to the work Hume remarks: "The whole frame of nature bespeaks an intelligent author; and no rational enquirer can, after serious reflection, suspend his belief a moment with regard to the primary principles of genuine Theism and Religion" (NHR Intro, 4: [309]).

Similar affirmations appear at least five times in the main text. Seventeen years earlier, in a footnote to the Appendix to the *Treatise*, Hume had unequivocally countermanded whatever damage to belief in God the *Treatise* might have been supposed guilty of: "The order of the universe proves an omnipotent mind; that is, a mind whose will is *constantly attended* with the obedience of every creature and being. Nothing more is requisite to give a foundation to all the articles of religion" (T App, 633). And yet the argument to God's existence from the order of the universe, described in the first *Enquiry* as the "chief or sole argument for a divine existence" (EHU 11, 135) is there, and again and most celebratedly in the *Dialogues*, subjected to devastating criticism. Most paradoxically of all, this criticism is itself followed by an affirmation from the sceptic Philo that "a purpose, an intention, or design strikes everywhere the most careless, the most stupid thinker" (DNR 12, 214). Another instance of Hume's arguments apparently being at odds with his conclusion is in his onslaught upon miracles. There his attack upon the credentials of revelation concludes with a direction to faith: "Our most holy religion is founded on *Faith*, not on reason" (EHU 10.2, 130). Somewhat similarly, his aphoristic demolition of the grounds for believing in immortality in "Of the Immortality of the Soul" begins and ends with a direction to "the gospel alone, that has brought life and immortality to light" (E-IS, 590).

It is not possible within present constraints of space to discuss these issues in full. They are complex and have, moreover, already been examined at depth in recent Humean exegeses.[5] But an outline interpretation will be useful. In the first place, neither Hume nor any other writer in eighteenth-century Britain (or elsewhere in Europe, for that matter) was free to express atheistical or anti-religious views without the threat or actuality of prosecution or social penalties of a very nasty sort. Hence, we would expect Hume to cover his apparently sceptical views with protestations of orthodoxy with which he could defend himself when need arose. In this he is in company with most other eighteenth-century expressions of religious scepticism or atheism.[6] His isolated direction to faith as the foundation of "our most holy religion" is thus almost certainly a defensive irony following upon his attack on miracles, or a rueful acknowledgement of the ultimate irrationality of religious belief, not a sincere fideistic defence of what religious belief "really" is. It would also be possible to construe some of his blander affirmations of belief in God as the designer in this way, particularly the fulsome and then highly qualified concession by the sceptic Philo in the *Dialogues*, Part 12.

But having acknowledged the prudential irony, there remains an impression, both from the careful complexity of his arguments, from his scepticism about metaphysical arguments, and from letters and anecdotal evidence, that Hume really was unwilling to deny the existence of God and all lesser supernatural agents in the unequivocal sense now conveyed by the notion of atheism. It is as if he was too consistent a sceptic to pronounce positively on any "remote and abstruse subjects" (EHU 1, 12), atheism included; and, moreover, it is as if the closer he looked at the defects of the design argument, the more something of it remained unrefuted, so that, at the end of the *Dialogues*, in a paragraph added just before his death, he can write, surely without hint of irony:

If the whole of natural theology, as some people seem to maintain, resolves itself into one simple, though somewhat ambiguous, at least undefined proposition, *that the cause or causes of order in the universe probably bear some remote analogy to human intelligence*: If this proposition be not capable of extension, variation, or more particular explication: If it afford no inference that affects human life, or can be the source of any action or forbearance: And if the analogy, imperfect as it is, can be carried no farther than to the human intelligence; and cannot be transferred, with any appearance of probability, to the other qualities of the mind: If this really be the case, what can the most inquisitive, contemplative, and religious man do more than give a plain, philosophical assent to the proposition, as often as it occurs; and believe that the arguments, on which it is established, exceed the objections which lie against it?   (DNR 12, 227)

So I would suggest for working purposes that one should take as prudential irony Hume's affirmations where they are blandly at variance with any straightforward reading of what precedes or follows them. But one should also acknowledge that his regard for the limitations of human understanding, and his caution concerning "so extraordinary and magnificent a question" as the being and nature of God (DNR 12, 227), make him genuinely unable to advocate straightforward atheism of the sort later associated with d'Holbach or Russell. Thus, his scepticism about all theological and other claims based upon "abstruse metaphysics" does not at the end permit him to reject *in toto* "obvious" claims based upon the order apparent in the universe. But these "obvious" claims amount to very little, as far as any real religion is concerned. They imply no duties and no action or forbearance from action. They involve no devotion. I have elsewhere suggested that such an emasculated concession to the proposition "there is a god" should be called "attenuated deism."[7] This is deism in which such evidence and reasons as remain uncontroverted add up to no more than a dim possibility that some non-providential god exists, a possibility too ill-understood to be affirmed or denied by a "wise man."

But whether the designation "attenuated deism" is appropriate or not, it is Hume's actual arguments which contribute to the philosophy of religion, together with the excitement of the challenges which he brings to bear on questions concerning religion and the existence of God or gods. These arguments and challenges for the most part stand or fall on their own philosophical merits without need to refer to Hume's own hard-to-identify stance. In what follows, and for present purposes, I shall therefore take Hume to be identified with any interesting position set out in his own works.[8]

II. ARGUMENT AND OUTCOME

The core of natural religion

In the first *Enquiry* Hume refers to the design argument as "the chief or sole argument for a divine existence" (EHU 11, 135). He is here not making a judgement but reporting a fact. There are strong hints of the argument in the Bible.[9] It played a significant part in Greek philosophical monotheism.[10] In its teleological version, it appears as the Fifth Way of Aquinas. In eighteenth-century literature, its soundness is virtually taken for granted and the same applies for much nineteenth-century literature. It has even enjoyed some rehabilitation in the twentieth century.[11]

Apart from numerous short references, Hume attempts three statements of the argument.[12]

1. [The religious philosophers] paint, in the most magnificent colours, the order, beauty, and wise arrangement of the universe; and then ask, if such a glorious display of intelligence could proceed from the fortuitous concourse of atoms, or if chance could produce what the greatest genius can never sufficiently admire. (EHU 11, 135)

2. The curious adapting of means to ends, throughout all nature, resembles exactly, though it much exceeds, the productions of human contrivance; of human design, thought, wisdom, and intelligence. Since therefore the effects resemble each other, we are led to infer, by all the rules of analogy, that the causes also resemble; and that the Author of nature is somewhat similar to the mind of man; though possessed of much larger faculties, proportioned to the grandeur of the work, which he has executed. (DNR 2, 143)

3. Consider, anatomize the eye: Survey its structure and contrivance; and tell me, from your own feeling, if the idea of a contriver does not immediately flow in upon you with a force like that of sensation. (DNR 3, 154)

In effect (although I do not think it can be shown that Hume intended anything so systematic), these three statements show the design argument in distinct versions. In (1), the argument is presented as what I have elsewhere suggested should be called the nomological argument,[13] namely, as the appeal to the inexplicability of natural *order* if this is not accounted for as the outcome of intelligent design. In (2), Hume makes a careful attempt to represent the form of what is usually called the teleological argument: the appeal to the significance of the *purposes* supposedly evident in natural phenomena. In (3), Cleanthes, the advocate of the argument in the *Dialogues*, is not so much presenting a new version of the argument as suggesting that its conclusion is something verging upon the perceptually obvious. We cannot see the structures of nature, or become *aware* of the all pervading regularities we express as laws of nature, without "feeling" their source as intelligent. The question then becomes whether this "feeling" is justifiably related to what elicits it (like our feeling of fear about atomic radiation) or unjustifiably related (like some people's feeling of fear about darkness per se).

In the *Dialogues* and the first *Enquiry*, Section 11, Hume subjects these arguments to an intricate and cumulatively devastating series of objections, the majority of which apply to both the nomological and the teleological arguments. His main objections are as follows:

a. If we suppose God (or gods) to be the cause of order in the world, then since all that we can infer about God (or gods) is inferred from the world, we can *only* attribute to God (or the gods) whatever degree of power, intelligence, foresight, and so forth is sufficient to produce what we actually find in the world (EHU 11, 136–42). In particular, Hume argues, when applied to divine providence, it is impossible to *infer* from the world infinite or even very great benevolence in its designer (DNR 10–11). As Philo in the *Dialogues* puts it, "The whole presents nothing but the idea of a blind nature, impregnated by a great vivifying principle, and pouring forth from her lap, without discernment or parental care, her maimed and abortive children" (DNR 11, 211). Hume is also at pains to point out in the *Dialogues* and first *Enquiry* that we may "torture our brains" into *reconciling* the suffering of living things with the presupposition that God is perfectly benevolent; what we cannot do is justify that presupposition by *inference* from the given suffering.

b. If valid, the inference from design could equally well establish a number of conclusions incompatible with monotheism; for example, that the universe, like most human contrivance, is the product of co-operating designers; that it is a discarded experiment in universe making or the product of a second-rate god; that it is the creation of a deistic god, that is, one who has set it all going and then let it run on at its own devices, and so on (DNR 5, 166–9).

c. If, as Hume argues extensively in his general philosophy, the concept of cause only applies to *species* of objects (*C*s, whenever they occur, cause *E*s), then it makes no sense to talk about a unique object such as "the universe as a whole" being causally produced by a unique and otherwise unknown entity "outside" (in the sense of not being one among) the repeating causal sequences of the universe itself (EHU 11, 148; DNR 2, 149–51).

d. The analogy, Hume contends, between artifacts – objects known to proceed from design – and natural objects is too weak and remote to suggest similar causes. (This objection is developed almost throughout the *Dialogues*).

e. The relation between order and design is experience based: "order, arrangement, or the adjustment of final causes" is not *a priori* proof of design, it is indicative of design "only so far as it has been experienced to proceed from that principle" (DNR 2, 146).

f. If an intelligent agent is required to explain the order in nature, then the intelligent agent will in turn need to be explained (DNR 4, 160–4). "But if we stop [at the agent explanation] . . . why go so far? Why not stop at the material world?" (DNR 4, 161).[14]

Each of the above requires, and is given by Hume and the secondary literature which follows his agenda, detailed philosophical discussion which cannot be attempted here. But at least one other important and highly original counter to the design argument is suggested by Hume. We can all agree that the inference to a designer depends upon the assumptions that the order in nature *needs* explanation, and that no explanation is possible other than by reference to some designing intelligence. In Part 8 of the *Dialogues*, both these assumptions are questioned.

The first had been classically challenged by a tenet of the Epicurean (or Greek Atomist) system which attracted much ancient ridicule and criticism. This was Epicurus's contention that the world just happened by the unguided collision and grouping of numberless primary particles taking place over an infinite time in infinite space. Thus, Balbus, a Stoic, one of Cicero's characters in his dialogues in *De Natura Deorum* (2.37), derides the Epicureans:

Should it not astound me that anyone . . . can persuade himself . . . That a world of the utmost splendour and beauty is created by an accidental combination of those [primary particles]? I do not see how the person who supposes that this can happen cannot also believe that if countless instances of the twenty-one letters were thrown into a container, then shaken out onto the ground, it were possible they might form a readable version of the *Annals* of Ennius. I'm not sure that luck could manage this to the extent of a single line!

The fundamental claim against the Epicureans is that order, beauty, and the arrangement of the universe *need* explanation, and random collisions of infinite numbers of primary particles do not provide a probable one. The same claim is elicited by the seventeenth-century revival of Epicurean atomism.

In 1682, at Oxford, a translation into English verse of Lucretius's "six books of Epicurean philosophy" appeared, to be followed by paraphrases by Dryden and others. An angry reaction to the popularity of such an irreligious work followed, and in 1712 there appeared an answer on an epic scale: *The Creation* by Sir Richard Blackmore. At several points, Blackmore confronts the Epicurean account of the origin of the *ordered* universe in precisely the manner in which it had been confronted by Balbus in Cicero's dialogue seventeen hundred years earlier:

> Could Atomes, which with undirected flight
> Roam'd thro' the Void, and rang'd the Realms of Night;
> Of Reason destitute, without Intent,
> Depriv'd of Choice, and mindless of Event,
> In Order march, and to their Posts advance
> Led by no Guide, but undesigning Chance?

The challenge is again clear: the order manifested by the universe *needs* explanation. But does it? Hume is inclined to answer – see (f) above – that it does not; or rather, if we think it does, then having traced its origin to a divine orderer, the order in *that* ought just as much to require explanation as the order in matter:

> To say, that the different ideas, which compose the reason of the supreme Being, fall into order, of themselves, and by their own nature, is really to talk without any precise meaning. If it has a meaning, I would fain know, why it is not as good sense to say, that the parts of the material world fall into order, of themselves, and by their own nature? Can the one opinion be intelligible, while the other is not so?   (DNR 4, 162)

Hume adds that we have indeed "experience of ideas, which fall into order, of themselves, and without any *known* cause" (presumably our own ideas) but "we have a much larger experience of matter, which does the same." A reply to Hume is that the reduction of two sorts of autonomous order, material and mental, to one, mental order, effects a desirable elimination of a superfluous explanatory entity.[15] The problem for the theist, however, is to show, against the ever-rising tide of scientific evidence, that mental order, and not material order, has explanatory primacy: that material order is explainable in terms of mental order and not vice versa, and that mental order and material order are genuinely different categories.

But there is a further reason to think that the order manifested in the universe is *not* in need of special explanation. The point is that Cicero's Balbus, and Blackmore, and others who have walked in

their footsteps, have assumed that in some sense a chaotic universe is more probable, at least would be less in need of explanation, than the orderly cosmos we find. But this assumption is in need of justification. Why? Because the assumption implies that we can compare the ordered cosmos which actually exists with a chaos which does not exist, and find the existent cosmos less probable than the non-existent chaos. But the crucial point is that we cannot make such a comparison. We have absolutely *no* grounds for supposing that what actually exists has any probability at all by comparison with anything else, since in this special instance *there is nothing else*. Similarly, we have absolutely no grounds for holding that order in nature is more (or less) in need of explanation than chaos would have been. Order is what we have got, and there is nothing else by contrast with which that order is in any sense probable or improbable.

Even if at best Hume himself can do no more than shed doubt upon the need to explain natural order, or upon the usefulness of doing so, the second assumption required for inference to a designer remains, namely, that there can be no other explanation of natural order if we do not attribute it to a designing intelligence. However, we (but not Hume) might be able to argue, in the light of the big bang theory favoured by modern cosmology, that the initial event out of which all subsequent sequences of events emerged could (at least we have no reasons to think that it could not) have set absolutely any sort of universe developing. But having set going this universe, those first developments were continuous with what we subsequently read as the laws of nature. The initial event having set things going in *one* way (that is, the way it actually did), that *one* way is what we see as natural order, and indeed no existent things can develop in any other way given the initial event. There is even a hint of this type of thinking in the *Dialogues* (although it is arrived at in a somewhat different way): "Instead of admiring the order of natural beings, we should clearly see, that it was absolutely impossible for them, in the smallest article, ever to admit of any other disposition" (DNR 6, 175). But in the pages of the *Dialogues* which follow this remark, Hume develops without aid from our big bang theory an extensive reply to the traditional Stoic and Christian assumption that order *could not* have emerged from chaos without intelligent design.

Hume's "new hypothesis of cosmogony" (DNR 8, 183) is a form of the Epicurean theory revised by the assumption that the number of

primary particles of matter is very large but not, as Epicurus supposed, infinite. Suppose, says Hume, in a passage of remarkable insight, "matter were thrown into any position, by a blind, unguided force" and that this force was not exhausted at the moment of the first throw, but remained active in every part of matter so that movement continued (DNR 8, 184). Is what we actually find – namely, stable structures composed of disorderly primary particles – not a possible outcome of such a finite amount of matter undergoing transpositions over a very long period of time? In particular, will not certain structures and sequences, once struck upon, be of a character that enables them to endure?

In effect, Hume is suggesting that given an initial blind force (a big bang?), subsequent random movements of a large but finite amount of matter *could* produce the stable entities and sequences we now observe in the universe. Laws of nature and inorganic structures, just as much as natural species, *could* be arrived at by a process akin to that of natural selection: "It is in vain, therefore, to insist upon the uses of the parts in animals or vegetables, and their curious adjustment to each other. I would fain know how an animal could subsist, unless its parts were so adjusted?" (DNR 8, 185)

Even if the best reading of the available evidence would now seem to show that the most fundamental laws of nature have not evolved, but have operated uniformly from the remotest accessible past, Hume's "new hypothesis" remains astonishingly impressive as an attempt to provide an alternative to the "religious hypothesis" (EHU 11, 139). It is, moreover, an attempt which, when fleshed out by Darwin's observations, vastly devalues the teleological argument even if the nomological argument partly escapes.

What, then, is Hume's achievement in this area? At the very least he put a massive and permanent question mark against a crucial piece of religious apologetics previously taken as unquestionable. In the process, he brilliantly anticipated later ideas and established the grounds on which all subsequent philosophical discussions have taken place.

The credentials of revelation

Two-and-one-half centuries after its publication, "Of Miracles," Section 10 in the first *Enquiry*, is still spawning book-length responses together with an unabated stream of discussion articles.[16] Indeed, "Of

Miracles" is manifestly one of those rare philosophical pieces whose very inconsistencies and ambiguities are more fruitful than the cautious balance of a thousand lesser works. Its main structure is simple.

In Part 2, a number of case histories and what have been called *a posteriori* arguments are reproduced (for the most part, they are not original to Hume) to show that "there never was a miraculous event established on so full an evidence" (EHU 10.2, 116). In effect, Part 2 is concerned with the criteria for good evidence, with the significance of incompatible religious claims based upon rival miracles,[17] and with the general conclusion Hume draws from his arguments – that "a miracle can never be proved, so as to be the foundation of a system of religion" (EHU 10.2, 127). Given the contemporary background of controversy concerning miracles,[18] and the use of miracles to validate the particular revelation of Christianity, I have suggested that this guarded conclusion should be unpacked as "The Resurrection can never be proved in such a way that it can function as a good reason to accept the Christian revelation."

In Part 1, an *a priori* argument (so called by commentators on Hume) is produced to act as a "check" on superstition. The argument purports to show that no "wise man" (that is, one whose belief is proportioned to the evidence) could believe reports of miracles. A paraphrase of Hume's argument is as follows:

1. A weaker evidence can never destroy a stronger.
2. A wise man proportions his belief to the evidence.
3. Some things happen invariably in our experience, for example, that men die. In matters of fact these invariable experiences constitute certainties and are called, or form the basis of, laws of nature – "a firm and unalterable [unalterable because *past*] experience has established these laws" (EHU 10.1, 114).
4. Other things happen less than invariably in our experience, for example, that one will survive a heart attack. In matters of fact these variable experiences constitute probabilities which admit of degrees ranging from strong (almost always happens) to weak (very seldom happens).
5. The veracity of human testimony is, from experience, normally a strong probability and as such amounts to a proof that what is reported took place. But sometimes the veracity of human testimony is a weak probability (as is always the

case, according to Hume's arguments in Part 2, with reports of miracles). *Therefore,* from 3 and 4, when testimony is given which is contrary to our invariable experience, a probability, whether weak or strong, is opposing a certainty and (from 1 and 2) the wise man will believe the certainty.

6. But a miracle is *"a transgression of a law of nature* [see 3] *by a particular volition of the Deity"* (EHU 10.1, 115n). *Therefore,* "There must . . . be a uniform experience against every miraculous event, otherwise the event would not merit that appellation. And as a uniform experience amounts to a proof, there is here a direct and full *proof,* from the nature of the fact, against the existence of any miracle" (EHU 10.1, 115).

The above argument has provoked many questions. Among them the following have been conspicuous: (i) What is meant by a law of nature, and how can one distinguish between an event which falsifies a law (shows that it is an inaccurate description of the way things are in the natural world) and an event which results from a suspension of the law or an intrusion into the natural world by a supernatural agent such as a god or other invisible spirit? (ii) Can Hume, on the basis of what he says elsewhere in the *Treatise* and first *Enquiry,* formulate any concept of natural causation strong enough to give content to the notion of its violation? (iii) Is Hume's definition of a miracle (which is entirely reportive) in need of supplementation, particularly by the qualification "of religious significance," so that mere inexplicable freaks of nature do not get counted as miracles? (iv) Is Hume correct in implying (EHU 10.1, 114–16) that in order for something to be called a miracle it must not happen more than once? And if, as biblical reports would seem to suggest, he is not correct, at what stage will repeated "miracles" become clusters of "paranormal" phenomena in need of explanation *within* the natural world? (v) Can Hume, or anyone arguing on his behalf, or on behalf of those who need such a concept in their definition of what a miracle is, give adequate content to the notion of a physically impossible event? (vi) With what justification can we use the exceptional nature of an event as grounds for rejecting testimony that the alleged event took place? It is this final question which is crucial in assessing and understanding Hume's *a priori* argument since the argument is addressed to *reports* of events, not to our own eye-witnessing of them.

The position I would defend with regard to question (vi) is this: Hume's argument is an accurate formal representation of the norm of rationality we all in fact apply, or try to apply, in our search for historical truth. Furthermore, when applied to the reports to which Hume has to apply it in order to damage the credentials of the Christian revelation – namely, to the biblical reports of miracles in general and to the Resurrection in particular – the norm is successful in showing that these reports would be rejected for the reasons he gives, if they occurred in contexts in which religious faith was not involved.

Consider a non-biblical example. Towards the end of his dialogue *Agricola*, the august Roman historian Tacitus describes a decisive battle with the aboriginal tribes north of Perth in Scotland at "Mount Grampius." The location of the battle has never been identified, but supporting archaeological traces of Agricola's campaign have been discovered, and there is nothing improbable about a battle, in the circumstances Tacitus describes, that would invite the application of Hume's argument. *Hence* we accept the testimony. Now at the end of the same historian's account of Germany, when he surveys the land to the east, he concludes: "What comes after them is the stuff of fables: Hellusii and Oxiones with the faces and features of men, but the bodies and limbs of animals. Concerning such unverifiables I will express no opinion." Since the judicious Tacitus merely itemizes fables and then suspends judgement, we are not faced with a report to assess, however far-fetched. But suppose he had written:

In the borderlands of the world to the east of the Dneiper there are human-like creatures who (A) have a single eye in the middle of their skulls, and (B) do not move as other creatures do, but when they desire to traverse a distance they merely wish it so, whereupon they disappear in the place they were in and reappear in the place where they wish to be. These creatures are called cyclopoids.

What would be the result of applying Hume's norm of historical rationality to this supposed report? Item (A) has some trace of corroboration in the *Odyssey* but lacks any zoological or archaeological support, and never has occurred in our experience. Hence, despite Tacitus's reputation, we are unlikely to accept as true the report I am supposing him to have given. It is too *improbable*. Item (B) is of a different order. Like the reconstitution of a dead body into a living man, such wish-locomotion would be violation of a whole cluster of what we are justified in taking as laws of nature, and as such there is a "direct and full *proof*, from the nature of the [alleged] fact" against its existence. Cyclopoids (B) just do not exist. The report is at variance with the norm of historical rationality formalized in Hume's argument because the report concerns *the impossible* as that concept would normally be understood and is commonly applied.

Now it is largely agreed that despite his obvious *inclination* to regard miracles as impossible, Hume did not put forward the official version of his *a priori* argument in order to *prove* that miracles are impossible. What he set out to show was that it would never be reasonable to believe on the basis of reported evidence that a miracle had taken place. But once it is granted that he, and you and I, never have ourselves experienced a miracle in the sense of something which is clearly at variance with what we call laws of nature, the effective *practical* difference between "never reasonable to believe" and "impossible" becomes negligible. In terms of what we have rational warrant to believe, there is no difference between rejecting ancient testimony to cyclopoid (B) – or the Resurrection – on the grounds that it conflicts with all our experience as codified in the laws of nature, and saying that cyclopoid (B) – or the Resurrection – is "impossible" as that word is commonly employed. It is this, I suggest, which gives Hume's *a priori* argument, his "check to all kinds of superstitious delusion" (EHU 10.1, 110), its peculiarly sharp ambiguity in which one feels, and is, taken to a more radical conclusion than one believes to be warranted.[19]

The "preposterous distribution . . . of praise and blame"

The attention justly given to the *Treatise* as, among other achievements, Hume's main contribution to analytic moral philosophy has tended to eclipse his other account of social and personal morality in the second *Enquiry*.[20] This account, supplemented by the final part of the *Dialogues* and the essay "Of Suicide," has two things to say about religion which to many people are as unacceptable at the end of the twentieth century as they were when Hume first published his ideas in the middle of the eighteenth. The first is that the precepts of morality and our practical obligations to observe them are independent of religious beliefs and religious sanctions. The second is that when religion does intrude into morality, it serves only to distort natural morality by the introduction of "frivolous species of merit" and the creation of artificial crimes. This distortion results in "a preposterous distribution . . . of praise and blame" and in gratuitous human suffering (DNR 12, 222).

1. The independence of morality. It is a matter of fact everywhere observable, Hume contends in the second *Enquiry*, that normal human beings are not absolutely indifferent to the weal and woe of others physically or imaginatively near to them. This responsiveness to other people is, according to Hume, ultimately traceable to the operation of "sympathy," the natural trait by means of which we actually share in, or are directly moved by, the feelings of others. Now, continues Hume, since human beings have to a certain extent a common nature, what is misery to one, is misery to most; and what produces happiness in one, produces happiness in most. Thus it is that certain devices and doings attract our *general* condemnation because they commonly produce misery, while others attract our *general* approval because they commonly promote happiness. This generality of approval for whatever promotes happiness in human society is, according to Hume, the ultimate source of moral discriminations. On this showing, moral rules (and the particular laws of a state) will, in the absence of distorting prejudices or misinformation, express the general policies which have been found to promote the objectives of minimizing misery and maximizing happiness. The sources of moral rules are thus located in the good of society and its members, and not in man's relation to God or to some other non-worldly or "spiritual" entity. The point was well made by the Emperor Julian in A.D. 361 when he rejected the Judeo-Christian claim to have had a special moral revelation in the Ten Commandments: "Except for the commandment 'Thou shalt not worship other gods' and 'Remember the sabbath day,' what nation is there . . . which does NOT think it ought to keep the other commandments?"[21] Hume would have agreed. The *other* commandments commend themselves to us quite apart from religion because they are perceived to codify some of the conduct generally needed to ensure

the happiness of any society, and this perception is true, as a matter of common human experience, not as a result of surprising information conveyed by a God on Mount Sinai.

But even if it is conceded that moral rules have, or need have, no source beyond our open-minded and "natural" (I return to this word shortly) approval of what is generally useful in promoting happiness, surely our commitment to observing them depends upon religion? Do we not to this day, and not infrequently, come across utterances by politicians, religious believers, and laymen, blaming the increase of crime and the drop in standards of behaviour upon *lack* of religious belief and teaching? And if religious teaching (as Hume and the Emperor Julian would have it) is not a necessary precondition for "discovering" that, for example, stealing and murder have to be prohibited, then it must at least be the case that religion is a necessary condition for our enforcement of these commandments upon ourselves as individuals when we are disinclined to obey them. In short, religion is the source of moral *obligation*.

Hume would disagree: "the *moral obligation* holds proportion with the *usefulness*" (EPM 4, 206). Yes, but that is to assert a proportion between obligation and usefulness, not to give an account of the source of the obligation. We may agree that the more something contributes happiness to individuals or to society, the more we ought to do it. But the nature of "ought" is not thereby explained.

Hume's explanation, his highly distinctive secular analysis of obligation, is for the most part located in the conclusion to the second *Enquiry* (EPM 9.2). What he there produces is an account of what he calls "our interested *obligation*" to virtue. It is "interested" because it is a combination of all the factors which press upon us, as mentally normal people in our normal social relations. These factors include our self-interest in doing to others what we would wish others to do to us; our natural interchange of sympathy; our desire to be well thought of by our neighbours; our wish to live at ease with ourselves when "inward peace of mind, consciousness of integrity, a satisfactory review of our own conduct" is part of what is required to be a happy person (EPM 9.2, 283). But if these are some of the factors which interest us in what is called morality, how do they add up to an *obligation*? Because, apart from being understandable and capable of analysis into separate influences, they constitute something naturally *felt*, and feelings, unlike thoughts or facts in Hume's estimation, constitute direct sources of action. Feelings, or, in Hume's preferred term, "passions," are the mainsprings of action.

Now, clearly, a lot more deserves to be said and will no doubt be said about Hume's account of social morality, but for present purposes the point is that however debatable the outcome, what Hume offers is a serious account of morality that makes no reference whatsoever to God, or to religious belief or teaching. But Hume goes further than a separation of religion and morality. He also holds that the input of religion into morality is positively mischievous in the sense that religion invents crimes (such as suicide or the use of contraceptives) which are not natural crimes, that is, are not activities which normally produce misery; and it invents virtues (such as self-mortification or doctrinal orthodoxy) which are not natural virtues, that is, are not activities which normally promote happiness in oneself or others.

2. The religious distortion of morality. The key to the point Hume is making is to be found in my insistent use of such phrases as "in the absence of distorting prejudices," "natural approval," and "normal people." The point is that Hume is attempting to characterize morality as it is or would be when it operates between *normal* people in *natural* conditions: "normal" in the sense (a) that the person or persons concerned are not pathologically defective (from whatever cause) in their emotional responses, feelings, or levels of intelligence, and "natural" in the sense (b) that the conditions do *not* include special influences which overcome normal feelings. Item (a) will make a special case of, for example, the criminally insane, or those whose conduct is explainable in terms of their real lack of the feelings which commonly operate between persons (for example, the person whose hurt to children really does not feel to him or her as a hurt because that was the way they themselves were treated). In such cases, those who follow the direction of Hume's thought would conclude that special treatment, not *moral* disapproval, is called for: *moral* disapproval being reserved for the voluntary actions of people who are normal in the sense just given. Item (b), vastly more serious because capable of vastly more general operation than (a), attempts to single out as "unnatural" conduct which over-rides the natural system of morality (based upon happiness) in the interests of non-moral "superstitions." The superstitions Hume was thinking about

as over-riding natural morality were religious, those in which the commitment to the religion overcame all sense of natural good, for example, in the burning of witches and heretics and the righteous infliction of pain on others for their (non-natural) good, or for the good of the religion per se. But the twentieth century could add political superstitions – National Socialist and Marxist – in which all feelings of natural good have given way (and have *really* given way in the feelings of the many concerned) to the non-natural good which consists of loyalty to the party or state irrespective of the happiness resulting, or the misery caused to actual men and women.

Hume's substantial account of secular, this-worldly, utilitarian morality in the second *Enquiry* is certainly polished literature, but it is also, as I hope to have shown, revolutionary thought of ever-widening application. The revolution is still going on, and the thought is still contentious.[22] If it were not, it is difficult to see why so often religion and morality are still popularly linked, or how, for example, a major religion can still stigmatize as sinful the natural (Hume's sense) good inherent in effective family planning.

Natural belief

If, as Hume maintains, the evidence of natural religion is at best highly problematic and ambiguous, if the evidence of revelation is such as would not be accepted if it came from a non-religious source, if we can both understand the natural causes of religion and deplore its unnatural effects upon conduct, and if, as seems to be Hume's argued position at the beginning and end of both the first *Enquiry* and the *Dialogues*, all speculations about "the powers and operations of one universal spirit" are beyond our understanding (DNR 1, 135), why is it that religious belief persists, even among well-informed people?

One possible answer is that which seems to be implied by a full reading of Hume on religion: that belief in the Divine retains just enough wisps of rational support for our propensity to see the world as intelligible, in conjunction with the still-operating causes of religion, to sustain religion despite philosophical criticism. Another answer, not strictly an answer at all, is characterized by the gesture of astonishment with which Hume ends his essay on miracles in the first *Enquiry*: the gesture which has led some apologists into the false view that Hume is advocating fideism as a defensible account of how we do, and why we should, retain religious belief. But a third, and potentially fruitful answer, is sometimes given on Hume's behalf: that belief in the Divine is a natural belief.

The concept of a natural belief is assembled from the characteristics of those few and very general beliefs which Hume identifies as ultimately resistant to all sceptical argument – belief in the continuous existence of an external world independent of our perception of that world, belief that the regularities of the past will continue into the future, that our senses are normally reliable, are examples. The characteristics of these "instincts and propensities of nature," as Hume sometimes calls them, are

a. That they are arrived at prior to any process of reasoning, and cannot for long be dislodged by any process of sceptical reasoning because:

b. They are indispensable as presuppositions of knowledge and conduct for any sentient being who lives in a coherent relation to the given appearances of things. In practical terms, no one can act in the world unless he has these beliefs. Hence:

c. These beliefs are universal – not merely the cherished or dominant or unquestioned assumptions of a particular culture or of a learned or unlearned population, but such as all human beings always and everywhere have.

Set out thus, it is all but obvious that belief in the Divine does not have the characteristics of a natural belief.[23] Even if it could be shown that for most, or at least for many people, religious belief is attained and retained according to (a), it is an incontrovertible matter of fact that religious belief is not universal in the manner of (c). It is also evident that individuals can and do act perfectly adequately in the world without religious belief, and that religious belief is not an epistemic requirement for any coherent relation to the given appearances of things, that is, (b) does not hold either.

There is, moreover, no clear evidence that Hume ever seriously entertained the thought that belief in the Divine might be an instinct of nature impervious to scepticism in the way that our belief in an external world is. The nearest we get to such a thought is Cleanthes' restatement of the design argument in which there is an appeal: "tell me, from your own feeling, if the idea of a contriver does not immediately flow in upon you with a force like that of sensation" followed by a reference to the universal and "irresistible" influence of the argument (the design argument) for theism (see DNR 3, 154, quoted as (3) in Section II above). The force of Cleanthes' point seems to be that our natural propensity to see and expect order in nature is so close to seeing an *orderer* that our natural belief in the former brings with it the latter. But even if Cleanthes, contrary to the majority view among commentators, can be taken to be speaking for Hume, his view is defective in this matter. In the first place, as Philo points out near the end of Part 4 of the *Dialogues* and again in Part 7, the activity of an ordering agent is not the only possible explanation of order; and second, even if the *feeling* that "a contriver" is responsible for the ordered universe is difficult to keep at bay with sceptical argument, it is not "irresistible" because it is resisted, and it is not "universal" because at least some people do not succumb to the influence of the argument for theism. That something is widely felt, influential, and difficult to dislodge by argument is not of itself sufficient to give it the exceptionally privileged status of a natural belief. But this still leaves Hume with the difficulty – which he partly faces in the *Natural History of Religion* – of explaining the persistence of religious belief once the arguments and evidence for it are shown to be all but negligible.

Hume did not and perhaps could not have anticipated the nineteenth-century explanation for this persistence developed by Schopenhauer, Feuerbach, and above all by Freud: namely, that we are so constituted that emotionally and psychologically (but not rationally and epistemically) we *need* some sort of religious belief. Nor could Hume have expected that his sceptical philosophy of religion would lead to a re-deployment of fideism or that his "natural belief," counter to extreme scepticism, would suggest the development of other and new defences of Christianity. How did this come about?

In the first place Hume's undermining of the traditional rational grounds for belief in God was so thorough that once his position had been absorbed into the mainstreams of European thought (via, among others, d'Holbach, Kant, and Shelley) a fundamental reappraisal of the nature of religion commenced. Thus, first Schleiermacher (1768–1834) and later Kierkegaard (1813–55) sought to make religion rely less on evidence and reason, and more upon feeling, subjective experience, and faith. Such a fideistic reliance largely evades Hume's rationalistic critique, but it does so at the risk of making religious belief arbitrary, while at the same time both inviting Hume-type accounts of its "natural history" and leaving intact his criticism of its moral and social effects.

Theological fideism has a philosophical counterpart in what Terence Penelhum has called "The Parity Argument."[24] The argument can be used by someone who agrees, as Hume does, with the sceptical tradition "that at least some of the fundamental philosophical commitments of secular common sense are without rational foundation" but who nevertheless yields to our natural tendency to believe them: "The Parity Argument suggests to such a person that he is inconsistent if he refuses to yield also to the demands of religious belief merely because he considers that it, too, does not have a rational foundation."[25]

The core objection to this argument is that the inconsistency claimed is not an inconsistency unless it can be shown that the pressure to yield to religious belief is *equal in all respects* to the pressure to yield to natural beliefs. But set against the criteria (a), (b), and (c) mentioned earlier in this section, we have already seen that the meta-rational demands to believe in the Divine are in many respects *not* equal to the demands to believe in, for example, an external world. An additional objection to the Parity Argument is that if it justifies belief in the Divine, it also justifies *any* cherished personal or group belief for which there is no rational foundation, for example, that there are witches with diabolical and supernatural powers. It will be noted that Hume's account of "natural beliefs" cannot be used to justify such cherished irrationalities because the criteria for a natural belief are enormously tougher than the irrationality criterion appealed to in the Parity Argument.

Despite the failure to identify belief in the Divine as a genuine natural belief, modern philosophical theology is marked with attempts to employ some notion of natural belief for apologetic purposes. Thus, for example, John Hick asserts an analogy between "the religious person's claim to be conscious of God and any man's claim to be conscious of the physical world as an environment, existing independently of himself."[26] The same thought turns up in the writings of John Macquarrie: "It is not inappropriate to compare the conviction of the independent reality of God to the conviction of the independent reality of the world or of other selves,"[27] and again, more recently, in the writings of Hans Kung: "The history of modern epistemology from Descartes, Hume and Kant, to Popper and Lorenz, has – it seems to me – made clear that the fact of any reality at all independent of our consciousness can be accepted only as an act of trust"; *hence* a like act of trust is appropriate to belief in God.[28] A similar move, but differently presented, is evident in the American school of "Basic Belief Apologists," associated with Alvin Plantinga.[29]

These moves derive from Hume's "natural belief" counter to excessive scepticism, but the derivation is less acceptable than Hume's original counter for the two reasons already identified in connection with the Parity Argument; namely, the derivation admits *any* belief which one may choose to assert baselessly, and it fails to differentiate between an optional belief like belief in God (optional since plainly some of us do not have it) and a non-optional belief like belief in an external world:

To whatever length any one may push his speculative principles of scepticism, he must act, I own, and live, and converse like other men; and for this conduct he is not obliged to give any other reason than the absolute necessity he lies under of so doing.   (DNR 1, 134)

No such absolute necessity attaches to any particular belief in the Divine.

I said above that there are three possible ways in which Hume could have responded to the puzzle about the resistance of religious belief to sceptical reasoning. He does not take the way of natural belief. He works at the way of causal explanations for religion coupled with a vestigial rationality. The third way, characterized by the gesture of astonishment with which Hume ends his essay "Of Miracles," is perhaps a very realistic perception of the fundamental irrationality of man concerning those specially cherished beliefs called religious: "So that, upon the whole, we may conclude, that the *Christian Religion* not only was at first attended with miracles, but even at this day cannot be believed by any reasonable person without one" (EHU 10, 131). This is not, as some would have it, to clear the way for fideistic Christianity – a conception alien both to Hume's mitigated scepticism and to his worldly morality. It is simply to note the "continued miracle" by which religious faith survives in the secular world against all the intellectual odds.

NOTES

1 See my "Hume's Attenuated Deism," *Archiv für Geschichte der Philosophie* 65 (1983): 160–73.

2 For more on Hume's distinction between superstition and enthusiasm and true religion, see his unpublished Preface to the *History of England*, quoted in full in Ernest Campbell Mossner, *Life of David Hume* (Edinburgh, 1954) pp. 306–7. For a discussion of the political dimensions of the distinction, see Knud Haakonssen, "The Structure of Hume's Political Theory," in this volume.

3 Norman Kemp Smith, *The Philosophy of David Hume* (London, 1941), particularly chaps. 5 and 21.

4 The suggestion is endorsed in David Wootton's important article "Hume's 'Of Miracles'," in *Studies in the Philosophy of the Scottish Enlightenment*, ed. M. A. Stewart (Oxford, 1990), p. 199. Wootton is mainly concerned with the background influences on Hume.

5 For a full development of the interpretation that follows, see my *Hume's Philosophy of Religion*, 2d ed. (London, 1988). For further works in the same area and other recent exegesis of the *Dialogues*, see note 8.

6 The matter is well documented by David Berman in his *A History of Atheism in Britain* (London, 1988).

7 See my *Hume's Philosophy of Religion*, pp. 219–23.

8 The only case where this may need special justification is the *Dialogues*, where the three speakers are in evident conflict and it is not always clear who has the better of the argument. Given that Hume's model is Cicero, and the balanced presentation exemplified by *De Natura Deorum*, and not Plato, with (generally) his pro-Socratic yes-men, it is still possible to say that (a) Demea speaks very little for Hume and in good part for both the high rationalism of Samuel Clarke and, somewhat perversely, for such "blind belief" as Hume admits into the discussion; (b) Cleanthes speaks somewhat more for Hume, especially when he opposes Demea, but mostly for the moderate rationalists and users of the *a posteriori* arguments whose best-known representative is Joseph Butler; (c) Philo is closest to Hume's mouthpiece but inclined to overstate his position so that retreat is occasionally possible. There is a considerable literature on the interpretation of the *Dialogues*. See, in particular, Norman Kemp Smith's introductory material to his edition of the *Dialogues* (Oxford, 1935); James Noxon, "Hume's Agnosticism," *Philosophical Review* 73

(1964): 248–61; my *Hume's Philosophy of Religion*, chap. 12; *Hume's Dialogues concerning Natural Religion*, ed. Nelson Pike (New York, 1970); *Hume: Dialogues concerning Natural Religion*, ed. Stanley Tweyman (Toronto, 1990); Stanley Tweyman, *Scepticism and Belief in Hume's Dialogues* (The Hague, 1986).

9 Note, for example, Psalm 19; 2 Maccabees 7:28; Romans 1:20.

10 See, for example, Xenophon: *Memorabilia*, 1.4, 6–7; Plato: *Timaeus*, 47; Cicero: *De Natura Deorum*, 2, 34–5.

11 Note particularly the remarkably modern sounding *The Fitness of the Environment* by L. J. Henderson (New York, 1913), and, among more recent books, Alvin Plantinga, *God and Other Minds* (Ithaca, 1967), and R. G. Swinburne, *The Existence of God* (Oxford, 1979), chap. 8.

12 It is difficult even now to identify any definitive statement of the design argument, and we know Hume encountered the same problem. See HL 1: 155.

13 See *An Encyclopaedia of Philosophy*, ed. G. H. R. Parkinson (London, 1988), pp. 339–42.

14 For a critical discussion of this and some of Hume's other objections to the design argument, see "The Argument from Design," R. G. Swinburne, *Philosophy* 43 (1968): 199–212. See also L. Dupre, "The Argument from Design Today," *Journal of Religion* 54 (1974): 1–12; Gary Doore, "The Argument from Design: Some Better Reasons for Agreeing with Hume," *Religious Studies* 16 (1980): 145–61; and my *Hume's Philosophy of Religion*, chaps. 2–3.

15 This and related matters were investigated in the Swinburne – Olding exchange in the early 1970s. See A. Olding, "The Argument from Design – a Reply to R. G. Swinburne," *Religious Studies* 7 (1971): 361–73; R. G. Swinburne, "The Argument from Design – a Defence," *Religious Studies* 8 (1972): 193–205; A. Olding, "Design – A Further Reply to R. G. Swinburne," *Religious Studies* 9 (1973): 229–32.

16 The first book-length reply was William Adams, *An Essay on Mr. Hume's Essay on Miracles* (London, 1752). George Campbell's reply, *A Dissertation on Miracles* (Edinburgh, 1762), elicited from Hume one of his rare philosophical replies: see HL 1: 348–51. The latest that I have seen are R. A. H. Larmer's *Water into Wine?* (Montreal, 1988) and Michael Levine's *Hume and the Problem of Miracles: A Solution* (Dordrecht, 1989).

17 See my "Contrary Miracles Concluded," *Hume Studies* (Supplement 1985): 1–14.

18 The controversy is most readably documented by Sir Leslie Stephen in his *History of English Thought in the Eighteenth Century*, chap. 4, sec. 4 (originally published in 1876). The area has been more thoroughly and

more recently worked over by R. M. Burns in *The Great Debate on Miracles* (London, 1981). For the interpretation of "Of Miracles" as a comment on the evidential significance of the Resurrection, see my "David Hume and the Eighteenth Century Interest in Miracles," *Hermathena* 99 (1964): 80–92. See also note 5 here.

19 As already indicated, the literature is very extensive. Among modern discussions of the logic and the interpretation of Hume's argument, the following provide some of the basic discussion: Antony Flew, *Hume's Philosophy of Belief* (London, 1961), chap. 8; *David Hume* (Oxford, 1986), chap. 5; my *Hume's Philosophy of Religion*, chap. 8. The above paraphrase of Hume's *a priori* argument is drawn from this latter work, pp. 152f. A useful collection of highly relevant articles (including Hume's essay) is provided in *Miracles*, ed. R. G. Swinburne (New York, 1989). Recent additions to the article literature include Dorothy Coleman, "Hume, Miracles and Lotteries," *Hume Studies* 14 (1988): 328–46; Robert J. Fogelin, "What Hume Actually Said about Miracles," *Hume Studies* 16 (1990): 81–6. See also notes 16–18 here.

20 For example, in *Hume's Moral Theory* (London, 1980), J. L. Mackie mentions the second *Enquiry* in his first sentence and then continues an otherwise admirable book as if only the *Treatise* existed. Similar treatment of the two works is evident in Jonathan Harrison's *Hume's Theory of Justice* (Oxford, 1981). Both Mackie and Harrison typify the standard and disproportionate emphasis on the *Treatise* as the only worthwhile source for Hume's contribution to ethics. A recent and useful study that gives some attention to *An Enquiry concerning the Principles of Morals* is Nicholas Capaldi, *Hume's Place in Moral Philosophy* (New York, 1989). For further discussions of Hume's ethics, see, in this volume, Terence Penelhum, "Hume's Moral Psychology," and David Fate Norton, "Hume, Human Nature, and the Foundations of Morality."

21 The Emperor Julian, *Against the Galilaeans*, 152D (Spanheim-Neumann pagination).

22 For further discussion, see David Fate Norton, "Hume, Atheism, and the Autonomy of Morals," in *Hume's Philosophy of Religion*, ed. M. Hester (Wake Forest, N.C., 1986), particularly pp. 120–33.

23 For a thorough examination of this thesis, see my *Hume's Philosophy of Religion*, chaps. 6–7.

24 See Terence Penelhum's important work, *God and Skepticism* (Dordrecht, 1983), particularly chaps. 2, 5, and 6.

25 Penelhum, *God and Skepticism*, p. 139.

26 John Hick, *Arguments for the Existence of God* (London, 1970), p. 110.

27 John Macquarrie, *God-Talk* (London, 1967), p. 244.

28 Hans Kung, *Eternal Life* (New York, 1984), p. 227. See also his *Does God*

Exist? (London, 1980), pp. 568–83. I am indebted to Philip Barnes for these references.

29 See particularly Alvin Plantinga, "Rationality and Religious Belief," in *Contemporary Philosophy of Religion*, ed. S. Kahn and D. Shatz (New York, 1982); and *Faith and Rationality: Reason and Belief in God*, ed. Alvin Plantinga and N. Wolterstorff (Notre Dame, 1983).

APPENDIX: HUME'S AUTOBIOGRAPHIES

I. A KIND OF HISTORY OF MY LIFE

In the spring of 1734, Hume accepted a position with a Bristol merchant. His philosophical endeavours were not going well, and so he determined to put these "aside for some time, in order the more effectually to resume them." As he travelled to Bristol, he wrote to an unnamed physician, probably John Arbuthnot, to ask advice about dealing with "the Disease of the Learned" that afflicted him. Whether or not Hume actually sent another copy of this letter is not known, but the surviving manuscript furnishes us with a valuable account of the first years of his adult life. The text printed here is based on the original manuscript deposited in the National Library of Scotland, and is published with the permission of the Royal Society of Edinburgh. The title is taken from the letter itself.

Sir

Not being acquainted with this hand-writing, you will probably look to the bottom to find the Subscription, & not finding any, will certainly wonder at this strange method of addressing to you. I must here in the beginning beg you to excuse it, & to perswade you to read what follows with some Attention, [and] must tell you, that this gives you an Opportunity to do a very good-natur'd Action, which I believe is the most powerful Argument I can use. I need not tell you, that I am your Countryman, a Scotchman; for without any such tye, I dare rely upon your Humanity, even to a perfect Stranger, such as I am. The Favour I beg of you is your Advice, & the reason why I address myself in particular to you need not be told. As one must be a skilful Physician, a man of Letters, of Wit, of Good Sense, & of great Humanity, to give me a satisfying Answer, I wish Fame had pointed out to me more Persons, in whom these Qualities are united, in order to have kept me some time in Suspense. This I say in the Sincerity of my Heart, & without any

345

Intention of making a Complement: For tho' it may seem necessary, that in the beginning of so unusual a Letter, I shou'd say some fine things, to bespeak your good Opinion, & remove any prejudices you may conceive at it, yet such an Endeavor to be witty, wou'd but ill suit with the present Condition of my Mind; which, I must confess, is not without Anxiety concerning the Judgement you will form of me. Trusting however to your Candor & Generosity, I shall, without further Preface, proceed to open up to you the present Condition of my Health, & to do that the more effectually shall give you a kind of History of my Life, after which you will easily learn, why I keep my Name a Secret.

You must know then that from my earliest Infancy, I found alwise a strong Inclination to Books & Letters. As our College Education in Scotland, extending little further than the Languages, ends commonly when we are about 14 or 15 Years of Age, I was after that left to my own Choice in my Reading, & found it encline me almost equally to Books of Reasoning & Philosophy, & to Poetry & the polite Authors. Every one, who is acquainted either with the Philosophers or Critics, knows that there is nothing yet establisht in either of these two Sciences, & that they contain little more than endless Disputes, even in the most fundamental Articles. Upon Examination of these, I found a certain Boldness of Temper, growing in me, which was not enclin'd to submit to any Authority in these Subjects, but led me to seek out some new Medium, by which Truth might be establisht. After much Study, & Reflection on this, at last, when I was about 18 Years of Age, there seem'd to be open'd up to me a new Scene of Thought, which transported me beyond Measure, & made me, with an Ardor natural to young men, throw up every other Pleasure or Business to apply entirely to it. The Law which was the Business I design'd to follow, appear'd nauseous to me, & I cou'd think of no other way of pushing my Fortune in the World, but that of a Scholar & Philosopher. I was infinitely happy in this Course of Life for some Months; till at last, about the beginning of Septr 1729, all my Ardor seem'd in a moment to be extinguisht, & I cou'd no longer raise my Mind to that pitch, which formerly gave me such excessive Pleasure. I felt no Uneasyness or Want of Spirits, when I laid aside my Book; & therefore never imagind there was any bodily Distemper in the Case, but that my Coldness proceeded from a Laziness of Temper, which must be overcome by redoubling my Application. In this Condition I remain'd for nine Months, very uneasy to myself, as you may well imagine, but without growing any worse, which was a Miracle.

There was another particular, which contributed more than any thing, to waste my Spirits & bring on me this Distemper, which was, that having read many Books of Morality, such as Cicero, Seneca & Plutarch, & being smit with their beautiful Representations of Virtue & Philosophy, I undertook the Improvement of my Temper & Will, along with my Reason & Understanding. I was continually fortifying myself with Reflections against Death, & Poverty, & Shame, & Pain, & all the other Calamities of Life. These no doubt are exceeding useful, when join'd with an active Life; because the Occasion being presented along with the Reflection, works it into the Soul, & makes it take a deep Impression, but in Solitude they serve to little other Purpose, than to waste the Spirits, the Force of the Mind meeting with no Resistance, but wasting itself in the Air, like our Arm when it misses its Aim. This however I did not learn but by Experience, & till I had already ruin'd my Health, tho' I was not sensible of it.

Some Scurvy Spots broke out on my Fingers, the first Winter I fell ill, about which I consulted a very knowing Physician, who gave me some Medicines, that remov'd these Symptoms, & at the same time gave me a Warning against the Vapors, which, tho I was laboring under at that time, I fancy'd myself so far remov'd from, & indeed from any other Disease, except a slight Scurvy, that I despis'd his Warning. At last about Aprile 1730, when I was 19 Years of Age, a Symptom, which I had notic'd a little from the beginning, encreas'd considerably, so that tho' it was no Uneasyness, the Novelty of it made me ask Advice. It was what they call a Ptyalism or Watryness in the mouth. Upon my mentioning it to my Physician, he laught at me, & told me I was now a Brother, for that I had fairly got the Disease of the Learned. Of this he found great Difficulty to perswade me, finding in myself nothing of that lowness of Spirit, which those, who labor under that Distemper so much complain of. However upon his Advice, I went under a Course of Bitters, & Anti-hysteric Pills. Drunk an English Pint of Claret Wine every Day, & rode 8 or 10 Scotch Miles. This I continu'd for about 7 Months after.

Tho I was sorry to find myself engag'd with so tedious a Distemper yet the Knowledge of it, set me very much at ease, by satisfying me that my former Coldness, proceeded not from any Defect of Temper or Genius, but from a Disease, to which any one may be subject. I now began to take some Indulgence to myself; studied moderately, & only when I found my Spirits at their highest Pitch, leaving off before I was weary, & trifling away the rest of my Time in the best manner I could. In this way, I liv'd with Satisfaction enough; and on my return to Town next Winter found my Spirits very much recruited, so that, tho they sunk under me in the higher Flights of Genius, yet I was able to make considerable Progress in my former Designs. I was very regular in my Diet & way of Life from the beginning, & all that Winter, made it a constant Rule to ride twice or thrice a week, & walk every day. For these Reasons, I expected when I return'd to the Countrey, & cou'd renew my Exercise with less Interruption, that I wou'd perfectly recover. But in this I was much mistaken. For next Summer, about May 1731 there grew upon [me] a very ravenous Appetite, & as quick a Digestion, which I at first took for a good Symptom, & was very much surpriz'd to find it bring back a Palpitation of Heart, which I had felt very little of before. This Appetite, however, had an Effect very unusual, which was to nourish me extremely; so that in 6 weeks time I past from the one extreme to the other, & being before tall, lean, & rawbon'd became on a sudden, the most sturdy, robust, healthful-like Fellow you have seen, with a ruddy Complexion & a chearful Countenance. In excuse for my Riding, & care of my Health, I alwise said, that I was afraid of a Consumption; which was readily believ'd from my Looks; but now every Body congratulate me upon my thorow Recovery. This unnatural Appetite wore off by degrees, but left me as a Legacy, the same Palpitation of the heart in a small degree, & a good deal of Wind in my Stomach, which comes away easily, & without any bad Gout, as is ordinary. However, these Symptoms are little or no Uneasyness to me. I eat well; I sleep well. Have no lowness of Spirits; at least never more than what one of the best Health may feel, from too full a meal, from sitting too near a Fire, & even that degree I feel very seldom, & never almost in the Morning or Forenoon. Those who live in the same Family with me, & see me at all times, cannot observe the least Alteration in my Humor, & rather think me a better Companion than I was before, as choosing to pass more of my time with them. This gave me such Hopes, that I scarce ever mist a days riding, except in the Winter-time; & last Summer undertook a very laborious task, which was to travel 8 Miles every Morning & as many in the Forenoon, to & from a mineral Well of some Reputation. I renew'd the Bitters & Anti-hysteric Pills twice, along with Anti-scorbutic Juices last Spring, but without any considerable Effect, except abating the Symptoms for a little time.

Thus I have given you a full account of the Condition of my Body, & without staying to ask Pardon, as I ought to do, for so tedious a Story, shall explain to you how my Mind stood all this time, which on every Occasion, especially in this Distemper, have a very near Connexion together. Having now Time & Leizure to cool my inflam'd Imaginations, I began to consider seriously, how I shou'd proceed in my Philosophical Enquiries. I found that the moral Philosophy transmitted to us by Antiquity, labor'd under the same Inconvenience that has been found in their natural Philosophy, of being entirely Hypothetical, & depending more upon Invention than Experience. Every one consulted his Fancy in erecting Schemes of Virtue & of Happiness, without regarding human Nature, upon which every moral Conclusion must depend. This therefore I resolved to make my principal Study, & the Source from which I wou'd derive every Truth in Criticism as well as Morality. I believe 'tis a certain Fact that most of the Philosophers who have gone before us, have been overthrown by the Greatness of their Genius, &

that little more is requir'd to make a man succeed in this Study than to throw off all Prejudices either for his own Opinions or for th[ose] of others. At least this is all I have to depend on for the Truth of my Reasonings, which I have multiply'd to such a degree, that within these three Years, I find I have scribled many a Quire of Paper, in which there is nothing contain'd but my own Inventions. This with the Reading most of the celebrated Books in Latin, French & English, & acquiring the Italian, you may think a sufficient Business for one in perfect Health; & so it wou'd, had it been done to any Purpose: But my Disease was a cruel Incumbrance on me. I found that I was not able to follow out any Train of Thought, by one continued Stretch of View, but by repeated Interruptions, & by refreshing my Eye from Time to Time upon other Objects. Yet with this Inconvenience I have collected the rude Materials for many Volume; but in reducing these to Words, when one must bring the Idea he comprehended in gross, nearer to him so as to contemplate its minutest Parts, & keep it steddily in his Eye, so as to copy these Parts in Order, this I found impracticable for me, nor were my Spirits equal to so severe an Employment. Here lay my greatest Calamity. I had no Hopes of delivering my Opinions with such Elegance & Neatness, as to draw to me the Attention of the World, & I wou'd rather live & dye in Obscurity than produce them maim'd & imperfect.

Such a miserable Disappointment I scarce ever remember to have heard of. The small Distance betwixt me & perfect Health makes me the more uneasy in my present Situation. Tis a Weakness rather than a Lowness of Spirits which troubles me, & there seems to be as great a Difference betwixt my Distemper & common Vapors, as betwixt Vapors & Madness.

I have notic'd in the Writings of the French Mysticks, & in those of our Fanatics here, that, when they give a History of the Situation of their Souls, they mention a Coldness & Desertion of the Spirit, which frequently returns, & some of them, at the beginning, have been tormented with it many Years. As this kind of Devotion depends entirely on the Force of Passion, & consequently of the Animal Spirits, I have often thought that their Case & mine were pretty parralel, & that their rapturous Admirations might discompose the Fabric of the Nerves & Brain, as much as profound Reflections, & that warmth or Enthusiasm which is inseperable from them.

However this may be, I have not come out of the Cloud so well as they commonly tell us they have done, or rather began to despair of ever recovering. To keep myself from being Melancholy on so dismal a Prospect, my only Security was in peevish Reflections on the Vanity of the World & of all humane Glory; which, however just Sentiments they may be esteem'd, I have found can never be sincere, except in those who are possest of them. Being sensible that all my Philosophy wou'd never made me contented in my present Situation, I began to rouze up myself; & being encourag'd by Instances of Recovery from worse degrees of this Distemper, as well as by the Assurances of my Physicians, I began to think of something more effectual, than I had hitherto try'd. I found, that as there are two things very bad for this Distemper, Study & Idleness, so there are two things very good, Business & Diversion; & that my whole Time was spent betwixt the bad, with little or no Share of the Good. For this reason I resolved to seek out a more active Life, & tho' I cou'd not quit my Pretensions in Learning, but with my last Breath, to lay them aside for some time, in order the more effectually to resume them.

Upon Examination I found my Choice confin'd to two kinds of Life; that of a travelling Governor & that of a Merchant. The first, besides that it is in some respects an idle Life, was, I found, unfit for me; & that because from a sedentary & retir'd way of living, from a bashful Temper, & from a narrow Fortune, I had been little accustom'd to general Companies, & had not Confidence & Knowledge enough of the World to push my Fortune or be serviceable in that way. I therefore fixt my Choice upon a Merchant; & having got Recommendation to a considerable Trader in Bristol, I am just now hastening thither, with a Resolution to forget myself, & every thing that is past, to engage myself, as far as is possible, in that Course of Life, & to toss about the World, from the one Pole to the other, till I leave this Distemper behind me.

As I am come to London in my way to Bristol, I have resolved, if possible, to get your Advice, tho' I shou'd take this absurd Method of procuring it. All the Physicians, I have consulted, tho' very able, cou'd never enter into my Distemper; because not being Persons of great Learning beyond their own Profession, they were unacquainted with these Motions of the Mind. Your Fame pointed you out as the properest Person to resolve my Doubts, & I was determin'd to have some bodies Opinion, which I cou'd rest upon in all the Varieties of Fears & Hopes, incident to so lingering a Distemper. I hope I have been particular enough in describing the Symptoms to allow you to form a Judgement; or rather perhaps have been too particular. But you know 'tis a Symptom of this Distemper to delight in complaining & talking of itself.

The Questions I wou'd humbly propose to you are: Whether among all these Scholars, you have been acquainted with, you have ever known any affected in this manner? Whether I can ever hope for a Recovery? Whether I must long wait for it? Whether my Recovery will ever be perfect, & my Spirits regain their former Spring & Vigor, so as to endure the Fatigue of deep & abstruse thinking? Whether I have taken a right way to recover? I believe all proper Medicines have been us'd, & therefore I need mention nothing of them.

II. MY OWN LIFE

By April 1776, Hume was convinced that the bowel disorder that had afflicted him for some months would soon lead to his death. Just prior to setting out for Bath, there to seek a cure from the waters, he prepared his will and the brief autobiography that follows. The title is Hume's own; the text printed here is that of the first edition of this work, The Life of David Hume, Esq. Written by Himself, *London, 1777.*

It is difficult for a man to speak long of himself without vanity; therefore, I shall be short. It may be thought an instance of vanity that I pretend at all to write my life; but this Narrative shall contain little more than the History of my Writings; as, indeed, almost all my life has been spent in literary pursuits and occupations. The first success of most of my writings was not such as to be an object of vanity.

I was born the 26th of April 1711, old style, at Edinburgh. I was of a good family, both by father and mother: my father's family is a branch of the Earl of Home's, or Hume's; and my ancestors had been proprietors of the estate, which my brother possesses, for several generations. My mother was daughter of Sir David Falconer, President of the College of Justice: the title of Lord Halkerton came by succession to her brother.

My family, however, was not rich, and being myself a younger brother, my patrimony, according to the mode of my country, was of course very slender. My father, who passed for a man of parts, died when I was an infant, leaving me, with an elder brother and a sister, under the care of our mother, a woman of singular merit, who, though young and handsome, devoted herself entirely to the rearing and educating of her children. I passed through the ordinary course of education with success, and was seized very early with a passion for literature, which has been the ruling passion of my life, and the great source of my enjoyments. My studious disposition, my sobriety, and my industry, gave my family a notion that the law was a proper profession for me; but I found an unsurmountable aversion to every thing but the pursuits of philosophy and general learning; and while they fancied I was poring upon Voet and Vinnius, Cicero and Virgil were the authors which I was secretly devouring.

My very slender fortune, however, being unsuitable to this plan of life, and my health being a little broken by my ardent application, I was tempted, or rather forced, to make a very feeble trial for entering into a more active scene of life. In 1734, I went to Bristol, with some recommendations to eminent merchants, but in a few months found that scene totally unsuitable to me. I went over to France, with a view of prosecuting my studies in a country retreat; and I there laid that plan of life, which I have steadily and successfully pursued. I resolved to make a very rigid frugality supply my deficiency of fortune, to maintain unimpaired my independency, and to regard every object as contemptible, except the improvement of my talents in literature.

During my retreat in France, first at Reims, but chiefly at La Fleche, in Anjou, I composed my *Treatise of Human Nature*. After passing three years very agreeably in that country, I came over to London in 1737. In the end of 1738, I published my Treatise, and immediately went down to my mother and my brother, who lived at his country-house, and was employing himself very judiciously and successfully in the improvement of his fortune.

Never literary attempt was more unfortunate than my Treatise of Human Nature. It fell *dead-born from the press*, without reaching such distinction, as even to excite a murmur among the zealots. But being naturally of a cheerful and sanguine temper, I very soon recovered the blow, and prosecuted with great ardour my studies in the country. In 1742, I printed at Edinburgh the first part of my Essays: the work was favourably received, and soon made me entirely forget my former disappointment. I continued with my mother and brother in the country, and in that time recovered the knowledge of the Greek language, which I had too much neglected in my early youth.

In 1745, I received a letter from the Marquis of Annandale, inviting me to come and live with him in England; I found also, that the friends and family of that young nobleman were desirous of putting him under my care and direction, for the state of his mind and health required it. – I lived with him a twelvemonth. My appointments during that time made a considerable accession to my small fortune. I then received an invitation from General St. Clair to attend him as a secretary to his expedition, which was at first meant against Canada, but ended in an incursion on the coast of France. Next year, to wit, 1747, I received an invitation from the General to attend him in the same station in his military embassy to the courts of Vienna and Turin. I then wore the uniform of an officer, and was introduced at these courts as aid-de-camp to the general, along with Sir Harry Erskine and Captain Grant, now General Grant. These two years were almost the only interruptions which my studies have received during the course of my life: I passed them agreeably, and in good company; and my appointments, with my frugality, had made me reach a fortune, which I called independent, though most of my friends were inclined to smile when I said so; in short, I was now master of near a thousand pounds.

I had always entertained a notion, that my want of success in publishing the Treatise of Human Nature, had proceeded more from the manner than the matter, and that I had been guilty of a very usual indiscretion, in going to the press too early. I, therefore, cast the first part of that work anew in the Enquiry concerning Human Understanding, which was published while I was at Turin. But this piece was at first little more successful than the Treatise of Human Nature. On my return from Italy, I had the mortification to find all England in a ferment, on account of Dr. Middleton's Free Enquiry, while my performance was entirely overlooked and neglected. A new edition, which had been published at London of my Essays, moral and political, met not with a much better reception.

Such is the force of natural temper, that these disappointments made little or no impression on me. I went down in 1749, and lived two years with my brother at his country-house, for my mother was now dead. I there composed the second part of my Essays, which I called Political Discourses, and also my Enquiry concerning the Principles of Morals, which is another part of my treatise that I cast anew. Meanwhile, my bookseller, A. Millar, informed me, that my former publications (all but the unfortunate Treatise) were beginning to be the subject of conversation; that the sale of them was gradually increasing, and that new editions were demanded. Answers by Reverends, and Right Reverends, came out two or three in a year; and I found, by Dr. Warburton's railing, that the books were beginning to be esteemed in good company. However, I had fixed a resolution, which I inflexibly maintained, never to reply to any body; and not being very irascible in my temper, I have easily kept myself clear of all literary squabbles. These symptoms of a rising reputation gave me encouragement, as I was ever more disposed to see the favourable than unfavourable side of things; a turn of mind which it is more happy to possess, than to be born to an estate of ten thousand a year.

In 1751, I removed from the country to the town, the true scene for a man of letters. In 1752, were published at Edinburgh, where I then lived, my Political Discourses, the only work of mine that was successful on the first publication. It was well received abroad and at home. In the same year was published at London, my Enquiry concerning the Principles of Morals; which, in my own opinion (who ought not to judge on that subject), is of all my writings, historical, philosophical, or literary, incomparably the best. It came unnoticed and unobserved into the world.

In 1752, the Faculty of Advocates chose me their Librarian, an office from which I received little or no emolument, but which gave me the command of a large library. I then formed the plan of writing the History of England; but being frightened with the notion of continuing a narrative through a period of 1700 years, I commenced with the accession of the House of Stuart, an epoch when, I thought, the misrepresentations of faction began chiefly to take place. I was, I own, sanguine in my expectations of the success of this work. I thought that I was the only historian, that had at once neglected present power, interest, and authority, and the cry of popular prejudices; and as the subject was suited to every capacity, I expected proportional applause. But miserable was my disappointment: I was assailed by one cry of reproach, disapprobation, and even detestation; English, Scotch, and Irish, Whig and Tory, churchman and sectary, freethinker and religionist, patriot and courtier, united in their rage against the man, who had presumed to shed a generous tear for the fate of Charles I. and the Earl of Strafford; and after the first ebullitions of their fury were over, what was still more mortifying, the book seemed to sink into oblivion. Mr. Millar told me, that in a twelvemonth he sold only forty-five copies of it. I scarcely, indeed, heard of one man in the three kingdoms, considerable for rank or letters, that could endure the book. I must only except the primate of England, Dr. Herring, and the primate of Ireland, Dr. Stone, which seem two odd exceptions. These dignified prelates separately sent me messages not to be discouraged.

I was, however, I confess, discouraged; and had not the war been at that time breaking out between France and England, I had certainly retired to some provincial town of the former kingdom, have changed my name, and never more have returned to my native country. But as this scheme was not now practicable, and the subsequent volume was considerably advanced, I resolved to pick up courage and to persevere.

In this interval, I published at London my Natural History of Religion, along with some other small pieces: its public entry was rather obscure, except only that Dr. Hurd wrote a pamphlet against it, with all the illiberal petulance, arrogance, and scurrility, which distinguish the Warburtonian school. This pamphlet gave me some consolation for the otherwise indifferent reception of my performance.

In 1756, two years after the fall of the first volume, was published the second volume of my History, containing the period from the death of Charles I. till the Revolution. This performance happened to give less displeasure to the Whigs, and was better received. It not only rose itself, but helped to buoy up its unfortunate brother.

But though I had been taught by experience, that the Whig party were in possession of bestowing all places, both in the state and in literature, I was so little inclined to yield to their senseless clamour, that in above a hundred alterations, which farther study, reading, or reflection engaged me to make in the reigns of the two first Stuarts, I have made all of them invariably to the Tory side. It is ridiculous to consider the English constitution before that period as a regular plan of liberty.

In 1759, I published my History of the House of Tudor. The clamour against this performance was almost equal to that against the History of the two first Stuarts. The reign of Elizabeth was particularly obnoxious. But I was now callous against the impressions of public folly, and continued very peaceably and contentedly in my retreat at Edinburgh, to finish, in two volumes, the more early part of the English History, which I gave to the public in 1761, with tolerable, and but tolerable success.

But, notwithstanding this variety of winds and seasons, to which my writings had been exposed, they had still been making such advances, that the copy-money given me by the booksellers, much exceeded any thing formerly known in England; I was become not only independent, but opulent. I retired to my native country of Scotland, determined never more to set my foot out of it; and retaining the satisfaction of never having preferred a request to one great man, or even making advances of friendship to any of them. As I was now turned of fifty, I thought of passing all the rest of my life in this philosophical manner, when I received, in 1763, an invitation from the Earl of Hertford, with whom I was not in the least acquainted, to attend him on his embassy to Paris, with a near prospect of being appointed secretary to the embassy; and, in the meanwhile, of performing the functions of that office. This offer, however inviting, I at first declined, both because I was reluctant to begin connexions with the great, and because I was afraid that the civilities and gay company of Paris, would prove disagreeable to a person of my age and humour: but on his lordship's repeating the invitation, I accepted of it. I have every reason, both of pleasure and interest, to think myself happy in my connexions with that nobleman, as well as afterwards with his brother, General Conway.

Those who have not seen the strange effects of modes, will never imagine the reception I met with at Paris, from men and women of all ranks and stations. The more I [recoiled] from their excessive civilities, the more I was loaded with them. There is, however, a real satisfaction in living at Paris, from the great number of sensible, knowing, and polite company with which that city abounds above all places in the universe. I thought once of settling there for life.

I was appointed secretary to the embassy; and, in summer 1765, Lord Hertford left me, being appointed Lord Lieutenant of Ireland. I was *charge d'affaires* till the arrival of the Duke of Richmond, towards the end of the year. In the beginning of 1766, I left Paris, and next summer went to Edinburgh, with the same view as formerly, of burying myself in a philosophical retreat. I returned to that place, not richer, but with much more money, and a much larger income, by means of Lord Hertford's friendship, than I left it; and I was desirous of trying what superfluity could produce, as I had formerly made an experiment of a competency. But, in 1767, I received from Mr. Conway an invitation to be Under-secretary; and this invitation, both the character of the person, and my connexions with Lord Hertford, prevented me from declining. I returned to Edinburgh in 1769, very opulent (for

I possessed a revenue of 1000 l. a year), healthy, and though somewhat stricken in years, with the prospect of enjoying long my ease, and of seeing the increase of my reputation.

In spring 1775, I was struck with a disorder in my bowels, which at first gave me no alarm, but has since, as I apprehend it, become mortal and incurable. I now reckon upon a speedy dissolution. I have suffered very little pain from my disorder; and what is more strange, have, notwithstanding the great decline of my person, never suffered a moment's abatement of my spirits; insomuch, that were I to name the period of my life, which I should most choose to pass over again, I might be tempted to point to this later period. I possess the same ardour as ever in study, and the same gaiety in company. I consider, besides, that a man of sixty-five, by dying, cuts off only a few years of infirmities; and though I see many symptoms of my literary reputation's breaking out at last with additional lustre, I knew that I could have but few years to enjoy it. It is difficult to be more detached from life than I am at present.

To conclude historically with my own character. I am, or rather was (for that is the style I must now use in speaking of myself, which emboldens me the more to speak my sentiments); I was, I say, a man of mild dispositions, of command of temper, of an open, social, and cheerful humour, capable of attachment, but little susceptible of enmity, and of great moderation in all my passions. Even my love of literary fame, my ruling passion, never soured my temper, notwithstanding my frequent disappointments. My company was not unacceptable to the young and careless, as well as to the studious and literary; and as I took a particular pleasure in the company of modest women, I had no reason to be displeased with the reception I met with from them. In a word, though most men any wise eminent, have found reason to complain of calumny, I never was touched, or even attacked by her baleful tooth: and though I wantonly exposed myself to the rage of both civil and religious factions, they seemed to be disarmed in my behalf of their wonted fury. My friends never had occasion to vindicate any one circumstance of my character and conduct: not but that the zealots, we may well suppose, would have been glad to invent and propagate any story to my disadvantage, but they could never find any which they thought would wear the face of probability. I cannot say there is no vanity in making this funeral oration of myself, but I hope it is not a misplaced one; and this is a matter of fact which is easily cleared and ascertained.

April 18, 1776.

BIBLIOGRAPHY

This bibliography provides the reader with information about Hume's principal philosophical, historical, and literary works (to adopt his own classification of those works). It includes bibliographies of Hume's writing; a selection of biographical accounts; a selection of the principal early discussions of or responses to his work; and a selection of monographs and recent articles, primarily those cited earlier in this volume, on his work. Readers who wish to extend their researches into Hume and his thought will be able to consult the more extensive bibliographies listed. Books and articles cited in the essays, but not explicitly on Hume and his work, are not included in this bibliography. However, the names of authors and editors cited in the volume are included in the "Index of Names and Subjects."

For a list of the editions and abbreviations used in this volume, see "Method of Citation" in the front matter.

I. HUME'S WRITINGS

There is as yet no standard, critical edition of any of Hume's philosophical or historical publications. The closest thing to a critical edition of the principal philosophical writings is *The Philosophical Works of David Hume*, edited by T. H. Green and T. H. Grose (4 vols. London, 1874–5. Facsimile reprint. Darmstadt, 1964). This edition omits the *Abstract* and *A Letter from a Gentleman* and was based on an incomplete collation of the editions of Hume's own collection, *Essays and Treatises on Several Subjects*. Oxford University Press has recently undertaken to publish, under the editorship of Tom L. Beauchamp, David Fate Norton, and M. A. Stewart, a critical edition of Hume's philosophical, political, and literary works. As yet no publisher has undertaken a critical edition of *The History of England*.

For the present, then, it is necessary to rely on a melange of editions of Hume's works. With this in mind, the following list presents, in the approxi-

357

mate chronological order of original publication, the works of Hume mentioned in this volume.

A Treatise of Human Nature: Being an Attempt to introduce the experimental Method of Reasoning into Moral Subjects. 3 vols. London, 1739–40.

An Abstract of a Book lately Published; Entituled, A Treatise of Human Nature, &c. Wherein the Chief Argument of that Book is farther Illustrated and Explained. London, 1740. Prior to its rediscovery in the mid-1930s by J. M. Keynes and P. Sraffa and their publication of it (*An Abstract of a* Treatise of Human Nature *1740: A Pamphlet hitherto unknown by David Hume.* Cambridge, 1938. Reprint. Hamden, Conn., 1965), this work was often attributed to Adam Smith, but scholars are now widely agreed that Hume was its author.

Essays, Moral and Political. 2 vols. Edinburgh, 1741–2. Most of the essays in this work were published in 1758 as *Essays, Moral, Political, and Literary* in *Essays and Treatises on Several Subjects.* From 1760 to 1777 this collection was reprinted seven times under Hume's direction.

A Letter from a Gentleman to His Friend in Edinburgh: Containing Some Observations on A Specimen of the Principles concerning Religion and Morality, said to be maintain'd in a Book lately publish'd, intituled, A Treatise of Human Nature, &c. Edinburgh, 1745.

An Enquiry concerning Human Understanding, first published as *Philosophical Essays concerning Human Understanding.* London, 1748.

An Enquiry concerning the Principles of Morals. London, 1751.

Political Discourses. Edinburgh, 1752. The essays in this work were eventually to be included in *Essays and Treatises on Several Subjects,* a collection first published 1753–6, and from 1758 to 1777, reprinted eight times under Hume's direction.

Four Dissertations. London, 1757. The items in this work were eventually to be included in *Essays and Treatises on Several Subjects,* a collection first published 1753–6, and, from 1758–77, reprinted eight times under Hume's direction.

The History of England, from the Invasion of Julius Caesar to The Revolution in 1688. The work now published under this title was first published in six volumes over an eight-year period, 1754–62. It will be seen that Hume wrote his history, in one sense, backward. He first wrote about the period 1603–88, then about the period 1485–1603, and, finally, about the period from c. 50 B.C. to A.D. 1485. Following the publication of the last-written volumes, the work was re-published as a set and in chronological order. Complete new editions, prepared for the press by Hume, were published in 1763, 1767, 1770, 1772, 1773, and 1778. Between 1780 and c. 1900 the work was republished nearly two

hundred times. For further details about the posthumous editions of the
History, see *David Hume: Philosophical Historian*, ed. David Fate Norton and Richard H. Popkin. Indianapolis, 1965. Appendix A.

The original titles and dates of publication, in chronological order,
were

*The History of Great Britain. Vol. I. Containing the Reigns of James I and
Charles I.* Edinburgh, 1754.
*The History of Great Britain. Vol. II. Containing the Commonwealth,
and the Reigns of Charles II and James II.* London, 1757.
*The History of England, under the House of Tudor. Comprehending the
Reigns of K. Henry VII. K. Henry VIII. K. Edward VI. Q. Mary, and Q.
Elizabeth.* 2 vols. London, 1759.
*The History of England, from the Invasion of Julius Caesar to the Acces-
sion of Henry VII.* 2 vols. London, 1762.

The Life of David Hume, Esq. Written by Himself. London, 1777.
Dialogues concerning Natural Religion. London, 1779. Edited and published
by Hume's nephew, David Hume the Younger.
"Hume's Early Memoranda, 1729–1740." Edited by E. C. Mossner. *Journal
of the History of Ideas* 9 (1948): 492–518.
The Letters of David Hume. Edited by J. Y. T. Greig. 2 vols. Oxford: Claren-
don Press, 1932; reprinted 1969, 1983.
New Letters of David Hume. Edited by Raymond Klibansky and E. C.
Mossner. Oxford: Clarendon Press, 1954; reprinted 1970, 1983.

Many additional letters of Hume have been published since 1954, in
several different journals and books. A new edition of the Hume correspondence is being prepared for Oxford University Press by David
Raynor.

Computer readable collections

There are at the time this volume goes to press three computer readable (e-
text) collections of Hume's texts. The most comprehensive of these is
HUMETEXT 1.0, prepared by Tom L. Beauchamp, David Fate Norton, and
M. A. Stewart, and available from the Department of Philosophy, George-
town University. This collection includes Hume's philosophical, political,
and literary works, that is, all of the works listed above except *The History
of England*, letters, and "Early Memoranda." A slightly less extensive collection of these same works is available in the PAST MASTERS Series of the
Intelex Corporation. In addition, Hume's *Treatise* and two *Enquiries* are
available from Oxford University Press.

II. WORKS ON HUME

A. Bibliographies

Jessop, T. E. *A Bibliography of David Hume and of Scottish Philosophy from Francis Hutcheson to Lord Balfour.* London: Brown and Son, 1938. Reprint. New York, Garland, 1983. This is the standard bibliography of Hume's works. Additional information about the earliest editions of Hume's works may be found in Todd.

Hall, Roland. *Fifty Years of Hume Scholarship: A Bibliographical Guide.* Edinburgh, 1978. This bibliography includes the principal writing on Hume for the years 1900–24 and a comprehensive list of Hume literature from 1925 through 1976. Annual bibliographies for the years 1977–85, also prepared by Roland Hall, appeared in *Hume Studies,* a journal specializing in work on Hume, from 1978 to 1988. For literature on Hume published after 1985, the *Philosopher's Index* should be consulted.

Ikeda, Sadao. *David Hume and the Eighteenth Century British Thought: An Annotated Catalogue.* Tokyo: Chuo University Library, 1986. *Supplement,* 1988.

Todd, W. B. "David Hume, A Preliminary Bibliography," *Hume and the Enlightenment: Essays Presented to Ernest Campbell Mossner.* Edited by W. B. Todd. Edinburgh: Edinburgh University Press, 1974.

B. Bibliographies of Hume manuscripts

Greig, J. Y. T. and Harold Beynon. *Calendar of Hume MSS. in the Possession of the Royal Society of Edinburgh.* Edinburgh: Royal Society of Edinburgh, 1932. Reprint, Garland, 1990. Most of Hume's manuscripts and a large collection of his surviving correspondence were given to the Royal Society of Edinburgh by his nephew, David Hume, in 1838. These materials are now located in the National Library of Scotland.

Cunningham, Ian C. "The Arrangement of the Royal Society of Edinburgh's David Hume Collection," *The Bibliotheck* 15 (1988): 8–22.

C. Biographies and biographical accounts

Boswell, James. "An Account of My Last Interview with David Hume, Esq." In *Dialogues concerning Natural Religion.* Edited by Norman Kemp Smith. Oxford: Oxford University Press, 1935. Second edition with supplement. London: Thomas Nelson, 1947. Reprint. Indianapolis: Bobbs-Merrill [1962].

Burton, John Hill. *Life and Correspondence of David Hume*. Edinburgh, 1846. Reprint. New York: B. Franklin, 1967.

Graham, H. G. *Scottish Men of Letters in the Eighteenth Century*. London, 1901.

Greig, J. Y. T. *David Hume*. Oxford: Oxford University Press, 1931. Reprint. New York: Garland, 1983.

Mossner, Ernest Campbell. *The Forgotten Hume: Le bon David*. New York, Columbia University Press, 1943; reprint, 1967.

—*The Life of David Hume*. Edinburgh: Edinburgh University Press, 1954. Second edition. Oxford: Clarendon, 1980.

Ritchie, Thomas E. *An Account of the Life and Writings of David Hume*. London, 1807.

Smith, Adam. "Letter from Adam Smith, LL.D. to William Strahan, Esq." In *Hume's* Dialogues concerning Natural Religion. Edited by Norman Kemp Smith. Second edition. London: Thomas Nelson and Sons Ltd., 1947. Also in HL 2: 450–2.

D. Selected early responses*

Adams, William. *An Essay on Mr. Hume's Essay on Miracles*. London, 1752.

Anonymous. *An Essay on the Academical or Sceptical Philosophy, as applied by Mr. Hume to the Perception of External Existence*. London, 1827.

[Balfour, James (of Pilrig)]. *A Delineation of the Nature and Obligation of Morality. With Reflexions upon Mr. Hume's Book, Intitled,* An Inquiry concerning the Principles of Morals. Edinburgh, 1753.

—*Philosophical Essays*. Edinburgh, 1768.

Beattie, James. *An Essay on the Nature and Immutability of Truth; in Opposition to Sophistry and Scepticism*. Edinburgh, 1770.

Brodie, George. *History of the British Empire . . . including a particular Examination of Mr. Hume's Statements . . . .* Edinburgh, 1822. Reviewed by John Stuart Mill, who used the occasion to attack Hume's *History of England*.

Brown, Thomas. *Observations on the Nature and Tendency of the Doctrine of Mr. Hume concerning the Relation of Cause and Effect*. Edinburgh, [1805].

—*Lectures on the Philosophy of the Human Mind*. Edinburgh, 1820.

Campbell, George. *A Dissertation on Miracles: Containing an Examination*

---

*I am indebted to Manfred Kuehn for assistance with the early German response to Hume.

of the Principles Advanced by David Hume, Esq; in an Essay on Miracles. Edinburgh, 1762.

[Gerard, Alexander]. *The Influence of the Pastoral Office on the Character Examined; with a View, especially, to Mr. Hume's Representation of the Spirit of that Office*. London 1760.

Hamann, Johann Georg. *Sokratische Denkwürdigkeiten für die lange Weile des Publicums zusammengetragen von einem Liebhaber der langen Weile* [Socratic Memorabilia, compiled for the boredom of the public by a lover of boredom]. Amsterdam, 1759. *Hamann's Socratic Memorabilia*. Translation and commentary by James C. O'Flaherty. Baltimore: Johns Hopkins Press, 1967.

Hegel, Georg Wilhelm Friedrich. *Glauben und Wissen oder die Reflexionsphilosophie der Subjektivität in der Vollständigkeit ihrer Formen Als Kantische Jacobische und Fichtesche Philosophie* [Believing and knowing or the philosophy of reflection in all its forms as the Kantian, the Jacobian and Fichtean]. 1802.

—*Verhältnis des Skeptizismus zur Philosophie. Darstellung seiner verschiedenen Modifikationen und Vergleichung der neuesten mit der alten* [The relation of scepticism and philosophy. An account of its different forms and a comparison of the most recent one with the ancient one]. 1802.

Home, Henry, Lord Kames. *Essays on the Principles of Morality and Natural Religion*. Edinburgh, 1751.

Jacobi, F. H. *David Hume über den Glauben oder Idealismus und Realismus* [David Hume on belief or idealism and realism]. The 1787 edition with the Preface of the 1815 edition. Edited by Hamilton Beck. New York: Garland, 1983.

Jakob, Ludwig Heinrich. *Kritische Versuche über David Humes erstes Buch der Abhandlung über die menschliche Natur* [Critical essays on David Hume's first book of the Treatise of Human Nature]. Appended to Jakob's translation of the *Treatise of Human Nature*. 1790.

Kant, Immanuel. *Prolegomena zu einer jeden künftigen Metaphysik die als Wissenschaft wird austreten können* [Prolegomena to any future metaphysics]. 1780.

—*Kritik der praktischen Vernunft* [Critique of practical reason]. 1788.

—*Kritik der reinen Vernunft* [Critique of pure reason]. 1781.

Leland, John. *A View of the Principal Deistical Writers of the Last and Present Century*. London, 1755.

[Lyall, Alfred]. *A Review of the Principles of Necessary and Contingent truth, in Reference Chiefly to the Doctrines of Hume and Reid*. London, 1830.

Maimon, Salomon. *Versuch einer neuen Logik und Theorie des Denkens.*

Nebst angehängten Briefen des Philaletes an Aenesidemus [Essay on a new logic and theory of thought. Together with appended letters of Philates to Aenesidemus]. 1794.

[M'Queen, Daniel]. *Letters on Mr. Hume's History of Great Britain*. Edinburgh, 1756.

Mendelssohn, Moses. "Gedanken von der Wahrscheinlichkeit" ["Thoughts on Probability"]. 1756; revised editions, 1761, 1771. Available in *Gesammelte Schriften*. Edited by F. Bamberger and others. Stuttgart/ Bad Canstatt, 1931, 1: 147–64.

Oswald, James. *An Appeal to Common Sense in Behalf of Religion*. 2 vols. Edinburgh, 1766–72.

Paley, William. *View of the Evidences of Christianity*. London, 1794.

Pistorius, Hermann Andreas. "Notes and Additions to Dr. Hartley's *Observations on Man*." Appended to the German translation of Hartley's *Observations*, with a lengthy discussion of miracles. Pistorius's notes were translated into English and published in the third edition of Hartley's works. London, 1781.

Platner, Ernst. *Gespräche über die natürliche Religion von David Hume*. . . . Translation of the *Dialogues concerning Natural Religion*. Platner is the editor, the translator is said to be Karl Schreiter. Leipzig, 1781.

Priestley, Joseph. *Letters to a Philosophical Unbeliever*. Bath, 1780.

Reid, Thomas. *An Inquiry into the Human Mind, on the Principles of Common Sense*. Edinburgh, 1764.

—*Essays on the Intellectual Powers of Man*. Edinburgh, 1785.

—*Essays on the Active Powers of Man*. Edinburgh, 1788.

Reinhold, Karl Leonhard. *Über die Möglichkeit der Philosophie als strenge Wissenschaft* [On the possibility of philosophy as a strict science]. 1791. Mit einer Einleitung herausgegeben von Wolfgang Schrader. Hamburg, 1978.

—"Über den philosophischen Skepticismus" in *Untersuchungen über den menschlichen Verstand*. ["On philosophical skepticism," in *An Enquiry concerning Human Understanding*, newly translated by W. G. Tenneman]. 1793.

Schulze, Gottlob Ernst. *Aenesidemus oder über die Fundamente der von Herrn Professor Reinhold in Jena gelieferten Elementar-Philosophie* [Aenesidemus, or on the foundations of the elementary philosophy of Professor Reinhold in Jena]. 1792.

[Shepherd, Lady Mary] *An Essay upon the Relation of Cause and Effect, Controverting the Doctrine of Mr. Hume*. London, 1827.

Smith, Adam. *Lectures on Rhetoric and Belles Lettres*. Edited by J. C. Bryce. Oxford: Clarendon Press, 1983. First published in 1762–3.

—*The Theory of Moral Sentiments.* Edited by D. D. Raphael and A. L. Macfie. Oxford, 1976. First published in 1759.

—*An Inquiry into the Causes of the Wealth of Nations.* Edited by R. H. Campbell, and others. Oxford, 1976. First published in 1776.

Stewart, Dugald. *Elements of the Philosophy of the Human Mind.* London, 1792, 1814, 1827.

[Warburton, William and Richard Hurd]. *Remarks on Mr. David Hume's Essay on the Natural History of Religion.* London, 1757.

Tetens, Johann Nicolaus. *Über die allgemeine speculativische Philosophie* [On universal speculative philosophy]. 1775.

—*Philosophische Versuche über die menschliche Natur und ihre Entwicklung* [Philosophical essays on human nature and its development]. 2 vols. Leipzig, 1776–7.

Towers, Joseph. *Observations on Mr. Hume's* History of England. London, 1778.

Voltaire, F. M. A. de. Notice of *The History of England* in *La Gazette Litteraire*, 1764. Reprinted in *Oeuvres complètes de Voltaire*, Paris, 1877–85, 25: 169–73.

[Wallace, Robert.] *A Dissertation on the numbers of Mankind in Antient and Modern Times . . . with . . . some remarks on Mr. Hume's Political Discourse, of the Populousness of Antient Nations.* Edinburgh, 1753.

[Whately, Richard]. *Historic Doubts Relative to Napoleon Buonaparte.* London, 1819.

E. Selected monographs

Anderson, Robert Fendel. *Hume's First Principles.* Lincoln: University of Nebraska Press, 1966.

Árdal, Páll S. *Passion and Value in Hume's* Treatise. Edinburgh: Edinburgh University Press, 1966.

Ayer, A. J. *Hume.* Past Masters. New York: Hill and Wang, 1980.

Baier, Annette. *A Progress of Sentiments: Reflections on Hume's* Treatise. Cambridge, Mass.: Harvard University Press, 1991.

Beauchamp, Tom L. and Alexander Rosenberg. *Hume and the Problem of Causation.* New York: Oxford University Press, 1981.

Beck, Lewis White. *Essays on Kant and Hume.* New Haven: Yale University Press, 1978.

Bennett, Jonathan. *Locke, Berkeley, Hume: Central Themes.* Oxford: Clarendon Press, 1971.

Berry, Christopher J. *Hume, Hegel and Human Nature.* The Hague: Martinus Nijhoff, 1982.

Bongie, Laurence L. *David Hume: Prophet of the Counter-Revolution*. Oxford: Clarendon Press, 1965.

Box, M. A. *The Suasive Art of David Hume*. Princeton: Princeton University Press, 1990.

Bricke, John. *Hume's Philosophy of Mind*. Princeton: Princeton University Press, 1980.

Broiles, David. *The Moral Philosophy of David Hume*. The Hague, 1964; second edition, 1969.

Brunius, Teddy. *David Hume on Criticism*. Stockholm, 1951.

Buckle, Stephen. *Natural Law and the Theory of Property*. *Grotius to Hume*. Oxford: Clarendon Press, 1991.

Calderwood, Henry. *David Hume*. Edinburgh, 1898. Reprint. Books on Hume and on the Scottish Enlightenment. Bristol: Thoemmes, nd.

Capaldi, Nicholas. *David Hume the Newtonian Philosopher*, Boston: Twayne, 1975.

—*Hume's Place in Moral Philosophy*. New York: Peter Lang, 1989.

Christensen, Jerome. *Practicing Enlightenment: Hume and the Formation of a Literary Career*. Madison: University of Wisconsin Press, 1987.

Church, Ralph W. *Hume's Theory of the Understanding*. Ithaca: Cornell University Press, 1935. Reprint. Hamden, Conn.: Archon Books, 1968.

Danford, John W. *David Hume and the Problem of Reason: Recovering the Human Sciences*. New Haven: Yale University Press, 1990.

Flage, Daniel E. *David Hume's Theory of Mind*. New York: Routledge, 1991.

Flew, Antony. *David Hume, Philosopher of Moral Science*. Oxford: Blackwell, 1986.

—*Hume's Philosophy of Belief: A Study of His First* Inquiry. London: Routledge & Kegan Paul, 1961.

Fogelin, Robert J. *Hume's Skepticism in the* Treatise of Human Nature. London: Routledge & Kegan Paul, 1985.

Forbes, Duncan. *Hume's Philosophical Politics*. Cambridge: Cambridge University Press, 1975.

Gaskin, J. C. A. *Hume's Philosophy of Religion*. New York: Macmillan, 1978; second edition, 1988.

Glathe, A. B. *Hume's Theory of the Passions and of Morals: A Study of Books II and III of the* Treatise. Berkeley: University of California Press, 1950.

Green, Thomas Hill. *Hume and Locke*. New York: Thomas Y. Crowell, 1968. Reprint of the "General Introduction" to the Green and Grose edition of Hume's *Treatise*.

Haakonssen, Knud. *The Science of a Legislator: The Natural Jurisprudence of David Hume and Adam Smith*. Cambridge: Cambridge University Press, 1981.

Harrison, Jonathan. *Hume's Theory of Justice*. Oxford: Clarendon Press, 1981.

—*Hume's Moral Epistemology*. Oxford: Clarendon Press, 1976.

Heinemann, F. H. *David Hume: The Man and His Science of Man, Containing Some Unpublished Letters of Hume*. Paris, 1940.

Hendel, Charles W. *Studies in the Philosophy of David Hume*. Princeton: Princeton University Press, 1925. New edition. Indianapolis: Bobbs-Merrill, 1963.

Hurlbutt, Robert H., III. *Hume, Newton, and the Design Argument*. Lincoln: University of Nebraska Press, 1963; revised edition, 1985.

Huxley, T. H. *Hume*. London, 1879. Reprint. London: Macmillan, 1902.

Jones, Peter. *Hume's Sentiments: Their Ciceronian and French Context*. Edinburgh: Edinburgh University Press, 1982.

Knight, William Angus. *Hume*. Edinburgh, 1886.

Kuypers, Mary S. *Studies in the Eighteenth Century Background of Hume's Empiricism*. Minneapolis: University of Minnesota Press, 1930. Reprint. New York: Garland, 1983.

Kydd, Rachel M. *Reason and Conduct in Hume's Treatise*. Oxford: Clarendon Press, 1946; reprint, 1964.

Laing, B. M. *David Hume*. London: Methuen, 1932. Reprint. New York: Russell & Russell, 1968.

Laird, John. *Hume's Philosophy of Human Nature*. London, 1932. Reprint. New York: Garland, 1983.

Levine, Michael. *Hume and the Problem of Miracles: A Solution*. Dordrecht: Kluwer, 1989.

Livingston, Donald W. *Hume's Philosophy of Common Life*. Chicago: University of Chicago Press, 1984.

McCosh, James. *The Scottish Philosophy, Biographical, Expository, Critical, From Hutcheson to Hamilton*. New York, 1875.

Mackie, John L. *Hume's Moral Theory*. London: Routledge & Kegan Paul, 1980.

MacNabb, D. G. C. *David Hume: His Theory of Knowledge and Morality*. London: Hutchinson, 1951. Second edition. Hamden, Conn.: Archon Books, 1966.

Mall, R. A. *Experience and Reason: The Phenomenology of Husserl and its Relation to Hume's Philosophy*. The Hague: Martinus Nijhoff, 1973.

Maund, Constance. *Hume's Theory of Knowledge: A Critical Examination*. London: Macmillan, 1937. Reprint. New York: 1972.

Mercer, P. *Sympathy and Ethics: A Study of the Relationship between Sympathy and Morality, with Special Reference to Hume's Treatise*. Oxford: Clarendon Press, 1972.

Miller, David. *Philosophy and Ideology in Hume's Political Thought.* Oxford: Clarendon Press, 1981.

Neu, Jerome. *Emotion, Thought & Therapy: A Study of Hume and Spinoza and the Relationship of Philosophical Theories of the Emotions to Psychological Theories of Therapy.* Berkeley: University of California Press, 1977.

Norton, David Fate. *David Hume: Common-Sense Moralist, Sceptical Metaphysician.* Princeton: Princeton University Press, 1982; revised edition, 1984.

Noxon, James. *Hume's Philosophical Development.* Oxford: Clarendon Press, 1973.

Orr, James. *David Hume and His Influence on Philosophy and Theology.* Edinburgh, 1903.

Passmore, John. *Hume's Intentions.* Cambridge: Cambridge University Press, 1952. Revised edition. New York: Basic Books, 1968.

Pears, David. *Hume's System: An Examination of the First Book of His Treatise.* Oxford: Oxford University Press, 1990.

Penelhum, Terence. *David Hume: An Introduction to His Philosophical System.* West Lafayette, Ind.: Purdue University Press, 1992.

—*Hume.* London: Macmillan, 1975.

Phillipson, Nicholas. *Hume.* London: Weidenfeld & Nicolson, 1989.

Pompa, Leon. *Human Nature and Historical Knowledge: Hume, Hegel, and Vico.* Cambridge: Cambridge University Press, 1990.

Price, H. H. *Hume's Theory of the External World.* Oxford: Clarendon Press, 1940.

Price, John V. *David Hume.* New York: Twayne, 1986.

—*The Ironic Hume.* Austin: University of Texas Press, 1965.

Richetti, John J. *Philosophical Writing: Locke, Berkeley, Hume.* Cambridge, Mass.: Harvard University Press, 1983.

Salmon, C. V. *The Central Problem of David Hume's Philosophy.* In *Jahrbuch fur Philosophie und phanomenologische Forschung.* Edited by Edmund Husserl (Halle, 1929), 299–499. Monograph reprint. New York: Garland, 1983.

Schwerin, Alan. *The Reluctant Revolutionary: An Essay on David Hume's Account of Necessary Connection.* New York: Lang, 1989.

Seth, Andrew. *Scottish Philosophy. A Comparison of the Scottish and German Answers to Hume.* Edinburgh, 1885.

Siebert, Donald T. *The Moral Animus of David Hume.* Cranbury: University of Delaware Press, 1990.

Snare, Francis. *Morals Motivation and Convention: Hume's Influential Doctrines.* New York: Cambridge University Press, 1991.

Stern, George. *A Faculty Theory of Knowledge: The Aim and Scope of Hume's First* Enquiry. Lewisburg: Bucknell University Press, 1971.

Stewart, John B. *The Moral and Political Philosophy of David Hume.* New York: Columbia University Press, 1963.

—*Opinion and Reform in Hume's Political Philosophy.* Princeton: Princeton University Press, 1992.

Stove, David C. *Probability and Hume's Inductive Scepticism.* Oxford: Clarendon Press, 1973.

Strawson, Galen. *The Secret Connexion: Causation, Realism, and David Hume.* Oxford: Clarendon Press, 1989.

Stroud, Barry. *Hume.* London: Routledge & Kegan Paul, 1977.

Taylor, A. E. *David Hume and the Miraculous.* Cambridge: Cambridge University Press, 1927.

Taylor, W. L. *Francis Hutcheson and David Hume as Predecessors of Adam Smith.* Durham, N.C.: Duke University Press, 1965.

Tweyman, Stanley. *Reason and Conduct in Hume and His Predecessors.* The Hague: Martinus Nijhoff, 1974.

—*Scepticism and Belief in Hume's* Dialogues concerning Natural Religion. The Hague: Martinus Nijhoff, 1974.

Weinberg, Julius R. *Ockham, Descartes, & Hume: Self-Knowledge, Substance, and Causality.* Madison: University of Wisconsin Press, 1977.

Wexler, V. *David Hume and* The History of England. Philadelphia: American Philosophical Society, 1979.

Whelan, Frederick G. *Order and Artifice in Hume's Political Philosophy.* Princeton: Princeton University Press, 1985.

Wilbanks, Jan. *Hume's Theory of Imagination.* The Hague: Martinus Nijhoff, 1968.

Wilson, Fred. *Laws and Other Worlds.* Dordrecht: Reidel, 1986.

Wright, John. *The Sceptical Realism of David Hume.* Manchester: Manchester University Press, 1983.

Zabeeh, Farhang. *Hume: Precursor of Modern Empiricism.* The Hague: Martinus Nihjoff, 1960; revised edition, 1973.

F. Selected monographs in languages other than English

Baldi, Marialuisa. *David Hume nel settecento italiano: filosofia ed economica.* Florence, 1983.

Garcia Roca, J. *Postivismo e ilustracion: La filosofia de David Hume.* Valencia, 1981.

Gawlick, G. and L. Kreimendahl. *Hume in der deutschen Aufklärung. Umrisse einer Rezeptionsgeschichte.* Stuttgart-Bad Cannstatt, 1987.

Giarrizzo, Giuseppe. *David Hume politico e storico.* Turin, 1962.

Kreimendahl, L. *Humes verborgener Rationalismus*. Berlin, 1982.

Leroy, Andre-Louis. *La critique et la religion chez David Hume*. Paris, 1930.

—*David Hume*. Paris, 1953.

Linares, R. *Das politische Denken von David Hume*. Hildesheim, 1984.

Luthe, Rudolf. *David Hume: Historicker und Philosoph*. Freiburg, 1991.

Malherbe, Michel. *La philosophie empiriste de David Hume*. Paris, 1976; revised edition, 1984.

Mall, R. A. *Der operative Begriff des Geistes: Locke, Berkeley, Hume*. Freiburg, 1984.

Michaud, Yves. *Hume et la fin de la philosophie*. Paris, 1983.

Monteiro, Joao Paulo. *Hume e a epistemologia*. Sao Paulo, nd.

Nedeljkovic, M. *David Hume: approche phenomenologique de l'action et theorie linguistique du temps*. Paris, 1976.

Schaefer, A. *David Hume. Philosophie und Politik*. Meisenheim, 1963.

Vlachos, G. *Essai sur la politique de Hume*. Athens, 1955.

Wenzel, L. *David Humes politische Philosophie in ihrem Zusammenhang mit seiner gesamten Lehre*. Cologne, 1959.

G. Selected multiple-author anthologies

Capaldi, Nicholas and Donald W. Livingston, eds. *Liberty in Hume's History of England*. Dordrecht: Kluwer, 1990.

Chappell, V. C., ed. *Hume: A Collection of Critical Essays*. New York: Doubleday, 1966. Hardbound edition. Notre Dame, Ind.: University of Notre Dame Press, 1968.

Hester, Marcus, ed. *Hume's Philosophy of Religion*. Winston-Salem: Wake Forest University Press, 1986.

Hope, Vincent, ed. *Philosophers of the Scottish Enlightenment*. Edinburgh: Edinburgh University Press, 1984.

Livingston, Donald W. and James T. King, eds. *Hume: A Re-evaluation*. New York: Fordham University Press, 1976.

Merrill, Kenneth and Robert W. Shahan, eds. *David Hume Many-sided Genius*. Norman: University of Oklahoma Press, 1976,

Morice, G. P., ed. *David Hume Bicentenary Papers*. Edinburgh: University of Edinburgh Press, 1977

Norton, David Fate, Nicholas Capaldi, and Wade L. Robison, eds. *McGill Hume Studies*. San Diego: Austin Hill Press, 1976.

Pears, David F., ed. *David Hume: A Symposium*. London: Macmillan, 1963; reprinted 1966.

Stewart, M. A., ed. *Studies in the Philosophy of the Scottish Enlightenment*. Oxford Studies in the History of Philosophy, vol. 1. Oxford, 1990.

Todd, William B., ed. *Hume and the Enlightenment: Essays presented to Ernest Campbell Mossner.* Edinburgh, 1974.

H. Selected articles and essays

Adair, Douglas. "'That Politics May Be Reduced to a Science': David Hume, James Madison and the Tenth *Federalist.*" *Huntington Library Quarterly* 20 (1957): 343–60. Reprinted in *Fame and the Founding Fathers: Essays by Douglas Adair.* Edited by T. Colbourn. New York 1974.

Árdal, Páll S. "Some Implications of the Virtue of Reasonableness in Hume's *Treatise,* in *Hume: a Re-evaluation.* See Livingston and King, Section G.

Arkin, M. "The Economic Writings of David Hume – a Reassessment." *South African Journal of Economics* 24 (1956): 204–20.

Arnold, N. Scott "Hume's Skepticism about Inductive Inference." *Journal of the History of Philosophy* 21 (1983): 31–55.

Baier, Annette. "Good Men's Women: Hume on Chastity and Trust." *Hume Studies* 5 (1979): 1–19.

—"Master Passions." In *Explaining Emotions.* Edited by A. O. Rorty. Berkeley: University of California Press, 1980.

Barfoot, Michael. "Hume and the Culture of Science in the Early Eighteenth Century," in *Studies in the Philosophy of the Scottish Enlightenment.* See Stewart, Section G.

Battersby, Christine. "An Enquiry concerning the Humean Woman." *Philosophy* 56 (1981): 303–12.

Berman, David. "David Hume on the 1641 Rebellion in Ireland." *Studies: An Irish Quarterly Review* 65 (1976): 101–12.

—"David Hume and the Suppression of Atheism." *Journal of the History of Philosophy* 21 (1983): 375–87.

Biro, John. "Hume on Self-Identity and Memory." *Review of Metaphysics* 30, 1 (1976): 19–38.

—"Hume's Difficulties with the Self." *Hume Studies* 5 (April, 1979): 45–54.

—"Hume and Cognitive Science." *History of Philosophy Quarterly* 2 (1985): 257–74. Reprinted in *Historical Foundations of Cognitive Science.* Edited by J-C. Smith. Dordrecht: Kluwer, 1990.

—"Memory, Mind, and Society." Paper presented at the São Paulo Hume Conference, 1987.

Blackburn, Simon. "Hume and Thick Connections." *Philosophy and Phenomenological Research* 50 (1990): 237–50.

Bower, K. "Imagery: From Hume to Cognitive Science." *Canadian Journal of Philosophy* 14 (1984): 217–34.

Bracken, H. M. "Bayle, Berkeley, and Hume." *Eighteenth-Century Studies* 11 (1978): 227–45.

Bricke, John. "Hume's Conception of Character." *Southwestern Journal of Philosophy* 5 (1974): 107–13.

—"Hume's Volitions," in *Philosophers of the Scottish Enlightenment*. See Hope, Section G.

—"On the Interpretation of Hume's *Dialogues*." *Religious Studies* 11 (1975): 1–18.

Broad, C. D. "Hume's Theory of the Credibility of Miracles." *Proceedings of the Aristotelian Society* 17 (1916): 77–94.

Burnyeat, Myles. "Can the Sceptic Live His Scepticism?" In *Doubt and Dogmatism*. Edited by Malcolm Schofield, Myles Burnyeat, and Jonathan Barnes. Oxford: Clarendon Press, 1980.

Butler, R. J. "Natural Belief and the Enigma of Hume." *Archiv für Geschichte der Philosophie*. 42 (1960): 73–100.

Capaldi, Nicholas, James T. King, and Donald W. Livingston. "The Hume Literature of the 1980s." *American Philosophical Quarterly* 28 (1991): 255–72.

Chamley, P. E. "The Conflict between Montesquieu and Hume." In *Essays on Adam Smith*. Edited by Andrew S. Skinner and T. Wilson. Oxford: Clarendon Press, 1975.

Church, R. W. "Malebranche and Hume." *Revue Internationale de Philosophie* 1 (1938): 143–61.

Cohen, Michael F. "Obligation and Human Nature in Hume's Philosophy." *Philosophical Quarterly* 40 (1990): 316–41.

Coleman, Dorothy. "Hume, Miracles and Lotteries." *Hume Studies* 14 (1988): 328–46.

Davidson, Donald. "Hume's Cognitive Theory of Pride." *Journal of Philosophy* 73 (1976): 744–57.

Davie, George. "Edmund Husserl and 'the as yet, in its most important respect, unrecognized greatness of Hume,' " in *David Hume Bicentenary Papers*. See Morice, Section G.

Davie, William. "Hume on Morality, Action, and Character." *History of Philosophy Quarterly* 2 (1985): 337–48.

Doore, Gary. "The Argument from Design: Some Better Reasons for Agreeing with Hume." *Religious Studies* 16 (1980): 145–61.

Fieser, James. "Hume's Classification of the Passions and Its Precursors." *Hume Studies* 18 (1992): 1–17.

Flew, Antony. "Infinite Divisibility in Hume's *Treatise*," in *Hume: A Reevaluation*. See Livingston and King, Section G.

Fogelin, Robert J. "What Hume Actually Said about Miracles." *Hume Studies* (1990): 81–6.

—"The Tendency of Hume's Scepticism." In *The Skeptical Tradition.* Edited by Miles Burnyeat. Berkeley: University of California Press, 1983.

Forbes, Duncan. "Hume's Science of Politics." In *David Hume Bicentenary Papers.* See Morice, Section G.

—"Politics and History in David Hume." *Historical Journal* 6 (1963): 280–95.

Force, James E. "Hume's Interest in Newton and Science." *Hume Studies* 13 (1976): 166–216.

Gaskin, J. C. A. "Contrary Miracles Concluded." *Hume Studies* (Supplement 1985): 1–14.

—"David Hume and the Eighteenth Century Interest in Miracles." *Hermathena* 99 (1964): 80–92.

—"God, Hume, and Natural Belief." *Philosophy* 49 (1974): 281–94

—"Hume's Attenuated Deism." *Archiv für Geschichte der Philosophie* 65 (1983): 160–73.

Gauthier, David. "David Hume, Contractarian." *Philosophical Review* 88 (1979): 3–38.

Giarrizzo, Giuseppe. "Ancora su Hume storico." *Rivista storica italiana* 83 (1971): 429–49.

Haakonssen, Knud. "Hume's Obligations." *Hume Studies* 4 (1978): 7–17.

Hacking, Ian. "Hume's Species of Probability." *Philosophical Studies* 3 (1978): 21–37.

Hayek, F. A. von. "The Legal and Political Philosophy of David Hume." *Il Politico* 28 (1963): 691–704. Reprinted in Hayek. *Studies in Philosophy, Politics and Economics.* London, 1967.

Hearn, T. "General Rules and the Moral Sentiments in Hume's *Treatise.*" *Review of Metaphysics* 30 (1976): 57–72.

—"General Rules in Hume's *Treatise.*" *Journal of the History of Philosophy* 8 (1970): 405–22.

Hilson, J. C. "Hume: The Historian as Man of Feeling." In *Augustan Worlds.* Edited by J. C. Hilson, M. M. B. Jones, and J. R. Watson. Leicester: Leicester University Press, 1978.

Immerwahr, John. "The Anatomist and the Painter: The Continuity of Hume's *Treatise* and *Essays.*" *Hume Studies* 17 (1991): 1–14.

Jessop, T. E. "Hume's Limited Scepticism." *Revue Internationale de Philosophie* 30 (1976): 3–27.

Johnson, Clarence Shole. "Hume on Character, Action and Causal Necessity." *Auslegung* 16 (1990): 149–64.

Jones, Peter. "Cause, Reason, and Objectivity in Hume's Aesthetics," in *Hume: A Re-evaluation.* See Livingston and King, Section G.

—"Hume and the Beginnings of Modern Aesthetics." In *The Science of Man in the Scottish Enlightenment.* Edited by Peter Jones. Edinburgh: Edinburgh University Press, 1989.

King, James. "Hume's Classical Theory of Justice." *Hume Studies* 7 (1981): 32–54.

Kivy, Peter. "Hume's Standard of Taste: Breaking the Circle." *British Journal of Aesthetics* 7 (1967): 57–66.

—"Hume's Neighbour's Wife: An Essay on the Evolution of Hume's Aesthetics." *British Journal of Aesthetics* 23 (1983): 195–208.

Korsmeyer, C. M. "Hume and the Foundations of Taste." *Journal of Aesthetics and Art Criticism* 35 (1976): 201–15.

Kuehn, Manfred. "Kant's Conception of 'Hume's Problem.' " *Journal of the History of Philosophy* 21 (1983): 275–93.

—"Hume's Antinomies." *Hume Studies* 9 (1983): 25–45.

Lesher, James. 1973. "Hume's Analysis of Cause and the 'Two Definitions' Dispute." *Journal of the History of Philosophy* 11 (1973): 387–92.

Livingston, Donald W. "Hume on Ultimate Causation." *American Philosophical Quarterly* 8 (1971): 63–70.

McGilvary, E. B. "Altruism in Hume's *Treatise*." *Philosophical Review* 12 (1903): 272–98.

McIntyre, Alasdair C. "Hume on 'Is' and 'Ought.' " *Philosophical Review* 68 (1959): 451–68. Reprinted in Chappell, Section G.

McIntyre, Jane L. "Character: a Humean Account." *History of Philosophy Quarterly* 7 (1990): 193–206.

—"Is Hume Self Consistent?" in *McGill Hume Studies*. See Norton, Capaldi, and Robison, Section G.

—"Personal Identity and the Passions." *Journal of the History of Philosophy* 27 (1989): 316–41.

Mackie, John L. "Causes and Conditions." *American Philosophical Quarterly* 2 (1965): 245–64.

Martin, Marie A. "Utility and Morality: Adam Smith's Critique of Hume." *Hume Studies* 16 (1990): 107–20.

Merlan, Philip. "From Hume to Hamann." *Personalist* 32 (1951): 11–18.

Monteiro, J.-P. "Hume's Conception of Science." *Journal of the History of Philosophy* 19 (1981): 327–42.

—"Hume, Induction, and Natural Selection," in *McGill Hume Studies*. See Norton, Capaldi, and Robison, Section G.

Moore, James. "Hume's Political Science and the Classical Republican Tradition." *Canadian Journal of Political Science* 10 (1977): 809–39.

—"Hume's Theory of Justice and Property." *Political Studies* 24 (1976): 103–19.

Mossner, Ernest Campbell. "The Continental Reception of Hume's *Treatise*, 1739–1741." *Mind* 56 (1947): 31–43.

—"Was Hume a Tory Historian? Facts and Reconsiderations." *Journal of the History of Ideas* 2 (1941): 225–36.

Norton, David Fate. "How a Sceptic May Live Scepticism." In *Faith,*

Scepticism and Rationality: Essays in Honour of Terence Penelhum. Edited by J. J. MacIntosh and Hugo Meynell. Calgary: University of Calgary Press, forthcoming.

—"Hume and his Scottish Critics," in *McGill Hume Studies.* See Norton, Capaldi, and Robison, Section G.

—"Hume, Atheism, and the Autonomy of Morals," in *Hume's Philosophy of Religion.* See Hester, Section G.

—"History and Philosophy in Hume's Thought." In *David Hume: Philosophical Historian.* Edited by David Fate Norton and Richard H. Popkin. Indianapolis: Bobbs-Merrill, 1965.

—"More Evidence that Hume Wrote the *Abstract.*" *Hume Studies* 19 (1993).

Noxon, J. "Hume's Agnosticism." *Philosophical Review* 73 (1964): 248–61.

—"In Defence of 'Hume's Agnosticism'." *Journal of the History of Philosophy* 14 (1976): 469–73.

Peirce, C. S. "Hume on Miracles." In *Collected Papers of Charles Sanders Peirce.* Edited by C. Hartshorne and P. Weiss. Vol. 6. Cambridge, Mass.: Harvard University Press, 1935; reprint, 1960.

Penelhum, Terence. "Butler and Hume." *Hume Studies* 14 (1988): 251–76.

—"Hume on Personal Identity." *Philosophical Review* 64 (1955): 571–89. Reprinted in Chappell, Section G.

—"Hume's Skepticism and the *Dialogues,*" in *McGill Hume Studies.* See Norton, Capaldi, and Robison. Section G.

—"Hume's Theory of the Self Revisited." *Dialogue* 14 (1975): 389–409.

—"Natural Belief and Religious Belief in Hume's Philosophy." *Philosophical Quartery* 33 (1983): 166–81.

Pike, Nelson. "Hume on the Argument from Design." In *Hume: Dialogues concerning Natural Religion.* Indianapolis: Bobbs-Merrill, 1970.

—"Hume's Bundle Theory of the Self: a Limited Defense." *American Philosophical Quarterly* 4 (1976): 159–65.

Pitson, A. E. "Projectionism, Realism, and Hume's Moral Sense Theory." *Hume Studies* 15 (1989): 61–92.

Pocock, J. G. A. "Hume and the American Revolution: The Dying Thoughts of a North Briton," in *McGill Hume Studies.* See Norton, Capaldi, and Robison. Section G. Reprinted in Pocock. *Virtue, Commerce, and History.* Cambridge: Cambridge University Press, 1985.

Popkin, Richard H. "David Hume and the Pyrrhonian Controversy." *Review of Metaphysics* 6 (1952): 65–81. Reprinted in *The High Road to Pyrrhonism.* Edited by Richard A. Watson and James E. Force. San Diego: Austin Hill Press, 1980.

—"David Hume: His Pyrrhonism and his Critique of Pyrrhonism." *Philo-*

sophical Quarterly 1 (1951): 385–407. Reprinted in *Hume*. See Chappell, Section G.

—"Hume: Philosophical versus Prophetic Historian," in *David Hume Many-sided Genius*. See Merrill and Shahan, Section G.

Price, J. V. "Hume's Concept of Liberty and *The History of England*." *Studies in Romanticism* 5 (1966): 139–57.

Raynor, David. "Hume and Berkeley's *Three Dialogues*," in *Studies in the Philosophy of the Scottish Enlightenment*. See Stewart, Section G.

—"The Authorship of the *Abstract* Revisited." *Hume Studies* 19 (1993).

Robinson, J. A. "Hume's Two Definitions of 'Cause'." *Philosophical Quarterly* 12 (1962): 129–47. Reprinted in *Hume*. See Chappell, Section G.

Rotwein, Eugene. "Introduction." In *Hume: Writings on Economics*. Madison: University of Wisconsin Press, 1955; reprint, 1970.

—"The Shaping of Political Economy in the Enlightenment." *Scottish Journal of Political Economy* 37 (1990): 145–65.

Smith, Norman Kemp. "The Naturalism of Hume." *Mind* 14 (1905): 149–73, 335–47.

Stockton, C. N. "Economics and the Mechanism of Historical Progress in Hume's *History*," in *Hume: A Re-Evaluation*. See Livingston and King, Section G.

Swain, Corliss. "Being Sure of One's Self." *Hume Studies* 17 (November 1991): 107–24.

—"Passionate Objectivity." *Nous*, 27 (1993).

Swinburne. R. G. "The Argument from Design." *Philosophy* 43 (1968): 199–212.

—"The Argument from Design – a Defence." *Religious Studies* 11 (1972): 193–205.

Taylor, A. E., J. Laird, and T. E. Jessop. "The Present-Day Relevance of Hume's *Dialogues concerning Natural Religion*." *Proceedings of the Aristotelian Society* 18 (Supplement, 1939): 179–228.

Traiger, Saul. "Impressions, Ideas, and Fictions." *Hume Studies* 13: 381–99.

Vitek, William. "The Humean Promise: Whence Comes Its Obligation?" *Hume Studies* 12 (1986): 160–76.

Wilson, Fred. "Hume's Theory of Mental Activity," in *McGill Hume Studies*. See Norton, Capaldi, and Robison. Section G.

—"Was Hume a Subjectivist?" *Philosophy Research Archives* 14 (1988–9): 247–82.

Winkler, Kenneth. "The New Hume." *Philosophical Review* 100 (1992): 541–79.

Wolff, Robert Paul. "Hume's Theory of Mental Activity." *Philosophical Review* 69 (1960): 289–310. Reprinted in *Hume*. See Chappell, Section G.

Wood, Paul B. "David Hume . . . A New Letter to Hugh Blair from July 1762." *Mind* (1986), 411–16.

Wootton, David. "Hume's 'Of Miracles': Probability and Irreligion," in *Studies in the Philosophy of the Scottish Enlightenment*. See Stewart, Section G.

Yalden-Thomson, D. C. "Recent Work on Hume." *American Philosophical Quarterly* 20 (1983): 1–22.

INDEX OF NAMES AND SUBJECTS

This index does not list second or subsequent references to bibliographical data regarding authors and editors. Additional references to Hume's works are found in the Index of Citations and References.

Abrahamsen, A., 62n22
Abstract of . . . A Treatise of Human Nature, An, 3, 17, 31n23, 90, 121, 358
Act of Settlement, 203
Adair, Douglas, 219n26
Adam, 9
Adam, Robert, 257, 279n6
Adams, William, 342n16
Addison, Joseph, 210, 258–9, 265, 284
Advocates, Faculty of, 353
aesthetic judgement (*see also* criticism), 258, 260, 267–76
  and circularity, 274
  and comparison, 261, 268
  and context, 263–6, 274, 276
  and informed public, 265
  and interpretation, 268–9, 275, 276–7
  and moral assessment, 274–5
  objectivity of, 261–4, 268, 274–6
  and perceptual conditions, causes, 28n6, 261–2, 265, 267–8, 275–6
  and practice, 268–9
  and reason, 264–71
  and sentiment, 270–6
aesthetics, Hume's (*see also* aesthetic judgement)
  and artistic intention, 269–70
  and beauty, 258, 261–2
  context of, 255–6
  and focus on literature, 256–8
  influence of Dubos on, 259–60, 280n13

and unity, 269–70
and works of art, definition, 276, 279n11
agriculture, 231–2, 235–6
Alberti, Leon Battista, 257, 279n8
allegiance
  of British subjects, 203–4
  foundations of, 195–6
  and opinion, 192, 194–6, 197, 201–6, 293
  origins of, 172, 194
American Independence, Constitution, 213, 219n27, 297
analytic–synthetic distinction, 81–2
anatomy of human nature, 6, 29n10, 39, 45
ancient–modern controversy, 257, 259–60, 280n13, 288, 310n21
Anderson, Robert Fendel, 60n9
Annandale, George, Marquess of, 352
Anscombe, G.E.M., 72, 87n20
appetites, *see* desire(s)
approbation, 14–15, 162–3, 164–5, 168–70, 173–5, 227, 261, 275
Aquinas, Thomas, 146n22, 215n4, 322
Arbuthnot, John, 345
architecture, 257–8, 279n8,n9
Árdal, Páll S., 145n8,n9,n11
argument a posteriori, *see* argument from design
argument a priori, 314–15, 318–19, 329–30, 332

argument from design, 19–20, 314, 318–28, 329, 337–8, 342n9,n10,n12,n14,n15
Aristotelian philosophy, 66–7
Aristotle, 184
Arkin, M., 252n29
Arnauld, Antoine, 286
art, works of, see aesthetics, Hume's
artifice theory, see moral theories
artificial virtues, 16, 135–6, 165–8, 171
    development of, 165–8, 188–92
    framework dependent, 187–92
arts and sciences, 204–5, 264
association of ideas, 35, 40–1, 50, 54, 101, 120–2, 126
atheism, see religion
atomism, Epicurean, 325–8
Augustine, Saint, 286
Austin, J.L., 108, 115n21
authority, political, 192–7, 201–3, 303–5
Ayer, A.J., 74, 84n1, 86n14, 87n22
Ayers, Michael, 214n2

Bacon, Francis, 3
Baier, Annette, 115n16, 142, 145n8,n13, 147n26
Bailyn, Bernard, 219n24
Baldi, Marialuisa, 221n36
Balguy, John, 149, 153–4
Bankowski, Z., 220n32
Barbeyrac, Jean, 217n13
Barfoot, Michael, 28n2, 85n3, 278n2
Barker, Ernest, 218n20
Barnes, Jonathan, 115n19, 116n25
Barnes, Philip, 344n28
Bayle, Pierre, 7, 29n12, 89n34, 259
Beard, Geoffrey, 279n6
Beauchamp, Tom L., 87n17,n24, 114n5, 357
beauty, 258, 261–4
Bechtel, W., 62n22
belief, 10–12, 25, 30, 37–9, 41–6, 57–8, 60n11,n12, 61n17, 90–4, 98, 104–8, 110, 111, 112, 114n2, 122
    as "manner of conceiving," 10
    and "natural belief," 316, 336–41
    and personal identity, 47–9, 62n17, 140–1

political, 183, 194–6
religious, 178n15, 315, 316, 318–19, 321, 336–41
benevolence, 137, 154, 161–2, 164, 172, 179n23, 186
Bennett, Jonathan, 85n7
Bentivoglio, Guido, 283
Berkeley, George, 2, 7, 29n12, 68, 108–9, 116n23, 218n20, 253n40
Berman, David, 308n12, 341n6
Bernard, J.H., 146n17
Berry, Christopher, 218n22
Bible, 314, 318, 322, 330–1, 342n9
big bang theory, 327–8
Biro, John, 26, 58n1, 59n6, 62n16,n18,n20, 63n25,n26
Blackburn, Simon, 87n18
Blackmore, Sir Richard, 160, 326
Blair, Hugh, 86n8, 277
Boileau-Despréaux, Nicolas, 259, 279n12
Bolingbroke, Viscount (Henry St. John), 210, 217n19, 298, 311n40
Bongie, Laurence L., 214, 221n35
Borghero, C., 309n17
Boswell, James, 28n1, 32n29
Boyle, Robert, influence of, on Hume, 2, 65, 85n3
Brady, Robert, 298
Brentano, Franz, 50, 53
Bricke, John, 146n16
Britain (see also England), 182, 201, 204, 214, 239–40, 242, 277n1
British Constitution, 205–6, 209, 290, 293, 296, 298, 302–5, 354
    and Commons, 202, 209, 212, 234
    and Crown, 209, 304, 305
Broughton, Janet, 114n6
Brunius, T., 278n4
Bryce, J.C., 280n17
Buck, P.W., 249n2
Buckle, Stephen, 218n22
Burke, Edmund, 297
Burnet, Gilbert, 149
Burns, R.M., 343n18
Burnyeat, Myles, 115n19
Burrow, John, 220n34
Burton, John Hill, 222, 225
Butler, Joseph, 133, 136, 146n17,n20, 341n8

Cambridge Platonism, *see* Cudworth, Ralph
Campbell, Archibald, 149
Campbell, George, 277, 342*n*16
Campbell, R.H., 251*n*24
Campbell, T.D., 221*n*34
Cantillon, Richard, 246, 253*n*45
Capaldi, Nicholas, 63*n*25, 85*n*3, 145*n*8, 146*n*18, 178*n*16, 311*n*37, 343*n*20
Carnap, Rudolph, 84*n*1
Carte, Thomas, 218*n*19, 298
Cartesians, 1, 30*n*13, 38, 48, 56, 71, 92, 123, 267
Catholic, Catholicism, 286
causation (*see also* induction), 8–10, 22, 29*n*11, 37, 43, 49–50, 65, 67, 80, 85*n*5, 86*n*17, 87*n*18, 99, 114*n*5, 131
    and aesthetic judgement, 261–2, 269–71
    and argument from design, 324–8
    and causal necessity attributed to objects, 73–4, 87*n*18
    and constant conjunction, 9, 11, 71–5, 99–100
    and contiguity, 9, 71, 74, 86*n*16, 87*n*18
    and duty, 170–1
    and "heroic Humeanism," 75, 87*n*24
    Hume's definitions of, 71
    idea of, copied from impression of reflection, 72–3
    and laws of nature, 329–30
    and the mind, 71–2
    and priority, 9, 71, 74, 110
Chambers, Ephraim, 278*n*4
Chambers, Sir William, 258, 279*n*9
Chambray, Roland Fréart, Sieur de, 258, 279*n*8
Chamley, P.E., 310*n*26
chance, 22, 131
Chappell, V.C., 86*n*15
character, 133–4, 137–8, 179*n*22, 191, 311*n*31
Charles I, 233, 282, 289–90, 293, 297, 298–9, 301–2, 304–5, 306, 354
Charles II, 300, 303, 312*n*46
Charon the boatman, 23–4
Chippendale, Thomas, 258
Chisholm, R.M., 147*n*25

choice, 128, 129, 130, 139
Christensen, Jerome, 308*n*3
Church of England, 305
church(es), *see* religion
Cicero, Marcus Tullius, 2, 260, 276, 280*n*14, 325–7, 341*n*8, 342*n*10, 346, 351
Civil War (English), 285, 293, 303
civilization, process of, 204–5, 230, 232–5, 292–3
Clarendon, Edward Hyde, Earl of, 211, 285, 302, 312*n*45
Clarke, Samuel, 153, 189, 314, 341*n*8
classical republicanism, 212–13
Cochrane, E., 308*n*10
cognitive science, 33, 36, 45–7, 51–8, 61*n*14,*n*15, 62*n*22
Coleman, Dorothy, 343*n*19
Collini, Stefan, 220*n*34
commerce, rise of, 230–8, 246, 292–3
common sense, 42, 58, 63*n*26, 124, 139–40, 145*n*7
compatibilism, 129
Comte, Auguste, 64
concept formation, 13–15, 66–7
connection, causal, *see* causation
conscience, 133, 137, 146*n*17
constant conjunction, *see* causation
contiguity, *see* causation
contract theories, 150, 188, 192–4, 200–1, 215*n*4, 216*n*9, 300
convention, 15, 135–6, 153, 166–8, 172, 180*n*26,*n*28, 228, 262, 272, 274, 276
Conway, Seymour, General, 355
Coste, Pierre, 259
counterfactuals, 74–5, 78
Craftsman, The, (Bolingbroke), 210
Crimmins, J.E., 215*n*5
criticism (*see also* aesthetic judgement), 267–8, 271, 277, 348
    French influences on, 257
    Hume's proposed treatise on, 255, 260
    and mistaken critics, 271–5
Cromwell, Oliver, 293, 310*n*22
Crow, Thomas E., 278*n*1
Cudworth, Ralph, 149, 152–3, 157, 177*n*5, 189
Cumberland, Richard, 190, 200, 215*n*6, 217*n*13
custom, *see* habit

d'Alembert, Jean Le Rond, 266, 310n28
Darnley, Henry Stewart, Lord, 310n22
Darwin, Charles, 124, 328
Davenant, Charles, 223
Davila, Enrico, 283
Davis, Natalie Zeman, 308n6
de Boisguilbert, Pierre, 224
de Piles, Roger, 257, 278n3
de Pouilly, Lévesque, 287, 309n19
debt, national, see public credit
Defoe, Daniel, 216n8
deism, 315, 322
Deity, deities, see God, gods
Dennett, Daniel, 53–6, 63n24
Descartes, René, 37, 52, 66, 115n21,
    120, 123, 145n4, 223, 340
design argument, see argument from
    design
desire(s), 12, 122, 126–8, 133, 227–8
determination of mind, 100
"Dialogue, A," 251–2
Dialogues concerning Natural Religion,
    3, 19, 27, 316, 341n8, 359
Dickie, George, 280n22
Diderot, Denis, 310n28
dispositions, 15, 68–9, 72
Dissertation on the Passions, A, 17,
    179n24
divine right, 192
Domat, Jean, 215n4
Don Quixote (Cervantes), 270
Donne, John, 260
Doore, Gary, 342n14
Dryden, John, 256, 278n2, 326
du Fresnoy, Charles Alphonse, 256, 257,
    278n2,n3
Dubos, Abbé Jean-Baptiste, 257, 259,
    264–70, 273, 277, 279n5,
    280n13,n14
Ducasse, C.J., 72, 87n20
Dupre, L., 342n14
Dutens, Louis, 279n5
Dutot, 225
duty, duties, 125, 132–3, 136–7,
    143, 168–71, 180n30, 189, 191,
    193–4
    derivation of, 168–71, 334–5
    sense of, 135, 191

Echard, Laurence, 217n19
economics, see political economy

Edinburgh, 1, 257–8, 266, 279n10,
    307n2, 351, 353, 355
    University of, 32n26, 318
education, 228, 273
    and morality, 148, 155, 164, 180n29
egoism, see selfish theory
Elizabeth I, 284, 299, 303, 354
emotions, see passions
empiricism, 5, 36, 56, 65–8, 91
    and aesthetics, 277
    and mathematics, 80–2
Encyclopédie, (Diderot and d'Alembert),
    258, 266, 279n9, 310n28
England (see also Britain), 294, 298–307,
    354
    Star Chamber in, 305
Enquiry concerning Human Under-
    standing, An, 3, 17, 18–19, 316–17,
    353, 358
Enquiry concerning the Principles of
    Morals, An, 17, 171–6, 208, 212,
    266–7, 343n20, 353, 358
enthusiasm, see religion
Epicurus, 325, 328
epistemology, see belief; knowledge
Erskine, Sir Harry, 352
Essays, Moral and Political; Essays,
    Moral, Political, and Literary, 3, 18,
    259, 352–3, 358
Essays and Treatises on Several Subjects,
    3, 17, 21, 196, 205, 208, 246, 266
    economic essays, 231, 248, 251n26
    "Idea of a Perfect Commonwealth,"
    213
    "Of the Origin of Government," 194
    "Of the Populousness of Ancient Na-
    tions," 235–6, 288
    "Of the Standard of Taste," 259, 266
ethical scepticism, see scepticism
ethics, see morality
Europe, 182, 184, 204, 214, 230, 232,
    236–7, 255
evidence, historical, see history;
    testimony
evil, 127, 151–2, 175
existence, see external existence
experience, 10, 11, 90–1, 329–30
experimental method, 2, 149
    Hume's use of, 3–5, 18, 25, 28n6, 34,
    35, 57, 84, 91, 120–2, 136, 226, 231,
    256

explanation, 59n6, 77–80, 88n32, 140
extension, idea of (see also space),
  31n19, 60n9
external existence, 8, 11–12, 30n16, 41–
  3, 90–3, 106–8, 115n21, 337
  and naive realism, 108–11
  and theory of "double existence" (representational realism), 69, 106–9,
  112
external world, proof of, see external
  existence

fact and value, 143–4, 168–9
factions, parties, 205–9, 215n3, 294
faith, see belief, religious
Falconer, Sir David, 351
Falkland, Lucius Carey, viscount, 302
fallibilism, 91, 113
fancy, see imagination
Fearnley-Sander, M., 307n2
Federalist, The, Hume's influence on,
  213
Feigl, Herbert, 84n1
Félibien, André, 257, 278n3
Feuerbach, Ludwig, 338
fictions, 40, 41–2, 69–71, 109–11, 283
fideism, 316, 337, 339, 340
Filmer, Robert, 216n8
Fleming, John, 279n6
Flew, Antony, 89n35, 96, 115n8, 219n22,
  343n19
Fodor, Jerry, 59n3, 86n10
Fogelin, Robert J., 26, 60n9, 89n34,
  114n3, 343n19
Fontana, Biancamaria, 220n34
Fontenelle, Bernard le Bovier de, 259,
  265, 279n5
Forbes, Duncan, 211–12, 213, 216n10,
  217n17, 220n31, 251n25, 301,
  311n34, 312n44
Force, James, 85n3
Four Dissertations, 266, 358
France, 201, 204, 205, 215n4, 217n17,
  260, 278n1, 297, 305, 352, 354, 355
Frede, Michael, 116n25
free trade, 224, 243–4, 245, 249
freedom and necessity, 122–3, 125, 129–
  32, 138–9, 144
  and liberty of indifference, 130–2,
  141–2
  and liberty of spontaneity, 130

Fréret, Nicholas, 287
Freud, Sigmund, 338
Furniss, Edgar S., 249n2

Galiani, Ferdinando, 248
Galileo, 120
Garber, Daniel, 214n2
Gaskin, J.C.A., 27, 148, 341n1,n5,
  342n17, 343n18,n19
Gauden, John, 289–90
Gawlick, Gunther, 221n36
general rules, 28n6, 44, 60n12, 167,
  197–9, 263
generosity, see benevolence
geometry (see also mathematics), 79,
  81–2
Gerard, Alexander, 257, 266, 277, 278n3
Gervaise, Isaac, 224
Gettier problem, 61n13
Giarrizzo, Giuseppe, 218n21, 311n33
Gibbon, Edward, 295, 307n2
God, gods, 19–20, 21, 150–2, 157–8,
  177n5, 178n14, 185, 189–90, 214n2,
  313–16, 318–20, 324, 330, 335, 338,
  339–40
Gödel, Kurt, 81–2
Goldman, Alvin, 60n14
good, 127, 151–2, 154, 175, 189–90
government, 159
  ecclesiastical, 312n47
  right of, 201–6, 229, 304
  and security, 294
  stability of, 197–9
Grant, James, 352
Graunt, John, 223
gravity, 86n16
Great Britain, see Britain
Greece, ancient, 260
Green, T.H., 357
Grose, T.H., 357
Grotius, Hugo, 149–51, 158, 184, 185,
  199, 200, 214n2, 225
Guicciardini, Francesco, 308n9
Guichard, Octavie, Madame Belot,
  308n6
Guthrie, William, 218n19

Haakonssen, Knud, 27, 214n2,
  215n6,n7, 216n11, 219n27,
  220n32,n33,n34
habeas corpus, 294, 305–6

habit, 12, 24–5, 39, 41–2, 50, 76, 90, 91,
    92, 99, 140, 196, 202–3, 232–3, 235,
    237, 241, 266
Hacking, Ian, 115n18
Halkerton, Lord, 351
Halley, Edmund, 223
Hampden, John, 301, 306
Hanoverians, 203, 208
happiness, 162, 172, 180n30, 226, 233,
    239, 264, 333–6
Harre, Rom, 87n21
Harrington, James, 202, 217n14, 290–3
Harrington, Kevin, 279n9
Harris, Eileen, 279n7
Harrison, Jonathan, 219n22, 343n20
Hayek, F.A. von, 218n21
Hearn, Thomas K., 61n12
Heckscher, Eli, 249n2
Hempel, Carl, 84n1, 88n32,n33
Henderson, L.J., 342n11
Henry VIII, 230, 299, 303
Herring, Thomas, Archbishop of Canter-
    bury, 354
Hertford, Francis Seymour Conway, Earl
    of, 355
Hervey, John, Baron, 298, 311n41
Hester, Marcus, 343n22
Hick, John, 339, 343n26
Higgs, Henry, 253n45
Hilson, J.C., 308n5
history, 203–4, 208, 211, 229–39,
    241
    criticism of sources of, 286–90
    and economics, 229–39
    Hume's views of, 281–5
    and method, 285–90, 294–5, 309n15,
        331–2
    and morality, 282
    and parties, 294
    and the passions, 282
    philosophy of, 285–95,
        309n14,n15,n17
    and probability, 286–7
    and providence, 295
    and reading public, 281–2
    use of, 203–4, 208, 211, 229–39, 307
History of England, The, 3, 5, 21–2,
    28n7, 196, 205, 208, 229–30,
    251n22, 281, 308n9, 341n2, 358–9
    aim of, 283–5, 288, 296

and analytical digressions, 294–5,
    311n31
favours Court Whigs, mixed constitu-
    tion, 297–300, 302, 306–7, 308n6
and Hume's models, 282–5
and impartiality, 5, 211, 288, 296–8,
    300–3, 307, 312n45, 353–4
and liberty, 296–7
literary judgements in, 260
as narrative of change, 298–9
reception of, 211, 214, 285, 297,
    308n6, 353–4
and religion, 319, 341n2
writing of, 282–5, 353–4
Hoadly, Benjamin, 216n8
Hobbes, Thomas, 136, 146n14, 149,
    151–5, 159, 176n3, 177n12, 184,
    185, 186, 200, 214n2, 215n4, 291
Holbach, Paul Henri, Baron d', 322, 338
Home, John, 260
Homer, 260, 274
Hont, Istvan, 218n21, 253n39
Hooke, Robert, 65
Hope, Vincent, 146n16
Hopfl, H.H., 309n14
Horace, 260, 273
House of Commons, see British
    Constitution
Howe, D.W., 220n27
human nature, 3, 6, 24–5, 33–6, 101,
    119–24, 159, 164–5, 167–8, 229
    as foundation of morality, 148–81
        (esp. 158–60), 185, 195, 348–9
    Hume's view of, 21–4, 144, 172–5,
        180n30, 182–3, 186, 225–9, 231,
        235, 249–50, 266, 309n14, 333
    and original condition, 16, 165–6,
        180n28, 189
    rationalist view of, 122–3, 125, 127,
        132, 133, 136, 139, 143–4, 145n8
    science of, 1, 3, 6, 24–5, 33–6, 39,
        101, 119–24, 125–6, 129, 131, 138–
        40, 178n16, 226, 260
Hume
    on common sense and morality, 136–
        40, 145n7
    constructive aims of, 1, 117–20
    on essences, 179n24
    "first principle" of, 60n8
    and Hume's Fork, 96–8

and knowledge of science, 64–5
and materialism, 52
and "mental world," 6–7, 158
moral objectives of, 117
naturalistic interpretation of, 76–7
neo-Hellenism of, 143
phenomenological turn of, 8, 30n17
philosophical character of, 23–6,
   32n31, 117–20, 351, 353
post-sceptical stance of, 1, 5–7, 25
psychology of, 119–22
relation philosophy and political
   theory of, 211–12
traditional interpretation of, 5, 36,
   59n4
Hume, life of, 1–2, 279n10, 345–56,
   360–1
   and Bristol merchant, 345, 350
   character, 23–6, 32n31, 117–20, 351,
      353, 356
   deathbed conversation, 23–4, 32n29
   early writing, 2, 347–9
   family, 351
   health, 346–50, 351, 356
   letter to a physician, 345–50
   literary fame, 24, 356
   philosophical anxiety, 118–19, 124,
      345–50
   self-analysis, 346–7
   wealth, 355–6
   youth, education, and reading, 1–3,
      213–14, 255–9, 278n2,n4,n5, 346–
      7, 349, 351–2
Hume, works of (see also individual titles and Index of Citations and References), 3–5, 16–22, 345–8, 351–6,
   357–9
   articles and monographs on, 364–76
   bibliographies, 360
   computer readable editions, 359
   critical edition, 357
   early responses to, 361–4
   Hume's account of, 351–4
Hume as reformer, 23–5, 179n22, 210–
   14, 332–6
"Hume's Early Memoranda," 259,
   280n13, 359
Hume's political theory
   and America, 212–13
   impact of, 210–14

and writings as political acts, 183
Hunter, J. Paul, 278n1
Hurd, Richard, 354
Husserl, Edmund, 30n17
Hutcheson, Francis, 2, 149, 158, 177n11,
   189, 190, 225, 250n15, 259, 261,
   280n12,n14
   moral views of, 154–5, 161
Hutchison, Terence W., 249, 250n7,
   253n40
"hypothetico-deductivism," see
   explanation

ideas, 30n15, 40, 120, 153
   characteristics of, 6, 127
   derive from impressions, 8, 13–14,
      30n16, 60n8, 65–71, 85n8
   refer to impressions, 8, 30n16, 66
   relations of, 96–7, 114n7, 115n9, 270

identity (see also personal identity),
   109–10, 116n24
Ignatieff, Michael, 218n21
imagination, 8–9, 11, 39, 41–3, 59n7,
   60n12, 101, 105, 109–10, 113, 259,
   262
immortality, see religion
impartiality, 164–5, 175
impressions, 6–7, 11, 30n15, n16, 40,
   60n8, 85n8, 120, 270
   characteristics of, 6, 65–6, 127
   of reflection, 12, 14–15
   of sensation, 6–8, 30n16, 66, 85n8
induction (see also causation), 30n14,
   46, 75–7, 88n25,n31, 114n5,
   115n10,n20
   and Hume's inductive scepticism, 94–
   100
   Hume's view of, 75–7
   and inductive over-generalization, 41–
   2, 46, 60n12
infinite divisibility, 82–3
instinct(s) (see also dispositions), 39,
   100–1, 113, 124, 126, 144, 164, 337
intention, see motivation, motives
intentionality, 50, 53–5, 62n23, 128
interest, see self-interest, selfishness
interest, rate of, 237–8, 252n30,n34, 288
international trade, 239–40, 247–8
introspection, 56–7

Ireland and massacre of 1641, 289, 310n22
irony, 59n5, 118, 306, 321–2
is-ought passage, 59n4, 168–9

Jacobites, 208, 245, 289, 310n22
James I, 310n22
James II, 302–3, 310n22, 312n46
Joan of Arc, 28
Johnson, David, 277n1
Johnson, E.A.G., 250n4,n7
Jones, M.M.B., 308n5
Jones, Peter, 27, 85n3, 120, 278n4, 280n21
Jones, R.F., 310n21
judgement, see aesthethic judgement
Julian, Emperor, 333–4
Julius Caesar, 230, 286
justice (see also property), 135, 146n19, 165–8, 180n26, 195, 216n12, 228
    distribution of, 197–9
    and liberty, 198–9
    moralized, 167
    and personal merit, 197–8
    as social artifice, 180n28,n29, 186–92 (see also conventions)
    two foundations of, 167–8
    usefulness of, 172

Kahn, S., 344n29
Kahneman, Daniel, 60n15
Kames, Henry Home, Lord, 243, 251n19, 253n39, 257, 265, 277, 278n3
Kant, Immanuel, 81, 115n9, 140, 277, 280n16, 338, 340
Kaye, F.B., 177n10
Kemp Smith, Norman, 76, 88n27,n34, 124, 145n9, 316, 341n8
Kennett, Basil, 217n13
Kennett, White, 217n19
Kenny, E.J., 116n25
Kierkegaard, Søren, 338
King, Gregory, 223
King, James T., 89n35
Kivy, Peter, 280n14,n20
Kloppenberg, J.T., 219n24
knowledge (see also belief; probability; scepticism), 37–9, 61n13, 91, 100, 102–3, 120–1, 153, 272, 316
Koran, 314

Kornblith, H., 60n14
Kramnick, I., 311n40
Kreimendahl, Lothar, 221n36
Kuehn, Manfred, 361
Kung, Hans, 340, 343n28
Kuypers, Mary Shaw, 85n3, 86n16
Kydd, Rachel M., 145n13

La Bruyère, Jean de, 259, 279n12
Lacey, Michael, 216n9
Larmer, R.A.H., 342n16
Laslett, Peter, 215n4
Laud, Archbishop William, 305
Laugier, Marc-Antoine, 258, 279n9
Law, John, 253n40
laws of nature, 19, 290, 323, 327–30, 332
    and explanation, 77–80
    themselves inexplicable, 3, 35, 78–9, 158–9
Lee, R.W., 278n2
Lehrer, Keith, 147n25
Leibniz, Gottfried, 38
Leslie, Charles, 216n8
Letter from a Gentleman to His Friend in Edinburgh, A 32n26, 358
Letwin, William, 250n7
Levellers, 198
Levine, Michael, 342n16
Lewis, David, 87n23
liberty (see also freedom and necessity), 215n3, 293, 295, 297–300, 303, 305, 307, 310n28, 311n29,n37, 354
    and commerce, 252n31, 292
    English, 215n3, 293–4, 307, 354
    of the press, 306
    protected, 198–9
    and religious bigotry, 306
Life of David Hume, The, see My Own Life
literary criticism, see aesthetic judgement
literary theory, see aesthetics
Livingston, Donald W., 89n35, 212, 218n22, 309n15
Livy (Titus Livius), 284, 287
Locke, John, 2, 7, 29n12, 68–9, 72, 85n6, 106, 115n21, 177n12, 184, 212, 215n4, 216n8, 218n20, 225, 251n18, 259, 286, 300

logical positivism, 64–71, 84n1
Lorenz, Conrad, 340
Louis XVI, 297
Lucian, 23
Lucretius, 325–6

Macaulay, Catherine, 211, 217n19, 308n6
Macaulay, T.B., 211
MacCormick, D.N., 220n32
McCulloch, J.R., 249n3, 250n5
Macfie, A.L., 251n20
Machiavelli, Niccolo, 283, 290–1, 308n9
McIntyre, Jane L., 62n25
MacIntyre, M.M., 116n25
Mackie, J.L., 88n24, 114n3,n5, 343n20
Mackintosh, James, 221n34
Macpherson, James, 260
Macquarrie, John, 339, 343n27
Madden, Edward, 87n21
Madison, James, 213, 219n26
Magna Carta, 300
Mandeville, Bernard, 148, 154–6, 160, 179n23, 224, 232
Martyn, Henry, 224
Marx, Karl, 225
Mary Queen of Scotland, 289, 290, 310n22
mathematics (see also geometry), 80–4
matters of fact (see also ideas, relations of), 96–7, 128
Maxwell, J., 217n13
meaning, theory of (see also concept formation), 31n21, 63n26, 65–71, 80, 85n6,n7, 86n9, 111
Meek, Ronald L., 216n10, 253n45,n46, 310n25
Melon, Jean-François, 225
mercantilism, 222–3, 240, 249n2
Merrill, Kenneth R., 308n10
Middle Ages, 299, 300
Middleton, Conyers, 353
Mill, J.S., 80, 88n26
Millar, Andrew, 353, 354
Miller, David, 212, 218n22, 311n37
mind, science of the, see human nature, science of; philosophy of mind and Hume
minima sensibilia, 83

Mirabeau, Marquis de, 246
miracles, 28n7, 286–8, 318, 320, 328–32, 342n16,n18, 343n19
missing shade of blue, 67
monarchy, 202–6, 205, 217n17, 303–5
Monder, S., 61n12
money, 235–9, 241, 242–3, 247, 250n7
monotheism, 20
Montaigne, Michel, 149
Monteiro, J.-P., 59n6
Montesquieu, Charles-Louis de Secondat, baron de, 225, 241, 251n19, 252n32,n33, 266, 290, 305, 310n27,n29, 311n30
  on climate and culture, 241, 293
  influence of, on Hume, 293–5
Moore, James, 310n23
moral scepticism, see scepticism
moral sentiments, moral sense, 12, 14–15, 133–5, 154, 162–3, 164–5, 168, 171, 175, 189, 334–6
moral theories, 148–58
  artifice theory, 155–6
  Hume's criticisms of, 155–8
  Hume's moral theory, 158–81
morality
  ancient, 346, 348–9
  an artifact, 15–16
  and civilization, 299
  and common sentiments, 175–6
  and the Deity, 150–1, 157–8, 189–90
  distorted by religion, 317, 332–6
  foundations of, 148–81, 348–9
  and history, 282
  and moral distinctions, 14–15, 138–9, 148, 150–8, 160–4, 171, 174–5, 180n25, see also moral sentiments
  and moral vocabulary, 156, 172, 173, 175
  and motivation, 150–1, 154–5, 157
  and origin of moral ideas, 13–15
  rationalist views of, 152–3, 156–7, 169, 177n13
  science of, 190
  secular basis of, 137, 143, 156, 178n15, 186–92, 200, 332–6
  and society, 333–5
  and teleology, 190–1
  and usefulness, 172–4, 180n25, 190–1
  and will theories, 188–92

morals, *see* morality
Morellet, Abbé André, 247, 251*n*19
Morice, G.P., 218*n*21
Morris, Robert, 258, 279*n*9
Mossner, E.C., 32*n*26, 279*n*10, 280*n*13, 312*n*42, 341*n*2
Mothersill, Mary, 280*n*22
motivation, motives, 15, 155, 160–1, 166–7, 169–70, 179*n*22, 191, 335
Munn, Thomas, 222, 249*n*3
Mure, William of Caldwell, Baron, 245
music, 257
My Own Life, 3, 351–6, 359

National Library of Scotland, 345
"natural belief," 316, 336–41
Natural History of Religion, The, 3, 18– 19, 20–1, 32*n*26, 309*n*14, 316, 338, 354
natural law, 184–5, 199–201, 213, 214*n*2, 216*n*11, 217*n*13, 220*n*32
natural religion, 314–15
natural virtues, 16, 135, 164–5, 171, 186–7
naturalism, 91–2, 100
nature, natural, defined, 164, 316, 335
Neal, Daniel, 217*n*19
necessary connection, *see* causation
necessity, *see* freedom and necessity
Nero, 14, 15
Netherlands, 201
Newton, Sir Isaac, 2, 34, 38, 55, 80
   influence of, on Hume, 59*n*2, 62*n*25, 64–5, 120–1 138, 140–1
   and Newtonian mechanics, 78–9
   and second causes, 68–9
Nicole, Pierre, 286
Nidditch, P.H., 85*n*6
"no-argument argument," 98
normative claims, *see* fact and value
North, Roger, 223
North, Sir Dudley, 223
Norton, David Fate, 26, 29*n*9, 31*n*23, 32*n*34, 60*n*7, 63*n*25, 85*n*3, 114*n*3, 145*n*7,*n*13, 146*n*20, 176*n*2, 178*n*15, 278*n*4,*n*5, 308*n*13, 357
Norton, Mary J., 278*n*4,*n*5
novels, 278*n*1, 282, 308*n*4
Noxon, James, 64, 85*n*2, 341*n*8

Oakeshott, Michael, 176*n*3
obligation, moral, *see* duty, duties
obligation, political, *see* allegiance
"Of a particular Providence and of a fu- ture State," *see* argument from design
"Of Miracles," 19, 287, 289–90, 309*n*16
   publication of, 18, 31*n*26, 287, 317
offices, *see* duty, duties
Olding, A., 342*n*15
Oldmixon, John, 217*n*19, 312*n*45
Onuf, Peter S., 219*n*24
opinion, *see* allegiance; belief
Oswald, James, of Dunnikier, 242, 251*n*19, 253*n*39
Ovid, 64, 273

pain, *see* pleasure, pain
painting and poetry, 256, 278*n*2
Palladio, Andrea, 257, 279*n*8
Paris-Duverney, Joseph, 225
"Parity Argument, The," 339
Parliament (*see also* British Constitu- tion), 234, 293, 301, 304, 305, 306
parties, 205–9, 215*n*3, 294
Pascal, Blaise, 316
passions, 12–13, 62*n*19, 122–3, 125–9, 132–3, 144, 145*n*9, 156, 311*n*31
   calm, 127, 145*n*11, 272
   direct, 12, 125–7
   as impressions of reflection, 6, 12, 125
   indirect, 12–13, 125–6, 135, 142
   influence conduct, 127, 335
   not representational, 128
   and reason, 125–9, 139–40, 163
   violent, 127, 145*n*11
Paul, Saint, 316
Pears, Iain, 278*n*1
Penelhum, Terence, 26, 146*n*16,*n*24, 148, 339, 343*n*24
perceptions (*see also* ideas; impres- sions), 6–8, 30*n*15, 40, 55–6, 106, 108–9, 120
Perrault, Claude, 257–8, 278*n*5
personal identity, 11, 38, 47–56, 61*n*16, 62*n*25, 121–2, 140–3, 319
   and impression of self, 134
   and the passions, 62*n*19, 140–3
personal merit, 171–6
Petty, William, 223

Petyt, William, 222–3, 250n5
phenomenalism, 30n16, 70–1, 80
phenomenology, 8, 30n17
Phillipson, Nicholas, 217n17
Philosophical Essays concerning Human Understanding, see *Enquiry concerning Human Understanding, An*
philosophy, value of, 24
philosophy of history, *see* history
philosophy of mind and Hume, 51–6
physical necessity, *see* causation
Physiocrats, 246–7, 253n45
Pike, Nelson, 146n24, 342n8
Plantinga, Alvin, 340, 342n11, 343n29
Plato, 12, 120, 122–3, 159, 341n8, 342n10
pleasure, pain, 62n23, 126, 134, 160, 162–3, 165, 179n24, 275
Plutarch, 346
Pocock, J.G.A., 211–12, 218n21, 219n25, 220n32
political authority, 192–7, 201–3, 303–5
Political Discourses, 210, 251n26, 353, 358
political economy, 244–5, 250n7
  and historical dynamics, 231–5
  and human nature, psychology, 224–9
  Hume's influence on, 245–8
  methodology of, 223–4, 235–6, 241
  and stages theory, 231–3, 248, 292–3
political institutions, 5, 195–6, 291, 304
  theories of, 184–5
political theory, *see* Hume's political theory
polytheism, 21
Pompa, L., 309n14
Popish Plot, 289, 302, 310n22
Popkin, Richard H., 29n12, 115n19, 308n10
Popper, Sir Karl, 340
population, 235–6, 247, 252n32, 288
Port-Royal Logic, The (Arnauld and Nicole), 286
Pothier, Robert-Joseph, 215n4
power, *see* causation
power, political, *see* political authority
Price, J.V., 59n5, 311n37
prices, 236–9, 240, 243
pride, 12–13, 126, 142, 227

probability (*see also* belief; induction), 77, 95, 102–4, 115n18, 286–7, 327, 329–30
propensity, *see* disposition; instinct(s)
property (*see also* justice), 135, 144, 165–7, 172, 180n28, 184–5, 187–8, 190–1, 193, 197–202, 210, 212, 227, 234, 291–2, 300, 304
  and egalitarian schemes, 198, 234–5
Protagoras, 113, 152
Protestants, Protestantism, 286, 288, 303
  and moral theory, 185, 189–90
providence, 315
psychological egoism, *see* selfish theory
public credit, 210, 233, 244–5, 252n30, 295
Pufendorf, Samuel, 149, 152–3, 157, 176n4, 178n14, 184, 200, 217n13, 225
Puritans, 198
Pylyshyn, Zenon, 60n15
Pym, John, 301
Pyrrhonism, Pyrrho (*see also* scepticism), 12, 29n12, 90, 91, 94, 104, 112, 115n19, 116n25

qualities, primary and secondary, 7, 29n12, 68, 116n23
Quesnay, François, 246–7
Quine, W.V.O., 60n14

Racine, Jean, 260
Ralph, James, 217n19
Rameau, Jean Philippe, 257
Ramsay, Allan, 256, 266
Ramsay, Frank, 87n22
Raphael, D.D., 216n10, 221n34, 252n20
Rapin-Thoyras, Paul de, 217n19, 282, 298, 308n7, 311n42
rationalists, *see* human nature; morality
Raynor, David, 1, 29n12, 31n23, 116n23, 219n22, 359
realism
  and morality, 148
  naive, 108–11
  representational, 30n15, 69, 106–9, 112

reason, reasoning, 11, 43–4, 59n7,
    60n7,n12, 91–7, 100–6, 114n2,
    123–4, 127–8, 264
  and aesthetic judgement, 264–5, 266–
    71
  and beauty, 261–4
  demonstrative, 94–7, 115n17
  and dimunition argument, 101–3
  experimental or causal, 43–4, 99–100
  and morality, 14–15, 132–4, 150, 153,
    162, 163, 171
  and the passions, 125–9, 139–40,
    163–4
  and regression argument, 101–3
  scepticism regarding, 100–5
reflection, impressions of, 30n16, 126,
    128
reform, see Hume as reformer
Reformation, Protestant, 149, 184
Reichenbach, Hans, 84n1
Reid, Thomas, 85n8, 115n7, 220n33,
    277
relation(s)
  of ideas, 96–7, 114n7, 115n9, 127 (see
    also matters of fact)
  natural and philosophical, 44, 47
relativity, special theory of, 87n17
religion, 18–21, 31n26, 67, 144, 178n15,
    184, 200, 210, 288–9
  and affirmations of orthodoxy, 319–22
  and argument a priori, 314–5, 318–9
  and argument from design, 19–20,
    314–15, 318–28, 337–8, 342n12
  and atheism, 18–19, 32n26, 320–2,
    341n6
  and Christianity, 207–8
  enthusiasm in, 182–3, 198, 207,
    214n1, 232, 315–16, 341n2
  in Essays, 317
  and French mystics, 349
  Hume's criticisms of, 313, 318–22
  Hume's writings on, 313, 316–19
  and immortality, 317, 319, 320
  and morality, 317, 319, 322, 332–6
  natural, 314–15
  and origins of religious belief, 20–1,
    316, 318–19, 338
  and priestcraft, 207–8, 251n23
  and providence, 295, 315
  and prudence, 313, 321

revealed, 314–15, 317, 328–32
  and superstition, 182–3, 207, 295,
    315, 335–6, 341n2
  terminology in, 313–16
  in Treatise, 317–18
religious strife, 185–6, 207
Renaissance, 149, 212
representation, 53–5
Rescher, Nicholas, 59n3
Restoration, the, 289, 291
Resurrection, the, 314, 329, 331–2,
    343n18
Revolution of 1688, 208, 233, 354
rich country–poor country debate, 242,
    248, 253n39
Richardson, Jonathan, 257, 278n3
Richardson, Samuel, 308n4
Richmond, Charles Lennox, Duke of,
    355
rights, 199–201, 216n11,n12
Robertson, J.M., 177n9
Robertson, John, 219n23
Robertson, William, 281, 289, 307n2
Robinson, J.A., 86n15
Robison, Wade, 63n25
Rogin, Leo, 253n51
Rollin, Charles, 284
Roman Catholicism, 286
Roman law, 199, 215n4
Rosenberg, Alexander, 26, 114n5
Ross, Ian, 309n19
Rotwein, Eugene, 225–6, 251n19,n28,
    252n34
Rouet (Rouat, Ruet), William, 245
Rousseau, Jean Jacques, 257
Royal Society of Edinburgh, 345
Russell, Bertrand, 65, 85n5, 115n21, 322
Rye House plot, 303, 312n46
Rykwert, Anne, 279n6
Rykwert, Joseph, 278n1, 279n6
Ryle, Gilbert, 146n15

St. Clair, James, 256, 352
Sallust (Gaius Sallustius Crispus), 284
Salmon, Wesley, 85n4, 88n31
Sarpi, Fra Paolo, 283–4, 308n10
Say, J.B., 240, 247, 252n36
Scamozzi, Vincenzo, 257, 279n8
scepticism, 1, 5, 7, 8, 11–12, 25, 26,
    30n14,n18, 35, 36–9, 41–2, 45, 47–

8, 57–8, 76–7, 90–1, 93, 111–13, 124, 144, 149
ethical or moral, 114n3, 150–2, 154, 155, 171, 176, 176n3
and fallibilism, 91, 113
and history, 287–8, 309n13
Hume's inductive, 94–100
and Hume's sceptical strategies, 32n34, 93–4
mitigated, 113, 319
regarding reason, 100–5
regarding the senses, 105–8, 113n1
and religion, 1, 19–21, 32n26, 316, 321, 338, 340
and the senses, 105–8
Schaefer, A., 218n21
Schleiermacher, Friedrich, 338
Schmoller, Gustav von, 249n2
Schneider, H.-P., 217n13
Schofield, M., 115n19
scholastics, 215n4
Schopenhauer, Arthur, 338
Schumpeter, Joseph A., 248, 249n2, 250n7,n17, 252n32
science, early modern, 149, 151, 175–6
Hume's knowledge of, 64–5, 85n3
science of human nature, see human nature, science of
science of politics, 194–6, 195–6
Scotland, 1, 256, 258, 266, 277n1, 279n10, 281, 299–300, 303, 307n2, 331, 346, 351, 353, 355
Scott, George, 245
Scott, W.R., 250n15
Scottish Enlightenment, 213, 220n28
Seidler, Michael, 177n4
self, self-identity, see personal identity
self-interest, selfishness (see also selfish theory), 16, 148–9, 150–6, 155, 164, 166–8, 173–5, 179n23, 224, 227–9, 231, 290–1, 334
and aesthetic judgement, 265
and constraint, 228–9
and interest and allegiance, 193–4
and testimony, 287
selfish theory (psychological egoism), 136, 145n9, 173–4, 177n12, 178n18, 179n23
self-knowledge, 119–20
self-love, see self-interest

Seneca, Lucius Anneus 346
senses, 11, 105–8
sentiment(s) (see also moral sentiments, moral sense), 280n17, 261–4, 266–7, 270–6, 323
Serlio, Sebastiano, 257, 279n8
Sextus Empiricus, 113
Shaftesbury, Anthony Ashley Cooper, first Earl of, 310n22
Shaftesbury, Anthony Ashley Cooper, third Earl of, 154, 175, 177n9, 189, 259, 261, 266, 272, 279n12
Shahan, Robert, 308n10
Shakespeare, William, 260
Shalhope, R.E., 219n24
Shatz, D., 344n29
Shaver, Robert, 148
Shelley, Percy Bysshe, 338
Sher, R.B., 220n27,n28
Shope, R.K., 60n13
Sidney, Algernon, 300
skepticism, see scepticism
Skinner, Andrew S., 27, 218n21, 221n34, 250n10, 251n24, 252n36, 253n42, 280n21
slavery, 235, 288
Slovic, Paul, 61n15
Smith, Adam, 23–4, 27, 32n31, 210, 213, 216n12, 222, 225, 227, 230, 239, 240, 245, 251n20, 258, 260, 266, 277, 280n17,n21, 292, 309n19
and history, 248, 309n15
Hume's influence on, 213, 230, 246–7
Theory of Moral Sentiments, The, 246
Wealth of Nations, The, 247, 249
Smitten, J.R., 220n27
Smollett, Tobias, 307n2
sociability, 150, 185
social conventions, 166
society, 2, 166, 172, 195–6, 228–30, 264–6, 295, 333–6
Socrates, 119–20, 122
Sommerville, J.P., 216n8
Sosa, Ernest, 87n20
sovereignty, see government, right of
space, 8, 31n19, 41, 82–4, 88n34
and geometry, 79
as "manner of appearance," 8, 83
Spectator, The (Addison and Steele), 210, 258–9, 284

INDEX OF CITATIONS AND REFERENCES

This index locates both citations and discussions of particular passages in Hume's works. More general discussions of these works may be found through the Index of Names and Subjects.

An Abstract of . . . A Treatise of Human Nature (A)
[641] — 17
646 — 4, 29n10, 39
647 — 8–9
649–51 — 71
650–1 — 9
651 — 95
653–4 — 11
656 — 30n13
656–7 — 71, 72
657 — 12, 90, 92, 94
661 — 121

Dialogue, A (D)
333–4 — 180n30

Dialogues concerning Natural Religion (DNR)
Pt. 1 134 — 340
Pt. 1 135 — 336
Pt. 2 143 — 314, 323
Pt. 2 146 — 325
Pt. 2 149–51 — 324
Pt. 3 154 — 323, 338
Pt. 4 — 338
Pt. 4 160–4 — 325
Pt. 4 161 — 325
Pt. 4 162 — 326
Pt. 5 166–9 — 324
Pt. 6 175 — 327
Pt. 7 — 338

Pt. 8 — 325
Pt. 8 183 — 327
Pt. 8 184 — 328
Pt. 8 185 — 328
Pt. 9 — 319
Pt. 9 188 — 314
Pt. 9 188–9 — 315
Pts. 10–11 — 324
Pt. 11 211 — 324
Pt. 12 214 — 320
Pt. 12 222 — 333
Pt. 12 227 — 20, 321–2

Dissertation on the Passions (DP)
Sec. 2.6 4:147 — 179n24
Sec. 2.10 4:152 — 272

An Enquiry concerning Human Understanding (EHU)
Advertisement [3] — 18
Sec. 1 5 — 24
Sec. 1 12 — 321
Sec. 1 14 — 34
Sec. 2 20 — 66
Sec. 2 20–1 — 67
Sec. 3 W4:19 — 269
Sec. 3 W4:19–23 — 270
Sec. 4 — 99, 114n4
Sec. 4.1 25 — 81, 96–7
Sec. 4.1 26 — 65
Sec. 4.1 30 — 78
Sec. 4.2 32 — 95

stages theory, *see* political economy and stages theory
standard of taste, 266–76
Stanhope, Phillip, Earl of, 266
Steele, Sir Richard, 210
Stein, P.G., 216n10
Stephen, Sir Leslie, 342n18
Sterne, Laurence, 308n4
Steuart, Robert, 278n2,n6
Steuart, Sir James, 224, 245–6, 248
Stewart, Dugald, 221n34, 224–5, 253n43, 309n14
Stewart, John B., 32n32, 146n18, 178n16, 212, 218n22, 311n37
Stewart, M.A., 28n2, 215n6, 357
Stich, Stephen, 60n14
Stockton, Constant Noble, 310n24
Stoics, 12, 143, 194, 325, 327
Stone, George, Primate of All Ireland, 354
Stove, David, 77, 88n30
Strafford, Thomas Wentworth, Earl of, 301, 354
Strahan, William, 32n28
Strawson, Galen, 87n18
Stroud, Barry, 76, 88n28, 115n10
Stuarts, 202, 208, 297, 298–9, 301, 304, 306, 312n42, 354
substance, 66, 69–71, 109–11
succession (*see* causation and priority)
suicide, 317, 319
Summerson, John, 277n1
superstition, *see* religion
Swift, Jonathan, 282
Swinburne, R.G., 342n11,n14,n15, 343n19
sympathy, 15–16, 142, 146n18, 165, 167–8, 171, 178n16, 227–8, 250n20, 261, 272, 311n31, 333, 334
    as principle of communication, 15, 134, 136

Tacitus, Gaius Cornelius, 260, 273, 283, 284, 307, 331
Tasso, 260
taste, standard of, (*see also* aesthetic judgement), 266–76
taxation, 233
Taylor, A.E., 117–19, 144n1
Taylor, W.L., 250n15

Teichgraber, Richard F., 219n22, 241, 254n54
Ten Commandments, The, 333–4
Tertullian, 316
testimony, 286–90, 329–32
theism, 315
theology, *see* religion
theoretical entities, 67–71
Thomas, P.J., 249n2
time, 8–9, 41, 83–4, 88n34, 116n24
    as "manner of appearance," 8, 83
Todd, W.B., 253n24
Tories, 5, 192, 208, 211, 216n8, 288, 296–307, 311n32, 312n45, 354
trade, *see* international trade
tragedy, 265–6
Traiger, Saul, 86n12
Treatise of Human Nature, A, 3, 21–2, 90, 120, 208, 212, 226, 246, 261, 332, 343n20, 358
    Abstract as attempt to clarify, 17
    "Advertisement" urging that, be disregarded, 17–18
    as "*dead-born from the press,*" 16
    early work on, 2, 18, 118–19, 346, 349, 352
    ill-success of, 352–3
    Of Morals, 163–71
    recastings of, 16–21, 31n24, 171, 353
    and religion, 18, 317–18, 320
Tuck, Richard, 176n3, 214n2, 215n4
Tucker, Josiah, 225, 242, 248, 253n39
Tudors, 299, 303–4, 305, 312n42, 354
Tully, James, 177n4
Turgot, Anne-Robert-Jacques, baron de l'Aulne, 247, 251n19, 252n29, 290, 295
Turnbull, George, 257, 278n3
Tversky, Amos, 61n15
Tweyman, Stanley, 342n8
Tyrrell, James, 298

Ullman, Shimon, 61n15
understanding, the, 101–3, 115n15
universalizability, 175
usefulness, *see* morality

Vanderlint, Jacob, 224–5, 250n12
Vauban, Sebastian, 225

Vickers, Douglas, 250n7
Vignola, Giacome Barozzi da, 257, 279n8
Viner, Jacob, 249n2
Vinnius, Arnoldus (Arnold Vinnen), 351
Virgil, 260, 351
virtues, artificial, *see* artificial virtues
virtues, natural, 16, 135, 164–5, 171, 186–7
virtue(s), vice(s), 13–14, 133–5, 137–8, 146n22, 164–8, 170, 175, 180n30, 198, 302, 346–7
Vitruvius, Pollio, 257, 279n8
Vlachos, G., 218n21
Voet, Johannes, 351
Voltaire (François Marie Arouet), 266, 283, 295, 308n8
voluntarism, 152, 156, 157, 177n5, 185, 186, 189

Wallace, Robert, 235, 248, 252n32, 288
Walpole, Horace, 282–3, 284
Walpole, Sir Robert, 209, 311n41
Warburton, William, 353, 354
Waszek, N., 221n36
Watson, J.R., 308n5
"way of ideas," 8, 30n15, 56
Wenzel, L., 218n21
Wexler, V., 219n22
Whalley, P., 309n15

Whelan, Frederick, 212, 218n22
Whigs, 5, 192–3, 203, 208, 211, 216n 245, 288, 289, 296–307, 308n6, 310n22, 311n32,n41, 312n45, 35
Whitelocke, Bulstrode, 312n45
Wilkes, John, 205, 215n3, 295, 296, 2 306
will (*see also* freedom and necessity), 127, 129–32, 188–93
will theories, *see* contract theories
William of Orange, 203, 306
Wills, Garry, 219n27
Wilson, Fred, 146n23
Wilson, Thomas, 218n21
Winch, Donald, 220n30, 221n34
Wittgenstein, Ludwig, 86n9
Wolff, Robert Paul, 146n23
Wollaston, William, 149
Wolterstorff, N., 344n29
Wood, Gordon S., 219n24
Wood, P.B., 86n8
Woolf, Daniel, 309n18
Wootton, David, 27, 308n10, 309n16 341n4
Wotton, William, 278n5
Wright, John P., 87n18

Xenophon, 342n10

Zeno's paradoxes, 82

Sec. 4.2 32–9	4
Sec. 4.2 37–8	76
Sec. 4.2 39	43
Sec. 5	39, 45, 99
Sec. 5.1 41	25
Sec. 5.1 41–2	99
Sec. 5.1 43	99
Sec. 5.2 54	124
Sec. 5.2 55	100
Sec. 7.1 63	72
Sec. 7.1 63–4	73
Sec. 7.1 64–9	131
Sec. 7.1 73n	68
Sec. 7.2 74	73
Sec. 7.2 76–7	71
Sec. 8	129–30, 319
Sec. 8.1 83	226
Sec. 8.1 84	159
Sec. 8.1 95	130, 131
Sec. 9	100
Sec. 9 108	43, 100
Sec. 10	19, 93, 287, 317, 328
Sec. 10.1 114	329
Sec. 10.1 114–16	330
Sec. 10.1 115, 115n	330
Sec. 10.2 116	329
Sec. 10.2 127	329
Sec. 10.2 130	318, 320
Sec. 10 131	336, 340
Sec. 11	19–20, 316–17, 319
Sec. 11 135	320, 322, 323
Sec. 11 136–42	324
Sec. 11 139	328
Sec. 11 148	324
Sec. 12.1 150	92
Sec. 12.1 153	107
Sec. 12.1 155n	93–4
Sec. 12.2	93
Sec. 12.3 162	113
Sec. 12.3 165	4, 67, 317

An Enquiry concerning the Principles of Morals (EPM)

Sec. 1 169–74	171–2
Sec. 1 173	261, 264, 270
Sec. 1 174	4
Sec. 2.1 176	172
Sec. 2.1 181	172

Sec. 2.2 181	161
Sec. 3.1 183–204	172
Sec. 3.2 193	198
Sec. 3.2 193–4	199
Sec. 3.2 194	198, 235
Sec. 3.2 202	273
Sec. 4 206	334
Sec. 4 207	263
Sec. 5.1–2 215–19	155
Sec. 5.1 213n	173, 272
Sec. 5.1 214	156, 273
Sec. 5.1 214–15	173
Sec. 5.2 219–20n	159
Sec. 5.2 222	273
Sec. 5.2 229	263
Sec. 5.2 230	159, 162
Sec. 6.1 235–6	180n25
Sec. 6.2 245	270
Sec. 9.1 268–70	174
Sec. 9.1 270	143
Sec. 9.1 271	162, 174, 269
Sec. 9.1 271–3	175
Sec. 9.1 274	176
Sec. 9.1 278	176
Sec. 9.2	334
Sec. 9.2 278–84	180n30
Sec. 9.2 283	334
App. 1 285–6	163
App. 1 289	163
App. 1 292	257, 261
App. 2 296	178n18
App. 2 298	177n12
App. 2 300	179n23

Essays, Moral and Political (1741–2)
Advertisement

W 3:41–2	210

Essays Moral, Political, and Literary (E) [Alphabetized by abbreviation, in conformity with the list on front pages xi–xii.]

Whether the British Government inclines more to Absolute Monarchy, or to a Republic (E-BG)

47–53	291
47–8	217n14
51	293

Of the Balance of Trade (E-BT)

312	241
314	241
317	253n40

Of Civil Liberty (E-CL)

87–96	217n17
88–9	292
91	260, 282
92–3	292

Of Commerce (E-Co)

254	231
256	231
260	233
260–1	232
261	232
262	233
263	239
265	233, 243–4, 252n31, 292
267	241

Of the Coalition of Parties (E-CP)

493–501	312n42
493–501	216n8

A Character of Sir Robert Walpole (E-CR)

574–6	311n41

Of the Dignity or Meanness of Human Nature (E-DM)

80–6	155

Of the Delicacy of Taste and Passion (E-DT)

4	267
6	267

The Epicurean (E-Ep)

140	273

Of the First Principles of Government (E-FP)

21	291
32–3	195
33	197, 201
33–4	202

Of Impudence and Modesty (E-IM)

553	273

Of Interest (E-In)

297	237
300	226, 232
301	237
302–3	238

Of the Independency of Parliament (E-IP)

42–6	291
44–5	21

Idea of A Perfect Commonwealth (E-IPC)

512–29	291
514	25
514–16	217n14
522–3	217n14

Of the Immortality of the Soul (E-IS)

590–8	317
590	320

Of the Jealousy of Trade (E-JT)

324	241
327–8	239–40
328	239
329	240
331	240

Of the Liberty of the Press (E-LP)

9–13	21
10–11	217n17
604	306

Of Money (E-Mo)

281	236
283	242, 243
283–4	242–3
284	253n40
286	233
286–7	238–9
288	239
290	238
290–1	236
292–3	237
294	237

Of National Characters (E-NC)

197–215	241, 317

Of the Original Contract (E-OC)

465–86	300
469	263
470–1	194
479–80	165
480	4
485–6	217n17

Of the Origin of Government (E-OG)

37–8	197

39–40	194
40	304
40–41	294

Of the Populousness of Ancient Nations (E-PA)

377–464	288
379–80	252n32
381	235
383	235
396	235
416	235
419–20	236

Of Public Credit (E-PC)

353–4	233
354–5	242, 244
357–8	244–5
637	252n30

Of Parties in General (E-PG)

55	21, 206
59–60	206
60	207
62	207
63	208

Of the Parties of Great Britain (E-PGB)

64–72	311n32
69–72	216n8
71–2	208

That Politics may be reduced to a Science (E-PR)

18–19	242
21	291
22–4	217n17

Of the Protestant Succession (E-PS)

502–11	208, 291

Of Refinement in the Arts (E-RA)

268	232
269	226
270	226
271	234
272	275
277–8	234

Of the Rise and Progress of the Arts and Sciences (E-RP)

111–12	22
112–13	231
113	227, 292
113–19	217n17

124–33	217n17
125	303

The Sceptic (E-Sc)

163	271
164–6	261
170–1	24
172	263–4

Of Superstition and Enthusiasm (E-SE)

73–9	21, 317
73–4	316
74	182–3

Of the Study of History (E-SH)

563	282
566	229
566–7	282

Of Simplicity and Refinement in Writing (E-SR)

193	260

Of the Standard of Taste (E-ST)

226–49	259
229	267
230	267
231	4, 267
232	267, 274
232–3	28n6
234	267
235	270
236	271
237	269, 275
237–9	268
238	272
239	268
239–40	267
240	268, 271
241	270, 273–4
242	267
244	273
246	260
246–7	273

Of Suicide (E-Su)

577–89	317, 332
580–6	79

Of Taxes (E-T)

343	233
345–6	233
347–8	303

Of Tragedy (E-Tr)
216–25   266

The History of England (HE)
App. 3 4:355   304
App. 3 4:356–60   305
App. 3 4:360   303
App. 3 4:370   305
App. 4 5:151–2   260
Ch. 11 1:445   300
Ch. 20 2:398   29n7
Ch. 23 2:514   304
Ch. 23 2:518   306
Ch. 23 2:525   307
Ch. 26 3:76   234
Ch. 26 3:78   230
Ch. 29 3:135   230, 251n23
Ch. 33 3:323   303
Ch. 33 3:328   252n35
Ch. 39 4:388–9nF   283
Ch. 39 4:395nM   289
Ch. 45 5:18–19   306
Ch. 53 5:249–50   306
Ch. 53 5:250   305
Ch. 56 5:416–17   302
Ch. 57 5:441–3   214n1
Ch. 59 5:547–8   289
Ch. 62 6:140   229
Ch. 62 6:142–6   214n1
Ch. 62 6:148   233
Ch. 64 6:215   312n45
Ch. 66 6:307–8   301
Ch. 67 6:367   306
Ch. 68 6:381   216n8
Ch. 69 6:436   300
Ch. 71 6:523–34   216n8
Ch. 71 6:530–4   208–9
Ch. 71 6:531   307
Ch. 71 6:537   233

"A Kind of History of my Life"
(KHL)
345–50   2, 24, 118, 148

Letter to Hugh
   Blair   85n8

The Letters of David Hume (HL)
1:9   2
1:30   275
1:32   34, 39
1:32–3   29n10

1:34   161
1:38–9   17
1:40   15
1:109   284
1:118–27   257
1:138   311n30
1:142–3   242
1:142–4   253n39
1:158   17
1:170   282, 312n42
1:179   301
1:193   281
1:196   297–8
1:210   282
1:222   282, 301
1:226   308n8
1:237   301
1:244   281
1:251   283
1:255   281
1:258   312n42
1:264   312n42
1:266   281
1:270–1   253n39
1:270–2   250n14
1:271–2   243
1:284   283
1:285   284–5, 285
1:294   295
1:302   307n2
1:314   281
1:316   283
1:344   282
1:369   301
1:379   283, 312n42
1:401   260
1:461   312n42
1:512   256
2:93–5   252n29
2:106   281
2:133   275
2:173   257
2:180   250n14, 295
2:180–1   215n3
2:182   250n14
2:191–2   215n3, 297
2:196   281
2:205   247, 250n14
2:209–11   215n3
2:212–13   215n3

2:216	215n3, 297, 312n42	Sec. 1 4–5	66
		Sec. 1 5	66
2:229	281	Sec. 1 5–6	67
2:233	281	Sec. 4 10	121
2:242	281, 297	Sec. 4 12–13	80, 121
2:260–1	307, 312n42	Sec. 4 13	35, 158
2:261	215n3	Sec. 5 13–14	44
2:269	308n4	Sec. 7 16	70
2:303	297		
2:309–12	307n2	Book 1 Part 2	
2:310	295, 299–300	Sec. 1 27	83
2:347	282	Sec. 2 30–1	83
2:366–7	282	Sec. 2 32	14, 31n19,n21, 60n9

My Own Life (MOL)

351–6	16, 17, 24, 31n24, 171, 282	Sec. 3 34	8–9, 30n16, 83
		Sec. 3 35	9, 83
		Sec. 3 38	8–9

The Natural History of Religion (NHR)

		Sec. 4 48	41, 70
Intro. 4: 309–10	5, 20, 320	Sec. 4 51	41
		Sec. 4 51–2	41

New Letters of David Hume (NHL)

		Sec. 5 60	80
4	24		
13	319	Book 1 Part 3	
23	284	Sec. 1 71	79, 81, 82
53	295	Sec. 2	318
69–71	312n42	Sec. 2 73–4	44
196	215n3, 311n29	Sec. 2 75	86n16
		Sec. 2 76	86n17
198	299	Sec. 2 77	9, 87n18
199	215n3, 295	Secs. 4–14	115n12
		Sec. 5 84	6–7

A Treatise of Human Nature (T)

		Sec. 5 86	60n11
Book 1 *Of the Understanding*		Sec. 6	114n6, 115n12
Title-page	64		
Advertisement		Sec. 6 89	95
[xii]	246, 255	Sec. 6 90	95
Intro. xiv	6, 34, 39	Sec. 7 94–8	11
Intro. xv	24, 226	Sec. 7 96	13
Intro. xvi	3, 34, 35, 120, 226	Sec. 7 96n	44
		Sec. 7 97n	43
Intro. xvi–xix	158	Sec. 8 101–4	43
Intro. xvii	3, 34	Sec. 9 106	44
Intro. xviii	36	Sec. 9 117–18	59n7
Intro. xix	4, 22, 57, 226	Sec. 10 122	69
Book 1 Part 1		Sec. 11 124	9
Sec. 1 1	40, 66, 127	Secs. 13–14	317
Sec. 1 4	60n8	Sec. 13 145	287
Secs. 1–4 1–13	6	Sec. 13 146ff	60n12
		Sec. 14	100

Book 1 Part 3 (cont.)
Sec. 14 157   14
Sec. 14 161   13
Sec. 14 162   14, 31n21
Sec. 14 162–6   10
Sec. 14 165   73
Sec. 14 167   74
Sec. 14 167–8   74
Sec. 14 170   71
Sec. 14 171   131
Sec. 15 173   76
Sec. 15 173–6   60n12

Book 1 Part 4
Sec. 1   101
Sec. 1 180   102–3
Sec. 1 181–2   102
Sec. 1 182–3   102
Sec. 1 183   43, 104
Sec. 2 185   105
Sec. 2   29n11, 93
Sec. 2 187   70
Sec. 2 187–8   37, 41, 105–6
Sec. 2 187–93   11
Sec. 2 190   30n16
Sec. 2 193   43, 114n2
Sec. 2 194–7   29, 71
Sec. 2 195   93
Sec. 2 198   41, 42
Sec. 2 200–4   47
Sec. 2 201   61n16
Sec. 2 202   70, 106
Sec. 2 210–11   106
Sec. 2 211   109
Sec. 2 212   106–7
Sec. 2 215   109
Sec. 2 217   107–8
Sec. 2 218   112
Sec. 3 220   69, 110
Sec. 3 221   116n24
Sec. 3 222   111
Sec. 3 224   111
Sec. 4 225   38, 42, 60n12
Sec. 4   116n23
Sec. 4 230–1   30n16
Sec. 5   317
Secs. 5–6   319
Sec. 6   49, 134
Sec. 6 251   38
Sec. 6 252   11, 49
Sec. 6 253   122, 141

Sec. 6 253–9   47
Sec. 6 259   48
Sec. 6 261–2   49
Sec. 6 262   41, 50
Sec. 6 263   29n10
Sec. 7 263–74   118
Sec. 7 267   59n7
Sec. 7 268   105
Sec. 7 271–2   119
Sec. 7 272–3   35
Sec. 7 273   34, 35, 113
Sec. 7 273–4   116n26

Book 2 Of the Passions
Book 2 Part 1
Sec. 1 275–6   6
Sec. 1 276   12, 126, 127
Sec. 1 276–7   125
Sec. 2 277   134, 141
Sec. 3 280   126
Sec. 3 280–1   159
Sec. 4 284   178n17
Sec. 7 295–6   148
Sec. 7 296   162
Sec. 8 299   261, 262
Sec. 9 303   227
Sec. 10 309   227
Sec. 10 311   227, 262
Sec. 10 315   227
Sec. 11   142
Sec. 11 316   272
Sec. 11 317   134, 141

Book 2 Part 2
Sec. 1 331–2   227
Sec. 3 348   161
Sec. 4 353   270
Sec. 4 354   62n19
Sec. 5 357–8   227
Sec. 5 362   263
Sec. 5 363–4   261
Sec. 5 364   258, 261, 262,
                     270
Sec. 5 365   143
Sec. 8 372   261
Sec. 8 379–80   270
Sec. 10 390   272

Book 2 Part 3
Secs. 1–2   130
Sec. 1 402   159, 178n17

Sec. 1 402–3	159
Sec. 1 403	84
Sec. 1 406	131
Sec. 1 408	131
Sec. 2 407	130
Sec. 2 412	179n22
Sec. 3 413	127
Sec. 3 415	30n16, 123, 128
Sec. 3 415–16	163
Sec. 3 416	128–9, 139
Sec. 3 417	127
Sec. 4 419	127
Sec. 9 439	126, 126–7
Sec. 9 441	275
Sec. 10 450–1	226
Sec. 10 451	270

Book 3 *Of Morals*

Title-page	17

Book 3 Part 1

Sec. 1 455–70	157
Sec. 1 456	13
Sec. 1 456–68	14
Sec. 1 466	164
Sec. 1 468–9	13
Sec. 1 469–70	59n4, 169
Sec. 2 470	162
Sec. 2 471	179n24, 275
Sec. 2 472	134, 164
Sec. 2 474	270
Sec. 2 474–5	164

Book 3 Part 2

Sec. 1 477	16
Sec. 1 477–8	161
Sec. 1 478	167, 169
Sec. 1 478–9	170, 215n7
Sec. 1 479	133, 135, 143
Sec. 1 480–1	187
Sec. 1 483	169, 262
Sec. 1 483–4	188
Sec. 1 484	170, 180n26
Sec. 2 484	167
Sec. 2 484–5	166
Sec. 2 484–501	188
Sec. 2 486–7	187
Sec. 2 487	204
Sec. 2 487–8	198
Sec. 2 488–9	166

Sec. 2 490	180n28
Sec. 2 492	228
Sec. 2 495	228
Sec. 2 498	167
Sec. 2 498–501	215n7
Sec. 2 499	167
Sec. 2 499–500	168
Sec. 2 500	13, 156, 180n29
Secs. 3–5 501–25	188
Sec. 5 517	136
Sec. 5 517–19	215n7
Sec. 5 518–19	169
Sec. 5 522–3	215n7
Sec. 6 533	168
Sec. 6 533–4	180n29, 228
Sec. 7 534–7	229
Secs. 7–9 534–50	193
Sec. 8 541–2	194
Sec. 8 543	192
Sec. 8 545	193, 215n7
Sec. 9 551	178n17
Sec. 9 553	178n17
Sec. 10 556–63	202
Sec. 10 562	203
Sec. 10 564	303
Sec. 10 566–7	296
Sec. 11 566	203

Book 3 Part 3

Sec. 1 574	186
Sec. 1 574–91	215n7
Sec. 1 575	133, 161
Sec. 1 576–7	227–8
Sec. 1 577	251n20, 258
Sec. 1 578	156, 180n29, 186, 187
Sec. 1 579	13, 16, 165, 168, 186
Sec. 1 581–3	263
Sec. 1 584–7	262
Sec. 1 590	158
Sec. 1 591	263
Sec. 2 592	272
Sec. 2 593	261
Sec. 3 602–3	215n7
Sec. 3 603	263
Sec. 4	137
Sec. 4 608	137

Book 3 Part 3 (*cont.*)

Sec. 5 614	135
Sec. 5 615	262
Sec. 6 620–1	29n10

Book 3 Appendix

631–2	44
633	29n11, 320
636	44